PATTERNS OF DREAMING

A C. G. JUNG FOUNDATION BOOK

The C. G. Jung Foundation for Analytical Psychology is dedicated to helping men and women grow in conscious awareness of the psychological realities in themselves and society, find healing and meaning in their lives and greater depth in their relationships, and live in response to their discovered sense of purpose. It welcomes the public to attend its lectures, seminars, films, symposia, and workshops and offers a wide selection of books for sale through its bookstore. The Foundation also published *Quadrant,* a semiannual journal, and books on Analytical Psychology and related subjects. For information about Foundation programs or membership, please write to the C. G. Jung Foundation, 28 East 39th Street, New York, NY 10016.

PATTERNS OF
DREAMING

*Jungian Techniques
in Theory and Practice*

JAMES A. HALL, M.D.

Foreword by Edward C. Whitmont, M.D.

SHAMBHALA
Boston & London
1991

Shambhala Publications, Inc.
Horticultural Hall
300 Massachusetts Avenue
Boston, Massachusetts 02115

Shambhala Publications, Inc.
Random Century House
20 Vauxhall Bridge Road
London SW1V 2SA

9 8 7 6 5 4 3 2 1

First Paperback Edition

Printed in the United States of America on acid-free paper

Distributed in the United States by Random House, Inc.; in Canada by
Random House of Canada Ltd; and in the United Kingdom by Random
Century Group

Library of Congress Cataloging-in-Publication Data

Hall, James A. (James Albert), 1934–
    [Clinical uses of dreams]
    Patterns of dreaming: Jungian techniques in theory and practice /
  James A. Hall; foreword by Edward C. Whitmont.—1st paperback
ed.
        p. cm.
    Originally published: Clinical uses of dreams. New York: Grune &
Stratton, © 1977.
    Includes bibliographical references and index.
    ISBN 0-87773-621-9
    1. Dreams. 2. Psychoanalysis. 3. Jung, C. G. (Carl Gustav),
1875–1961. I. Title.
BF1078.H26 1991   90-53555
154.6'3—dc20   CIP

Contents

II. Jungian Dream Interpretation

To Thelma, Suzanne, Angela, and Sherry, who have been with me at the beginnings, the ends, the rebeginnings of dreams.

Foreword

The last few years have seen an ever increasing interest in Jung's lifework. Thus it is a peculiar paradox that what may be his most important contribution to clinical psychotherapy, namely, his novel method of dream interpretation on the "subject level," has received comparatively little attention, especially in the psychiatric community. Although Freud was the first to recognize intuitively that the dream was the *via regia* to the unconscious, the clinical effectiveness of his classical psychoanalytic method of dream interpretation remains controversial, and the method has been of limited usefulness.

Jung proposed that the dream presents us with allegorical or symbolic descriptions of the dreamer's unconscious psychological situation as it is, rather than as a censored wish. The dream attempts to reveal rather than conceal, and it will bring to the fore any aspect in the attempt to help resolve life problems, relationships, and emotional issues, as well as existential, philosophic, and religious conflicts. The seeming incoherence of the dream is not to be regarded as the result of repression but simply as the manner in which the unconscious psyche expresses itself, namely, prerational image sequences that encompass an intuitive perception of wholeness patterns; hence also the apparent condensation noted in dreams: one image representing a whole pattern. Conceptual logic, with its abstractive tendencies, is an expression of a later conscious development.

This postulate of a superior wisdom in the unconscious psyche was branded as mystical in Jung's own day, but it is now gaining respectability because of modern research on the activities of the brain's right hemisphere, studies of "peak" LSD experiences, and investigation of paranormal cognition.

The subject-level approach to dreams regards every detail, person, or object of the dream as representational of an element of the dreamer's psychological attitude. Nothing is considered to be haphazard, accidental, or irrelevant. When properly understood, all details fit, and each detail appears to be chosen to convey what needs to reach the dreamer's awareness (when these details are translated into terms that have meaning or emotional significance for the dreamer, not terms from a fixed symbolism of what someone else thinks the details ought to mean). By use of this method, the art of dream interpretation can be sharpened into a diagnostic tool, yielding a sort of x-ray picture of psychodynamics. Indeed, translation of shadowy dream images into psychodynamic conceptions requires interpretive skills and imaginative capacities similar to those needed to interpret x-ray pictures.

The therapeutic implications of this method for the patient are considerable: the patient will be confronted with specific images of the self coming from the depths of the self rather than being derived from the therapist's opinions and perhaps bias. Conscious confrontation with the "knower," the critic and guide within, can show the nature of the impasse and point the way toward growth and maturation.

Dr. Hall's systematic survey of the possibilities for clinical uses of dreams should be of inestimable value to the practitioner who wishes to examine the scope of Jung's methodology.

Edward C. Whitmont, M.D.

Preface to the Paperback Edition

I am pleased that this book is now available in an affordable paperback edition. In the years since it first appeared, under the title *Clinical Uses of Dreams: Jungian Interpretations and Enactments,* interest in the subject has become even more widespread in the therapeutic community. Specialized studies on dreams also have appeared in the Jungian literature. The need is even stronger now for a clear and basic presentation of classical Jungian dream theory, a need this volume satisfies. Two major trends have emerged since the original publication.

First, the wide acceptance of dream laboratories devoted to the investigation of sleep and dreaming has added a great deal to the understanding of sleep disorders. A useful outline of sleep disorders now appears in the standard psychiatric nomenclature. But such studies have added little, if anything, to the clinical use of dreams in psychotherapy and psychoanalysis. This has been a disappointment to me. I had hoped that a renewed laboratory study of dreaming would inevitably bring a renaissance in the psychodynamic investigation and use of dreams. It is a severe disappointment that even dream researchers who are sympathetic to the Jungian theory of dreams often do not understand in depth the use of dreams in analysis.

The laboratory studies have continued to be cast in the epiphenomenalist model of science, which asserts that dreams are "explained" by measuring brain activity and defining which areas are active during dreaming. This is nothing more than neurophysiological reductionism. What is missing is the openness of Jung's original vision—a broad net that not only takes in the fascinating correspondences between dream symbols and the patterns of the dreamer's life, but is open to the frontier questions of telepathic dreams, parallel dreams, dreams as diagnostic of bodily processes, and precognitive dreams. This last category, precognitive dreams of the future, is the most difficult area for the epiphenomenalist to discuss. In his work on synchronicity, Jung approached such questions more directly, yielding the insight that the archetypes, the basic structures of the psyche, can manifest both psychological and physical effects.

The second and most encouraging of the trends is the increased interest in "lucid" dreaming, particularly since the publication of Stephen LeBerge's book *Lucid Dreaming* (Los Angeles: Jeremy Tarcher, 1985). Lucid dreaming simply means being aware while dreaming that one *is* dreaming. The interest in lucid dreaming has been inspired by a simple innovation in dream-lab techniques, which enables the sleeping subject to signal, by means of prearranged eye movements, that he or she is aware of dreaming while the electroencephalograph recordings show the usual rapid-eye-movement (REM) tracing that is present during most dreaming. Like the discovery of the REM state as an indicator of dreams, the laboratory means of demonstrating lucid dreaming has produced an explosion of interest in this long-known clinical phenomenon.

Such increased clinical interest has led to attempts to induce lucidity while dreaming. Two major types of exercise have thus far been proposed. First, one can develop the habit of asking oneself, "Am I dreaming?" One will then presumably tend to ask the question when actually dreaming, in which case a "yes" answer will likely induce the lucid state.

The second technique for developing lucid dreaming is to attempt something that is impossible in the awake state but possible when dreaming, such as jumping into the air and staying there. This is an on-the-spot test as to whether or not one is dreaming. It can induce lucidity.

Lucid dreaming itself is nothing new. A large percentage of the population have experienced it. It is closely related to the experience of a dream-within-a-dream in which one "wakes up," remembering a dream, and then actually awakens and realizes that one had only *dreamed* of awakening.

In lucid dreaming, as in the dream-within-a-dream, we find ourselves concerned with "levels" of consciousness. Perhaps "compartments" of consciousness would be a more precise description. Both phenomena demonstrate a basic Jungian insight—the dissociability of the psyche. This is also a major aspect of hypnotherapy, which I have related to Jungian theory in *Hypnosis: A Jungian Perspective* (New York: Guilford, 1989). Hypnosis can be conceived from a Jungian perspective as a collection of techniques for using the dissociability of the psyche in an intentional and controlled way to dissolve pathological complexes and to rapidly form new complexes.

Both lucid dreaming and hypnotherapy techniques are quite similar to what Jung called *active imagination,* which is the closest waking equivalent to the activity of nocturnal dreaming. Since my book was originally published, there has been a proliferation of enactment techniques that border on active imagination. These have included description of "waking" dreams, shamanistic journeys, group rituals for women's and (more recently) for men's groups, and visualization techniques intended to enhance the body's immune system to fight cancer and other diseases. All of these enactment techniques utilize the dissociability of the psyche. An understanding of dreams, the *natural* dissociating experience, is a necessary ground for effective utilization of this range of enactment techniques.

The ego-image, what we call "I," is also only a fragment of the psyche, a complex among other psychological complexes. But the ego is that unique complex which has the property of consciousness, although all complexes have *partial* consciousness and constitute part-personalities. Complexes seem to act as if they "desire" to become part of the structure of the ego. Yet the ego is also the very center of consciousness and the bedrock of our sense of personal identity. A complex is not necessarily pathological, like an "inferiority complex," but is a natural building block of the mind.

A complex is like a computer program that can be accessed by a range of stimuli that have similar meanings, perhaps only unconsciously. Once activated, a complex distorts ordinary consciousness and can induce a number of related feelings and behaviors, although lacking the balance and discrimination of the mature ego.

Dreaming can be conceptualized as a natural dialogue between the ego-complex and the unconscious. At its core, dreaming is best seen as serving the process of *individuation,* the term Jung chose for describing an innate tendency to actualize the possibilities of the psyche in one's own actual life. The individuation process is always incomplete. Perhaps it is best conceived as an appropriate direction of life rather than a point of achievement.

The reader who understands the classical Jungian view of dreams, which this volume provides, will have the essence of Jungian clinical theory, a firm basis for the clinical use of dream interpretation and a wide range of other enactments.

James A. Hall
Dallas, Texas
1990

Acknowledgments

When I first began to realize the importance of dreams, I found that neither the psychiatry training I had experienced nor the psychoanalytic literature was of much help. I had gone into medical training with the impression that psychiatrists had deep respect for the dream, Freud's "royal road to the unconscious." This naive view was quickly shattered, for I was exposed to a spectrum of psychiatric opinion and practice during residency training at Duke University Medical Center, Durham, North Carolina, and Parkland Memorial Hospital, Dallas, Texas. I saw some very good clinicians functioning without any reference to the unconscious, let alone dreams. Others would inquire regarding dreams, but then they would relate the patient's dream to the transference, to general life situations, or worst of all to evidence of repressed childhood fears. Appreciation of the dream itself was missing. In many respects this neglect of the dream paralleled the neglect of hypnotherapy, both perhaps being symptomatic of the hope that rational explanations could be found for all unusual and borderline phenomena. Today this extreme objective stance continues, but it is tempered by increasing appreciation of the unconscious side of man, both in the academic setting and certainly among the public.

The one oasis in my early search for meaning in dreams was a seminar with Bingham Dai at Duke University. Dr. Dai, originally a sociologist, was trained by Harry Stack Sullivan, and for many years Dr. Dai was the principal psychoanalyst for the psychiatric residency training program at Duke. Later, as my first personal analyst, he instilled in me a deep and enduring respect for the purposeiveness of dreams and their movement toward growth and health of the psyche. Although he respects Jung's work, Dr. Dai is not a Jungian. In a remarkable fashion he is able to refer dream scenarios to the family constellation of the past and the interpersonal situations of the present. It was a series of dreams that caused me to enter my first analysis at a time when it was not financially convenient. The decision was fortunate, because during that same period of time the psychiatry residents at Duke invited Walter Bonime, M.D., to be a visiting lecturer; his warm, practical approach to dreams encouraged me, although he, too, was not allied with Jungian thought.

A series of fortuitous circumstances increased my interest in Jung's work. I had begun to read Jung in medical school, beginning with the writings and selections of the late Jolande Jacobi, who later became my friend and teacher. But the real turning point came when I met one of Jung's grandsons, Adrian Baumann, through an early "growth center," the Creative Center of Dallas, which was sponsored by Carr Collins, Jr., and administered by Jeanne Coffin. Together with Florence Wiedemann, Adrian Baumann gave a series of public lectures on his grandfather's life and work. Through him I learned that his brother, a psychiatrist and a practicing Jungian psychoanalyst in Zurich, was to visit the United States. An introduction by letter resulted in Dieter Baumann spending several days with my family in Durham, where he also lectured at J. B. Rhine's Parapsychology Laboratory (now part of the Foundation for Research on the Nature of Man) and visited the weekly psychosomatic conference of the Duke Psychiatry Department. At that conference I was most impressed with Dr. Baumann's discussion of our clinical case. He made the relevant observations that any competent psychiatrist would make, but then he continued the discussion in terms of the patient's individuation process, including the meaning of the dreams she had revealed to us. I was deeply moved. For the first time I saw that Jung's work was not excessively burdened with aesthetic symbology; it was not only a scholarly study but also a direct, practical, useful means of deepening human understanding of life in realms where traditional medical psychology had turned but a casual eye. Dieter Baumann suggested that I undergo analysis, if possible, with two analysts who had worked intimately with Jung himself: Rivkah Scharf Kluger, then in Los Angeles, and Marie-Louise von Franz of Kusnacht, near Zurich. At that time, such an undertaking was not within the bounds of possibility, and I consoled myself with informal seminar discussions (and culinary excursions) with several other psychiatry residents in the kitchen of Dr. Portia Bomar, a retired clinical psychologist who had undergone Jungian analysis in London years before.

After deciding to enter private practice, I returned to Dallas to complete my training and open an office. The following year, during a trip to a meeting of the American Group Psychotherapy Association, I arranged an hour to meet Dr. Rivkah Kluger in Los Angeles. That was a fortunate turning point. As we discussed a number of dreams I had experienced, she brought to them a viewpoint that revealed unexpected ranges of meaning, although I was perhaps as much concerned at my lack of understanding as I was excited about meeting someone who embodied this Jungian technique in such a practical way. At that time, I was on the waiting list of a Freudian psychoanalyst in Dallas; also, it seemed that the commuting distance between Dallas and Los Angeles would be too great. Dr. Kluger then made a suggestion for which I am continually grateful. Perhaps, she tentatively suggested, we might arrange for me to come to Los Angeles for intensive analysis several times a year, with weekly discussion of my dreams by telephone between visits. She had tried this arrangement only once before, with an analysand who had worked with her in person for quite some time and then had moved away. She was hesitant, and so was I, but we agreed to try it. There followed several years of weekly analysis by telephone, with frequent visits to Los Angeles. This continued through my first year in practice and 2 years in military service. Later it happened that Dr. Kluger and I were in Zurich at the same time, and I was able to resume analysis with her for several months as she and her husband were in the process of immigrating to Israel.

After military service, a grant from the Sangreal Foundation permitted me to arrange an extended time in residence at the C. G. Jung Institute, Zurich, where I worked concurrently with Marie-Louise von Franz and Dieter Baumann. Dieter Baumann taught me to appreciate the fine, intricate detail of dreams. His careful use of the sensation function often uncovered important meanings that my own first reading had missed. We often spent 2 hours of analysis on a single dream, turning it to many angles, seeing it refract diverse and unexpected meanings. From Dr. von Franz I learned a different approach to dreams. Sometimes at one sitting she would take the accumulated dreams of 2 weeks and find in them not only links to past dream material but also arrows toward future developments. Her vast knowledge of myths, fairy tales, and cultural amplifications would at times provide the precise key to unlock a difficult dream. I learned from her an abiding appreciation for the seemingly irrational movements of the psyche.

After my return to this country, I was very fortunate to be able to continue my analytical work with Edward Whitmont, M.D., of New York. His writings had been of great help to me, particularly *The Symbolic Quest*. Dr. Whitmont brought me back again to a careful consideration of the interrelationship between dream material and personal life, but with the depth dimension retained. I am indebted to him also for my initial understanding of the *enactment* of dream material being complementary to its interpretation. At the Sixth International Congress of Analytical Psychology, the day before we visited Stonehenge together, he demonstrated to me, using my own dream material, his application of *guided imagination* as a supplement to *active imagination.* I am also grateful that he permitted me to visit, as an observer, one of his ongoing therapy groups. I am honored that he has written the Foreword for this book.

I have learned as much about dreams from teaching as from being taught, and I am grateful to my former chief of psychiatry, Robert L. Stubblefield, M.D., for inviting me to give a seminar on dream interpretation to the advanced psychiatry residents at Southwestern Medical School, now part of the University of Texas Health Science Center, Dallas. Another meaningful chance to teach dream interpretation was provided by my friend Harville Hendrix, Ph.D., of Perkins School of Theology, Southern Methodist University, Dallas, with whom I have shared responsibility for several courses on dreams and other counseling techniques. In this regard, I am grateful also for the support of Dr. James Gwaltney, Perkins School of Theology, and to the Foundation for the Study of Theology and the Human Sciences. I would also like to single out my colleagues in the Inter-Regional Society of Jungian Analysts, a member organization of the International Association of Analytical Psychology (IAAP). The training program of the Inter-Regional Society has given me an opportunity to work with intelligent, deeply motivated analysts and trainees whose interest in their own dreams and those of their analysands has caused me to rethink my assumptions continually and has taught me much. I owe particular thanks to Dr. June Singer, with whom I have worked on the training committee of the Inter-Regional Society since its formation.

The Inter-Regional Society, which is devoted to the development of Jungian analysis outside the traditional centers of study in New York, Los Angeles, and San Francisco, owes much to the guidance of Joseph Wheelwright, M.D., former president of the IAAP, and to Gerhard Adler, Ph.D., president of the IAAP at the time the Inter-Regional Society was formed.

My insight into the use of dreams in group therapy has been increased by 8 years of close personal and professional collaboration with Gladys Guy Brown, Ph.D., who has functioned as co-therapist with me in two weekly groups and in many joint marathons involving our patients. In addition, we have worked together on the training committee of the Dallas Group Psychotherapy Society during three of the society's four 2-year training programs in professional group psychotherapy.

Eunice Dennis, the godmother of my daughters, did much to introduce me to the joys and pains of bibliographic research. Although we differed personally in many ways, the late Dr. Franz Riklin, former president of the Curatorium of the C. G. Jung Institute, Zurich, was kind and consistent in smoothing the way for my studies there. I am appreciative, too, of the help of Dr. Mario Jacoby of Zurich, the chairman of my thesis committee.

Harold B. Crasilneck, Ph.D., my former teacher, has been a friend and colleague for many years. Together we have published a number of papers on the clinical applications of hypnotherapy; this work culminated in our recent textbook *Clinical Hypnosis*. Although it is not primarily concerned with dreams, this work with Dr. Crasilneck has increased my appreciation for the important influences that the unconscious mind can exert in many clinical situations.

Sherry Gold Knopf has brought to this volume the same care in editorial preparation and advice that she exercised during the writing of *Clinical Hypnosis*. I am also indebted for proofreading and advice to Shirley McElya; and to Mary Kugler for permission to quote from her unpublished paper on dream telepathy. Howard P. Roffman, M.D. generously reviewed Chapter 3, although the publication schedule did not permit me to take full advantage of his excellent critique. Any errors are, of course, my own responsibility.

I also wish to express warm appreciation to my dedicated secretary, Cresse (Mrs. Frank) Holt, who has provided support and encouragement at all times. I am grateful to Nancy Yates for her careful proofreading and typing. Patricia Walther, senior editor at Grune & Stratton, has been a valued influence as adviser and friend.

The longer I have continued analysis of my own dream material, both formally and informally, the more it has seemed to me that one's closest relationships are a part of what Jung called individuation. Before my father's death, it was a pleasure to experience him as an individual, with the projections of the father imago diminished. My relationship with my mother continues to be a tapestry of past and present, and more and more I realize how her infinite patience with a small, troublesome boy did so much to mold the psyche I still explore.

To my wife Suzanne I owe a personal and professional debt so great as to be unpayable. She has been the container in which much of myself has formed, dissolved, and formed again. Virtually all the library research for this volume was done by Suzanne and our daughters Angela and Sherry; for their constant devotion to the work of verification of sources I am grateful.

Although I never met Dr. Jung, it seems appropriate here to express thanks and acknowledge his achievement in opening up for those of us who follow after him an avenue, a method, and a vision of the psyche of man broad enough and deep enough to touch both the tightly focused world of science and the misty Venetian shores of the soul.

Introduction

The purpose of this book is thoroughly practical: to make available to clinicians the concepts I have found useful during many years spent in the clinical study of dreams. I have reviewed a variety of approaches and have found the analytical psychology of C. G. Jung to be the most rewarding. Jung's conception of the psyche, particularly the central paradox of ego and Self, permits one to see the dream as reflecting not only the concerns of the everyday world but pointing beyond toward the archetypal foundations of human experience. Dreams are important in a number of contexts: in childhood development; in the process of individuation in which we literally become "more ourselves"; in the crisis times of birth, death, and initiation; in close personal relationships; and in giving us intimations of the deeper nature of reality, both physical and psychological.

Part of my motivation in writing this book is to try to fill the void left by neglect and lack of interest in dream interpretation in psychiatric teaching. In my own first years of residency at Duke University Medical Center we were fortunate to have a seminar on dreams, but it was offered only every other year; it was a special teaching effort on the part of a very remarkable therapist, my first psychoanalyst, Dr. Bingham Dai. He combined the insights of many dream theories into an extremely practical approach based primarily on the work of Harry Stack Sullivan, and therefore the approach emphasized the interpersonal and family meanings that may be found in dreams. Outside of this course, there seemed to be little interest among the staff in the practical use of dreams. My other residence experience at Parkland Memorial Hospital in Dallas (the teaching hospital of Southwestern Medical School) was equally devoid of any significant interest on the part of the staff in the use of dream material.

It was a shocking experience to find dreams so neglected. Prior to entering psychiatric training, I had thought that dreams would be a major part of psychotherapy work; this impression was based, not unreasonably, on the work of Freud, who referred to dreams as "the royal road to the unconscious."

The literature available at that time was also sparse. Outside of the psychoanalytic journals, little attention was paid to the use of dreams. The literature that was available seemed to be superficial, or else it was cast in the Freudian theoretical framework, which even then did not satisfy me. There was very little material available that embodied the quality and humanity I encountered in the dream seminar of Dr. Dai. Freud's own work, *The Interpretation of Dreams,* was at that time 60 years old, and most later writers had simply followed his approach.

While research and professional interest in dreams waned, popular enthusiasm for dreams remained undiminished. This pattern of neglect of dreams had appeared before in man's history. During the Middle Ages, the ancient and respectable practice of temple *incubation* for dreams fell into disrepute; it came to be regarded by the Church as a superstitious practice, based on the possibility that dreams might be sent by demons to deceive the faithful. In his valuable review of dreams, De Becker (1968) outlines their long religious, political, cultural, and creative history from antiquity to modern times. Quoting the magazine *Match* for 22 September 1938, De Becker cites a dream attributed to Adolph Hitler that occurred when he was a Bavarian corporal on the French front in 1917. The dream was said to have warned Hitler of an impending artillery barrage, thus possibly saving his life (De Becker, 1968, pp. 79–80). De Becker cites impressive accounts of dreams from such varied personages as the mother of Buddha and the author J. B. Priestly.

The idea that dreams are more expressive of unconscious material than other data has gradually begun to receive experimental support (Gordon, 1953). While any person seems always to exhibit some defensiveness in regard to whatever ordinary projective technique may be used to probe the deeper regions of the mind, the dream is a dialogue of self with self; in Jungian terminology it is a dialogue of the ego with the Self. When one realizes that the process of the Self (or central archetype) is the foundation process of the entire mind, the significance of the interaction between ego and Self in the dream becomes central in understanding both normal and pathologic processes.

Much of the current scientific interest in dreams derives from the vast amount of laboratory work on sleep and dreaming that has been carried out since the pioneering observations of Aserinsky and Kleitman (1953); they showed that high percentages of dreams were reported when persons were awakened from ascending stage I sleep when that stage was accompanied by rapid eye movements (REM). Although an overview of such work will be presented, it is not directly relevant to the clinical uses of dreams. In fact, it may have "no impact on the debate concerning the function of dreams" (Giora and Elam, 1974), in spite of laboratory studies that provide increased understanding of the conditions necessary for dreaming to occur.

Up to now, the dominant force in the clinical study of dreams has been Freud's theory, which will be outlined later. Jungian concepts have been neglected, both clinically and experimentally, in spite of Jung's early major contributions to psychoanalysis, to laboratory study of word-association experiments (out of which grew polygraph testing), and to the phenomenology of dreaming. Most projective testing has paid slight attention to Jung's concepts of analytical psychology, even though Jung's work inspired Rorschach and other early workers (Spiegelman, 1955; Klopfer, 1955; McCully, 1971). This is perhaps due in part to Jung's early humanistic insistence that the science of psychology must be concerned with the whole man. As Edinger (1962) remarked in speaking before a memorial meeting honoring Jung, the great Swiss psychiatrist was not content to study "just a convenient fragment" of man, as is done in so many disciplines. Thus, said Edinger, "all factions with partial viewpoints have trouble relating to him."

While laboratory studies continue to find the personal meanings of dreams confusing, fragmented, and reflective of physiologic processes in the brain, the popular mind is uncritically ready to accord them oracular and predictive meaning. The truth lies somewhere in between, and balance is a primary requirement in approaching this fascinating and confusing subject. Long ago Aristotle wrote that "the most skilled interpreter of dreams is he who has the faculty of observing resemblances" (Aristotle, 1941). It might be added that it is of the utmost importance to *observe* resemblances without *reducing* the dream to that which it resembles (e.g., not to waking personal relationships, not to archetypal images, not to any procrustean frame of reference). My friend Albert C. Outler, distinguished professor of theology at Southern Methodist University, brought to my attention a remark made by John Wesley in his sermon "Human Life a Dream." It is one of the best images I have encountered of what a dream really is: "A dream is a fragment of life, broken off at both ends, leaving us with one end of it [our remembrance] in our hands." It is the search for the other end of the dream, the one that is still attached to the autonomous processes of the objective psyche and to one's deeper life, that constitutes the core of working with dreams. We must continually remind ourselves that the other end of the dream *is* hidden, that what we begin with is not the whole dream; and we must understand beforehand that our reward is in the search for it, not in bringing it home to display as a trophy.

The need for a concise presentation of Jungian dream work became clear to me during my work as a training analyst for the Inter-Regional Society of Jungian Analysts, a group that itself is the result of an attempt to make available in the United States more analysts trained in Jung's techniques of analytical psychology. Since it covers a wide geographic area, the Inter-Regional Society program has had to rely on dedicated work by isolated Jungian analysts, together with intensive workshops. To increase the availability of this information to students in that program, I began to collect notes from various lectures, primarily those at the Department of Psychiatry, Southwestern Medical School, University of Texas Health Science Center, Dallas, and those at the pastoral counseling program of the Perkins School of Theology, Southern Methodist University. Those lectures formed the skeleton of this book. It has been fleshed out with many clinical examples and has been adapted for easy reference to some recurring clinical problems of dream interpretation.

No book on such a topic can be exhaustive, and I do not mean to imply that perusal of this or any other volume can possibly substitute for personal analysis and supervision of ongoing psychotherapy cases by an analyst skilled in the use of dreams. However, it can serve as an introduction to dream work, as a textbook for the teaching of dream interpretation, and as an aid to interested members of the lay public in deciding whether they wish professional help with their own dreams. Dream interpretation is an art, not a science, and like all arts it can best be learned by apprenticeship. The most satisfactory way of learning about dream interpretation is psychoanalytic education, where personal analysis ensures that the student carefully considers his own dreams, those with which he is most intimate, and where supervision of his control cases brings his understanding of dreams into focus alongside those of more experienced analysts. I am speaking of psychoanalytic education in a broad sense, not limiting it to Freud's school or to the school of Jung; rather, I use it in a generic sense to cover all those in-depth approaches, whether therapeutic or growth-oriented, that involve careful, open, and extended application of one trained person to facilitate the growth processes of another. Those who know my own type of practice realize that this also includes psychoanalytic group therapy.

Neither I nor anyone else can say definitively what any particular dream actually means. It is sufficient that we have a feeling that we understand the dream, and it is imperative that we never come to believe that the dream has been finally and fully interpreted. The dream life is a living process, the remembered dream only a reflection. Even dreams from the laboratory (which usually detail a higher percentage of total dream life than do spontaneously remembered dreams) are subject to the distortion inherent in a laboratory situation; they, also, may be only partially remembered, and they do not seem to be accompanied by the same freedom of expression as ordinary dreams.

The concept of focal and tacit knowing, which was introduced into scientific theory by Michael Polanyi (1958), is used as a heuristic aid to understanding how consciousness relies on the structures of psychological complexes, which have at their core the transpersonal archetypes of the collective unconscious (the objective psyche.) There are some tentative thoughts on the profound but confusing problem of how the archetypal foundations of the mind may be related to parapsychological phenomena in the physical world and to mystical religious experience. The book is otherwise devoted to practical, day-to-day clinical uses of dreams in diagnosis, prognosis, and interpretation.

Noninterpretive uses of dreams are expounded in order to broaden the range of clinical application of dream work. Suggestions are given for enactment of dreams, which should sometimes take precedence over classical interpretation.

Michael Polanyi, in his book *Personal Knowledge* (1958), clearly described the role of the maxim, and it is in that form that this book is presented. Maxims are rules of thumb created by those who know a skill and are used to guide those learning that skill. They are not the same as instructions given to a machinist to reproduce a model. Maxims can be false as well as true, and only intuitive understanding of the work makes it possible to apply maxims correctly. Jung emphasized this quite clearly. Dream interpretation can be guided by maxims, in the sense that Polanyi used the term; it cannot be accomplished by rules, by specified steps, or by formula.

I have taken great care that no individual can be identified in this work. At times, small alterations in clinical data have been made in the interest of anonymity, never affecting the illustrative value of the dream cited. Some dreams are taken entirely out of their clinical matrix and are used as examples or illustrations of technical points. This may result in emphasis on an aspect of the dream that would be insignificant in the clinical setting, where each dream is seen as one vision in an ongoing process of meaning.

In virtually every instance, written permission has been obtained from the analysand for the use of dream material. Nevertheless, I want to add a further word of caution, both to my former and present analysands and to those who may find similarities between the dreams described here and dreams or fantasies of their own: *There are recurrent types of dreams.* But a given dream experienced by two different people (or experienced by a single person in two different situations) may have two different meanings. What the reader may take to be a dream from his past may be only a similar dream from another person. Please do not make the mistake of reading any personal meaning for yourself, or anyone you know, from the teaching examples in this book.

It is possible that someone may be disappointed that I requested permission to use a dream but then did not use it in this book. There were many possible examples of each illustrative dream type actually described, and the choice was not always easy. I am grateful to all my analysands, past and present, who have trusted me with their intimate and personal views of their dreams, allowing me to observe with admiration the heroic and passionate efforts, often unseen by the world, that have gone into their own processes of individuation.

Although these maxims and examples will of themselves teach no one the art of dream interpretation, I hope that they may make such teaching easier by providing a source of reference. It is also my hope that this book will give the reader an appreciation of the immense value of dream interpretation, particularly from a Jungian standpoint, in helping the many people who otherwise do not respond well or rapidly to various modes of psychotherapy. Man's recent technologic advances have been amazing, but our next frontier is clearly psychical: we must delve more fully into the nature of each person's consciousness and uniqueness. This is the borderland in which science, our greatest achievement, and religion, our most basic concern, may finally be reconciled.

REFERENCES

Aristotle: De somnis (on dreams), in McKeon R (ed): The Basic Works of Aristotle. New York, Random House, 1941, p 630

Aserinsky E, Kleitman N: Regularly occurring periods of eye motility and concomitant phenomena during sleep. Science 118:273–274, 1953

De Becker R: The Understanding of Dreams, or The Machinations of the Night. (Trans: M Heron) London, Allen & Unwin, 1968

Edinger EF: The ego-self paradox. J Anal Psychol 5:3–18, 1960

Edinger E: Opening Remarks, in Carl Gustav Jung: A memorial meeting. New York: The New York Association for Analytical Psychology and the Analytical Psychology Club of New York, 1962, pp. 1–3

Edinger EF: Ego and Archetype: Individuation and the Religious Function of the Psyche. New York, Putnam, 1972

Giora Z, Elam Z: What a dream is. Br J Med Psychol 47:283–289, 1974.

Gordon HL: A comparative study of dreams and responses to the thematic apperception test. J Pers 22:234–253, 1953

Gordon R: Symbols: Content and process, in Fordham M, Gordon R, Hubback J, et al (eds): Analytical Psychology. London, Heinemann, 1973, pp 52–65

Klopfer B: Editorial dedication honoring Jung's 80th birthday. J Projective Techniques 19:110, 1955

McCully RS: Rorschach Theory and Symbolism: A Jungian Approach to Clinical Material. Baltimore, Williams & Wilkins, 1971

Polanyi M: Personal Knowledge: Towards a Post-critical Philosophy. Chicago, University of Chicago Press, 1958

Spiegelman M: Jungian theory and the analysis of thematic tests. J Projective Techniques 19:253–263, 1955

PART I

History of Dream Interpretation

Those who attribute far too much hidden meaning to dreams should be treated with contempt since they have no insight into the structure of a dream and they are accusing the gods of malice and ill will.

Artemidorus, *Oneirocritica*

1
Dreams from Antiquity to Freud

Dreams are reported in the oldest existing records of mankind. The Babylonian epic of Gilgamesh is known to us largely through clay tablets incised in cuneiform characters. The tablets were found about the middle of the nineteenth century in the ruins of the temple of the god Nabu, the biblical Nebo (Isaiah 46:1), a Sumerian god of wisdom and writing, and in the remains of the palace library of the Assyrian king Ashurbanipal (668– ?633 B.C.) at Nineveh (Heidel, 1946).

At the beginning of the epic the king Gilgamesh has grown too powerful; he is forcing his people to build the city walls higher and higher, and he is expending the excesses of his energy in such fashion that there are hardly any virgins left in the kingdom. Psychologically, the king is showing inflation, hubris, overweening of ego. His harassed people pray for relief from Gilgamesh, and the gods send his counterpart, a wild, untamed man named Enkidu, who at first does not even realize that he is different from the animals who dwell in the forest with him. At this point Gilgamesh is being troubled by dreams. He takes his dreams to his mother, the goddess Ninsun, who then makes the first recorded dream interpretation. In each of the dreams there is a repeated theme, and it is interpreted to mean that there is now one as mighty as Gilgamesh, that neither can conquer the other, and that they will be companions and will do mighty deeds. The psychological meaning of this epic story, as expounded by Rivkah Kluger in her Zurich seminar in 1968, is that excessive inflation of Gilgamesh's ego complex has been compensated by his confrontation with his shadow (Enkidu).

3

Many adventures befall the two companions after they test their strengths against one another and realize, as the dream interpretation had said, that neither can prevail.

Dreams continue to be important in the development of the story. Gilgamesh has a dream the night before he and Enkidu slay the giant Humbaba, guardian of Ishtar's cedar forest. A dream warns Enkidu that he is to die, and in another dream he sees a personage with nails like eagle's talons who beckons for him to follow into the underworld. The story eventually becomes a moving tale of how Gilgamesh realizes his own mortality, strives to overcome it by visiting Utnapishtim (the Babylonian equivalent of Noah), and finally comes to accept the existential reality of man's fate.

Another early account of dreams comes from a somewhat later time (ca. 1450 B.C.); it describes a dream of Thotmes IV, pharaoh of Egypt (Thorndike, 1923).

CLASSICAL SOURCES

The most institutionalized form of dream study in the ancient world was the temple sleep of *incubation,* which was practiced in the cult of Aesculapius, the Greek god of healing and a son of Apollo. The principal sanctuary of the cult was at Epidaurus, near Athens, although it may have originated at Tricca in Thessaly. Meier (1967) described the cult of Aesculapius and compared its use of dreams to the uses of dreams in modern psychotherapy. He described (Meier, 1967, p. 23) how Aesculapius was at first a mortal physician (as reported by Homer) who then seems to have taken on the qualities of a chthonic oracular demon with a fixed habitation, only later to be considered one of the gods. According to Papageorgiou (1975), the practice of incubation has survived in some Christian monasteries in modern Greece, but its use is declining.

During the early period of ancient Greece, it appears that the events in dreams were considered to have actually happened (Bergmann, 1966); this same attitude was found by Piaget to be characteristic of small children. In some instances in the tragedies of Aeschylus (525–456 B.C.) there is even the suggestion that the dream is inhaled by the dreamer (Devereux, 1967).

In the ancient world there were about 410 Aesculapian sanctuaries, most linked with Epidaurus, which was active from the sixth century B.C. until the third century A.D. Satellite temples were usually established by a rite of "translation," in which an image of the god, often in the form of a serpent, was sent from Epidaurus to the new site. Ovid described in *Metamorphoses* how a delegation was sent from Latium to Delphi to ask the help of Apollo in combating a plague (Meier, 1967, p. 18). However, the priestess Pythia at Delphi reported that Apollo wished them to seek help instead from his son Aesculapius at Epidaurus.

When the delegation reached Epidaurus, one of the Romans dreamed that the god of healing would accompany them in the form of a serpent, and indeed a serpent boarded their ship the next day. Six days later, when the galley reached Rome, the serpent swam to the Tiber Island, where a sanctuary honoring Aesculapius was established (291 B.C.); later this became the site of the church of San Bartolomeo, which incorporated parts of the ancient temple, and the hospital of the Fatebenefratelli. The emperor Claudius decreed that slaves cured at the sanctuary must be freed (Meier, 1967, p. 68). Other temples were established at Athens (420 B.C.) and Pergamum (fourth century B.C.).

At an Aesculapian temple an ill person went through the customary rites of purification and then slept in the temple until a significant dream occurred; the dream was thought to give either the cure itself or directions for the treatment of the affliction. Both birth and death were prohibited within the sacred temple precinct; this prohibition is also found in other cults, as in the Shinto temple on the island of It-sukushima (Meier, 1967, p. 54). Similar rites of incubation were practiced from the fourth century B.C. in Egypt. Even the deified lover of the emperor Hadrian, Antinous, was said to cure through dreams. Islam also adopted the practice, calling it *istigâra*; it supposedly was recommended by Mohammed (De Becker, 1968, p. 155).

Dreams are discussed in Hesiod's *Theogony* and in Homer's *Odyssey,* where the distinction between false and true dreams is made: false dreams come through gates of ivory; true dreams come through gates of horn. In the *Aeneid*, Vergil assigned false dreams to the time before midnight, with true dreams occurring after midnight. Herodotus, who lived from the time of the Persian War (431–404 B.C.) until the Peloponnesian War, related 17 dreams experienced by personages of his day. Plutarch, writing in the first century A.D., recorded 34 dreams.

At the beginning of the ninth book of the *Republic*, Plato (427–347 B.C.) had Socrates say that dreams reveal violence and lawlessness in us all (Diamond, 1974, p. 496), which is a striking parallel to Freud's thought. Plato also admitted the occurrence of "superior dreams" in a balanced personality dominated by reason.

Aristotle (384–322 B.C.) wrote three essays on dreams in the *Parva*

Naturalia. His thesis was essentially that dreams are illusions produced by the faint after-activity of sense impressions influenced by
emotion; however, he thought it possible for the dreamer to become
aware that he is asleep, and in that case, the images are not judged as
real, thus producing what has been called a lucid dream (Green, 1968).
Unlike many of his predecessors, Aristotle took a skeptical attitude
toward any divine inspiration of dreams, although he admitted that
they may be joined to the future as token, cause, or as coincidence
(McCurdy, 1946). "The dream proper is a presentation based on the
movement of sense impressions, when such presentation occurs during
sleep" (Aristotle, 1941, p. 625).

Lucretius (96?–55 B.C.) was an Epicurean who taught that dream
images are actual atomic combinations "whether shed from the surface
of solid objects or generated spontaneously in mid-air" (McCurdy,
1946, p. 47). Attributing dream images ("idols") to chance, Lucretius
had difficulty in explaining how supposedly chance images may have
deep meaning for the dreamer. But he simply raised the problem and
admitted that he did not deal with it adequately. He described in *De
Rerum Natura* a phenomenon that any dog owner has seen: dogs apparently dream of tracking prey.

By far the best source we have for the dream interpretation practices of antiquity is the *Oneirocritica* of Artemidorus of Ephesus, from
the second century A.D. There were many dream books in use at the
beginning of the Christian era (Thorndike, 1923), but the work of Artemidorus is the most comprehensive and most impressive example
that survives. The many sources quoted by Artemidorus, although now
lost to us, indicate that there was a flourishing tradition of dream interpretation (White, 1975, p. 6). Artemidorus talked of two classes of
dreams: *somnium,* which forecasts the future, and *insomnium,* which
refers to contemporary matters and is affected by the state of the body
and the mind. He stated that the interpreter should know certain facts:
the images that are natural, lawful, and customary for the dreamer; the
circumstances at the time of the dream; the dreamer's occupation and
personality—all of which are important to a modern clinical study of
dreams (McCurdy, 1946).

Pliny's *Natural History,* which appeared about A.D. 77 and was
dedicated to the emperor Titus, is also an important source of information about dream interpretation in antiquity. He suggested chance,
accident, and dreams (or divine revelation) as means of discovering the
medicinal virtues of plants (Thorndike, Vol. 1, 1923, p. 42). Pliny related how the root of the wild rose was revealed in a dream to be a cure
for hydrophobia. The dreamer sent the information to her son in the
Praetorian guard, who was said to be healed.

In the first century A.D., Apollonius of Tyana was reputed to be skilled in dream interpretation. When he went to Rome during Nero's reign, some of his followers, being afraid to accompany him, excused themselves by citing warning dreams (Thorndike, 1923).

It is McCurdy's (1946) opinion that Freud's dream theory is closer to the theories of Aristotle and Plato than to those of later writers. Certainly the material covered in Chapter 1 of Freud's *The Interpretation of Dreams* bears a strong resemblance to Aristotle's thought about natural causes. Freud's own theory, however, plumbs for deeper meanings, although not the guidance that Socrates saw in dreams. Aristotle wrote, perhaps humorously, that if dreams were sent by the gods surely they would choose the recipients with more discrimination.

Galen was born in Pergamum about A.D. 129 and practiced for a time as physician to the gladiators of that city. A number of his writings survive, including the treatise *On Diagnosis from Dreams*. He emphasized the need to observe dreams carefully for clues to healing (Thorndike, Vol. I, 1923, p. 122).

Iamblichus (d. ca. A.D. 330) distinguished human dreams (which are sometimes true and sometimes false) from visions that are divinely sent, thus foreshadowing the question that was to becloud the natural study of dreams during the Middle Ages: Is the dream sent by God to a person of superior virtue, or is it sent by demons to a person who has fallen from grace?

ARABIC STUDIES

Alkindi (Ya kûb ibn Ishâk ibn Sabbâh al-Kindî), who died between A.D. 850 and A.D. 873, wrote the treatise *De Somno et Visione* discussing why some dreams reveal the future without interpretation, why others reveal the future only when properly understood, and why some seem to be contrary to what is to be (Thorndike, Vol. 1, 1923, p. 642). Kurland (1972) expressed the opinion that the medieval Arabic code of oneirocritics contained some quite modern ideas about precognitive dreams, dream symbols, semantic distinctions, and the use of disguise in dreams, as well as the fact that dreams do not speak in terms of contraries, which are only forms of avoiding disagreeable insights.

BIBLICAL SOURCES

Dreams are valued differently in different traditions. De Becker (1968) remarked that although there are dreams recorded in both the Old Testament and New Testament, the Gospels do not record a single dream experienced by Jesus; on the other hand, the Pali scriptures relate five of Gautama Buddha's dreams. The apocryphal Gospel of Nicodemus relates that Jesus was accused of causing Pilate's wife to dream. This ability to incite dreams was also attributed to Nectanebus, who is reputed to have sent a dream to Olympias, mother of Alexander the Great (Thorndike, Vol. 1, 1923, p. 561). De Becker (1968) suggested that the Bible preferentially mentions dreams that conform to messianic expectations: of approximately 15 dreams related in the Old Testament, most seem to have occurred at crucial periods of change in the history of Israel. De Becker called them "the compensatory power dreams of a conquered people." On the other hand, De Becker judged the dreams of the New Testament as having "a freshness, an 'evangelical' simplicity that would suggest authenticity." These are impressionistic judgments, but it is nevertheless true that dreams play a prominent part in both the Old Testament and the New Testament. However, biblical authors had mixed attitudes toward dreams. On the one hand, dreams were seen as a means by which God communicates with the prophets (Numbers 12:6), and yet divination by dreams was proscribed (Deuteronomy 18:10). Job (33:15–16) states that God talks to men "in a dream, in a vision of the night" and "sealeth their instruction."

Consider the important episode (Genesis 40:5–19) in which Joseph is released from prison because of his ability to interpret dreams correctly. He predicts from the repeated dreams of the Pharaoh, that a time of plenty in Egypt will be followed by a time of famine, thus allowing time for planning for the future of the state (Genesis 41:1–32). This parallels an approach to dreams that was not uncommon in early antiquity: the dreams of the ruler or king may refer to the fate of the kingdom rather than to his own personal psychodynamics. There are similar modern examples. Consider the dream that Bismarck recorded in 1881 (De Becker, 1968, pp. 78–79): In a letter to Emperor William I, Bismarck told of a dream of being on an Alpine path that was blocked by a rock; the path was so narrow that his horse refused to proceed. Bismarck called on God and struck the rock with his riding whip. The rock fell like stage scenery, revealing a broad open path and troops already in enemy country. Simultaneously, Bismarck's riding whip grew to a longer length. Freud, in *The Interpretation of Dreams,* approvingly quotes Hans Sachs as relating this dream to a probable masturbation inhibition in Bismarck; but to my mind the dream is exactly suited to exemplify the principle of compensation. The constricted path opened precisely in response to the dream ego taking action. This was a compensation to the conscious feeling of tiredness and limitation that

Sachs mentioned. It would be quite appropriate for Bismarck to be concerned with the Bohemian campaign as for the pharaoh to be concerned with the fate of Egypt, and the dream is understandable in those terms without being reduced to conjecture about a sexual problem. The whip seems less a disguised phallus when its increase in length is seen as a parallel image to the opening of the rock into an extended highway.

The dream of Jacob (Genesis 28:12) in which angels ascended and descended from heaven by means of a ladder was an important cultural dream; it also changed the life of the dreamer, who later took a new name (Israel) (Genesis 32:24–29). The ladder can have cultural amplifications, as in Egyptian imagery where it is a method of reaching heaven. Likewise, the dream in which Bismarck struck the rock can easily be construed to parallel the story of Moses striking the rock to bring forth water (Numbers 20:11). But these questions of amplification lead quickly into other areas of discussion, such as the role of opposites in the Moses story, and it is not appropriate to pursue such questions at this time.

Daniel's interpretation of the dream of Nebuchadnezzar (Daniel 4:10–18) is another important Old Testament instance of a dream having an impact, both for Daniel and for the king at a crucial turning point in history.

In the New Testament it is because of a dream that Joseph accepts the pregnancy of Mary as being of divine origin. Both the instructions to flee into Egypt and the instructions to return are sent by dreams (Matthew 1:20–21, 24; 2:12–13, 19–22). There are also instances in which people in the Bible have visions, which may possibly be related to dreams in intent. Peter is thrice given a vision of a net with animals (Acts 10:1–32); a parallel vision experienced by Cornelius tells him to send for Peter.

MEDIEVAL SOURCES

Coincidence of two visions or dreams is illustrated by the dreams of Francis of Assisi and Pope Innocent III. Before his crucial interview with the pope, Francis dreamed that he stopped to admire a large tree; then he grew as tall as the tree and was able to bend it easily. The pope dreamed that a minor monk restored the balance of the basilica of the Lateran, which was in danger of falling (De Becker, 1968, p. 26).

Beginning with the Christian era and continuing until the time of Freud, dreams increasingly came to be held in disrepute. As society became more structured, at least in its beliefs, less allowance was made for the individual insight that dreams furnished. Many manuscripts that have survived from the Middle Ages deal primarily with the question of true and false dreams. Whereas for Homer the distinction was between gates of ivory and gates of horn, in the Middle Ages the question became divinely inspired dreams versus dreams sent by demons to deceive; but the emphasis was much the same. In the Church there was little appreciation for those uses of dreams that were much like modern uses of dreams, which are closer to the Aesculapian attitude and to Socrates and Plato than to the atomism of Lucretius, the scientific reductionism of Aristotle, or complete denigration of the importance of dreams. Preoccupied with their struggle to preserve morality, the Christian priests apparently lost touch with the ancient interpretive skills. Dream interpretation might have been advanced significantly during those centuries had the Church devoted some of its considerable energies to such work. There is evidence that some interest in classical methods continued, but largely through popular dream books such as the so-called Dream-Books of Daniel (Thorndike, Vol. 2, 1923, pp. 290–302).

Tertullian, writing about A.D. 203, considered dreams to be the movement of the soul when separated from the body, coming in contact with realities reflecting God, nature, or demons. This bore some similarity to the opinion of Lucretius that dreams were "real" (McCurdy, 1946).

Origen, in the first half of the third century A.D., believed that some dreams might foreshadow the future, but this did not extend to accurate prophesy. During discussion with Celsus regarding the angel's warning to the Holy Family to flee to Egypt, Origen made the point that the warning came in a dream and thus was not marvelous, since dream warnings were well known to occur (Thorndike, Vol. 1, 1923, p. 459).

Gregory of Nyssa, one of the Cappadocian fathers, was an enlightened exception to the early Christian attitude toward dream interpretation. In *The Making of Man* (written about A.D. 380) he devoted several passages to dreams (McCurdy, 1946). In general, he affirmed the naturalistic attitudes of Aristotle and the physicians, but he also allowed for prophetic dreams sent by God. In contrast to Tertullian, he did not regard prophetic dreams as miraculous; he considered them not dreams at all in the ordinary sense. He thus avoided endless rumination on how the good dreams are to be distinguished from the bad. He thought that dreams were open to naturalistic study. The content of ordinary dreams he referred to memories or to the state of the body. This latter point he illustrated with a remarkable insight into the ravings of a relative who was ill. The sick man accused his relatives, including Gregory, of throwing water on him, and then moments later he broke into a profuse sweat. Gregory's alert mind saw the delusion to be a foreshadowing of the bodily event that was about to occur; by analogy, dreams can make visible what is only tacitly known in the body of the dreamer. Gregory also allowed a place for the passions, particularly sexual passions, in the origin of dreams. He distinguished between the qualities that were "brute life" and the transformation of such qualities into human passions by the "allegiance of thought." Thus animal feelings work for the good of the organism, but when taken over by the conscious function, they can become the human problems of "malignity, envy, deceit, conspiracy, hypocrisy" (McCurdy, 1946). In this respect Gregory of Nyssa was stating the converse of the opinion of Freud, who would place the irrational impulses of the id in the deeper recesses of the mind. Gregory saw the natural mind as balanced, like that of the animal, but becoming unbalanced when natural impulses are taken over and made into secondary conscious goals, cut off from their origins. In this formulation, Gregory of Nyssa came nearer to the Jungian view of the mind as inherently working toward wholeness and balance.

Synesius of Cyrene, the somewhat unorthodox Bishop of Ptolemais in the latter part of the fourth century A.D., wrote *De Insomniis Liber*; it was translated from Greek into Latin in the seventeenth century (McCurdy, 1946). He pictured the world as being interrelated such that events in one part might have effects in another through sympathetic vibrations; thus dreams might reflect true events. He also recommended dreams above other forms of divination because they were available to all persons and they could not be prevented by legal sanctions. While admitting that dreams might be obscure, he found them no more so than oracles.

In the eleventh century St. Peter Damien questioned the neglect of dreams and quoted a supposed remark of Alexander that he dreamed that he did not believe in dreams.

Saint Hildegard of Bingen (1098–1179) wrote in her *Causae et Curae* that the dreams sent by God to Adam before the Fall were true prophecy and that such dreams were still possible but could be confused with diabolic illusions (Thorndike, Vol. 2, 1923, p. 124). For true dreams, the body was to be in a "temperate condition" and the marrow "warmed," while there were to be no moral discrepancies in the dreamer. Hildegard had visions that were quite important in her own life, but they seem to have come to her in the waking state.

John of Salisbury, writing in 1159 (Thorndike, Vol. 2, 1923, p. 155), gave very conflicting views of dreams, seemingly without being much aware of the contradiction. That dreams are sometimes true he attributed to experience and "the authority of our ancestors." The reference of the dream is varied and may include the dreamer himself, someone other than the dreamer, common interests, or the public welfare. He cited the ancient idea that a king's dream concerned matters of state. Among the factors to be considered in understanding a dream, he listed the season of the year, the place of dreaming, and the personal characteristics of the dreamer—considerations not unlike those recommended by Artemidorus.

Michael Scot was an astrologer at the court of Frederick II in the first half of the thirteenth century. He considered the age of the dreamer, the phase of the moon, and the stage of digestion to be important factors in dream interpretation. A dream that took place before digestion had started was considered to be of no significance, and it dealt with the past. Dreams occurring during the process of digestion were thought to be concerned with the present. Only after digestion was complete did dreams signify the future. This is a curious blend of physiologic and psychological concerns, not unlike some of our present scientific difficulties, but expressed in a simple and intuitive way. Scot thought that dreams were diagnostic of imbalances of blood, red cholera, phlegm, and melancholy, or imbalances of heat, cold, dryness, and humidity. It would seem that he saw them as potentially diagnostic of physical illness.

Bartholomew of England, a Franciscan of the thirteenth century who lectured at Magdeburg in Saxony, counseled that one should neither reject nor easily accept the information of dreams, since they are sometimes true and sometimes false. He believed that some are evident, while others require interpretation. The possible origins of dreams were divine inspiration, angelic activity, diabolic illusion, and natural bodily causes.

The great theologian Thomas Aquinas (1225–1274) condemned most divinations, contrasting them to divinely inspired prophesy, which was able to speak with certainty even about matters that were contingent. Some natural divination was permissible, however, if not extended to accidental matters or to acts of will. Dreams produced by natural causes, either within or without the body, he considered possible sources for forecasting the future. In *Summa Theologica* Aquinas said that one could err in using dreams as sources of knowledge about the future either by making a pact with demons or by trying to extend divination beyond its possible limits.

Vincent of Beavais, in the thirteenth century, wrote his *Speculum Maius* in three "mirrors," or reflections. One of these, the *Speculum Naturale,* maintained that dreams are powerfully affected by motions of the stars, which motions are scarcely noticed by the awake mind. Similarly, dispositions of the sleeper might be ignored in waking hours but might be discernible during sleep; this is an early antecedent of Freud's position that repressed infantile wishes come to the surface when the energy available for repression is lessened during sleep. Vincent thought that dreams are not causes of future events but might be signs of them, and he thought that they require interpretation for that purpose, since it is not possible to represent an event clearly when the event has not yet occurred (Thorndike, Vol. 2, 1923, p. 457).

Albertus Magnus, who died in 1280 at the age of 80 years, was the principal teacher of Thomas Aquinas, and he outlived Aquinas by six years. It appears that he believed that interpretation of dreams was possible, and he linked dream interpretation with magic and astrology; but he did not censure the activity. Instead, he criticized Aristotle and others for not investigating dreams further in order to determine which dreams are suitable for interpretation. The writings of Roger Bacon inform us that study of Aristotle's works on natural philosophy was not permitted at Paris before 1237, one reason being his treatise *De Somno et Viglia,* dealing with dreams, although this prohibition may have been partially because of attached commentaries by others (Thorndike, Vol. 2, 1923, p. 576). Albertus Magnus linked the foretelling of future events by dreams with medical diagnosis. In both arts the predicted events do not always occur because of conflicting causes. He taught that dreams requiring interpretation do not come from God and that the future cannot be foretold by dreams that have accidental causes. He also thought that the actions of the stars might be a cause of dreams, since man was seen as a microcosm or image of the larger universe.

Cecco d'Ascoli, an early martyr to science, was condemned by the Inquisition and burned at the stake in Florence in 1327. He is known for his poem *l'Acerba,* which has been cited as an unkind parody of Dante's *Divine Comedy,* although more recently it has been suggested that he imitated the style of Dante out of admiration and respect. The work for which he was condemned was a commentary on the *Sphere* of Sacrobosco. Cecco ascribed any prophetic quality of dreams to astrologic influences; dreams were true when the moon was in the fixed astrologic signs (Taurus, Aquarius, Leo, and Scorpio) and either true or false in other signs.

FROM RENAISSANCE TO FREUD

Toward the end of the Middle Ages, people began to lose interest in the long argument about the divine or demonic origin of dreams; but unfortunately the abandonment of that argument did not lead to any revival of interest in constructive uses of dreams, such as those pursued by the Aesculapian priests in antiquity. The energy of the Renaissance was directed into exploration of the outer world and examination of the mind in relation to the world, as in the memory studies of Giulio Camillo, Ramon Lull, Giordano Bruno, Peter Ramus, and Robert Fludd (Yates, 1966). It is as if the preoccupation with the inner life that characterized the Middle Ages led to a rebound into the visible world; the imagainative capabilities that would have been essential to an intuitive understanding of the mind were directed instead toward experimentation in science and art. Even the elaborate memory systems, which certainly are impressive imaginative constructions, are primarily for the purpose of enlarging the ego's abilities; they attempt to impose structure on the unconscious mind rather than learn from it.

From the Renaissance to modern times the study of dreams fared little better. Thomas Hobbes (1599–1679) attributed the apparently disordered sequence of dream thoughts to the uneven influences of internal organs during sleep (Diamond, 1974). In *Humane Nature* (1650) he claimed that what coherence there is in dreams occurs by chance. The uneven influences on the brain cause dream thoughts to appear "like the Stars between the flying Clouds" and not in the order in which the waking man "would choose to observe them."

Marin Cureau de la Chabre (1594–1669), who was physician to Richelieu and Louis XIV, considered many dreams to be the aftermath of violent emotions experienced in the waking state; and dreams could accomplish such things as bringing plans for revenge "to a successful conclusion, since in sleep [the mind] is no longer governed by sense or by reason." He also considered physiologic causes of dreams, such as presumed imbalances in bile and blood (Diamond, 1974).

William Smellie (1740–1795), in his *Philosophy of Natural History,* recommended that dreams be written down as soon as the dreamer awakens in order to develop the capacity to remember dreams in greater detail. This advice is quite valid today. Although he offered no interpretations of dreams, he did record a dream of his own in which his breeches fell down during an important social occasion. We can recognize in this a typical form of the persona anxiety dream.

Descartes had three dreams on the night of November 10, 1619, on the way back from the emperor's coronation; these are discussed by von Franz (1975) as illustrations of the deep reworking of the personality that is possible through dreams. Descartes seems to have had no hesitation in taking these dreams as a serious occurrence in his life, a crucial turning point, without being at all troubled by whether they seemed true or false.

Thomas Willis (1621–1675) echoed the attitude of Lucretius toward dreams, emphasizing organic causes.

It is clear that in 1900, as Freud reviews the scientific literature on dreams in Chapter 1 of *The Interpretation of Dreams,* the old sense of dreams having meaning has been lost. In place of the medieval concern about true and false dreams, echoing the thoughts of antiquity, there are accounts of experiments concerning the roles of external and internal stimuli in evoking dreaming. Dreams were looked on as the products of the mind working with insufficient energy, without the coherence of its waking synthetic abilities. Amid these deintegrated studies of dreaming, Freud's significant and lasting achievement was to recapture the sense of personal meaning of the dream for the dreamer, a perspective that had been lost with the decline of the Aesculapian sanctuaries. Even though we may disagree with Freud's theoretical constructions regarding the dream, this in no way detracts from his truly heroic achievement in rehabilitating the study of dreams as a serious and meaningful enterprise after nineteen centuries of neglect.

With Freud begins the modern era of dream research and resumption of dream interpretation as a valid approach to the unconscious mind.

THE PSYCHOANALYTIC REVOLUTION

Freud's major work, *Die Traumdeutung* (*The Interpretation of Dreams*), carries the publication date 1900, although it was actually released in 1899. Interest in psychology was rising, and it carried with it fashions (such as phrenology) that would soon fade and those (such as psychic research) that would persist on a minimal level. This first major psychoanalytic work met with indifference rather than with the immediate antipathy that some writers have retrospectively imagined. The first printing did not sell well, and only gradually did the book gain the universal recognition it enjoys today as Freud's major and most original work (Jones, 1953). In many ways the psychoanalytic revolution appeared to spring full grown from Freud, primarily because of the preceding nineteen centuries of neglect of the art of dream interpretation (De Becker, 1968). In his *Introductory Lectures on Psycho-*

Analysis Freud acknowledged this hiatus and proposed to "embrace the prejudice of the ancients" and retrace the footsteps of "the dream interpreters of antiquity" (SE 15:87).*

Unlike the ancients, however, Freud totally dismissed the vexing question of true and false prophetic dreams, the conundrum that had troubled so many medieval Christian writers. He wrote (SE 19) that prophetic dreams would "disappear into nothing," but he indicated that he believed in the possibility of telepathic dreams between persons, and he even said that he had conducted telepathy experiments in his "private circle." In this opinion Freud was totally modern, for interest in scientific study of paranormal dreams had been increasing ever since the founding of the Society for Psychical Research in 1882 in England. There was no longer the ancient presumption of true and false dreams, nor the concern of the medieval churchmen with divine and demonic origins. Instead, the question of paranormal information in dreams was seen, as Freud indicated, to be a question for scientific examination.

Freud's theory of dreams changed only slightly from that set forth in his 1900 work (Pontalis, 1974). Of particular interest is Chapter VII, "The Psychology of the Dream Process," which contains his major insights. It is also historically instructive to review section G of Chapter I, in which Freud summarized the theories of dreaming and the functions of dreams that were being discussed in scientific circles at that time. His own insights and far-reaching intuitions are thrown into favorable relief by comparison. It is obvious that Freud's theory did not simply grow out of the researches of others; he had more affinity for the dream theories of antiquity than for the dissective laboratory experiments of his contemporaries.

In addition to *The Interpretation of Dreams,* important sources of information on Freud's thought are the essays "On Dreams" (SE 5), "Remarks on the Theory and Practice of Dream-interpretation" (SE 19), and "Some Additional Notes on Dream-interpretation as a Whole" (SE 19). Concern with dream interpretation is encountered throughout Freud's other works. In the wider psychoanalytic literature, references to dreams and dreaming are also legion, and only representative sources will be cited in this discussion. An early and clinically interesting presentation concerning dreams can be found in

---

*References to Freud's writings are to *The Complete Psychological Works of Sigmund Freud (Standard Edition),* published by Hogarth Press, London, 1966, indicated by the letters SE, followed by volume number and sometimes page number: (SE 15) or (SE 15:87).

Ella Freeman Sharpe's *Dream Analysis* (1937). The monographs by Nagera (1969) and Waldhorn (1967) offer modern statements of the clinical and theoretical positions on dreams and their interpretation in contemporary Freudian psychoanalysis. It is my impression that the dream has been relatively neglected, as compared to the importance it had in Freud's early thought and in his discoveries (sometimes mistaken) about the nature of unconscious processes.

NEGLECT OF DREAMS IN PSYCHOANALYSIS

In 1975 at the International Psychoanalytic Conference in London, Dr. Harold P. Blum was quoted as saying that dreams are no longer considered "the royal road to the unconscious" (Blum, 1975). Similar thoughts were expressed by Brenner (1969), who wrote that the view of dreams as the quickest and easiest road to understanding of the unconscious is at present backed by "no convincing evidence," although he added that it doubtless was sixty-five years ago. Summarizing the conclusions of a group of psychoanalysts, Waldhorn (1967) recorded that the analysis of dreams "should be handled in the same manner as the analysis of other mental productions," with no "predetermined precedence" being given to dream material. He added that "no longer can it [dream analysis] be considered the sole or even the primary or preeminent technique at the disposal of the analyst." Pontalis (1974) identified two opposing tendencies in the use of dreams in psychoanalysis, and these two tendencies are often manifested in the work of a single analyst. The first, which he does not wish to call classical, would maintain the royal-road status of dreams; the opposing tendency would consider a report of a dream no different than any other material in the patient's session. This second view has some support from Freud himself, who wrote in "Some Additional Notes upon Dream Interpretation as a Whole" (SE 19) that "no one can practice the interpretation of dreams as an isolated activity: it remains a part of the work of analysis."

Although the general trend in Freudian psychoanalytic work seems to be away from special emphasis on the dream, this is by no means a uniform attitude. Protests for retention of a special place for the dream also appear in the Freudian literature. Altman (1969) reaffirmed the dream as "essential to the exploration of the unconscious." This rests on the theoretical position that the dream is representative of an altered form of consciousness in which the intersystemic dynamics (id, ego, superego) function differently. The dream is therefore qualitatively different than waking productions. Also, as a practical clinical matter, information arrived at through interpretation of a dream may have greater impact on the patient than the same insights achieved through analysis of other aspects of behavior and experience.

In spite of conflicting views about dreams within the Freudian school, it seems fair to cite the statement of Pontalis (1974) that the current turning away from Freud's original emphasis on dreams "is strangling the eloquence of oneric [dream] life." In many ways the Jungian school of psychoanalysis has preserved Freud's original emphasis on dreams, although they are seen from a quite different theoretical stance. As I shall show later, the decline of the dream may have been inevitable in Freudian theory because of the basic theoretical assumption that what is dreamed and remembered is a disguise, a mere "manifest" dream, while the real meaning of the dream is said to lie behind the presumed disguise.

BASIC STATEMENT OF FREUD'S DREAM THEORY

Freud's position on dreams, as written in 1899, was later modified slightly by his elaboration of other models of the psychic apparatus. The original topographical model was based on the idea of spatial metaphors—the unconscious was "below" the conscious mind. He later talked more in structural terms, speaking of such different psychic entities as *ego, id,* and *superego.* The id was the original matrix of the mind; it contained *drives,* or psychologic representations of the basic biologic needs of the body. The ego was formed as an executive organ of the id, and with its elaboration the immediate pressure for gratification of id desires (*the pleasure principle*) was modified by the *reality principle,* allowing postponement of pleasure in order to enhance it or to avoid pain associated with immediate discharge. The ego saw reality and understood the need for a synthesis of various needs, while the id seemed only to wish decrease of instinctual tension, which it felt as pleasurable. The superego was a psychic entity that was developed later, based on the introjected image of the dominant parent, who represented the model of the society in which the ego was developing. The ego was seen as the mediator of tension between the outer demands of reality (including their representation in the superego) and the instinctual demands of the id.

Modifications in Freud's original theory of dreams seem to be little more than restatements of concepts in the later and more elaborated conceptual terms. The exception occurs in *Beyond the Pleasure Prin-*

ciple (SE 18), where Freud considered that there might be death instincts as well as life instincts, a revision in which he was not followed by many later Freudians. If a death instinct exists side by side with the libido of a life instinct, then dreams may satisfy one or the other or may satisfy both to varying degrees. The death instinct, for example, might be manifest as underlying repetition compulsions, repetitive dreams, and dreams of traumatic neuroses that exactly reproduce, in apparent disregard of the pleasure principle, extremely frightening situations that have actually occurred.

Freud (SE 18:53) claimed that his views had from the very first been dualistic, but had moved from the opposition of ego instincts and sexual instincts to a more comprehensive opposition of life instincts and death instincts. In contrast, he considered Jung's libido theory to be monistic because it described only one basic instinctual force. As will be shown later, Jung did indeed understand the need for duality in many conceptualizations, seeing a primary area of stress between the archetypal and the personal modes of existence; but Jung also pushed the concern with duality (which he usually referred to as "opposites") to its most extreme conceptualization—that of the central archetype being a *coincidentia oppositorum,* a union of opposites, something not thinkable in the usual modes of discourse and represented symbolically in such strange images as the alchemical *lapis.*

Freud's view of the dream was that during sleep the censor that ordinarily kept unacceptable wishes out of consciousness had at its disposal for this purpose much less energy (libido), and thus repressed wishes might arise during sleep. In sleep there was decathexis (removal of energy, libido) from all three parts of the psychic apparatus (ego, id, and superego); in psychosis, energy was deficient in the ego; in neurosis, there was a decrease of libido in the preconscious system (Waldhorn, 1967, p. 84). Since repressed wishes, usually of a childhood sexual nature, had been excluded from the conscious mind because they were unacceptable to the ego's image of itself, anxiety was produced by their attempt to enter unconsciousness when censorship was relaxed in sleep. Essentially the dream was seen as a compromise between the unacceptable wish and the desire to remain asleep. The dream work elaborated from the wish a disguised version that would permit partial discharge of the repressed wish without becoming so clear as to arouse anxiety and disturb sleep.

Thus the purpose or function of the dream was seen by Freud as preservation of sleep. Freud believed that when the dreamer awoke from the dream, especially if wakened by anxiety in the dream, the function of the dream had failed and the underlying anxiety had appeared in consciousness.

What is the dream? For the clinician it is whatever the patient reports as a dream (Waldhorn, 1967), although experienced therapists can often differentiate nocturnal dreams from other forms of imaginal activity such as reveries on the way toward sleep. Although Freud referred to dreams as transient psychosis (SE 14:230), he quite clearly did not consider them pathological in themselves, but rather as a normal part of mental functioning. Nagara (1969) offered perhaps the most succinct statement of Freud's view of the dream: "a dream is the [disguised] fulfillment of a [repressed] wish." Thus the dream is a repressed desire presented to consciousness in a disguised form.

In *An Outline of Psycho-Analysis,* published in 1938, Freud (SE 23) added to the id impulses as instigating sources of dreams the possibility that dreams could also arise from a preconscious chain of thoughts that contained conflict or from an ego desire based on the day residues, events of the day preceding the dream that had not been fully attended to in consciousness. *Day residues* are thought of as affective processes that have to some extent escaped the lowering of energy produced by sleep, possibly because they are indifferent elements that have resisted censorship (Nagara, 1969, pp. 40–41). The id impulse would most characteristically be a repressed wish, but it might in some instances be the result of somatic demands, such as the need to urinate. Thus the formation of the dream is the result of dream work done on the wish to prevent it from disturbing sleep.

As summarized by Nagara (1969), the elements that can be considered part of the dream work are *condensation, displacement, plastic representation,* and *secondary revision.* It is not considered that such "higher" functions as judgment, criticism, reasoning, etc., are part of the dream work itself; they may appear in the dream only because they are already in existence in the latent dream thoughts. This is in marked contrast to Jungian dream theory, in which the dream is seen as often highly creative. What Nagara called plastic representation was referred to earlier by Sharpe (1937) as symbolization; it can be described more accurately as the use of a semiotic sign, reserving the term *symbol,* as Jung does, for its more basic and traditional use.

The term *condensation* refers to the manner in which one idea is thought to be able to carry the energy charge of a number of related ideas. The process of energy moving from one idea to another is called *displacement,* and these two processes are thus closely related. Considerations of which ideas are appropriate for the displacement of energy include their similarity, consonance, and common attributes (SE 14:81). It follows from this theoretical model that the so-called manifest dream will have less content than the sum of the many latent dream thoughts that have found a disguised representation in it. By means of this process of displacement, the movement of energy from the latent thought to the manifest dream image can involve movement from a thing of greater interest to an image of lesser interest or movement from something important to something unimportant. Dream distortion is considered to be governed by two factors: it is greater when the wish that is to be censored is more frightening or when the demands of censorship are higher than usual. Obviously these two factors may be thought of as being of variable intensities (SE 15:143). The dual functioning of condensation and displacement produces distortion of the latent dream thoughts; in Freudian theory this distortion is necessary so that the unacceptable unconscious and preconscious material may be included in the manifest dream images (Nagara, 1969, p. 68).

Both *plastic representation* and *secondary revision* are theoretically required because the verbal expression available to the conscious mind (part of *secondary process*) is presumably not available for the dream work and because the dream, if not made believable by secondary revision, might attract the attention of the ego's reality sense and fail in its function of preserving sleep.

Processes in the unconscious are thought of as occurring according to a *primary process,* the tendency of which is to seek discharge without delay (Waldhorn, 1967, p. 82). The primary process is essentially an objective language for the same process that when experienced subjectively is called the *pleasure principle* (Hinsie and Campbell, 1960, pp. 577–578).

One particularly helpful model of Freudian dream theory pictures the "excitations" aroused during sleep as being denied their customary outlet in action. This is seen as analogous to a reflex arc in which the efferent action-taking limb of the reflex is prohibited by the state of sleep (SE 5:537). Impulses reaching their normal motor outlet are denied access to the motor apparatus because it is not functioning during sleep. These impulses then turn retrogressively through the unconscious toward the perceptual system, which is consequently activated and produces images. This is topographical regression and is seen as a return to "the primitive level of hallucinatory wish fulfillment" (Nagara, 1969, p. 63). Regression can be thought of as having three aspects: topographical, temporal, and formal. Topographical regression is from consciousness toward the content of the unconscious; temporal regression moves toward the awakening of earlier memories and images; formal regression refers to a more primitive mode of functioning of the mental apparatus. Although regression may also take place during the waking state, it ordinarily simply brings to consciousness mnemonic

images from the stored memory, not progressing to the point of hallucinatory perceptual images as in dreams.

Although Freud listed three sources of dreams (recent and indifferent material, infantile material, and somatic sources) he thought that
the motivating power was always an infantile wish that had been repressed (Nagara, 1969, p. 20). Thus the basic formulation that dreams
defend against repressed infantile wishes still holds a central theoretical
place in Freudian theory.

Since all subsequent work on interpretation of dreams, including
that of Jung, tends to be seen in contrast to the position of Freud, it
may be useful to elaborate more fully the basic components of Freud's
position.

Wish for Sleep as Motive for Dreams

Freud's postulation of the dream as the preserver of sleep was a
good approximation, considering what was known at the time he
wrote. Modern laboratory sleep studies, which will be reviewed in a
following chapter, have shown that the threshold for arousal is higher
during dreaming. But laboratory studies generally do not support
Freud's basic assumption that sleep is preserved by dreams. Indeed,
the converse may be true: one of the motives for sleeping may be to
dream. Even prior to the accumulation of data from laboratory sleep
studies, however, there were reasons for questioning Freud's model.
For example, a great number of dreams occur just prior to waking,
when it would seem that the need to sleep has been met (Hollender,
1962). Also, ascribing to dreams so universal a motive as the desire to
sleep obscures the intricate linkage that can be observed between the
content of the dream and the current life situation of the dreamer. If
preserving sleep were the principal aim, it would seem to be "on the
whole a matter of indifference to the sleeping ego what may be
dreamed," so long as sleep is preserved (SE 19). Freud's position
likewise did not allow for any actual creative activity or problem-
solving in dreams, although many people seem to think that their
dreams accomplish these functions (Lipton, 1967).

Sexual Nature of Repressed Wishes

There had been many instances of recognition of the sexual aspects of childhood prior to Freud, but his theory served to unify a
number of observations (Kern, 1973). Today there is no doubt about
the many sexual impulses of children. In the clinic the practitioner may

see problems caused by inadequate repression of such fantasy, as well as problems caused by the more common response of excessive repression. The presumption of a sexual nature in the repressed wishes behind dreams has been based to a great extent on the distinction between manifest content and latent content, a theoretical position that will be critiqued later. In fact, it might be said that the primary difference between the approaches of Freud and Jung to the dream lies in this distinction. Although the dream is not simply transparent for Jung, he does not speak in terms of a hidden latent meaning. By way of analogy, it would not be useful to maintain that a foreign language one does not understand is a disguised form of English; it is simply an unknown language, and one can learn its rules and meanings.

Freud (SE 19) remarked on the multiplicity of dreams dealing with incest, as compared to the scarcity of straightforward dreams of a sexual relationship with one's mother. This is because he believed that a large number of disguised versions of such wishes are to be found in dreams. It would appear that Freud was alluding to the frequency of such incest themes in the *latent* dream, which carries the supposed "true" meaning of the dream after it has been subjected to analysis. An example of such disguised sexuality of an incestual nature was given by Sharpe (1937, p. 178). A young woman patient dreamed that she was making love to Douglas Fairbanks, who gradually became her own brother. In the interpretation of this dream, Sharpe believed that the dreamer's father was there by implication: (1) the brother implied the family situation and may have been a displacement from the father; (2) there were two actors named Douglas Fairbanks: they were father and son, senior and junior. Sharpe therefore thought that father-daughter incest was the hidden meaning of the latent dream. Similar interpretations would seem to be the basis for Freud's assertion of the frequency of incest in psychoanalytic interpretations of dreams. The dream of Bismarck in which his riding whip grew longer is another example of sexual interpretation of dream motif that may carry other meanings, although sexual implications cannot be entirely dismissed.

Openly sexual dreams do occur, but they are not always interpretable as the result of repressed incest themes. Since the personal mother may represent other mothering images, it is possible that incest with the mother could itself be a symbol in the Jungian sense. A famous example of such symbolization by means of sexual imagery is Caesar's dream before crossing the Rubicon, an act that changed the course of Roman history. After weeks of indecision about marching on Rome, Caesar dreamed of intercourse with his mother, whereupon he decided to march his legions into Rome, the mother city. As De Becker (1968) explained, the dream interpreters of Caesar's day would have had no difficulty in seeing maternal incest as a symbol for territorial conquest. Today we are still familiar with the concepts mother earth, mother country, alma mater, and other similar usages.

Sexuality does occur in explicit form in dreams, but its specific meaning must always be considered. Is it a direct image (objective level of interpretation), or is it subjective, referring to parts of the dreamer's psyche? Whether objective or subjective, how symbolic is the sexual imagery? These are questions better examined after an exposition of Jung's theory.

There is no question that the fin de siècle society in which Freud worked in Vienna exhibited many forms of sexual repression, and for the more open society in which we live today we owe a considerable debt to Freud for his pioneering crusade against hypocrisy and disregard of natural instincts. However, it does not always follow that it is sexuality that will be revealed when repression is lifted. Perhaps the society that Freud observed was not representative of mankind as a whole—hence the early debate as to whether the oedipal complex was universal. Societies and individuals are equally capable of repressing other aspects of natural behavior. Indeed, it may be inevitable that some degree of repression occurs during the maturational process from child to adult; that which is repressed would seem likely to vary from culture to culture, from family to family, from one historical situation to another. Jung's principle of *compensation* does not specify what is likely to be found in unconscious material, but it asserts that the material will be compensatory to the conscious situation. An example may make clear the nature of compensation and sexuality.

A man in his forties who was separated from his wife was quite active sexually. In addition to sleeping with his wife several times a week, he had a mistress whom he saw regularly, and in his available free time he tended to seek casual sexual encounters with other women, frequenting for that purpose a bar well known as a place for such meetings. However during this period of very active and unrepressed sexuality, his dreams were in startling contrast—he dreamed of going to church and taking communion. The principle of compensation was clearly at work in this case. At one time earlier in his life he had wanted very much to become a minister, but had decided against those feelings and taken a different direction in his life work. The dreams were adding back to his consciousness, or attempting to do so, the element that was neglected at that moment in his ego activity. If he had been in Freud's Vienna, and if he had repressed his sexuality, his dreams would surely have been equally as forceful in representing back to his consciousness the missing sexual feelings.

One last point about sexuality and Freud's theory should be made. Pontalis (1974) made the interesting observation that to Freud himself the dream may have been "a displaced maternal body." If that is allowed, Freud's interest in his own dream life, the basis for his famous self-analysis, could symbolically have represented maternal incest. Freud's penetration of the "maternal" dreams (incest?) led to his understanding and conquering, he thought, the unexplored land of the unconscious mind. Given Pontalis' assumption, it is easy to see a parallel with the dream of Caesar that led to his crossing the Rubicon and becoming preeminent in Rome.

In Jungian thought the deeper layers of the unconscious contain opposites. The shadow, which is in many ways equivalent to Freud's *id,* is not simply the repository of repressed unacceptable wishes or the psychic representations of the needs of the body. In order to adapt to the particular family in which he is born, a child may have to repress perfectly natural and acceptable parts of his personality. But below the personal level of the unconscious, the opposites also occur in the archetypal images of the objective psyche (what Jung had originally called the collective unconscious). Out of the archetypes arise both instinctual impulses and instinctual counterimpulses. This is particularly well illustrated by Harding (1965) in *The 'I' and the 'Not-I'.* Her diagram V of the archetypal images shows clearly that what may appear to be opposites at the "upper" and more personal levels of consciousness arise from and remain in articulation with deeper archetypal layers of the psyche in which the unification of opposites is possible. If this relationship is read in a developmental way (that is, if one looks at it as the emergence of a personality out of the original unity of the psyche of the child), then it is clear that the deeper archetypal images contain both aspects of what will appear as instinctual motives in the more developed mind of the adult. This is an image of the self-regulating activity of the psyche, which appears in dream interpretation as the principle of compensation. Hillman (1968) also noted this self-regulation in discussing the masturbation inhibition.

Day Residue

Freud believed that the events of the day preceding the dream were involved in dream formation. His observation is without doubt correct, although the theoretical reasons he gave can be seen in other ways. Freud described two types of day residue. The first, composed of usually indifferent events, was to be seen in the manifest content of the dream, the dream as it was actually remembered and reported. The other type of day residue was more important psychodynamically; it touched more areas of conflict and could be determined only through the process of (Freudian) dream analysis. In analogy to business enterprises, Freud (SE 4, 5:561) spoke of the daytime thought that became the day residue as an *entrepreneur*, while the repressed unconscious wish that found expression through it was the possessor of the capital (libido) to actually produce the dream. Freud (SE 19:3–63) later spoke of similar differences in dreams that were "from below" and were provoked by the strength of the repressed wish, as compared to dreams "from above," which owed their origin primarily to thoughts from the previous day that obtained reinforcement from the repressed wish. In his final structural comments on dream interpretation, Freud (SE 23:141–207) repeated the opinion that dreams may arise from the id (unconscious wish) or from the ego (more precisely, from preconscious trains of thought carrying conflicting material). This is simply a restatement in structural terms (ego, id, superego) of his previous position of "dreams from above and dreams from below." In either case, however, it is the repressed wish that is crucial.

As a technical maneuver, Freud (SE 19:3–66, 22:3–182) twice recommended beginning the dream interpretation by identifying the day residues. In this respect he suggested much the same procedure as Jung, who insisted that the dream be placed in the context of life in which it occurred, although the theoretical reasons of the two oneiro-critical approaches are different.

Day residues were for Freud one of three ways in which memories could influence dreams, the others being unrepressed past memories (in hypermnesic dreams) and repressed past memories that appear in the manifest dream only in distorted and disguised form (Nagara, 1969, p. 50).

Hartman (1968) published interesting comparisons of the times of occurrence of the events that become day residues in dreams. From 88 dreams he identified 463 items of day residue. The day preceding the dream accounted for 94% of these items; 65% were from the evening hours of 6 P.M. to 9 P.M., with those occurring 2 hours before bedtime being most frequently seen in the manifest dreams. Items experienced just prior to sleep were linked to psychodynamically important material, but they were in themselves rather indifferent. If the day-residue item had occurred as much as a day prior to the dream, which was rare, it was more likely to have strong dynamic importance.

Let me make clear, with an example from a dream of my own, the manner in which day-residue material may be incorporated: I was discussing with RO (who in the dream seemed similar to DM) whether he was to pull a tooth with his thumb and forefinger. I don't think it was my tooth. There was playful sparring after the discussion. Then we were in the garage of the house where I grew up, looking at some old refrigerators, apparently trying to find one for DM's younger daughter, who had just married. She seemed to be inside the house talking to my parents. Leaving aside any psychodynamic meaning of the dream, let us consider several points of day-residue material. The evening prior to the dream I had addressed a dinner meeting of a dental honorary society. DM had been my dentist in childhood, and his *older* daughter had been one of my close childhood friends. The previous night I had visited friends in Dallas, where I unexpectedly saw their daughter, whom I knew, and met for the first time her new husband. There may have been day-residue associations linked to the couple I was visiting. She had come from a larger town just next to the small East Texas town where I grew up. A topic of conversation with her husband had been the importance of trying to enjoy life, an attitude that I associated with RO, the father of a high school friend.

Thus in this short dream there were a number of links to day residue: the talk to the dental society, the new marriage, links to my hometown, and two men associated with the thought of enjoying one's life. These day-residue associations may help to locate the dream in relation to events of concern at the time, but they do not in themselves offer significant information about dynamic meanings of the dream.

Bergler and Jekels (1940) suggested that day residue is not neutral in meaning but may be actively chosen by the superego to express guilt. This is a position derived from Freud's later dual-instinct theory. Langs (1971) introduced the term *recall residues* to designate those events of the day following the dream that serve as reminders for the recall of the forgotten dream. Several Freudian writers have moved in the direction of Jungian theory in suggesting that the dream may influence the events of the day following, not simply acting to protect sleep. Leveton (1961), for example, suggested the term *night residue* to refer to pieces of the dream that are retained in memory and may influence the actions and perceptions of the day following the dream. Kanzer (1955) emphasized the dream's tendency to communicate, not simply preserve sleep; and he showed that this tendency to establish contact with reality may be served by use of day residues in the dream. These similarities to Jungian thought do not appear to have been intentional, as the similarities were not noted by the authors.

Plastic Representation

Considerations of representability in dreams were thought by Freud to result from the unconscious presumably not having access to the use of language (a part of secondary or waking processes). It is certainly true that dreams are primarily visual in content, but sentences and conversation do occur in dreams, as do (more rarely) the sense modalities of smell, touch, taste, etc. In fact, some dreams consist entirely of words; thus it would not appear to be the incapacity of use language but rather preference for or suitability of visual representation that accounts for the predominance of plastic imagery in dreams. My own speculation in this regard is that the dream ego is relating to other intrapsychic "objects," which in the language of Jungian complex theory are the representations or personifications of complexes, emotionally toned collections of images held together by a similar affective component. As in waking life, most interaction with objects is phenomenologically nonverbal, with verbal interchange being characteristic of subject–subject interaction. At times it seems that the dream, although having access to the use of language, is deliberately impelled to use a visual image for the sake of a pun or humor that will attract the attention of the waking ego.

Secondary Revision

Freudian theory and Jungian theory diverge greatly in the way they view the dramatic form of the dream. Freud (SE 4–5) originally pictured this as part of the dream work, although he later placed it with the secondary process (SE 18:241). In Jungian analysis of dreams, the dramatic form of the dream is an intrinsic part of the meaning of the dream. Important information is sometimes conveyed by the manner in which scenes change or by the way the flow of the dramatic process is altered by activity of the dream ego.

Bresnitz (1971) identified three ways in which Freud used the concept of secondary revision: Primary revision is used to denote the process in the dream work; secondary revision is used to denote the alterations after a dream has been put in basic form by the dream work; tertiary revision denotes revision that operates after waking. These distinctions have not been widely noted.

Free Association

The technique Freud devised for uncovering what he thought to be the latent meanings in dream images was free association, a now well-known procedure in which the analysand is asked to verbalize whatever comes to mind in relation to each motif of the manifest dream. Although there has been no direct confirmation, it is likely that Freud knew of the prior report by Galton as to how Galton's mind associated to the various objects he saw while walking down Pall Mall (Roth, 1975). Inability on the part of the patient to comply completely with the rule of free association discloses resistances (Kaplan, 1973). The value of free association has been doubted, particularly in working with psychosomatic problems (Nemiah, 1976).

Jung's procedure of *amplification,* an alternative to free association, grew out of his work on word-association experiments (CW 2).* In those experiments he noted that supposedly indifferent stimulus words presented to a subject elicited varying responses. On occasion the time required before the subject could provide an associated word was unduly prolonged. Jung discovered that this was due to the activation of what he called complexes, groups of images with a common emotional tone as their core. Similar use of the term *complex* has become part of popular terminology. Although Jung's criticism of free-association will be discussed more fully in the exposition of the amplification process in a later chapter, the essence of his argument is as follows: When engaging in free association, the patient will inevitably reveal those complexes that are at that time activated in the patient's mind, and this will occur whether the stimulus for the association is indifferent or dynamic material. But the dream image is, in Jungian theory, a response of the unconscious mind to the state of the ego, and therefore the dream image itself may be a commentary on the complexes that are activated. It will be seen that similar striking differences between Jung and Freud appear in their disagreement about the concept of latent dream thoughts.

LATENT DREAMS

The difficulties inherent in Freud's dream theory can be focused in the question of whether there is a latent level of dream thought behind the manifest dream (the dream as it is actually experienced and recalled). Freud called the remembered dream the manifest dream, and he considered it to embody disguised forms of latent dream thoughts that in themselves had no pictorial character and could, if undisguised,

---

*References to Jung's *Collected Works* are indicated by the letters *CW,* followed by volume number and sometimes page number: (CW 2) or (CW 2:130). Jung's *Collected Works* have been translated by R.F.C. Hull (deceased) and edited by Sir Herbert Read (deceased), Michael Fordham, and Gerhard Adler, with William McGuire as executive editor. The *Collected Works* are published in English by Routledge and Kegan Paul, London, and for the Bollingen Foundation by Princeton University Press. Additional volumes are still being issued.

appear in the consciousness as waking thoughts or memories. Latent dream contents are considered by Freud to be those parts of the dream discoverable only through the analytic process: wishes (largely sexual), preconscious material (largely day residues), and bodily stimuli (Nagera, 1969, pp. 28–30). It is clear that for Freud the real meaning of the dream was not to be found in the actual remembered dream, but in what was presumed to lie behind it. Affects in a dream, often the most crucial aspect of a dream, were also attributed by Freud to the latent content (SE 5:466). The manifest dream is so different from the latent dream thoughts that "no one would suspect the presence of the latter behind the former" (Nagera, 1969, p. 59). Freud did mention the possibility that some manifest dreams could coincide with their latent contents, and these he called dreams of convenience; but these were considered to be the undisguised dreams of children or similar adult dreams in response to such needs as thirst. Also, Freud believed that the superego's wish to punish because latent content has been insufficiently disguised may at times appear in the manifest content (Nagera, 1969, p. 27).

In a 1925 essay, "Some Additional Notes on Dream Interpretation as a Whole," Freud commented on an insufficiently investigated observation that at times the manifest dream expresses both concrete ideas *and* abstract thoughts based on them (SE 19). In the same essay there was also the implication that one of the important motives in Freud's formulation was to shift the responsibility for the manifest dream away from the ego. These admissions did not alter Freudian theory in any basic fashion.

Foulkes (1964), among others, decried the fact that today there is only an "occasional episode" in which analysis includes classic reworking of dreams from the manifest meaning to the latent meaning. He also pointed to the increased significance given to the manifest dream itself, especially in the analysis of the transference.

The problem of the manifest dream was recognized by other psychoanalytic writers (Bernstein and Glenn, 1969; Babcock, 1966). Pontalis (1974) suggested that Freud's emphasis on the true dream work being different from both the manifest dream and the latent dream thoughts may have been in opposition to Jung's growing influence, since for Jung the manifest dream was the actual dream. What Freudian theory emphasized as the discrepancy between the manifest dream and the latent dream thoughts was seen by Jung as a tension between the symbols of the manifest (and only) dream and the unknown contents of the unconscious mind toward which they gestured. For Jung the dream was a symbol, for Freud it was a disguise.

In spite of Freud's unaltering position about the façade nature of the remembered dream, there has been growing concern that the manifest dream itself is of value. Epstein (1969) studied the dreams of 15 pregnant women and discovered that their manifest dreams, without interpretation, resembled their waking cognitive efforts to cope with the possible threats of the pregnancy and the approaching delivery. Spanjaard (1969) believed that in most patients the major conflict could be seen in the manifest dream.

This tension between classic Freudian theory and other approaches to dream interpretation was clearly demonstrated several years ago at the annual banquet gathering of Dallas psychiatrists, psychiatric social workers, and clinical psychologists. The speaker was Montague Ullman, M.D., the director of dream research at Maimonides Hospital in New York City and a pioneer in the investigation of telepathic dreams. In the discussion following Dr. Ullman's presentation, one of the leading Freudian psychoanalysts asked a lengthy question, ending with this comment: "It seems you're saying that there is no latent dream!" Dr. Ullman's answer was simple. "Yes," he said, "there *is* no latent dream." This brief interchange was the clearest statement I have seen of this conflict over the problem of a hidden, disguised, or latent dream. Perhaps there is no latent dream, but if we discard the concept of the latent dream, we must find other ways of accounting for the clinical phenomena that traditionally have been explained by this concept. The contents of the dream, for example, may have clear reference to problems that are not explicitly shown in the dream. I believe that these phenomena that traditionally have been associated with latent dream thoughts are better described by Jung's conceptions of symbolization (different from the Freudian use of the term *symbol*), emotionally toned complexes (different from the usual popular use of the term *complex*), and the central archetype (Self), which is the origin of the dream in Jungian theory.

NEED FOR NEW PSYCHOANALYTIC CONCEPTS

In the psychoanalytic literature there is no shortage of suggestions for basic revisions in theoretical concepts (Peterfreund and Schwartz, 1971; Waldhorn, 1967; Wolstein, 1969). Historically, psychoanalysis has been an attempt to construct a purely psychological theory of the mind, and this may at present be limiting new growth in the field (Peterfreund and Schwartz, 1971). Elaborated as a treatment, psychoanalysis has been more valuable as a training technique (Grotjahn,

1965). Some indications of the directions in which theoretical growth might occur have been given by Lichtenberg and Slap (1971), who emphasized the ego's use of nondefensive processes, such as cognitive control to modify the unconscious material that arises spontaneously and even to influence what material appears in consciousness.

Many difficulties have arisen during attempts to validate these various psychoanalytic concepts in a scientific manner. These difficulties are partly the result of such problems as are inherent in the latent dream, which is not open to empirical study in the same manner as is the manifest dream specimen. Brenner (1968) showed that introspection alone does not differentiate psychoanalysis from other natural sciences. Wolman (1964) stated that there is no direct evidence that can either confirm or refute the propositions of psychoanalytic theory in their present form. He called for new methods of research. Graves (1973) echoed the need for more testable formulations. Ambitious long-term attempts to study psychoanalytic impact in a clinical setting have been difficult to carry out and hard to interpret (Wallerstein, 1964). At the present time the utility of classic psychoanalysis is being reassessed, and its areas of particular application are being defined more precisely (Rawn, 1974).

In an important historical summary by Sandler, Dare, and Holder (1972), the course of psychoanalysis was divided into four major phases, based on Freud's work. A possible fifth phase was seen as having current potential. The fourth phase began with Freud's structural theory and continued into ego psychology and the work of Kris, Erikson, D. Rapaport, and, in a germinal way, A. Freud (Lustman, 1967). Melanie Klein's work was considered part of this fourth phase, as was Jung's work on psychosis. Other significant contributors that should be listed are Ernest Jones, Ronald Fairbairn, D.W. Winnicott, Frieda Fromm-Reichmann, and Franz Alexander. This historical perspective correctly acknowledged the contributions of Jung, which are more congruent with modern Freudian theory than they were with Freud's thinking at the time of his break with Jung. The projected fifth phase of psychoanalytic psychology is seen as a development resulting from new findings in general psychology and other scientific disciplines; laboratory studies on sleep and dreaming will contribute significantly to this development.

Hartmann, Kris, and Lowenstein (1953) carefully examined the role of theory in psychoanalysis, where theory and empirical observations that might confirm or refute theory are more intimately related than in most scientific enterprises. This interdependence is one reason that any alteration of the theoretical structures is so difficult: a challenge to theory can be countered by citing supportive experimental results; an attack on experimental results can be diluted by theoretical speculation. This is possible because the theory is founded on intuitive grounds, on belief, and is not the direct result of extrapolation from experiments. A situation in which theory and experiment alternately defend the status quo constitutes what Polanyi (1958) termed a dynamo-objective coupling, an arrangement that is particularly difficult to change. A basic fault in current psychoanalytic theory is that the constructs are impersonal causal models, while the clinical activity of psychoanalysis focuses strongly on meaning, a subjective experience that is crucial in behavior (Wachtel, 1969). Jungian theory, in contrast, has been concerned from its inception with the role of meaning, which can be deficient (as when the ego is too far removed from its own archetypal foundations) or overwhelming (as in schizophrenia, when activated archetypal imagery submerges the reality sense of the ego).

A counterpoint to the problem of validation in psychoanalysis was made by Wallerstein (1973): quoting Polanyi, he emphasized that the factor of personal involvement of the scientist is *always* present in the equation, although the scientist's personal commitment is more visible in psychoanalysis than in the physical sciences.

A particularly difficult problem of conceptualization in depth psychology is the use of spatial or structural metaphors, which tend to be reified and discussed as if they were localizable objects. Distinguishing the ego from the id was shown by Hayman (1969) to present conceptual problems in Freudian theory. A similar problem in Jungian theory is the actual inseparability of the personal unconscious from the deeper layers of the objective psyche, the collective unconscious (Williams, 1973).

In summary, the time has long passed when the problems of psychoanalytic theory could be excused as being the result of growing pains of a young science. The psychoanalytic enterprise, under whatever name, must be seen as the intensive study of individual subjective life (what Jung called the individuation process) that is not the exclusive property of any particular approach. The various schools of psychoanalysis, which often were based on overelaboration of specific aspects of theory, are today receiving less emphasis (Rangell, 1970). The important and impressive findings in other areas of scientific inquiry could be the stimulus for rebirth of the psychoanalytic movement in a more comprehensive form that is more viable, more accessible, and more true to the present moment in science.

FREUD

Aside from his importance as the revolutionary who ended nineteen centuries of neglect of dreams, Freud was a major force in determining the direction that psychoanalysis would develop. As Neumann (1956) said, we have only recently emerged from the heroic age of psychology, during which it burst the bounds of its traditional role as appendage to philosophy and completely changed man's view of himself and his psyche. In such an age of heroes it was perhaps unavoidable that the leaders would stamp their work with what Jung called the "personal equation." Although they were deeply divergent in crucial ways, Jung never repudiated the value of a Freudian (reductive) analysis in certain cases. Jung wrote two appreciative essays on Freud (CW 15:33–40, 41–49) and credited Freud with the "great achievement" of putting dream interpretation on the proper course by recognizing that "no interpretation can be undertaken without the dreamer" (CW 8:284). Biographies of both Freud and Jung continue to be written, each new publication giving fresh insights and correctives. Ellenberger (1973, p. 54) questioned many of the facts cited by Freud's foremost biographer, Ernest Jones (1953). The biographies of Jung have just begun to appear, two notable examples being *C. G. Jung: His Myth in Our Time* (von Franz, 1975) and *Jung, His Life and Works: A Biographical Memoir* (Hannah, 1976); von Franz and Hannah were both close associates of Jung. Also, much of the Jung-Freud correspondence is now available (McGuire, 1974), allowing fresh nuances to be seen in their interaction at the very beginnings of depth psychology. Frey-Rohn (1974) published a scholarly comparison of the basic concepts of Jung and Freud.

The intellectual environment in which both Freud and Jung worked did not aid them in their revolutionary insights (Rubiner, 1961; Schick, 1968–1969), and many writers discussed their cultural antecedents (Strotzka, 1969; D'Alessandro, 1968; Gupta, 1975). It was suggested that study of military tactics had a significant influence on Freud's concepts (Berkower, 1970). The role of the nursemaid in Freud's dreams was emphasized by Grigg (1973).

Both Freud's dreams and his famous case studies were reviewed frequently in the literature, including the Dora case (Deutsch, 1970) and the dream of the botanical monograph (Grinstein, 1961). A great number of studies focused on the Irma injection dream, about which Erikson (1954) wrote an impressive study. More critical views were presented by Bowler (1973), Cournut (1973), and Moore and Rojcewicz (1973).

A few studies linked Freud with the tradition of Judaism, which may have had both conscious and unconscious influences on his life. Bakan (1958) suggested that Freud's work could be seen as similar to the *Zohar* in rabbinic literature and to the tractate *Berakoth*. It is a striking coincidence that Freud died on Yom Kippur, the day of atonement (September 23, 1939), particularly since he may have had some influence over the date of his death by means of the amount of pain medication he took for his cancer. Severson (1976) pointed out the resemblances between Freud's concepts and some alchemical images. Jung's interest in the psychological aspects of religious phenomena is well known (CW 11, 13, 14), and the ways in which these giants of psychiatry may possibly have carried forward the older religious traditions of Western culture have yet to be explored adequately.

The Jungian psychoanalyst Neumann (1956), writing in honor of the centenary of Freud's birth, discussed the differences between Freud and Jung in the matter of the father archetype. He mentioned the two occasions on which Freud fainted during disagreements with Jung. The first was when Freud converted Jung from his antialcohol stance; Freud likened this to a fantasized destruction of his younger brother, who had died in childhood. The second occasion was psychodynamically more significant. He and Jung were disagreeing about the pharaoh Ikhnaton (Amenhotep IV). Freud focused on the fact that Ikhnaton erased his father's name from monuments, seeing in this a destructive wish against the father. Jung countered that the most important act of Ikhnaton had been the establishment of monotheism. Freud fainted. According to Neumann, this event highlighted the difference between Freud, who emphasized the personal relation to the father, and Jung, who spoke of the archetypal imagery behind the personal father. Neumann (1963) himself emphasized the importance of maternal archetypal material that was not appreciated in Freud's writing. In reviewing an important personal memoir of Freud by his physician Max Schur (1972), Williams (1974) suggested that an assessment of the murder of a supposed primal father for the sake of stealing away the father's women, of which Freud wrote in *Totem and Taboo* (SE 13), would benefit from the Jungian viewpoint, which would add that the women might symbolize the relationship of the father to his anima, his creativity, and (in mythological terms) his muse.

Ellenberger (1970) discussed the concept of creative illness, which was anticipated in literature by Novalis. As a prime example, he examined in detail the illness of Fechner, a professor at Leipzig University, who injured his eyesight performing visual experiments on himself. In 1840, at 39 years of age, he collapsed and did not work for 3 years. When he recovered, following a dream that he would be cured on the 77th day following, he went through a short period of elation; he thought he had discovered a universal truth, *das Lustprinzip,* the principle of pleasure. After his creative illness, Fechner became a philosopher of nature. Ellenberger also believed that Mesmer, the progenitor of hypnotism, underwent such a creative illness. Among the founders of dynamic psychiatry, however, he cited only Freud and Jung, who went through personal transformation processes resembling the initiatory illnesses of Siberian shamans. Both men emerged, Freud from his self-analysis and Jung from his "confrontation with the unconscious" (Jung, 1965, pp. 170–199), with a sense of having touched something of deep value for the world. The notable differences between Freud and Jung and between their respective systems of psychoanalysis and analytical psychology do not obscure their essential connection in enlarging our world to contain the still unmapped inner worlds of subjectivity. As the heroic age of depth psychology recedes into history, the works of Freud and Jung will be seen to be less divergent and closely related to the same important enterprise that still engages us today.

FREUDIAN DREAM THEORY AND LABORATORY DREAM RESEARCH

Today the relevance of psychoanalytic training is being reassessed in the light of social pressures for faster and less expensive treatment, and increasing numbers of questions are being asked about laboratory studies of dreams: Do such studies support, refute, or leave untouched Freud's classic views of dreaming and the psychological functions of dreams? It is difficult to test most psychoanalytic propositions (Etchegoyen, 1973; Mayman, 1973; Murray, 1965; Sarnoff, 1965), but the element of Freud's theory that has been clearly disproved by laboratory studies is his belief in the instantaneous nature of dreaming (Trosman, 1963), which held that a number of dream elements apparently experienced over an extended period of time in the dream may occur over a much shorter period of time. On the basis of laboratory sleep studies, it now appears that it takes about as long to experience the dream as it would to view the same events on television. However, refutation of the theory of the instantaneous nature of dreams does not affect any major point in Freud's position.

The basic proposition that dreams preserve sleep must be reconsidered (Hawkins, 1966). It now appears that the rhythmic occurrences of the REM state and the similarities between REM states in human neonates and other mammals argue for a neurophysiological basis for REM sleep. The psychological functions of the dream, far from causing REM sleep, may utilize it for other purposes. Hawkins (1966) suggested that a diffuse stimulation of the visual cortex from lower centers produces the potential for visual illusions, which may then be organized according to psychological needs. Jones (1962) judged Freud's sleep-preservation hypothesis to be moot, and the weight of opinion seems to be that it is in need of revision. Waldhorn (1967) suggested the possibility of reversing the dream-in-order-to-sleep theory of Freud. It is perhaps more likely that we sleep in order to dream, since sufficient REM deprivation increases the attempts to dream to such a degree that the subject is virtually unable to fall asleep without a dream occurring.

Jones and Oswald (1968) argued that a distinction should be made between Freud's theory of why we dream and his theory of clinical dream interpretation; they contended that Freud himself frequently confused the two activities. The dream may be the characteristic human response to the D state (dream state) of the species. Wish fulfillment may follow rather than cause the dream. Jones and Oswald made a particularly useful suggestion: instead of the defensive function of dreams, we should speak of the transformation function of dreaming. They convincingly argued that this was Freud's actual position, which would move the function of dreams closer to Jung's conception.

One of the clearest and most useful discussions of Freudian dream theory in the light of sleep research was presented by Altshuler (1966). He cited the increased cortical activation of the D state (dream state), as well as greater cardiovascular and respiratory activity, as suggesting a mastery process "in the face of libidinal upsurge." He also cited conflicting evidence, such as the fact that while amphetamines increase wakefulness they interfere with REM rather than call forth more dreams to aid in sleep. First-night subjects in dream laboratory studies, because of anxiety, might be expect to experience rapid onset of initial dreams to aid them in going to sleep, but actually they often tend to skip the first REM period. Altshuler showed that many REM periods are terminated by brief wakefulness, which indicates failure if the purpose of the dream is to preserve sleep. He believed that the regular 90-min periodicity of the dream cycle was unlikely to be the result of a balance between instinctual wishes and defenses against them. Altshuler argued for a careful examination of psychoanalytic concepts.

There seems to be increasing awareness of the need for basic revisions in Freudian psychoanalytic theory in response to the increased data now available from laboratory studies. The outcome is uncertain; rather than diminishing the importance of the dream in clinical practice, such revision may possibly lead to an appreciation of dreamlike activity underlying all of waking life. Kubie (1966) suggested "preconscious dream flow" for such a process.

REFERENCES

Abenheimer KM: The ego as subject, in Wheelwright JB (ed): The Reality of the Psyche. New York, Putnam, 1968, pp. 61–73

Altman L: The Dream in Psychoanalysis. New York, International Universities Press, 1969

Altshuler KZ: Comments on recent sleep research in relation to psychoanalytic theory. Arch Gen Psychiatry 15:235, 1966

Aristotle: De somnis (on dreams), in McKeon R (ed): The Basic Works of Aristotle. New York, Random House, 1941, pp 618–625

Babcock C: The manifest content of the dream. J Am Psychoanal Assoc 14:154–171, 1966

Bakan D: Sigmund Freud and the Jewish Mystical Tradition. New York, Van Nostrand, 1958

Bergler E, Jekels L: Instinct dualism in dreams. Psychoanal Q 12:353–370, 1940

Bergmann MS: The intrapsychic and communicative aspects of the dream: Their role in psychoanalysis and psychotherapy. Int J Psychoanal 47:356–363, 1966

Berkower LR: The military influence upon Freud's dynamic psychiatry. Amer J Psychiat 127:85–92, 1970

Bernstein I, Glenn J: Masturbation and the manifest content of dreams. In: The Manifest Content of the Dream, The Kris Study Group of the New York Psychoanalytic Institute, Monograph III, Fine B, Joseph E, and Waldhorn H (eds). New York: International Universities Press, 1969, pp 101–109

Blum HP: Quoted in: Dreams no longer 'royal road to unconscious.' Clinical Psychiatry News 3(10):6, 1975

Bonime W: The Clinical Use of Dreams. New York, Basic Books, 1962

Bowler JV: Irma injection flops. Psychiatr Q 47:604–608, 1973

Brenner C: Some comments on technical percepts in psychoanalysis. J Am Psychoanal Assoc 17:333–352, 1969

Brenner C: Psychoanalysis and science. J Am Psychoanal Assoc 16:675–696, 1968

Breznitz S: A critical note on secondary revision. Int J Psychoanal 52:407–412, 1971

Cournut J: An open letter to Irma. Rev Fr Psychanalyse 37:73–93, 1973

Dai B: Science and wisdom, in Kernodle RW (ed): The Sixth Decade of Our
    Century: The Developing Fabric of American Society. Williamsburg, Va,
    College of William and Mary, 1958, pp 35–52
D'Alessandro AJ: An historical review of "Die Symbolik des Traumes," Chap-
    ters I–VI. Psychiatr Q [Suppl] 42(2):337–343, 1968
De Becker R: The Understanding of Dreams, or The Machinations of the
    Night. (Trans: M Heron) London, Allen & Unwin, 1968
Deutsch F: Una "nota al pie de pagina" al trabajo de Freud "Analisis Frag-
    mentario de una Hiteria." [Footnote to Freud's work "Fragment of an
    Analysis of a Case of Hysteria."] Revista de Psicoanalisis 27:595–604,
    1970
Devereux G: Observation and belief in Aischylos' accounts of dreams.
    Psychother Psychosom 15:114–134, 1967
Diamond S (ed): The Roots of Psychology: A Sourcebook in the History of
    Ideas. New York, Basic Books, 1974, p xvii
Ellenberger HF: The Discovery of the Unconscious. New York, Basic Books,
    1970
Ellenberger HF: The urgency of getting the record right (interview). Psychol-
    ogy Today Mar 1973, pp 52–60
Epstein LS: Dreams of pregnant women. Doctoral dissertation, University of
    Kansas, 1969; abstract in Diss Abst Intern 30(7-B):3370, 1969
Erikson EH: The dream specimen of psychoanalysis. J Am Psychoanal Assoc
    2:5–56, 1954
Erikson EH: Childhood and Society. New York, W.W. Norton, 1950
Etchegoyen RH: A note on ideology and psychoanalytic technique. Int J Psy-
    choanal 54:485, 1973
Foulkes SH: Therapeutic Group Analysis. London, Allen & Unwin, 1964
French TM, Fromm E: Dream Interpretation: A New Approach. New York,
    Basic Books, 1964
Frey-Rohn L: From Freud to Jung. New York, Putnam, 1974
Fromm E: Spontaneous autohypnotic age-regression in a nocturnal dream. Int
    J Clin Exp Hypn 13:119–131, 1965
Gershman H: Dream power. Am J Psychoanal 33:167–177, 1973
Gibson JJ: The legacies of Koffla's principles. J Hist Behav Sci 7:3–9, 1971
Graves JD: Psychoanalytic theory: A critique. Prospectives in Psychiatric care
    11:114–120, 1973
Green CE: Lucid Dreams. Oxford, Institute of Psychophysical Research, 1968
Grigg KA: All roads lead to Rome: The role of the nursemaid in Freud's
    dreams. J Am Psychoanal Assoc 21:108–126, 1973
Grinstein A: Freud's dream of the botanical monograph. J Am Psychoanal
    Assoc 9:480–503, 1961
Grotjahn M: Psychoanalysis twenty-five years after the death of Sigmund
    Freud. Psychol Rep 16:965–968, 1965
Gupta RK: Freud and Schopenhauer, J History of Ideas 36:721–728, 1975
Guntrip H: Schizoid Phenomena, Object Relations and the Self. London,
    Hogarth, 1968

Hall C, Donmoff B: Aggression in dreams. Int J Psychiatry 9:259–267, 1963

Hannah B: Jung, His Life and Works: A Biographical Memoir. New York, Putnam, 1976

Harding M: The 'I' and the 'Not-I': Study in the Development of Consciousness. New York, Pantheon, 1965

Hartman E: Longitudinal studies of sleep and dream patterns in manic-depressive patients. Arch Gen Psychiatry 19:312–329, 1968

Hartmann EL: The Functions of Sleep. New Haven, Yale University Press, 1973

Hartmann H, Kris E, Lowenstein M: The function of theory in psychoanalysis, in Lowenstein M (ed): Drives, Affects, Behavior. New York, International Universities Press, 1953, pp 13–37

Hawkins DR: A review of psychoanalytic dream theory in the light of recent psycho-physiological studies of sleep and dreaming. Br J Med Psychol 39:85–104, 1966

Hayman A: What do we mean by "id"? J Am Psychoanal Assoc 17:353–380, 1969

Heidel A: The Gilgamesh Epic and Old Testament Parallels. Chicago, University of Chicago Press, 1946

Hillman J: Toward the archetypal model of the masturbation inhibition, in Wheelwright JB (ed): The Reality of the Psyche. New York, Putnam, 1968, pp 114–127

Hinsie LE, Campbell RJ: Psychiatric Dictionary (ed 3). New York, Oxford University Press, 1960

Hollender M: Is the wish to sleep a universal motive for dreaming. J Am Psychoanal Assoc 10:323–328, 1962

Jones E: The Life and Work of Sigmund Freud. New York, Basic Books, 1953

Jones HS, Oswald I: Two cases of healthy insomnia. Electroencephalogr Clin Neurophysiol 24:378–380, 1968

Jones RM: Ego Synthesis in Dreams. Cambridge, Mass, Schenkman, 1962

Jung CG: Memories, Dreams, Reflections. New York, Vintage Books, 1965

Kanzer M: The communicative function of the dream. Int J Psychoanal 36:260–266, 1955

Kaplan DM: A technical device in psychoanalysis and its implications for a scientific psychotherapy. Psychoanal Contem Sci 2:25–41, 1973

Kern S: Freud and the discovery of child sexuality. History of Childhood Quarterly: Journal of Psychohistory 1:117–141, 1973

Krohn AS: Level of object representation in the manifest dream and projective tests: A construct validation study. Doctoral dissertation, University of Michigan 1972; abstract in Diss Abst Intern 33(11-B):5520, 1973

Krohn A, Gutmann D: Changes in mastery style with age: A study of Navajo dreams. Psychiatry 34:289–300, 1971

Kubie LS: A reconsideration of thinking, the dream process, and "the dream." Psychoanal Q 35:191–198, 1966

Kurland ML: Oneiromancy: An historic review of dream interpretation. Am J Psychother 26:408–416, 1972

Langs RJ: Day residues, recall residues and dreams: Reality and the psyche. J Am Psychiatry Assoc 19:499–523, 1971

Leveton A: The night residue. Int J Psychoanal 42:506–516, 1961

Lichtenberg J, Slap J: On the defensive organization. Int J Psychoanal 52:451–457, 1971

Lichtenstein PE: A behavioral approach to "phenomenological data." Psychological Record 21:1–16, 1971

Lipton SD: Freud's position on problem solving in dreams. Br J Med Psychol 40:147–149, 1967

Lustman SL: The scientific leadership of Anna Freud. J Am Psychoanal Assoc 15:810–827, 1967

McCurdy H: The history of dream theory. Psychol Rev 53:225–233, 1946

McGuire W (ed): The Freud/Jung Letters. Princeton, Princeton University Press, 1974

Mayman H: Reflections on psychoanalytic research. Psychol Issues 8:1–10, 1973

Meier CA: Ancient Incubation and Modern Psychotherapy. (Trans: M Curtis) Evanston, Northwestern University Press, 1967

Moore RW, Rojcewicz S: Are all dreams Freudian? Am J Psychoanal 33:207–210, 1973

Murray EJ: Sleep, Dreams and Arousal. New York, Appleton, 1965

Nagera H (ed): The Hampstead Clinic Psychoanalytic Library, Vol II: Basic Psychoanalytic Concepts on the Theory of Dreams. New York, Basic Books, 1969

Nemiah JC: Quoted in: Value of free association doubted for some patients. Psychiatric News Aug 6, 1976

Neumann E: In Honour of the Centenary of Freud's Birth. J Anal Psychol vol 1, no 2, Mar 1956

Neumann E: The Great Mother: An Analysis of the Archetype. New York, Pantheon, 1963

Nichols C: The myth of the Negro. Unpublished paper presented to Mental Health Luncheon, Southern Methodist University, Dallas, 1967

Papageorgiou M: Incubation as a form of psychotherapy in the care of patients in ancient and modern Greece. Psychother Psychosom 26:35–38, 1975

Perry JW: The Self in Psychotic Process. Berkeley, University of California Press, 1953

Peterfreund A, Schwartz JT: Psychoanalysis: A science in an early stage of development. Psychol Issues 7:87–92, 1971

Polanyi M: Personal Knowledge: Toward a Post-Critical Philosophy. Chicago, University of Chicago Press, 1958

Pontalis JB: Dream as an object. Int Rev Psychoanal 1:125–133, 1974

Rangell L: Psychoanalysis and neuropsychiatry: A look at their interface. Am J Psychiatr 127:43–49, 1970

Rawn M: The present utility of classical analysis. Psychoanal Rev 61:457–473, 1974

Rosenthal H: Horney theory and child analysis. Am J Psychoanal 31:174–181, 1971

Roth N: Free association and creativity. J Amer Acad Psychoanal 3:373–381, 1975

Rubiner W: Concerning dream life. Am Imago 18:318–329, 1961

Sandler J, Dare C, Holder A: Frames of reference in psychoanalytic psychology. II. The historical context and phases in the development of psychoanalysis. Brit J Med Psychol 45:133–142, 1972

Sarnoff I: The experimental evaluation of psychoanalytic hypotheses. Trans NY Acad Sci 28:272–290, 1965

Schick A: The Vienna of Sigmund Freud. Psychoanal Rev 55:529–551, 1968–1969

Schur M: Freud: Living and Dying. London, Hogarth, 1972

Severson RW: The alchemy of dreamwork: Reflections on Freud and the alchemic tradition. Presented at Inter-Regional Society of Jungian Analysts training seminar, Dallas, 1976

Sharpe EF: Dream Analysis. London, Hogarth, 1937, 1961

Spanjaard J: Manifest dream content and its significance for interpretation of dreams. Int J Psychoanal 50:221–235, 1969

Strotzka H: Zur Kritik von Herbert Marcuses Freud-Interpretation (Criticism of Herbert Marcuse's interpretation of Freud). Dynamische Psychiatrie 2:134–143, 1969

Thorndike L: A History of Magic and Experimental Science. New York, Columbia University Press, 1923

Trosman H: Dream research and the psychoanalytic theory of dreams. Arch Gen Psychiatry 9:9–18, 1963

Ullman M: The social roots of the dream. Am J Psychoanal 20:180–196, 1960

Ullman M: Telepathy and dreams. Experimental Medicine and Surgery 27:19–38, 1969

Ullman M: Societal factors in dreaming. Contemporary Psychoanalysis 9:282–293, 1973

Ullman M: The transformation process in dreams. The Academy 19:8–10, 1975

Ullman M, Krippner S, Vaughan A: Dream Telepathy. New York, Macmillan, 1973

von Franz ML: CG Jung: His Myth in Our Time. New York, Putnam, 1975

Wachtel PL: Psychology, metapsychology, and psychoanalysis. J Abnorm Psychol 74:651–660, 1969

Waldhorn HF: The Place of the Dream in Psychoanalysis. New York, International Universities Press, 1967

Wallerstein RS: Psychoanalytic perspectives on the problem of reality. J Am Psychoanal Assoc 21:5–33, 1973

Wallerstein RS: The role of prediction in theory building in psychoanalysis. J Amer Psychoanal Assoc 12:675–690, 1964

White RJ (trans): The Interpretation of Dreams: Oneirocritica by Artemidorus. Park Ridge, NJ, Noyes Press, 1975

Williams M: The indivisibility of the personal and collective unconscious, in
    Fordham M, Gordon R, Hubback J. et al (eds): Analytical Psychology,
    Vol 1, Library of Analytical Psychology. London, Heinemann, 1973,
    pp 76–82
Williams M: Review of Schur M: Freud: Living and dying. London, Hogarth,
    1972. J Anal Psychol 19:111–112, 1974
Wolman B: Evidence in psychoanalytic research. J Amer Psychoanal Assoc
    12:717–731, 1964
Wolstein B: The new psychoanalytic structure. Am J Psychother 23:260–270,
    1969
Wykert J: Horney's later writings — her picture of women. Psychiatric News
    Nov 19, 1975
Yates F: The Art of Memory. Chicago, University of Chicago Press, 1966

2
Other Theories on Dreams

Before discussing Jung's views on dreams, it should be profitable to examine some of the other theories about dreams that contrast with the classic psychoanalytic position of Freud. In general, these alternative theories tend toward greater appreciation of the adaptive functions of dreaming, particularly in the area of interpersonal relationships. The unique feature of Jung's dream theory is its ability to encompass both the archetypal function of dreaming and the personal adaptation or change that is visible in the everyday world.

EMPHASIS ON THE INTERPERSONAL

Adler was one of the first psychoanalysts to insist on the importance of the fact that man is fundamentally related to others and to the world, which is in contrast to the heavy emphasis on instincts in early psychoanalytic writing (Brennan, 1968). This emphasis on the interpersonal sphere is often loosely termed culturist emphasis, and it has been carried forward notably in the work of Erikson (Mahl, 1974, Vol. 2). Erikson's psychosocial stages of epigenetic development clearly show the emergence of the individual life pattern through successive confrontation and mastery of age-specific conflicts, the most basic of which is trust versus fear. No conflict is perfectly resolved, but the developing individual must rely on whatever solution can be found and move on under the dynamism of the life process to the next task.

Retrospective reworking and strengthening of previous solutions is possible, principally in the work of psychotherapy and analysis. Erikson, in "The Dream Specimen of Psychoanalysis" (1954), applied his approach to the manifest content of Freud's Irma injection dream. Erikson demonstrated the usefulness of the manifest dream itself, and he also introduced the term dream configuration to discuss the various parts of the manifest dream. In the category of latent dream configuration, he not only mentions body stimuli and day residue ("delayed stimulus") but also four major areas of stress: acute life conflicts, transference conflicts, repetitive conflicts, and basic childhood conflicts. These are associated, according to Erikson, by wishes, drives, needs, methods of defense, denial, and distortion. In discussing the reconstruction of the dream in terms of social processes, he mentioned both ideal prototypes and evil prototypes, apparently approaching the Jungian idea of the persona (a more idealized social role) and the shadow (the hidden personal identity that is thought to be unacceptable). However, Erikson did not seem to appreciate fully the Jungian concept of autonomous movement of the archetypal images of the objective psyche as a motivating factor for change in the personality. Erikson's contributions have been widely accepted and appreciated, both theoretically (Green, 1972) and experimentally (Bauer and Snyder, 1972).

Ullman pioneered in awareness of the social roots of the dream and in the parapsychological nature of some dream experiences. As director of the Dream Research Laboratory at Maimonides Hospital, Brooklyn, New York, Ullman initiated the most convincing studies yet published on dream telepathy (1973). Ullman (1975) wrote that the most profound transformation of his professional life followed the "realization that Freud's theory of dreams was wrong." Instead of being defenses against unacceptable wishes, Ullman (1969) described dreams as "metaphors in motion." However, the term *metaphor,* borrowed from poetry, has a precise meaning here; it lies near to Jung's use of the term *symbol.* Metaphor is a statement that (1) binds together by its openness and multiple meanings significant events from the past and present, pointing toward the future, and (2) stimulates an emotional awareness in the dream that is not evoked by prosaic statements. Ullman even suggested that the proper study for psychiatrists is not dream interpretation but dream appreciation. He believed that dreams are creative forms that reveal in a metaphoric manner our relationships to the world. Although our waking and dreaming selves see the world differently, in some respects the dreaming self has a superior view— again an echo of Jung, who valued the interplay of both. Ullman suggested that the dream may be used to critique not only the ego image of the dreamer but the dreamer's view of society as well. In his foreword (1962) to Bonime's book, Ullman showed an appreciative awareness of Jung's contributions to the study of dreaming.

Ullman (1960, 1973) gave detailed examples of social factors in dreaming and examples of how the dream aids in adaptation to the dreamer's waking interpersonal world. In this social awareness, Ullman (1969) did not lose his symbolic perspective on the metaphoric quality of the elements of the dream and of the dream as a whole. Indeed, he suggested the possibility of ''metaphors within metaphors,'' a foreshadowing, perhaps, of the focal-tacit constitution of intra-psychic complexes that will be discussed in the later exposition of Jung's work.

In reviewing the laboratory work on dreams, Ullman (1970) placed emphasis on a vigilance hypothesis of dreaming: This hypothesis suggests that dreaming is an active vigilance operation. It is perhaps an attempt to master the disturbing content that produces a visual form of the dream. Past relevant experiences are explored in the dream. If the affect mobilized is too intense for active mastery, waking may occur, Murray (1965, p. 90) mentioned some difficulties with Ullman's vigilance hypothesis, principally that the heightened threshold for arousal during dreaming would make the dreamer more vulnerable to outside attack rather than alert for possible defense. Murray's criticism, however, does not adequately deal with the adaptive function of internal metaphoric restructuring of the dreamer's perceptual models, which may have adaptive advantage when the dreamer is again awake.

French and Fromm (1964) presented a comprehensive theory in which the dream is organized around problem-solving; this attempt at problem-solving is also seen in conscious rational behavior. The technique of dream interpretation suggested by Fromm and French involves the use of the therapist's intuitive imagination, followed by critical testing of the intuitions against other data from the dream and the dreamer's life. A focal conflict, seen as the core of the dream, is identified when the dream interpretation illuminates all parts of the dream and the associations in terms of a current emotional situation in the dreamer's life (French and Fromm, 1962). The approach of Fromm and French was criticized by Hartman (1973), who suggested that conscious recall of dreams could not be of importance in the functions of sleeping and dreaming because many persons function well and solve conflicts without recall of any dreams at all. Hartman's criticism is valid only if conscious understanding is the only goal of dream work, but it does not detract from the compensatory function of the unre-

membered dream, which will be discussed subsequently in terms of
Jung's theory of the psyche.

Fromm (1965), one of the leading clinical researchers in the field of
hypnotherapy, described a case of spontaneous autohypnotic age regression in a nocturnal dream. The focal conflict suggested in Fromm's
work on this dream did not seem to correspond to any current situation
in the dreamer's life, until he returned several months later to tell the
complicated story he had previously witheld, completing the gestalt of
the focal conflict.

Bonime, a major advocate of the theory of interpersonal emphasis
in dream interpretation, stated that the person always functions in
interpersonal terms, even while dreaming (Bonime, 1962, p. 157).
Dream images are seen as arising out of the individual's life experience,
often in the unconscious demand for an unrealized childhood (Bonime,
1962, p. 183). Like Fromm and French, Bonime used the dream to
understand concrete, troubling life situations. Feelings in dreams were
particularly emphasized by Bonime; they may be experienced through
the dream ego or may be symbolized. In spite of his primary interpersonal emphasis, Bonime (1962, p. 4) recognized that persons known to
the dreamer in waking life may appear in dreams either as themselves
or as representatives of certain qualities that may actually be subjective
parts of the dreamer. In this regard Bonime appreciated the Jungian
question of whether a dream image is objective or subjective. The
circumstances of the session in which the dream is remembered are
also significant; Bonime called this a contextual association. Bonime
was strongly influenced by Horney, an early psychoanalytic advocate
of both the interpersonal emphasis and a more balanced view of female
sexuality (Wykert, 1975). Gershman (1973), when working in the Horney Psychoanalytic Institute, mentioned his increasing appreciation for
the manifest content of the dream. Horney's approach also had importance for those who work with children (Rosenthal, 1971).

Dai had extensive experience with the complexities of interpersonal relationships, having been trained both as a sociologist and as a
psychotherapist; the latter training was undertaken with Harry Stack
Sullivan, a major force in guiding the focus of American psychiatry
primarily toward interpersonal models. Dai appreciated the Jungian
conception of the unconscious mind as containing growth-promoting
forces as well as shadow problems. His own emphasis was on the
primary ego identity, based on the child's initial view of himself in the
family structure. Given the chance to develop his own particular potentialities, said Dai (1958), the human being will relate to his more intrinsic nature and to others. To be kind and loving is not just essential for
the welfare of others; it promotes one's own essential health as well.

OBJECT-RELATIONS THEORY AND DREAMS

Object-relations theory grew out of Freud's work, as well as the work of Anna Freud, particularly the defense mechanism "identification with the aggressor" that she first defined (Freud, 1946). Although its origins can be traced to Freud, object-relations theory derives primarily from the work of Klein (Segal, 1964) and the elaborations of Fairbairn (1952) and Guntrip (1961, 1968, 1971). The primary focus in this theoretical approach is on "intrapsychic objects," which are formed in infancy through projection of the infant's own affective states onto outer objects, including, particularly, the person of the mother as perceived by the infant. These outer perceptions, contaminated by the infant's own projections, are then introjected, and they behave as inner objects that take definite attitudes toward the ego. The ego can make alliances or separate itself from inner objects. A particularly useful clinical picture based on object-relations theory is Fairbairn's (1952, p. 105) description of a central ego defending itself against both a libidinal ego attached to an exciting object and an "internal saboteur" (in later writings called the antilibidinal ego) related to a rejecting object.

In many respects the object-relations theories are compatible with Jungian thought. The work of Klein certainly influenced the British school of Jungians, represented primarily by the membership of the Society for Analytical Psychology. Object-relations theory is very close to Jungian theory in its conception of intrapsychic objects, which behave with some of the attributes of part-personalities. In this regard, the term *intrapsychic object* resembles Jung's picture of a personified complex described in his doctoral dissertation in 1902 (CW 1:3–88). The most obvious difference between Jungian thought and object-relations theory lies in Jung's conception of the multiplicity of archetypal patterns that can be activated in the psyche. Also, the Jungian model places less emphasis on pathological origins of complexes. The Jungian appreciation of imaginal materials in fairy tales, myths, and religious imagery, as well as in personal dreams and fantasies, reflects this theory of a multiplicity of patterns for ego development.

Although in object-relations theory childhood is emphasized (Fleming, 1974), and rightly so, it seems consistent with the theory that later events, if sufficiently charged with affect, can also produce enduring object-relations patterns. A similar entity originated in analytical psychology as "affect ego," and it has been related to the study of schizophrenia by Perry (1953). Affect ego refers to the form of the ego when it is under the influence of strong emotion; this is the way in which complexes are formed (if the affective ego and its object-relations models are dissociated). Also, the reexperiencing of the affect ego state is important in the dissolution of existing complexes.

In extreme situations, postchildhood experiences can produce complexes and patterns of complexes, such as are seen in survivors of political persecution, notably survivors of Nazi concentration camps (Engel, 1962; Hoppe, 1971). A less severe example is the trauma experienced by many normal children who undergo surgery. Shuster (1973) suggested that childhood traumatic experiences such as surgery can lead to later fantasies of monsters. He used the example of Bram Stoker's novel *Dracula,* making detailed parallels between the events of the story and presumed childhood surgical experiences of the author.

In his summary of Klein's work, Guntrip (1968) differentiated between persecutory anxiety, which is experienced when the ego is under attack by internal "bad objects," and depressive anxiety, which occurs when the ego experiences threatened loss of internalized "good objects." Persecutory anxiety was pictured as predominating in the first months of life, before attainment of the "depressive position," after which the ego attempts to defend its good objects from the rage of its bad introjects. Depressive anxiety is like a separation anxiety, but with the addition that the ego feels responsibility and guilt. The concept of internal objects admits a form of reality to the experience of the dream. Fantasy may be thought of as the same unconscious contents entering consciousness in a controlled form. This sense of the actual importance of what happens in the dream is similar to the Jungian position. It is a corrective contrast to the interpersonal emphasis on personal relationships as the final arbiter of the dream. Jung's differentiation of subjective and objective levels of interpretation maintains proper balance with the internal and external worlds, the complexes and their relationships to intrapsychic objects, and the person and his interpersonal relationships.

Fairbairn (1952, pp. 223–229) gave an excellent description of the connection between external events and intrapsychic objects. In 1936 he studied the effects of the death of King George V on the dreams of patients in analysis. From the reactions of the dream images, it was clear that the king represented both a subjective part of the patient's minds and a real figure in the external social world. More precisely, in the dream the intrapsychic object used the external event to clothe itself. I observed very similar dream responses in patients in Jungian analysis at the time of the assassination of President Kennedy.

Jones (1962) made extensive efforts to work out a system of dream interpretation incorporating Erikson's concepts (1954) of epigenetic development of psychosocial stages. His work had, to my mind, many similarities to the object-relations approach, and so it is mentioned here rather than with Freudian theory, although Jones himself was careful to make connections to Freud. Like most modern students of the dream, Jones emphasized the importance of the manifest dream, attacking the approach of equating the latent dream with profound meanings. Although he retained the idea that the motive for a dream may be found in a repressed wish, he suggested that the meaning of a dream is to be found in the actual manner of construction of the manifest dream. Although he mentioned Jung, Jones did not seem to be acquainted with the complexity of Jung's thought. He quoted from Silberer a description of the symbol that was almost identical to Jung's definition of the symbol, appreciating the ability of the symbol to offer an image of that which is not yet understandable in ordinary language. Jones pointed out that Erikson implied that the dream itself is engaged in reconstructive activity, a point that was clearly stated in Jungian theory and seems to have been an independent insight by Jones. Recognizing the artistry involved in the clinical use of dreams, Jones said that most clinically effective dream interpretations are "existential-phenomenological." Jones's study is worthy of more attention than it has received in the psychoanalytic literature.

An interesting application of object-relations theory has been the attempt to differentiate between active and passive psychotic behavior on the basis of images of self-threat or threat to others in the manifest content of patients' dreams (Framo and associates, 1962); the experimental evidence was highly supportive of their hypothesis. When the dream threat was directed toward the dream ego, the subject's later waking behavior was more likely to be judged overactive. Dreams of other-directed threats correlated with passive behavior. These observations are suggestive of the three modes of subjective awareness described by Abenheimer (1968): reestablishment of a passive identity with the environment, active mastery, and a third level of abstracting the ego identity and utilizing self-control. By comparing object representations in dreams and projective tests, Krohn and Mayman (1974) found that the manifest dream expressed the individual's range of internalized relationship models. Similar use of the manifest dream has been found in the mode of conceptualization of multiple personality (Berman, 1974).

A major contrast between the Jungian view of psychic development and the view provided by pure object-relations theory was clearly stated by Fordham (1958), one of the editors of Jung's *Collected Works*. Fordham saw (correctly, I think) object-relations theory as postulating that external objects in infancy shape the form of the infant's introjects. Fordham, in contrast, asserted the Jungian view that there is an inherent archetypal predisposition for certain images to be formed. As will be discussed in the section on archetypal levels of amplification, this predisposition is not equivalent to the actual inheritance of an image; rather, it shapes the forms of images that are based on experience. There are bridges to be built between this Jungian understanding and the structuralism of Lévi-Strauss (Rossi, 1974).

GESTALT THERAPY

Gestalt studies of perception have been important in the growth of modern psychology. Koffka's principles, such as figure–ground differentiation, have stimulated much experimentation (Gibson, 1971). The therapy developed by Perls bears the same name (gestalt), but it grew more directly out of Perls's early Freudian training, modified by such gestalt principles as those of Zeigarnik (Ellis, 1938, pp. 300–314), which suggested that unfinished tasks were more closely retained in memory. Much of Perls's clinical work tended toward closure and dispersal of repetitive neurotic patterns. Some Freudian principles were recast by Perls in suggestive fashion. The secondary process, for example, was considered "the loss of awareness of the self [ego] that *it* is exercising the inhibition" (Perls and associates, 1951, pp. 440–441). His understanding of dreams as creative was similar to Jungian understanding, and Perls seemed to be aware of this parallelism. A very good annotated bibliography of gestalt literature is available in *Counseling Psychologist,* Vol. 4, No. 4, 1974, pp. 60–63.

Perls published many examples of his technique used in working with patients. One (Perls, 1973, pp. 186–191) exemplified his method of dealing with "Madeline's dream." It was clear in that case that it was the intent of Perls to develop in the dreamer a sense of the meanings of the various parts of the dream. He did not seem to be concerned with a thinking interpretation that would link the dream in a conceptual way with the past history of the person. This general emphasis on the here and now and on experiencing emotion rather than remembering or understanding is characteristic of gestalt therapy (Gadol, 1977). In working with dreams, Zinker (1971) elaborated a gestalt group theater technique that suggested psychodrama.

The gestalt conception of immediate experience in dream work is quite Jungian. However, there does not seem to be an understanding of the tension between subjective and objective interpretations in most gestalt writings. For example, one famous team of gestalt therapists demonstrated their work with a dream by having a patient "be the ocean." This enactment of the ocean was fruitful for the patient, but it lost the Jungian sense of the ocean as a symbol for psychic content that was not (in the dream or in waking life) something to be integrated into the ego. Rather, it stood symbolically for an archetypal content that, should the ego successfully identify with it, could potentially overwhelm the sense of reality on which the ego relied. Another patient told me of his experience with gestalt work on a rather complicated dream. His therapist asked him during the course of the dream reenactment to "be the curb" of the street that was in the dream. In the process of "being the curb," the dreamer came to an awareness of many truths about himself: how people continually ran up against him without concern for his reactions, how he was immobile and fixed, how he felt cold and dead, etc.—all of which were useful insights into his neurotic character structure, but which left the symbolic meaning of the dream untouched.

Polster and Polster (1973) made an exceptionally clear and well-organized presentation of gestalt therapy. However, they relegated any mention of Jung to an appendix, and they did not seem to understand the Jungian approach. They maintained, for example, that the gestalt view of polarity "is more free-ranging than Jung's" because it is "not confined to archetype." Thus they seemed to miss entirely the profound way in which Jung traced opposites to the core of the archetypal problem, not simply in the more surface form of ego and shadow. Most gestalt work with polarities seems, in Jungian terminology, to be restricted to permitting the ego to reorient various identities that have been dissociated into the shadow complex, the rejected alter ego. Nevertheless, in their generally prospective and growth-promoting approach, the gestalt therapies come close to the Jungian understanding of the individuation process. However, they may not appreciate as fully the "dark" side of individuation: facing the personal shadow material and experiencing the "nigredo," an alchemical image that refers to the darkening of the substance that eventually can become the elixir.

PSYCHOSYNTHESIS

Focusing on synthesis, Assagioli developed a number of techniques that are detailed in a series of publications (1969, 1972, 1975) and in a major work entitled *Psychosynthesis* (1965). Assagioli was familiar with Jung and was generally appreciative of Jung's approach, although he assigned a lesser place to dream interpretation

than did Jung (Assagioli, 1965, p. 94). In 1966 Assagioli (1967) compared his system of psychosynthesis with Jung's analytical psychology. Although he called Jung "one of the closest and most akin to the
conceptions and practice of psychosynthesis," Assagioli criticized
Jung for omitting the imagination from his typology (two major attitudinal types, extraversion and introversion, with four functions of thinking, feeling, sensation, and intuition). In view of Jung's immense attention to imaginal thinking, notably the technique of active imagination,
this criticism is surprising. The Jungian concept of the Self (central archetype) was contrasted with the concept of Self in psychosynthesis
(Assagioli, 1967, p. 15), but I believe the comparison to be mistaken in
important respects. Assagioli apparently understood the central archetype to be merely psychological, perhaps only conceptual, while
the self as used in psychosynthesis was said to be experiential. The
diagrams that Assagioli used (1967, pp. 16–17) reveal similarities to
Jung's work, in that the Self is shown as the originator of the ego;
however, they do not reflect Jung's understanding of the central archetype as both the center and the totality of the psyche, in contrast to
the ego being the center of consciousness only. Assagioli also seemed
to break apart the opposites of the unconscious and divide them into a
lower unconscious and a higher unconscious (or superconscious). The
"higher self" was seen as the boundary between the superconscious
and the collective unconscious that is outside the personal sphere. Jung
had no such distinction of higher and lower in the unconscious, and the
Self in Jung's language was the center of the objective psyche (Assagioli used the older term collective unconscious). Both Jung and
Assagioli thought that it is possible to experience briefly the union of
the ego and the Self but that if this identity is held it can be pathological. Assagioli tended to maintain a continuous focus on promoting
positive aspects, while Jung seemed to have a greater awareness of the
negative material that must sometimes be first integrated. Rossi (1973)
suggested three hallmarks of the psychosynthesis process in dreams:
unusual content, active role of the ego, and vividness of inner experience. Rossi suggested that these may be related to protein synthesis in
the brain as a substrate for changes in memory and personality (the
dream–protein hypothesis).

HUMANISTIC PSYCHOLOGY

Humanistic psychology embarked on a distinct path in 1962 when
Maslow and others founded the Association for Humanistic Psychology. The emphasis in humanistic psychology is placed on the potential

for positive growth in man, and in that respect it closely parallels the focus of psychosynthesis. Maslow (1971), for example, clearly stated that neurosis may result from failure to unfold one's potentials. He was aware of the similarity of his concepts to the writings of Jung, and he freely acknowledged the humanistic content of Jung's theory. Maslow emphasized the importance of peak experiences and self-actualization: in the self-actualizing person, the peak experience of "being cognition," which usually occurs only during a peak experience, is a more regular feature of life (Stark, 1968). Maslow (1963) explored the relationships between these concepts and creativity.

Buhler (1974) outlined the history of humanistic psychology, tracing its roots in existential therapies, its compatibility with developmental psychology, and its similarity to group psychotherapy in its emphasis on improving interpersonal relationships. Buhler clearly defined one of the greatest problems of the humanistic psychology movement: the need to clarify the nature of conflict. Clearly, even a self-actualizing person will suffer tension in choosing between alternatives and may at times make the "wrong" choice. It would seem that humanistic psychology, like psychosynthesis, needs further understanding of the problem that in Jungian terms would be called the integration of the shadow. It is surprising that Buhler, unlike Maslow, did not mention Jung.

There is as yet no specific approach to dreams that is characteristic of the humanistic psychology movement. In discussing dreams and human potential, Krippner and Hughes (1970) emphasized the creative and healing functions of dreaming, with scant attention to shadow problems. They quoted with approval the so-called Senoi dream techniques; these are based on descriptions of the role of dreams in the Senoi tribe, a 12,000-member tribe on the Malay peninsula that Stewart visited in 1935 (Stewart, 1969, p. 159). The Senoi technique of seeing all dream images as positive resembles the general tone of humanistic psychology in its deemphasis of negative dream content. In a general sense, humanistic psychology, with its insistence on positive qualities, is the other pole of the pessimism found in early Freudian writings, expressed particularly in the concept of the id.

EXISTENTIAL PHENOMENOLOGY

In 1968 I spent an afternoon in Zurich discussing with Medard Boss, a leading existential psychiatrist, the differences between his approach to dream interpretation and that of Jung. Boss had studied with Jung and was quite familiar with his writings. Prior to this meeting

I had read *The Analysis of Dreams* (Boss, 1958) and had found it to be the clearest exposition of existential therapy I had seen.

Our discussion finally centered on the Jungian concept of archetype. In an effort to focus on a particular example, I recounted to Boss the dream of a giant tapir, which will be discussed in the section on archetypal amplification (p. 266). In previous work with this dream, the image of the giant tapir (see p. 270) had been assimilated (because of the structure of the dream) to a mother image. Only later did I learn that the giant tapir was a significant image in the mythological world of Cuña Indians, where it represented the "spirit of the earth mother's placenta" and symbolized the conservation of forms by nature. Thus the giant tapir had shown a similar meaning in the dream and in Cuña mythology, which was unknown to the dreamer at that time. It seemed to me (as it still does) an excellent example of an archetypal image in a dream where there is little possibility of forgotten prior knowledge (cryptamnesia). Finally, Boss said, "There are just some things in life that are best symbolized by a giant tapir!" With this, we agreed to disagree, Boss maintaining his consistent position that it is important not to impose any prior theoretical category on the immediate experience of the dream. I left with the same conviction that I had had on arrival: the concept of archetype is a useful way of ordering some experiences that are not fully amplified by personal and cultural associations.

This brief conversation, however, seemed to me to embody the characteristic tension between Jungian analysis and existential analysis, which are alike in some other very important respects. Leonard (1976), a professor of existential philosophy and also a Jungian psychoanalyst, carefully compared and contrasted Jung and Heidegger, the existential philosopher who was a major influence on Boss, Binswanger, Tillich, and others. Both Jung and Heidegger were concerned with the relationship of man to cosmos, and they saw this relationship as essentially a mystery. They both acknowledged the unknown. Both understood the importance of man facing the inevitability of his own death. Listening to and following his "call" (Heidegger) or pursuing his own process of "individuation" (Jung) is the way in which man develops his humanness, remaining open to the mystery of existence and acknowledging modes of consciousness superior to those that he ordinarily experiences. Both Heidegger and Jung claimed to use methods that were phenomenological, maintaining the importance of individual events. Both understood the creative process to involve the unknown realm as the origin of creativity: Heidegger saw the poet as mediator; Jung saw creativity as the actualization of archetypal possibilities.

Leonard (1976) presented the differences between Jung and Heidegger as setting up a tension similar to that experienced in my conversation with Boss. Jungians do objectify inner psychic phenomena and do use amplifications, archetypal and otherwise. The existentialists do not objectify phenomena, but they focus on "where one is open to the world." Jung found the distinction of an inner world and an outer world useful, as in the interpretation of dreams of a subjective or objective level. Heidegger maintained that man is never only in an inner world. Heidegger remained in the field of philosophy, while Jung related to psychology. Heidegger did not deal with development questions, while Jung and other psychoanalysts were quite interested in both the development of the particular individual and the developmental processes themselves. Leonard also pointed out that while Boss seemed opposed to amplification of images, Heidegger used essentially that approach when writing about myths and poetry. Also, the Jungian concern with synchronicity is an acknowledgement that the world is never finally split into an inner–outer dichotomy but is somehow still *unus mundus*.

Although we speak of existential phenomenology, the term *phenomenology* has more to do with method, while *existentialism* is primarily concerned with what it is like to be a concrete person. In therapeutic discussions it is almost impossible to make a significant distinction. The method of phenomenology is to let phenomena "announce" themselves, with the observing subject attempting to empty himself of any prior judgment categories. There is an emphasis on experience rather than on reason that suggests the gestalt therapies. The problem in the phenomenological approach, however, is that it is not possible to consciously give up one's categories. Pushed to extremes of divesting himself of observational bias, man is still dependent for all ordinary observation on the structure of the nervous system in which he is dwelling. In Polanyi's terminology, which will be used in defining the functions of dreams, the tacit contents of our minds (on which we must rely in order to know anything focally) may shift but do not vanish.

Heidegger's conception of *das man* focused on the everyday way of functioning in which one can lose one's sense of subjectivity and freedom. *Das Man* seems to be similar to the Jungian conception of identification with the persona, when the ego (the I, the center of subjectivity) identifies with one or more of its social roles, forgetting that the role is filled by but does not fill the ego. Such persona identification permits no sense of the mystery that remains when the ego still appreciates the dual nature of the ordinary sense of the I—one identity dependent on persona and ego image and another identity that is inher-

ent in the archetypal core of the ego itself. This phenomenon, although
not the archetypal explanation, was appreciated by Sartre (1957). In his
understanding that knowledge basically is not simply rational, Heidegger was similar to both Jung and Polanyi.

Elkin (1970) contrasted Husserl, the founder of phenomenology,
and Freud; both tried to establish rigorous sciences—Husserl a science
of consciousness, Freud a science of the unconscious.

The primary assumption of the existential approach to dream interpretation seems to be that the same limitations of a person's existence that are seen in waking life are also to be seen in that person's
dreams (Boss, 1958). By becoming aware of such limitations, the ego
can choose to be more open to possibilities that are outside of its usual
view of itself and its world. Cast in Jungian terms, this is equivalent to
saying that the ego is more than its images of itself. In the Jungian view,
the ego's limitations are not simply the result of "bad faith" that restricts the natural openness of the ego. In order to have an identity in
the world *(das man),* it is necessary to develop the ego in a one-sided
way, particularly in the first part of life when ego growth is the usual
goal. However, the pressure of individuation challenges each successive ego image to enlarge, until finally an ego is formed that is sufficiently integrated that it can again be presented with the archetypal
energies that were its own foundation. It is clear that in this Jungian
view the center of autonomous activity is not in the ego alone, as it
would appear to be in the existentialist view.

Existential phenomenology has had considerable impact on the
psychological literature of Europe (van Kaam, 1961); its influence has
been much greater than that achieved by Jungian views. There have
even been attempts to enlarge behavioral psychology to accommodate
the views of phenomenology (Lichtenstein, 1971) and other non-
behavorial approaches such as hypnotherapy, Jungian dream studies
and meditation practices. Clearly, behavioral psychology is beginning
to move toward deeper understanding.

Existential and phenomenological approaches to dreams have
been compared to the work of Horney (Kelman, 1965), particularly in
regard to the conception of responsibility. Kelman discussed experiments with the mind—Zen meditation, Descartes' *Cogito ergo Sum,*
Kant's *Critique of Pure Reason,* and Husserl's phenomenological concept of the epoché. The *epoché* involves bracketing the natural way of
observation; it is similar to Freud's free-association technique in that
ordinary choices are set aside and the mind is permitted to attempt
spontaneous revelation of itself. The occasionally highly abstract descriptions from Freudian metapsychology may sometimes be corrected

by the existential emphasis (Benda, 1960), but the often obscure and personalistic language of existential analysis presents equal difficulties (Khanna, 1969; Schmidl, 1960). Wolf (1968) gave a simple statement of the goal of much existential thought: the healthy person can risk his own self in a relationship that is revealing of the other. This is the same openness to another that Buber described as I–Thou (Friedman, 1960).

An important Jungian theorist (von Franz, 1964) described the existentialist approach as "stripping off the illusions of consciousness," but added that existentialists "go right up to the door of the unconscious and then fail to open it." Jung, too, was opposed to over-reliance on technique (Winthrop, 1966). In contrasting Freud and Karl Jaspers, the late existential psychiatrist, Oppenheimer (1974) saw the crucial difference as Freud's insistence on meaningful connections being seen as causal connections. Rybak (1971) also saw existentialism as a response to the free will or determinism controversy in psychology. Smillie (1971) asked that empirical psychology and phenomenology consider a common field of study. Oppenheimer (1974) stated that the acceptance of empathy as a means of observation introduces an entirely new approach, not present in the natural sciences. This is a common misconception of the way science progresses, and it is discussed by Polanyi in *Personal Knowledge* (1958).

Heuscher (1969) elaborated a single dream by three different approaches: Freudian psychoanalytic, behavioral, and existential. He concluded that each enriches the understanding of the dream. Suggesting that a common ground may be found between psychoanalysis and phenomenology, Elkin (1970) looked expectantly toward writers such as Erikson, Klein, Fairbairn, and Winnicott, i.e., toward the cultural and object-relations emphasis. Gargiulo (1976) expressed similar views.

Although he did not mention Jung or Polanyi, Hofstadter (1968) presented phenomenological philosophy in terms that can easily be related to their work. His description of the intentionality of consciousness ("consciousness of") is parallel to Polanyi's from–to structure of knowing. The other side of intentionality, the object of the intention "being for" the subject, touches on the question of the subjective but non-ego elements in the dream, which may be *in* the ego during the waking state. Hofstadter's description "I am conscious of myself by inhabiting my own acts" strikingly parallels Polanyi's analysis of how we understand a comprehensive entity by dwelling in its particulars.

It may be, as Van Dusen (1960) suggested, that existential analysis is a theoretical advancement that has outstripped its development of techniques. It is equally possible that the dislike of technique and the attempt to create each situation anew are the major blocks to integration of the phenomenological approach with other major areas of psychotherapy. Jung's work is the middle ground between these two theories, more structured than that of the existentialists, less conceptualized than that of the Freudians. Like the middle ground between two rivers, it is likely fertile soil.

BEHAVIORAL THERAPY

There is some disagreement about the definition of behavioral therapy. Marsh (1974) recommended that its definition be based on the application of experimental analysis to treatment endeavors but that the theoretical constructs be widened and not restricted to a conditioning model. Kantor (1968) distinguished six distinct periods in the development of behaviorism, and he distinguished Watsonian behaviorism from field behaviorism, which he saw as the current and most authentic form. One of these periods, the period of antibehaviorism, covered seventeen centuries, from the second century B.C. to the fifteenth century A.D. However, others have suggested that there were behavior-modification techniques being practiced during these dark ages of behaviorism, citing falconry as the equivalent of animal experiments in conditioning (Mountjoy and associates, 1969).

Pavlov, the great Russian behaviorist, apparently discussed dreaming only once, and that in passing response to a questioner (Cautela and Baron, 1974). Pavlovian theory is of some interest in conceptualizing the results of sleep and dream studies, although it offers little of interest in the psychodynamic study of dream content.

The generally accepted opinion that behavior therapy and psychodynamic therapies were incompatible was shown by Weitzman (1967) to be in error. He cited Jung's theory of complexes as an aid in conceptualizing the effectiveness of conditioning. If a stimulus activates an autonomous complex other than the ego, interference in conditioning is produced. If the same stimulus is presented during a state when the ego complex is stable, the autonomous nature of the previous response tends to be diminished through the attachment of the stimulus content to the integrated sphere of the ego (Weitzman, 1967, pp. 313–314). The complementary contributions of behavioral therapy and psychoanalysis were described by Wolf (1966) and by Marks and Gelder (1966).

Dreams were shown to change during the course of successful treatment of authority conflicts by desensitization techniques (Bergin, 1970). Behavior-modification treatment was also reported to be effective in causing cessation of recurrent nightmares by means of systematic desensitization of the motifs of the dream (Geer and Silverman, 1967).

It is evident from many clinical observations that in many instances changes in dream motifs can serve as indicators of subjective states. It is not surprising that dreams change during the course of successful behavior modification. My colleagues at the Medical Voluntary Control Laboratory in Dallas are collecting data on dreams of patients undergoing biofeedback treatment for a number of clinical problems (Timken and associates, 1975). Preliminary observations have suggested that it may be possible to understand failures in deconditioning treatment by the study of the conflicts shown in patients' dreams. There is no hesitation in that laboratory to use psychodynamic, biofeedback, behavioral modification, and hypnotherapy techniques if the situation warrants. The growing number of accounts of patients treated by mixed approaches suggests that cross-fertilization of psychodynamic and behavioral therapies may be profitable.

PIOTROWSKI SYSTEM

Piotrowski (1973) developed a system of dream interpretation, based on his work with the Rorschach test and Thematic Apperception Test, that was similar in some respects to the Jungian approach. One of his fundamental principles was that dreams do not distort the meaning of verbs; thus verbs mean the same in the dream as in waking life. This he called "the veridicity of verbs." Nouns can be treated in the same manner as verbs if they are abstract nouns. For instance, depression, as a dream noun, can be converted in Piotrowski's system into a waking state of functioning at a depressed level. Concrete nouns occurring in the dream, however, may have multiple meanings. In the sense that he considered conscious and unconscious thinking to be very much alike, Piotrowski's system resembled that of French and Fromm (1964). He saw little value in differentiating between the Freudian primary and secondary processes. Piotrowski worked only with the manifest dream, as do most theorists who are not orthodox Freudians.

In Piotrowski's system every dream figure is taken to be a different trait of the dreamer (axiom A); this is equivalent to Jung's interpretation on the subjective level. Axiom B postulates that different dream figures may reveal the dreamer's "thoughts, feelings, and action tendencies" toward actual persons who resemble the dream figures; this approaches Jung's interpretation of a dream on the objective level, with dream figures standing for the same figures in waking life.

In Piotrowski's system, the greater the physical distance between the dreamer in the dream and another figure, the more remote the trait represented by that figure is from the dreamer's conscious identity. Other rules, less well specified, involve symbolism, generalization, consistency, and implicit or contextual evidence. Piotrowski's rule of complementarity allows the interpreter to use general psychological laws "if their use helps to infer additional information from the manifest dream." A repetitive dream, for example, certainly indicates an unsuccessful and continuing struggle. Piotrowski's rule of overt and covert behavior involves an attempt to predict overt behavior from manifest dreams, which is not always a reliable indicator or a valid possibility. In the field of sociology there is similar difficulty in predicting overt behavior from measurements of an individual's attitudes (De Fleur and Westie, 1958).

ADLER SYSTEM

Like Jung, Adler was one of the early psychoanalytic pioneers. In 1911 he left Freud's group, taking 9 of the 23 other members with him (Hall, 1970). He argued with Freud over the role of early sexual trauma in neurosis, and he also disagreed on matters of dream interpretation. Adler was the first psychoanalyst to emphasize social factors in neurosis at a time when instinctual theory was predominant. He may be considered the progenitor of the culturist position that was elaborated by Horney and Harry Stack Sullivan.

Adler anticipated by many years the current emphasis on socialization of patients and their treatment by the least restrictive means within their community structure. He also foresaw the need for family therapy, reeducation techniques, and marriage counseling. Adler influenced American psychiatry far more than the references to his work would indicate to the casual reader. In his social emphasis, Adler was ahead of public awareness (Ferguson, 1968). Even the existential-humanistic therapists find much in Adler to support their own position (Dreyfus, 1968).

Adler's approach to dreams was consistent with his emphasis on overcoming one's innate sense of inferiority. He denied the notion of an unconscious (Ullman, 1962), but he held to the idea that dreams were for the gratification of desires, specifically the desire to increase security. He thus saw all psychological life as occurring in the polarization between a sense of mastery and a sense of inadequacy. This had many similarities to the Jungian description of persona (often an outward appearance of mastery) and shadow (alter ego that is considered by the ego to be inferior and unacceptable, although it may contain abilities needed for continued ego growth). However, Adler did not appreciate the more profound aspects of the objective psyche, and it is obvious that he focused his psychology primarily on the ego and its interaction with the social world. Brennan (1968) suggested that some of Adler's concern with the sense of inadequacy came from his childhood memories of suffering from rickets while his older brother appeared healthy.

In *Individual Psychology* (1929), Adler offered a number of examples of his approach to dreams. All were cast in the mold of the dream being reassuring, as if it were a fantasy, and working against any damage to the self-esteem of the dreamer. The dream was a sign that the dreamer was making "an attempt at anticipatory groping" to prepare for "some approaching difficulty" (Adler, 1929, p. 221). The dream had little meaning in itself; it was like "the smoke of a fire." The dream might present what was consciously desired as already existing, encouraging the awakened dreamer to put into effect what was anticipated in the dream. Much psychopathology was described as the manufacture of an acceptable excuse of sickness in order to escape the task of fulfilling one's potentialities.

In discussing a woman who dreamed that she danced with Napoleon, Adler (1929, pp. 224–225) concluded that she was covetous of her brother-in-law and wished to prove her superiority over her sister. Another patient dreamed that he was naked and was bitten on the thigh by his sweetheart; he woke with an attack of trigeminal neuralgia. Adler reduced this to the patient's avoidance of a position of inferiority; he interpreted the bite to mean that the patient thought that "she had degraded me to the position of a woman" (Adler, 1929, pp. 95–96) because the patient had been told in childhood that the stork bit his mother and made her pregnant. When the dream occurred, the patient had just received a postcard from his brother and learned that the brother was vacationing with a group that included the patient's former mistress. The first attack of neuralgia occurred the night before the patient's supervisor was to return from vacation, and the patient thought that the supervisor's wife had been making advances to him.

In summary, Adler's dream theory resembled the Jungian approach in its conception of the prospective functions of many dreams. Otherwise, Adler's approach gave no real autonomy to the dream; it reduced the dream to the status of servant of the waking ego in masking a sense of insecurity.

CONTENT ANALYSIS/COGNITIVE THEORY

Calvin Hall and his associates compiled extensive data developed by applying the method of content analysis to groups of dreamers (Hall, 1947, 1953a, 1953b, 1963). The most complete statement of the method is found in *The Content Analysis of Dreams* (1966) by Hall and Van de Castle. After chosen aspects of dreams are divided into categories, the method of content analysis is used to convert "verbal or other symbolic material into numbers in order that statistical operations may be performed" (Hall and Van de Castle, 1966, p. 1). The authors discussed some of the limitations of this method: it is reductionistic and ignores the unique. These are the same problems that are found in any statistical approach to psychodynamic material.

Hall also proposed a cognitive theory of dream symbols (1953a) and dreaming (1953b). In this theory, dream images were considered to be the embodiment of thoughts (Hall, 1959, pp. 123–134). Cognition was transformed by the dream into perceivable images. Dream interpretation was seen as reversing this process, retransforming images into their referent ideas in order to understand the dreamer rather than the dream. Hall (1959) seemed to imply that images are "the only means by which ideas find sensible expression in dreams," although other modalities of sensation also occur in dreams. He commented that dreams are relatively indifferent to political and economic questions, stating that during the last days of World War II the dreams of his students did not register a single identifiable response to the use of the first atomic bombs (Hall, 1959, p. 126). In contrast, I noted in several patients in analysis dream responses to the assassination of President Kennedy, and similar responses were found by Fairbairn to the death of the king in 1936; both of these were political events, but they were more obviously attached to the unconscious image of the father imago. It is also possible that the difference was between the dreams of students and the dreams studied in psychoanalysis.

Hall found that the number of times prominent people appear in dreams is very small. Common concerns in the dreams he studied were conceptions of self, conceptions of other people, conceptions of the world, conceptions of problems and conflicts, and conceptions of impulses, prohibitions, and penalties (Hall, 1959).

Like Jung, Hall was concerned with distinguishing between objective reality and subjective reality, cautioning against the use of dreams to form impressions of objective situations. Like Jung, he accorded to each a sense of reality, although his emphasis seemed to lie on the external problems and relationships. Hall visualized concepts as being organized into conceptual systems, which can then influence behavior. This is somewhat parallel to the Jungian model of emotionally toned complexes, which may be clustered in various groupings, the ego itself being a central grouping.

The cognitive theory of dream interpretation resembles the emphasis of Adler: "How a person sees himself is expressed in dreams by the parts the dreamer plays" (Hall, 1959, p. 61). There is a strong interpersonal referent as well. The persons in the dream are "not really strangers but personifications of our conceptions of people we know." The dream setting may also reveal the ways in which the dreamer sees his world: "If he feels the world is closing in on him he dreams of cramped spaces" (Hall, 1959, p. 61). This congruity of dream image and waking affective perception of the dreamer's world is close to the stance of the existential phenomenologists.

Hall (1959, p. 62) defined various recurrent themes in dreams: the struggle of maturity versus infantile security, the conflict between conceptions of good and evil, the opposition of integration and disintegration.

Dreams from "essentially normal persons" were analyzed according to the following categories: (1) setting, (2) characters, (3) plot, (4) emotions, and (5) color (Hall, 1959, pp. 55–63). The most frequent setting was a conveyance, usually an automobile (13%). Of those dreams whose actions occurred in a dwelling, Hall found the most common room to be the living room, followed in order by bedroom, kitchen, stairway, and basement; there seemed to be a tendency for dreams to be set in recreation or living surroundings, rather than in work settings.

Classification of action and behavior exhibited in 1000 dreams yielded 34% movement, 11% talking, 7% sitting, 7% watching, 6% socializing, 5% playing, 4% manual work, 4% thinking, 4% striving, 3% quarreling, 3% acquiring (Hall, 1959, p. 58). "Going somewhere" predominated over actively doing discrete things in fixed places. Play occurred more frequently than work. Many activities were passive.

Relationships between the dreamer himself and other figures in his dream were analyzed in 1320 dreams, using the basic categories of friendliness and hostility (Hall, 1959, p. 59); hostility characterized 448 dreams and friendliness 188 dreams. Of the hostile feelings, physical attack (28%) and denunciation (27%) were the leading categories. Of all dream emotions, 64% were unpleasant; only 18% were "positively pleasant." Somewhat paradoxically, the dreamers themselves more often rated the dream as a whole as pleasant rather than unpleasant (41% pleasant, 25% unpleasant). There was a tendency for older dreamers to report a higher percentage of unpleasant dreams.

Hall's cognitive theory of dreaming assumes that the dream image will represent the external referent according to the dreamer's feelings toward that person or situation (Murray, 1965). While this is similar to the existential phenomenological position, it is in contrast to Jung's basic idea that the dream is compensatory to the attitude of the ego. The cognitive theory assumes, as did Adler and Bonime, that the dream images are working on essentially the same problems that are being faced in waking life. Hall rejected the Freudian idea of dream symbols as disguises for repressed thoughts, but he believed that the thoughts of dreams are simplified and made more imaginal by the restricted nature of the cognitive process occurring during sleep. Hall's critique (1953a) of Freudian dream symbolism noted, in contrast to Freud's theory, the following points: (1) a series of dreams from the same subject will show frankly sexual dreams alternating with other images; (2) a naive subject can often provide the same sexual meanings as a trained interpreter; (3) slang expressions for sexual acts and organs are often similar to the supposed symbols.

Sex Differences in Dreams

Hall and Domhoff (1963) compared the dreams of 1399 men with those of 1418 women. The groups compared ranged over diverse cultural settings, from American children to Australian aborigines. They found that in all their nine groups studied, men dreamed more about men than about women, while women dreamed nearly equally about men and women. They related this finding to the possible difference in oedipal feelings of men and women—men having to endure rivalry with the also-loved father.

Husband (1959) compared the dreams of 25 men and 25 women who were interviewed by same-sex interviewers. Both men and women were active in the dreams studied. Although the men had a greater frequency of sexual dreams, few men awoke excited from such dreams, while about half the women who dreamed of sex awoke with sexual feelings. The women dreamed more often of persons whom they preferred, and their dreams were more emotional than those of the men; but the women also had a greater incidence of unpleasant emotions. The women's dreams contained more color and more everyday problems. One observation (Husband, 1959, p. 69) suggested Jung's principle of the compensatory nature of dreams: Men who were very shy tended to dream of sex relations, while men who "were rather casual about their sex relations" tended not to dream of intercourse at all. Perhaps along the same lines, the dreams of married persons involved less sex content than those of single persons.

Hall (1963) also collected a large number of dreams from college students, and these have been used in a number of studies by other workers.

Dreams of Patients

In one application of his technique, Hall (1966) studied the dreams of four groups of hospitalized male mental patients according to 46 variables in their dreams. A significant finding was that dreams of schizophrenics were shorter than those of nonschizophrenics. Alcoholics had more dreams that contained motifs of oral incorporation. Alcoholics also had fewer sex dreams. When compared to a sample of nonhospitalized males, the patients' dreams had a lesser number of friendly interactions with women.

Personality Factors

One of the motives for Hall's elaboration (1959) of content analysis of dreams was to permit large-scale studies of personality traits associated with dream motifs. He applied his technique in several areas. A hypothesis formulated by Harris, that people who have falling dreams are able to express more hostility toward the father than toward the mother, was confirmed by Hall (1955) at the 0.05 level of probability in the dreams of 517 college students. The proposition was based on the assumed equation between falling dreams and fear of loss of the mother's love. Hall and Van de Castle (1965) studied the castration complex in dreams. They concluded that male dreamers reported more castration anxiety than castration wish or penis envy, while the sequence was reversed for the female dreamers. Although they supported the oedipal theory, the authors admitted the possibility of other theoretical explanations.

Hall and Domhoff (1963) made extensive studies on aggression in dreams. They found that the greatest amount of aggression occurred in the dreams of children from 2 to 12 years of age; the level of aggression was the same for both boys and girls, although the dreams of boys had more physical aggression. After that age, the amount of aggression in the female dreams declined; thus a significant difference appeared between the dreams of men and those of women. Aggression in dreams declined after 30 years of age in both sexes, although the relatively greater amount of aggression in male dreams remained. Of all aggression in dreams, both male and female dreamers more often experienced aggression from unknown males. Until the age of 18 years, the dreamer was more likely to be the victim of aggression than the perpetrator of aggression.

Slang and Dream Symbols

Hall (1964) did not agree with the Freudian position that the dream image is a disguise; rather, he considered it a representation. However, he retained the distinction between preconscious unrepressed material and material that is in the unconscious because of repression. Some dream images seem to be slang associations.

Possible Prenatal Experiences

Hall (1967) examined 590 dreams for the presence of images of prenatal and birth experiences. He concluded that 370 of the dreams showed such images and that they occurred equally in the dreams of men and women. All dreams were collected for another purpose, and all were scored by the author himself. It is likely that this finding is a result of the number of items that were theoretically assumed to deal with fetal or birth experiences. For example, being in a room or part of a building was assumed to refer to a fetal experience, and these instances accounted for 38% of the supposed fetal dreams; but instances of being under water (which is probably more unambiguously associated with fetal life) accounted for only 4% of the supposed fetal dreams. The author readily admitted the uncertainty of his conclusions.

Authoritarian Attitudes

Meer (1959) studied the dreams of authoritarian and nonauthoritarian persons. An authoritarian person was defined as one tending to see the world in terms of black-and-white dichotomies. The dream events were also scored as to whether they occurred in interaction with in-group characters. Authoritarian subjects showed more aggression with out-group characters ($p = 0.05$). Authoritarian subjects had more friendly interactions with in-group characters than with out-group characters ($p = 0.05$), while there was no difference between groups for the nonauthoritarians.

Psychosomatic Implications

Saul and Sheppard (1956) ranked the dreams of hypertensives and normotensives according to the amount of aggression in the manifest dream. Three independent judges were able to discriminate accurately the dreams of the two groups. Although there were a number of variables, this was a striking finding, and it was consistent with the psychosomatic conception of hypertension as being related to repressed hostility. Further study of the relationship between manifest deam content and psychosomatic illness is needed.

Dreams and Literature

Hall and Lind (1970) introduced a radical innovation in the study of dreams and literature by applying the method of content analysis to the dreams and writings of Franz Kafka. Although there are many considerations that suggest caution in such a procedure, as in any analysis of a person from his artifacts, the approach deserves further elaboration.

Summary

Content analyses of dreams, and the work of Calvin Hall in particular, have done much to further appreciation of the meaningfulness of the manifest dream. Although Hall held to Freudian theory, he was in a sense contributing to the polar opposite of Freud's dream theory. The basic Freudian position stands or falls with the supposed meaning of the latent dream, which is uncoverable only through the analytic process. Hall focused in a number of meaningful ways on the reliable information available in collections of manifest dreams. However, it must be remembered that the most striking findings in content analysis and the cognitive theory of dreams apply to groups of dreamers. These findings are of less value in the primary situation of clinical dream interpretation—one dreamer trying to understand the deeper processes of his own mind as he examines his own ongoing dream life with the help of an analyst.

REFERENCES

Abenheimer KM: The ego as subject, in Wheelwright JB (ed.): The Reality of the Psyche. New York, Putnam, 1968, pp 61–73

Adler A: Individual Psychology. London, Routledge & Kegal Paul, 1929

Assagioli R: Psychosynthesis. New York, Psychosynthesis Research Foundation, 1965

Assagioli R: Jung and Psychosynthesis. New York, Psychosynthesis Research Foundation, 1967

Assagioli R: Symbols of Transpersonal Experiences. New York, Psychosynthesis Research Foundation, 1969

Assagioli R: The Balancing and Synthesis of the Opposites. New York, Psychosynthesis Research Foundation, 1972

Assagioli R: The Conflict between the Generations and the Psychosynthesis of the Human Ages. New York, Psychosynthesis Research Foundation, 1973

Assagioli R: The Resolution of Conflicts and Spiritual Conflicts and Crisis. New York, Psychosynthesis Research Foundation, 1975

Bauer R, Snyder R: Ego identity and motivation: An empirical study of achievement and affiliation in Erikson's theory. Psychol Rep 30: 951–955, 1972

Benda CE: Language, consciousness, and problems of existential analysis. Am J Psychother 14:259–176, 1960

Bergin AE: Brief note: A note on dream changes following desensitization. Behavior Therapy 1:546–549, 1970

Berman E: Multiple personality: Theoretical approaches. Journal of Bronx State Hospital 2:99–107, 1974

Bonime W: The Clinical Use of Dreams. New York, Basic Books, 1962

Boss M: The Analysis of Dreams. New York, Philosophical Library, 1958

Brennan JF: Upright posture as the foundation of individual psychology: A comparative analysis of Adler and Strauss. J Individ Psychol 24:25–32, 1968

Buhler C: The scope of humanistic psychology. Education 95:2–8, 1974

Cautela JR, Baron MG: Pavlovian theory of dreaming. Pavlov J Biol Sci 9:104–121, 1974

Dai B: Science and wisdom, in Kernodle RW (ed): The Sixth Decade of Our Century: The Developing Fabric of American Society. Williamsburg, Va, College of William and Mary, 1958, pp 35–52

De Fleur ML, Westie FR: Verbal attitudes and overt acts: An experiment on the salience of attitudes. Am Sociol Rev 23:667–673, 1958

Dreyfus EA: Humanness and psychotherapy: A confirmation. J Individ Psychol 24:82–85, 1968

Elkin H: Freudian and phenomenological approaches to the emergence of individual consciousness. Humanitas 5:287–305, 1970

Ellis WD: A Source of Gestalt Psychology. London, Routledge & Kegan Paul, 1938

Engel WH: Reflections of the psychiatric consequences of persecution. Am J
    Psychother 26:191–203, 1962
Erikson EH: The dream specimen of psychoanalysis. Am J Psychoanal Assoc
    2:5–56, 1954
Fairbairn WRD: Psychoanalytic Studies of the Personality. London, Tavis-
    tock, 1952
Ferguson ED: Adlerian concepts in contemporary psychology: The changing
    scene. J Individ Psychol 24:150–156, 1968
Fleming J: The problem of diagnosis in parent loss cases. Contemporary
    Psychoanalysis 10:439–451, 1974
Fordham M: The Objective Psyche. London, Routledge & Kegan Paul, 1958
Framo J, Osterweil J, Boszormenyi-Nagy I: A relationship between threat in
    the manifest content of dreams and active-passive behavior in psychotics.
    J Abnorm Soc Psychol 65:41–47, 1962
French TM, Fromm E: Dream Interpretation: A New Approach. New York,
    Basic Books, 1964
Freud A: The Ego and the Mechanisms of Defense. New York, International
    Universities Press, 1946
Friedman M: Dialogue and the "essential we": The basis of values in the
    philosophy of Martin Buber. Am J Psychoanal 20:26–34, 1960
Fromm E: Spontaneous autohypnotic age-regression in a nocturnal dream. Int
    J Clin Exp Hypn 13:119–131, 1965
Gadol I: Gestalt therapy. Presented to Dallas Group Psychotherapy Society,
    March 13, 1977
Gargiulo GJ: Sublimation, psychoanalysis and symbolic experience. Lecture
    series in phenomenology and depth psychology, University of Dallas,
    Texas, Nov 19, 1976
Geer JH, Silverman I: Treatment of a recurrent nightmare by behavior-
    modification procedures. J Abnorm Psychol 72:188–190, 1967
Gershman H: Dream power. Am J Psychoanal 33:167–177, 1973
Gibson J: The legacies of Koffka's principles. J Hist Behav Sci 7:3–9, 1971
Green B: The therapeutic stance: An Eriksonian approach to diagnosis and
    technique. Psychoanal Rev 59:73–87, 1972
Guntrip H: Personality Structure and Human Interaction. New York, Interna-
    tional Universities Press, 1961
Guntrip H: Schizoid Phenomena, Object Relations and the Self. London,
    Hogarth, 1968
Guntrip H: Psychoanalytic Theory, Therapy, and the Self. New York, Basic
    Books, 1971
Hall CS: Diagnosing personality by the analysis of dreams. J Abnorm Soc
    Psychol 42:68–79, 1947
Hall CS: What people dream about (pp 55–63); Cognitive theory of dreams
    (pp 123–124); Diagnosing personality by dreams (pp 193–211), in De-
    Martino MF (ed): Dreams and Personality Dynamics. Springfield, Ill,
    Charles C Thomas, 1959

Hall CS: A cognitive theory of dream symbols. J Gen Psychol 48:169–186, 1953a

Hall CS: A cognitive theory of dreams. J Gen Psychol 49:273–282, 1953b

Hall CS: The significance of the dream being attacked. J Pers 24:168–180, 1955

Hall CS: Dreams of American college students, in Baker R, Kaplan B (eds): Primary records in psychology publication No. 2, University of Kansas Social Science Studies, 1963

Hall CS: Strangers in dreams: An empirical confirmation of the oedipus complex. J Pers 31:337–345, 1963

Hall CS: Aggression in dreams. Int J Soc Psychiatry 9:259–267, 1963

Hall CS: Slang and dream symbols. Psycholanal Rev 51:38–48, 1964

Hall CS: A comparison of the dreams of four groups of hospitalized mental patients with each other and with a normal population. J Nerv Ment Dis 143:135–139, 1966

Hall CS: Are prenatal and birth experiences represented in dreams? Psychoanal Rev 54:157–174, 1967

Hall CS: Representation of the laboratory setting in dreams. J Nerv Ment Dis 144:198–206, 1967

Hall CS, Domhoff B: A ubiquitous sex difference in dreams. J Abnorm Soc Psychol 66:278–280, 1963

Hall CS, Lind RE: Dreams, Life and Literature: A Study of Franz Kafka. Chapel Hill, University of North Carolina Press, 1970

Hall CS, Van de Castle RL: An empirical investigation of the castration complex in dreams. J Pers 33:20–29, 1965

Hall CS, Van de Castle RL: The Content Analysis of Dreams. New York, Appleton, 1966

Hall E: Alfred Adler: A sketch. Psychology Today 3:45–67, 1970

Hartman E: The Functions of Sleep. New Haven and London: Yale University Press, 1973

Heuscher JE: The existential dimension in a dream. Compr Psychiatry 10:302–313, 1969

Hofstadter A: The vocation of consciousness. Rev Existential Psychol Psychiatr 9:64–77, 1968

Hoppe KD: Chronic reactive aggression in survivors of severe persecution. Compr Psychiatry 12:230–237, 1971

Husband RW: Sex differences in dream content, in DeMartino MF (ed): Dreams and Personality Dynamics. Springfield, Ill, Charles C Thomas, 1959

Jones RM: Ego Synthesis in Dreams. Cambridge, Mass: Schenkman, 1962

Jung CG: Memories, Dreams and Reflections. (Ed: A Jaffe) New York, Vintage Books, 1961

Kantor JR: Behaviorism in the history of psychology. Psychological Record 18:151–166, 1968

Kelman H: A phenomenologic approach to dream interpretation. Am J Psychoanal 25:188–202, 1965

Khanna P: A critique of existential guilt. Psychotherapy: Theory, Research & Practice 6:209–211, 1969

Krippner S, Hughes W: Dreams and human potential. J Humanistic Psychol 10:1–20, 1970

Krohn A, Mayman M: Object representations in dreams and projective tests. Bull Menninger Clin 38:445–466, 1974

Leonard L: Heidegger and Jung. Inter-Regional Society of Jungian Analysts training seminar, Dallas, Oct 23, 1976

Lichtenstein PE: A behavioral approach to "phenomenological data." Psychological Record 21:1–16, 1971

Mahl G: Fathers and sons, source material (two volumes). Catalog of Selected Documents in Psychology, Vol. 4, No. 47, 1974

Marks IM, Gelder MG: Common ground between behavior therapy and psychodynamic methods. Br J Med Psychol 39:11–23, 1966

Marsh EJ: Has behavior modification lost its identity? Canadia Psychologist 15:271–280, 1974

Maslow AH: The Creative Attitude. New York, Psychosynthesis Research Foundation, 1963

Maslow AH: The Farther Reaches of Human Nature. New York, Viking, 1971

Meer SJ: Authoritarian attitudes and dreams, in DeMartino MF (ed): Dreams and Personality Dynamics. Springfield, Ill, Charles C Thomas, 1959, pp 135–144

Mountjoy PT, Paul T, Bos JH, et al: Falconry: Neglected aspect of the history of psychology. J History Behavioral Sci 5:59–67, 1969

Murray EJ: Sleep, Dreams, and Arousal. New York, Appleton, 1965

Nikelly AG: Current Adlerian therapies. Compr Psychiatry 14:41–48, 1973

Openchaim IM: Psychoanalyse existentielle et spatialite onirique [Existential psychoanalysis and representation of space]. Psychother Psychosom 19:226–231, 1971

Oppenheimer H: Comprehensible and incomprehensible phenomena in psychopathology: A comparison of the psychology of Sigmund Freud and Karl Jaspers. Compr Psychiatry 15:503–510, 1974

Perls FS, Hefferline RF, Goodman P: Gestalt Therapy. New York, Julian Press, 1951

Perls F: The Gestalt Approach and Eye Witness to Therapy. Ben Lomond, Calif, Science and Behavior Books, 1973

Perry JW: The Self in Psychotic Process. Berkeley, Univ. Calif Press, 1953

Piotrowski ZA: A rational explanation of the irrational: Freud's and Jung's own dreams reinterpreted. J Pers Assess 35:505–518, 1971

Piotrowski ZA: The Piotrowski dream interpretation system. Psychiatr Q 47:609–622, 1973

Polanyi M: Personal Knowledge. Chicago, University of Chicago Press, 1958

Polster E, Polster M: Gestalt Therapy Integrated. New York, Brunner/Mazel, 1973

Rosenthal H: Horney theory and child analysis. Am J Psychoanal 31:174–181, 1971

Rossi EL: Psychosynthesis and the new biology of dreams and psychotherapy. Am J Psychother 27:34–41, 1973

Rossi I (ed): The Unconscious in Culture: The Structuralism of Claude Lévi-Strauss in Perspective. New York, Dutton, 1974, p xvii

Rybak D: Existential behaviorism: A transactionalistic approach to self-determination. Canadian Psychologist 12:243–247, 1971

Sartre JP: The Transcendence of the Ego: An Existentialist Theory of Consciousness. (Trans: F Williams, R Kirkpatrick) New York, Noonday Press, 1957

Saul L, Sheppard E: An attempt to quantify emotional forces using manifest dreams: A preliminary study. J Am Psychoanal Assoc 4:486–502, 1956

Schmidl F: Psychoanalysis and existential analysis. Psychoanal Q 29:344–354, 1960

Schuster S: Dracula and surgically induced trauma in children. Brit J Med Psychol 46:259–270, 1973

Segal H: Introduction to the Work of Melanie Klein. New York, Basic Books, 1964, p viii

Smillie D: A psychological contribution to the phenomenology of the other. Philosophical Phenomenological Res 32:64–77, 1971

Stark S: Being-cognition, peak-experience, and self-actualization: Some questions regarding interrelationship. Psychological Reports 23:836–838, 1968

Stewart K: Dream Theory in Malaya, in Tart CT (ed): Altered States of Consciousness. New York, Wiley, 1969

Timken KR, Chambers J, Hall JA, and Moore WT: Biofeedback: A demand for clinical expertise. Tex Med 71:44–47, 1975

Ullman M: The social roots of the dream. Am J Psychoanal 20:180–196, 1960

Ullman M: Foreword in Bonime W: The Clinical Use of Dreams. New York, Basic Books, 1962, pp vii–xix

Ullman M: Telepathy and dreams. Experimental Medicine and Surgery 27:19–38, 1969

Ullman M, Krippner S: An experimental approach to dreams and telepathy: II. Report of three studies. Amer J Psychiat 126:1282–1289, 1970

Ullman M: Societal factors in dreaming. Contemporary Psychoanalysis 9:282–293, 1973

Ullman M: The transformation process in dreams. The Academy 19:8–10, 1975

Van Dusen W: Existential analytical psychotherapy. Am J Psychoanal 20:35–40, 1960

van Kaam A: The impact of existential phenomenology on the psychological literature of Western Europe. Rev Existent Psychol Psychiatr 1:63–92, 1961

von Franz ML: The process of individuation, in Jung CG (ed): Man and His Symbols. London, Aldus Books, 1964, pp 158–229

Weitzman B: Behavior therapy and psychotherapy. Psychol Rev 74:300–317, 1967

Winthrop H: Existential and phenomenological frontiers. Part I: New dimensions for existential analysis: Major indictments of technological society. J Existentialism 6:343–354, 1966

Wolf E: Learning theory and psychoanalysis. Br J Med Psychol 39:1–9, 1966

Wolf M: Existential psychology and a romantic poem. Psychiatr Q [Suppl] 42:297–302, 1968

Wykert J: Horney's later writings—her picture of women. Psychiatric News Nov 19, 1975

Zinker JC: Dreamwork as theatre. Voices: The Art and Science of Psychotherapy 7:18–21, 1971

3

Laboratory Studies of Sleep and Dreams

Aristotle (1941, p. 620) suggested that in order to understand dreams we must study "the circumstances attending sleep." Until recently it was possible to make only gross measurements of the states of sleeping and waking, which tended to be considered polarized opposites. In 1903, when most theorists still considered sleep to be produced by an endogenous toxic substance, Claparède asserted that it was an active process, a view that has been confirmed by modern research in sleep and dreams (Bloch, 1974).

The great increase in scientific interest in sleep and dream studies began when Kleitman and Aserinsky (1955) demonstrated that dreaming is frequently associated with rapid eye movements (REM). This technical advance permitted external study of the process of dreaming, whereas previous studies of dreams had been dependent on the remembered subjective dream. Sleep was no longer considered a unitary phenomenon. We are still in the midst of an information explosion deriving from ongoing studies of sleep and dreams, and this state of flux must be considered in formulating theories on the clinical use of dreams (Kramer and associates, 1969).

When rapid eye movements are associated with ascending stage 1 sleep (light sleep that occurs as a change from a "deeper" electroencephalographic stage), dreaming is frequently reported. This dreaming sleep has been called by a variety of names: stage 1 REM sleep, D-state sleep, paradoxical sleep, third-state sleep, activated sleep, rhombencephalic sleep, etc. (Whitman and associates, 1967). Although it appears that dreaming is not exclusively associated with REM periods, dreams are reported predominantly by those waking from REM sleep.

In premature infants REM sleep constitutes 80% of total sleep time; full-term infants spend 50% of their sleep time in REM sleep. After about 2 years of age the percentage of REM sleep stabilizes at the adult level: 20%–25% of all sleep (Waldhorn, 1967). A number of studies have suggested that decreased dreaming, as indicated by decreased amounts of REM sleep, may be a factor in various psychiatric disorders, including depression, schizophrenia, and postpartum psychosis (Williams, 1969). Hartmann (1973) suggested that different stages of sleep may be associated with recovery from different types of tiredness: that resulting from physical effort (stage 4) and that associated with mental stress (REM). Rapid eye movement may be a mechanism for regulating the degree of cortical activity during sleep (Ephron and Carrington, 1969). In mammals there is no clear relationship between the complexity of the nervous system and the amount of REM sleep, but it appears possible that mammals with more highly developed nervous systems are more efficient in their sleep processes (Hartmann, 1973). In 1939 Kleitman suggested that sleep may be the primary state during the evolution of organisms and that wakefulness is an accomplishment, which poses the reverse of the usual question of why we need sleep.

Murray (1965) outlined stages for waking and sleeping as they correlate with electroencephalogram (EEG) recordings of brain activity. In *alert attentiveness* the EEG is partially synchronized with mostly fast, low-amplitude waves. In *relaxed wakefulness* there is more synchronicity, and alpha rhythm (8–13 cycles/sec) can be seen. The next stage, *drowsiness,* has reduced alpha activity and occasional low-amplitude slow waves. *Light sleep* shows loss of alpha activity together with occurrences of spindles and slow waves. As sleep progresses toward *deep sleep,* there are large slow delta waves (less than 4 cycles/sec). Many writers grade sleep by the deepening stages 1, 2, 3, and 4, referring to ascending stage 1 with REM as the REM period (REMP). A detailed description of the four stages as they are generally used is available in a government publication prepared by Luce (PHS publication 1389).

The implications of recent studies on sleep and dreaming are still being debated (Dement, 1974; Ullman, 1969; Wolpert and Trosman, 1958). The sleep-dream cycle, as described by REM and non-REM (NREM) stages, has been observed in all mammals studied. The duration of the sleep-dream cycle is inversely proportional to the pulse and respiratory rates (Hartmann, 1968a). In man the cycle of NREM-REM is approximately 90 min. Sleeping and dreaming may be alternating parts of one cycle linked to diurnal rhythm that adapts the organism to the 24-hour day. Hartmann (1966) pointed out that there seems to be a relationship between the length of a NREM sleep period and the length of the dream time that follows it; there does not appear to be a similar relationship between the length of a REM period and the length of the NREM period following it. This has been taken by some to indicate that the NREM period is a time in which physiological preparation is made for the following REM period dream.

The arousal that occurs during REM sleep is different from waking arousal, and it does not seem to be mediated by the same neural mechanisms. In animal experiments it is possible to evoke REM by stimulation of the pontine reticular formation when the animal is in slow-wave sleep, but not when the animal is awake (Murray, 1965). Fisher and Dement (1963), quoting Jouvet, characterized sleep as being divided into two phases: (1) telencephalic sleep, caused by inhibition descending from the cortex to the reticular activating system, that mediates waking arousal; and (2) rhombencephalic sleep, associated with dreaming, in which a rhombencephalic center activates the limbic midbrain circuit (thought to be associated with emotion) and simultaneously inhibits the reticular system.

Within the dream time itself, there seem to be fluctuations in REM density (Aserinsky, 1971). Just prior to a dream, there is suppression of muscle potentials in the face and neck; during this time there is an apparent "deepening" of sleep, as measured by the greater stimulus required to produce complete awakening (Larson and Foulkes, 1969).

Laboratory studies of dreaming are consistent in describing better recall of dreams from REM periods than from NREM periods, although the percentages of REM awakenings that are associated with dream recall vary. There is much more variation in the numbers of NREM awakenings that produce dream reports, and this had led to interest in the nature of NREM mentation. It has been reported that the longer a subject takes to awaken the less likely it is a dream will be remembered (Pivik and Foulkes, 1968); in the same study, the reports of NREM mentation became more dreamlike as the night progressed.

Subjects will subjectively rate their sleep as light or deep depending on the amount of REM time they experience. Greater amounts of REM are associated with feelings of deep sleep, less trouble returning to sleep during the night, and greater dislike of getting up in the morning. Analysis of all-night sleep EEGs suggests that less alpha activity and more beta activity (18–30 cycles/sec, characteristic of waking EEG records) correlate with a sense of poor sleep (Saletu, 1975).

Body movement varies throughout the night, with both eye and body movements being greatest in the lightest stage of sleep. However, with the onset of REM and dreaming, there is a sudden decrease in body motility (Dement and Kleitman, 1957). There have been some reports of a significant correlation between body movement during dreaming and the amount of dreamed action (Gardner and associates, 1975).

Artifacts of awakening may interfere with pure dream reporting (Goodenough and associates, 1965). Verbal reports of any form are probably subject to greater error than laboratory measurements (Kamiya, 1969). The only firm conclusion is that REM sleep and NREM sleep are physiologically different.

PHYSIOLOGICAL CHANGES

Physiological changes during dreaming have been reported in a number of areas: penile erections; irregularities in respiration, heart rate, and blood pressure; changes in blood levels of free fatty acids. Variations in respiration occur in REM. Strength of grip is weaker when the subject is aroused from REM sleep than when aroused from NREM sleep, but the difference is not significant (Tebbs and Foulkes, 1966).

Changes in heart rate during REM sleep are important because of the possibility that anxiety dreams may stress the heart excessively in persons with coronary disease. Premature ventricular beats are more frequent during dreaming (Rosenblatt and associates, 1973). Heart rate during sleep is increased by a 3-sec auditory stimulus, and no habituation to the response has been observed (Hord and associates, 1966). The response varies with the phase of respiration during which it occurs: it is greater on inspiration than on expiration. When subjects are deprived of sleep, heart rate and task performance tend to fall, unless the conditions are such that arousal is required. If alertness is demanded in the face of sleep loss, heart rate may be more variable.

Body temperature fluctuates on a diurnal basis, being lowest in the early morning hours. Fever induced by the injection of pyrogens decreases dream time (Karacan and associates, 1968).

In an unpublished study, Fahrion (1966) noted that with tachycardia patients the emotionality, hostility, and completeness of dream reports were related to variability of heart rate. The dream content ratings did not correlate with the variability.

Anxiety during dreaming has been suggested as the cause of catecholamine release, which in turn mobilizes increased levels of free fatty acids from body fat. Anxiety scores derived from manifest dream content have been shown to correlate with the rise in free fatty acids during the REM cycle (Gottschalk and associates, 1966). Changes in urine volume and osmolarity have been noted with dreaming. At the onset of REM, there is first a marked decrease in volume, with a corresponding increase in osmolarity, followed by a hypotonic diuresis (Mandell and associates, 1966). These urine changes probably indicate that dreaming anxiety affects the release of antidiuretic hormone. Periods of lying awake at night have been known to have the same biphasic effect on urine.

Studies of the secretion of luteinizing hormone, follicle-stimulating hormone, and growth hormone during the sleep of normal young men showed that only luteinizing hormone exhibited a small (14%) increase with onset of the REM state (Rubin and associates, 1973). Secretion of growth hormone showed a marked increase with the onset of slow-wave sleep (stage 4), but it was not correlated with dreaming.

EYE MOVEMENTS

An early study by Dement and Wolpert (1958) reported that the direction of eye movement during REM reflected the motion of the dream images being experienced. It seemed possible that the dreamer might be "watching" the activity in his dream from the point of view of his dream ego. Similar observations were reported by Roffwarg and associates (1962). They noted that the correlation between eye movement direction and the action of the dream was better when the dreams were remembered vividly. However, negative results were found by Moskowitz and Berger (1969) and Jacobs and associates (1972). The question is further complicated by the fact that REM occurs in all mammals; thus an exclusively human psychological function is unlikely for the basic REM process, but the psychological meanings of animal dreams are not accessible to study.

Impairment of ocular motility has been shown to decrease dreaming eye movements, but it is not known whether the subjective experience of movement in dreams is also impaired (Buscaino and associates, 1971); REM and clear dream reports reappeared in 2 patients when the disease process improved and ocular motility returned to normal. Related evidence was found that eye movements and dream are linked: when eye movement was induced by mechanical manipulation, photic stimulation, or caloric stimulation of the semicircular canals of the ear, in some cases dream fragments resulted (Baldridge and associates, 1968).

It appears uncertain at present whether the direction of eye movement is related to dream imagery. It may be possible that the REM state itself is phylogentically important in the establishment and maintenance of binocularly coordinated eye movements (Berger, 1968) and becomes secondarily available for the psychological functions of dreaming. No sleep study has come to my attention in which the direction of ocular movements during dreaming were correlated with the point of view of any figure in the dream other than the dream ego, there being an apparent assumption that if eye movements are correlated it is from the point of view of the ego in the dream. It would be difficult to investigate such a question, but such an investigation might provide additional information about the relationship between the dream ego and the waking ego.

LONG AND SHORT SLEEPERS

When subjects are divided into those who ordinarily sleep short times and those whose habitual sleep is longer, certain differences are found between the two groups. In one study, short sleepers (6.5 hours of sleep or less per night) spent less time in stage 3, but they achieved as much deep sleep (stage 4) and dreaming (REM) as the normal population. Their sleep might be characterized as more efficient (Webb and Agnew, 1970). Long sleepers tend to report more dreams than do short sleepers (Hartmann, 1973). Long sleepers tend to be more introverted, and in some ways they may be both more neurotic and more creative than short sleepers (Hartmann, 1973). It is possible that the longer time spent in sleep permits the establishment of more varied patterns for action. Hartmann (1973) suggested that it is not increased amounts of new facts learned during the day that make increased sleep necessary, but variations from the person's usual way of handling stress. Many persons are variable sleepers, and their amounts of sleep may fluctuate with changing needs.

AROUSAL

Dreaming sleep has been described as cerebral arousal in the absence of contact with the external world (Zimmerman, 1970). In view of the occurrence of dreamlike experiences in NREM sleep, such a definition may be more reasonable than relying solely on REM sleep as an indicator. It has been suggested that the REM dream state evolved as a means of periodically enhancing arousal during sleep and that it is functionally connected with pineal stimulation of the limbic system (Drew and Batt, 1972).

The amount of stimulation needed to arouse a sleeping subject has been found to be roughly the same in REM and in stage 2 sleep (low-voltage EEG with sleep spindles). Delta-wave deep sleep has a higher threshold for awakening. Throughout the night, thresholds for awakening become increasingly lower whatever the stage of sleep (Rechtschaffen and associates, 1966).

Subjects who are able to awaken themselves at a predetermined time seem to awaken as if from a dream, which raises the possibility that their motivation may somehow induce a dream that contributes to awakening (Orr and associates, 1968). Subjects sleep less on the nights they are scheduled to awaken. They have more dreams, and the dream content differs from that of their usual dreams, although not directly incorporating the arousal task. I recall that when sleeping as a dream-study subject in the laboratory of C. A. Meier in Zurich I once dreamed that I was awake in order (I thought in the dream) to cause EEG changes that would indice the technician to awaken me, which she did.

It is apparently usual for sleeping subjects to be able to awaken to motivating stimuli and to continue to sleep in the presence of more nearly neutral stimuli. This is the laboratory equivalent of the phenomenon wherein a person will awaken at the sound of a disturbed infant but will sleep through much more audible but emotionally meaningless sound. Wilson and Zung (1966) demonstrated that female subjects responded better to sounds that were more nearly neutral than did men at all stages of sleep except REM sleep, where scores were equivalent. The sexes discriminated meaningful sounds equally well at every stage of sleep. The authors suggested that there are at least two different alerting systems at work during sleep.

ENVIRONMENTAL INCORPORATION

The term *environmental incorporation* is used to describe the process whereby external stimuli that impinge on the sleeper are incorporated into the dream. These stimuli may include the setting, chance occurrences, or deliberate stimuli that are administered to the sleeper for experimental purposes. In dream research, the influence of the setting on the dream is called the laboratory effect, and it must be allowed for in considering the content of laboratory dreams.

Hall (1967) found the laboratory effect at work in 14.2% of 559 dreams that took place in the experimental setting, compared to only 2 of 264 home dreams that were reported; if only "significantly influenced" dreams were counted, the percentage fell to 6.2%. In the laboratory dreams, incorporation seemed not to be affected by the number of times the subject was awakened during the night, nor was it affected by whether the dreams were reported from earlier or later in the night. However, others have found that laboratory dreams recorded early in the night have a greater tendency to deal with the experimental setting (Dement and associates, 1965), a tendency also noted in first-night laboratory dreams although it declines on successive laboratory nights.

Baekeland (1971) compared two groups for their dream reactions to presleep laboratory procedures. The first group had no special presleep activity, but the second group was exposed to 30 min of anxiety-provoking tests focusing on laboratory procedures. The second group exhibited more laboratory effect and had more unpleasant dreams; they recalled their dreams less well and more often appeared as participants in their manifest dreams. In another study, male subjects incorporated more items from the laboratory setting than from an erotic movie shown prior to sleep (Cartwright and associates, 1969). Domhoff and Kamiya (1964) found that sexual elements may be actively screened out in laboratory dreams. Their subjects were used to compare laboratory dreams with dreams experienced at home. The laboratory dreams had fewer sexual and aggression-misfortune elements and had less personal involvement of the dream ego in the misfortunes. The authors concluded that the laboratory setting was perceived as threatening by women and as annoying and exhibitionistic by men.

Comparing presleep stresses, de Konick and Koulack (1975) showed subjects a presleep stressful film. Half of the subjects were then exposed to the sound track of the film while they were in REM sleep, but at a volume sufficiently low that it would not wake them. Those who were exposed to the sound track during sleep incorporated more elements of the film into their dreams, and they tended to show emotionality when they viewed the film a second time in the waking state. A control group of subjects also saw the film twice; then some of them slept during the 8-hour interval between showings, while some remained awake. In this control group, those who did not sleep between the showings experienced more anxiety on the second showing. These findings are open to interpretation. The anxiety levels of those subjects who heard the sound track during REM sleep resembled the anxiety levels of the waking subjects who saw the film twice without an interval of sleep. The control subjects who slept between showings exhibited less anxiety, as did the original subjects who slept undisturbed between showings. The sound-track presentation of previously seen traumatic film elements was apparently successful in causing more dream incorporation of stimuli, but this occurred at the expense of interfering with the normal adaptive function of assimilating new images to previous complex structures that would have functioned uninterrupted in the two groups that were permitted undisturbed sleep and dreaming between the two presentations of the film. If Freud were right, and dreams were for the preservation of sleep, those subjects who incorporated the stimuli would be expected to adapt better to the stress of the experiment, which otherwise might wake them from sleep. However, if dreams are a process of the unconscious mind compensating the distortions of ego images, as Jung thought, the stimuli presented during sleep could interfere with the adaptive activity already in process in the REM dream.

Castaldo and Shevrin (1968) presented sleeping subjects with two auditory stimuli (the words *pen* and *knee*) in both the REM state and the NREM state. NREM reports were conceptual in nature, as is consistent with the observed similarity of NREM mentation to waking thoughts. No effect was visible on the REM productions, although the authors had expected that the words might be combined into a rebus *penny* (from *pen* plus *knee*) which could then elicit associations of its own. Their findings are consistent with the Jungian position that the dream is not involved in adapting to immediate external stress but is involved in the psychological growth of the personality. If the rebus effect had occurred, it would have been because of the so-called clang (rhyming) association between the rebus words *pen* and *knee,* yielding their product *penny.* In his classic word-association experiments, Jung considered clang responses as evidence that the normal state of consciousness was being interrupted by an activated complex. The absence of the expected clang association in this experiment by Castaldo and Shevrin is very soft evidence that the dreamer is not analogous to the person unconsciously exhibiting an activated psychological complex. It is my own contention, to be elaborated in subsequent chapters, that the dream is in fact the manifestation of the mind's reworking of those previously formed complexes on which consciousness depends. It is important to remember that the word *complex* is a neutral term; it is not meant to carry the popular meaning of overactive complex, such as "mother complex."

In a thoughtfully designed experiment, Witkin and Lewis (1965) found that various experimentally induced presleep events could be identified in subsequent dreams, although sometimes in transformations. Unlike many dream studies, their study involved extensive preexperiment and postexperiment personal data about their subjects, and consequently they were able to understand some of the dream images in terms of the tension between the presleep stimulus and significant past events of the person's life. They tended to view their findings from a Freudian point of view, with its emphasis on regression, defensiveness, and disguise of disturbing dream elements. However, their results could as easily be viewed as demonstrating assimilation of the presleep stimulus to the complexes that were in the process of transformation in the dream life of the subject.

In the work of Portnoff and associates (1966), words presented for learning prior to the onset of sleep were retained better when the subject was forced to remain awake for a period. Words presented just before a return to sleep were less well retained. Their results were interpreted as demonstrating NREM sleep interfering with consolidation of learning. By extrapolation, these results are consistent with the loss of memory of a REM dream when longer periods of NREM sleep intervene before awakening.

Attempts to produce a more frequent appearance of the ego image in the dream through somatosensory stimulation have been unsuccessful (Koulack, 1969). However, there was an interesting suggestion in this study that the stimulus effect might have been represented by a person other than the dreamer in the dream. This observation is worthy of further study in the light of Jungian and object-relations theories of dreaming that might meaningfully assimilate consistent differences between the dream ego and other images within the dream.

The speed at which awakening takes place apparently has significant impact on reports of dreams. Goodenough and associates (1965) found that thinking reports were more frequent following gradual awakening, which suggested that the awakening process has an influence on what is reported from the immediately preceding sleep.

An interesting variation of the question of somatosensory stimulation affecting dream content was introduced by Rechtschaffen and Foulkes (1965). They taped open the eyes of their subjects, waited for them to sleep, and then illuminated various objects in front of them. The dreams obtained on awakening after these presentations contained occasional references to light stimulation, but no clear references to the specific forms of the stimulus objects. Their findings argue against dream images being induced by any form of retinal stimulation—part of the endogenous stimulation hypothesis.

Cartwright (1974) reported some studies that were in many ways consistent with Jungian dream theory. Testing problem-solving ability after matched intervals of either waking time or sleep time in which dreaming occurred, she found that performance on intellectual tasks was no better following dreaming than it was following the waking control period. However, solutions to emotion problems showed more change after dreaming than after waking. It was of interest that these solutions were "more likely to be biased toward failure" than waking solutions. Cartwright suggested that dreaming may better equip the subject to deal with the possibility of failure. While acknowledging that dreaming may produce solutions to problems, she suggested that such occurrences are rare. The more frequent outcome of dreaming appears to be "to provide additional associations to elements and possibilities previously unattended, making them more available for later conscious consideration" (Cartwright, 1974, p. 454). The similarity to Jung's concept of the compensatory function of dreaming is immediately obvious.

AGE

The amount of time spent in REM sleep varies with age. In the neonate, REM sleep is not necessarily preceded by the usual period of NREM sleep seen in the adult. Also, the association between erections and REM sleep is not as common in the infant as in the adult (Korner, 1968). It would appear that mechanisms for regulation of sleeping and waking are developed by 6.5 months of gestation (Frank and Chase, 1968). Observations have suggested that as early as 1 year of age children in an unstable environment (a foundling home) show more anxiety during REM sleep than children in a control group (Riva and Vitali, 1970).

Altshuler and associates (1963) studied the contents of dreams of noninstitutionalized persons with a mean age of 69 years. The only clearly defined problem in the dreams was "concern about lost resources for coping with problems." There were similar findings in manifest dreams of residents living in a home for the aged (Barad and associates, 1961). A marked tendency was found for the image of the psychiatrist to be incorporated into manifest dreams as an "omnipotent and controlled provider of magically satisfying services." The dreams of those residents with severe chronic brain syndrome were more stereotyped and repetitive, but they showed evidence of similar emotional concerns about decreased abilities to deal with stress. Sleep patterns normally change with increasing age, older persons requiring less sleep. This change is generally accomplished with little disturbance (McGhie and Russell, 1962). The number of night awakenings increases linearly with aging (Feinberg, 1968; Feinberg and Carlson, 1968). There is some variability with age in the number of dreams reported. Persons between 21 and 34 years of age and those between 50 and 64 years of age have been found to report more dreams than those between 35 and 49 years of age and those over 65 years of age (Winget and associates, 1972). Kahn and Fisher (1968) found a significantly smaller number of remembered dreams in a population over 70 years of age than in a young adult population.

Comparing the dreams of older women with those of a younger control group, Brenneis (1975) found that the manifest dreams of the older group showed a narrowing of personal investment, a decline in aggression, and less sense of the importance of the ego. The author was surprised to find increased images of active locomotor activity in the dreams of the older women. Although generalization must be done cautiously, the decreasing amount of ego concern is appropriate to what Jung called the problems of the second half of life, the time when relativization of the ego and reevaluation of life goals are the tasks. Increased locomotor activity in the dreams could be viewed as compensatory to the actually decreased body activity in the older group.

SLEEP LEARNING

The question whether useful learning can take place during sleep is still controversial, with both positive (Zukhar and associates, 1965) and negative reports (Lewis, 1968). Greenberg and Pearlman (1974) studied possible relationships between learning and various sleep stages. They concluded that "prepared" learning (that for which there is an instinctive tendency) is not decreased by REM deprivation, whereas new or "unprepared" learning can be considered REM-dependent. Again the implication is that REM dreaming is somehow involved in acquiring new adaptational responses. Feldman and Dement (1968) reported that REM deprivation did not affect retention of material learned prior to sleep, but the same subjects had more difficulty learning material presented after REM deprivation. In subjects deprived of dreams by amitriptyline, short-term memory deteriorated, and structured interviews showed more anger and confusion to be present (Adelman and Hartmann, 1968).

DRUGS AND DREAMS

The whole question of the function of the brain and the nature of dreams is brought into sharp focus in the question of drug influence on dreaming. It is possible not only to consider interference or enhancement of the D state by drugs but also to reverse the usual question and ask whether changes in the content of dreams show any psychodynamic impact from drugs that alter neurophysiology, the substrate of mental functioning.

Drug effects on dreams can be studied in dreams collected by patients in the home environment, thus circumventing some of the laboratory influences on dreaming (Morgan and associates, 1970). Numerous clinically useful drugs seem to decrease REM time (Hartmann, 1969; Rechtschaffen and Maron, 1964; Williams and Agnew, 1969). Such drugs as alcohol, barbiturates, and amphetamines suppress REM; there is rebound of REM catch-up time when these drugs are withdrawn, often with nightmares and anxiety dreams (Firth, 1974). The tricyclic antidepressants are associated with decreased REM (Hartmann, 1969), but they are not associated with the rebound effect. Reserpine was shown to increase REM time, but the REM time returned to normal after a week. Chlordiazepoxide HCl (Librium) did not alter REM.

In 1 subject the administration of LSD was shown to produce a profound change in REM (Green, 1969). On the night of administration there was an increase in REM sleep as a percentage of total sleep and an increase in the duration of the REM periods. This effect continued to increase the following day, and REM returned to normal only on the third day after LSD administration. The sole subject in this study was a chronic male alcoholic; reactions in other subjects might be different.

An approach to the study of manifest dream imagery in the evaluation of drug effects was made by Whitman and associates (1969). They concluded that the dream image of a gun firing harmlessly into the air might represent the mind's presentation to itself of the mode of action of imipramine (Tofranil). The gun was taken to represent a harmless discharge of aggressive energy. This was an isolated but striking observation, for it indicates a direction in which linkages may be found between psychophysiological actions and dream imagery.

Ethyl alcohol appears to be a dream-depriving agent (Gresham and associates, 1963; Martin, 1969). REM deprivation caused by alcohol consumption may contribute to some of the disorders of acute and chronic alcoholism.

It is possible that those drugs that decrease the "need" for dreaming act in man as antidepressants, possibly through their effects on serotonin metabolism (Hartmann, 1969). The antidepressant imipramine decreases the amount of REM sleep and produces a longer period of latency from onset of sleep until the first REM dream (Ritvo and associates, 1967). In discussing the relationship between antidepressant drugs and sleep, Zung (1969) speculated that these drugs may have an inhibitory effect on the arousal system, interfering with normal sleep and increasing the number of awakenings per night in the depressed patient.

DREAM AND SLEEP DEPRIVATION

Prior to the realization that REM sleep and NREM sleep were distinct states, studies concerned with total deprivation of a particular stage of sleep led to Dement's suggestion (1960) that deprivation of dreaming causes disorganization of the waking personality, in spite of the subject being permitted to have all the NREM sleep that he wishes. Therefore, Freud's designation of the dream as the protector of sleep from inner and outer stimuli that might cause wakening seemed in need of revision. The early dream-deprivation studies also raised the exciting speculation that schizophrenia might be a disorder in which deprivation of dreaming at night led to a breakthrough of the dream process into everyday waking life.

As is often the case in the sciences, the excitement of initial discovery dimmed when further studies did not clearly reproduce the same findings. NREM mentation was also found to contain dreamlike elements, increasingly so as the night progressed. The waking disturbances following dream deprivation were not uniformly replicated, and the psychological changes themselves were investigated with more subtle psychological instruments.

At the present stage of knowledge, it appears that dream deprivation does disturb the normal level of waking function, although this is not as uniform among subjects nor as simple as it appeared at first discovery. The implications for psychoanalytic insight are just beginning to emerge.

Four young men underwent 205 hours of sleep deprivation (Pasau and associates, 1968). After five days without sleep, they appeared to get a "second wind," perhaps indicating some adaptation to loss of sleep. As might be expected, they experienced increasing regression, hallucinations, labile affect, and decreased scores on performance tasks. One very regressive episode occurred after 160 hours of sleep deprivation; it resembled the night terrors the subject had experienced as a child, but he responded positively to reassurance by the experimenters and his fellow subjects. As the authors correctly pointed out, a true psychotic episode would not have responded so easily to reality testing and consensual validation. A subject who was deprived of sleep for 264 hours experienced fatigue and some sensory misperceptions, but was judged psychiatrically healthy (Ross, 1965). Others have also concluded that sleep deprivation is not in itself a sufficient cause for psychotic symptoms (Kollar and associates, 1966). Early dream-deprivation experiments were criticized methodologically (Barber, 1960), but these objections seem to have been met by changes in experimental design. The increasing numbers of studies in which drugs are used to modify the amounts of various stages of sleep circumvent some of the criticisms that the awakening process itself contributes to artifacts in the findings.

It has been found that when subjects are deprived of sleep and then monitored during the recovery sleeping time, all stages of sleep are not equally replenished (Tune, 1968). After sufficient sleep deprivation, stage 4 is first increased in amount over control levels, followed by increases in REM sleep (Murray, 1965). In milder states of deprivation, the increase in REM sleep after deprivation is more apparent than recovery of lost deep sleep.

Deprivation of stage 4 sleep in 5 adult males over 2 nights was followed by a significant increase in this stage of sleep during the monitored recovery night (Agnew and associates, 1964). Deprivation of stage 4 sleep tends to cause an increase in stage 2 sleep on the same night; deprivation of stage 1 REM sleep is associated with an increase in NREM stage 1 sleep during the experimental night. Deprivation of stage 4 sleep tends to cause depression, while deprivation of stage 1 REM sleep tends to produce irritability and lability of emotions (Williams and associates, 1967).

Saint-Laurent (1971) reviewed a number of studies on the detrimental effects of sleep loss, both total deprivation of sleep and selective REM sleep deprivation. Total deprivation of sleep was associated with headache and other muscular discomfort, reduced autonomic responses, decreased skin resistance, and vascular constriction. He cited no similar results from REM sleep deprivation alone. Total sleep loss may cause agitation, fatigue, apathy, decreased performance on skilled tasks, and drifting into sleep with the eyes open. Hypnagogic hallucinations may occur. The effects of REM sleep deprivation may cause increases in appetite and sex desire, increased startle reaction, hyperactivity, and a lowered seizure threshold—perhaps signs of undischarged "drive." Mood changes occur with both REM sleep loss and total sleep loss, but total loss may be more closely associated with depression and with loss of control over emotion. Cognitive difficulties involving concentration, disturbances of memory, and even paranoid delusions of grandeur may occur with both forms of deprivation. Total sleep loss is more likely to lead to fragmentation of ideation. Disturbances of body self-image and depersonalization-derealization phenomena are more likely with total sleep loss. Hallucinations may occur with total sleep loss or with REM sleep loss; those occurring with REM sleep loss are usually visual, while those associated with total sleep loss have been reported to be tactile as well. Misperceptions, illusions, and delusions are more likely to occur with loss of all stages of sleep.

In laboratory experiments with animals, electrically induced convulsions have been shown to decrease the need for REM sleep, suggesting that a discharge phenomenon may be involved (Giora, 1972). The association between sleep disturbance and depression, especially loss of stage 4 sleep, may have implications for the clinical use of electroconvulsive therapy.

Tolerance to sleep loss varies somewhat with the age of the subject (Vojtěcovský and associates, 1969). Younger subjects show an earlier onset of disturbance and more physical reactions, while older subjects are likely to have greater impairment of mental and perceptual abilities. Excessive sleep (when not in recovery from a sleep deficit) may impair the sense of rest. There is probably an optimal time of sleep for each person, and falling short of or exceeding that optimal time may cause some dysphoria of mood (Globus, 1969; Taub and associates, 1971).

It would appear that there are several factors involved in determining the different stages of sleep and their durations. The REM state may be part of a circadian rhythm that continues even after awakening, although the rhythm is easily experienced only in the sleeping state, when it is not obscured by attention to the outer world (Giora, 1972). Total or partial sleep loss may potentiate this circadian influence (Johnson and Naitoh, 1974). Some of the effects of sleep deprivation may be attributable to disturbance of the normal circadian rhythm rather than to loss of sleep itself. It has been suggested that stage 4 sleep is influenced more by the amount of sleep loss and that REM deprivation is influenced more by circadian factors (Berger and associates, 1971). There has been speculation that the requirement for REM sleep may be associated with personality and life-style, while the requirement for stage 4 sleep may be a more constant need (Hartmann and associates, 1971).

An observation made by Pivik and Foulkes (1966) and others is psychodynamically quite interesting. They found that subjects with high scores on the MMPI pathology scales tended to have shorter but more intense dreams.

PSYCHOSIS

The hypothesis of a relationship between dreams and psychosis was voiced early. In 1939 Jung (CW 3:241) said that it "is no metaphor," that insanity is like a dream that has become real. He referred to insanity as "a dream that has replaced normal consciousness," and he considered both dream and psychosis as evidence of what Janet called an *abaissement du niveau mental,* a lowering of the usual level of waking consciousness. As late as 1956 Jung (CW 3:258) referred to a "far-reaching analogy between schizophrenia and dreams."

Fleiss (1962) reiterated the similarities among psychosis, sleep, and the narcoleptic syndrome, referring to the "dissociation of the components of sleep." The developments of laboratory sleep studies again raised the question of these clinical observations. Gillin and associates (1974) found that active schizophrenics require fewer awakenings than controls to produce REM sleep deprivation, and they show less rebound phenomena in making up lost REM sleep time during monitored recovery nights. Snyder (1963) suggested again the "waking dream" model of psychosis, although he spoke in Freudian terms and did not mention Jung. He thus emphasized the image of instinctual drives pressing for discharge in the dream rather than the image of *abaissement* of ego functioning. The letter emphasis would raise the crucial question of the relationship between the waking ego and the phenomenological dream ego.

Hartmann (1968b) studied 4 acutely psychotic patients undergoing *Dauerschlaf,* a chemically induced prolonged sleep therapy that is still popular in Europe; the record of 1 patient was unscorable. The increased amounts of sleep were mostly stage 2 sleep. Two of the 3 patients experienced large amounts of dreaming sleep; the 1 patient not showing this increase had had repeated admissions, so that the absence of increased dreaming may have been because of adaptation to a familiar situation.

The clinical similarity of dreaming and psychotic symptoms suggested that a psychotic state might be produced by dream deprivation. Early reports that subjects deprived of REM sleep experienced deterioration of their waking psychological functions lent support to this possibility. But Vogel (1968) found no evidence to support a relationship between dream loss and psychosis, although he believed that REM abnormalities and depression were probably parts of the same brain mechanisms. The abnormalities of alcoholic hallucinations have been uncertainly related to dream deprivation. Ornstein and associates (1969) could not differentiate reliably between the dream content of schizophrenic subjects and that of control subjects. They suggested that dream deprivation might contribute to the acute disorganization of thought that occurs in psychosis but might not have etiologic connections with specific diagnostic entities such as schizophrenia. The limited discriminability of REM dream reports and reports of sleep-onset mentation must also be considered (Vogel and associates, 1972). Berger and Oswald (1962) reported that their subjects, who were deprived of all sleep for 4 nights and were closely observed by the experimenters, showed frequent psychotic features. They concluded that other studies, in which relays of observers participated, may have missed these symptoms because of the ability of a sleep-deprived subject to appear normal for short periods of time.

Vogel and Traub (1968) deprived 5 schizophrenic subjects of REM sleep for 7 consecutive nights and monitored their recovery sleep. Psychological testing did not demonstrate worsening of psychotic symptoms. The study did not support the theory that schizophrenia is causally related to increased REM pressure, or inability to compensate for loss of REM sleep. After reviewing a number of other studies, Vogel (1968) again reached the same conclusion.

The question of density of eye movements (eye-movement time/REMP time) in schizophrenic dreams was raised by Feinberg and associates (1965). They found that actively hallucinating schizophrenics had a greater density of eye movements during dreams.

DEPRESSION

Alterations in sleep patterns have long been known to be symptoms of depression: difficulty in falling asleep, more frequent awakenings, a tendency for the last morning awakening to be earlier. Clinicians have also stressed the characteristic diurnal variation in mood as a possible discriminant between the depression that results from acute stresses of living (in which the mood is better on awakening and worsens through the day) and the depression that is considered to arise endogenously (in which the patient awakens with severe depression but then improves throughout the following waking period).

After studying a subject with 48-hour cyclic swings from depression to hypomania, Kupfer and Heninger (1972) maintained that mood shifts and REM might be related throughout the sleep of a single night. The extent of depressed mood correlated inversely with the amount of REM during dreaming. On nights when the subject shifted toward the depressed phase of his illness, there was a decrease in REM in the second half of the night. Although based on only 1 subject, this study is consistent with the view that dreaming is a process that is compensatory to the waking state, even as the hypomania may be considered psychodynamically a compensation to depression.

Kramer and associates (1968) collected dreams from 10 severely depressed hospital patients who received imipramine. Early during the administration of the drug, the patients' dreams showed increased hostility and anxiety, but the long-range effect of imipramine was to decrease these unpleasant emotions and increase heterosexuality and motility. Sleep and dream disorders in the depressed patient have been found to revert to normal following ECT (Green and Stajduhar, 1966).

It is important to keep in mind that not all clinically depressed patients experience decreased sleep (Kupfer and associates, 1973). Some experience increased amounts of sleep and may respond to different medications.

Observations have suggested that those depressed patients who are likely to respond to antidepressant medication, in this case amitriptyline, may show changes in REM activity as early as the first 2 nights of drug treatment, long before improvement in the depression is clinically evident (Kupfer and associates, 1976). These changes include increases in REM sleep latency, decreases in total time in REM sleep, and decreases in percentage of REM sleep. An obvious extension of this observation is that deprivation of REM sleep, one of the effects of the drug, might in itself lead to improvement in the depression. This possibility was not supported in a study of REM sleep deprivation in 5 subjects (Vogal and associates, 1968).

At the present time there is no clear or simple relationship between psychosis or depression and disorders related to dreaming. This field of inquiry remains promising and potentially valuable, particularly in the study of drug effects; eventually it may yield information about the relationship between neurophysiology and conscious functioning.

AROUSAL DISORDERS

Some disorders traditionally thought to occur with dreaming have been shown by laboratory sleep studies to be unrelated to dreams (Karacan and associates, 1973). These include such phenomena as

sleep talking, somnambulism, night terrors (pavor nocturnus), narcolepsy, enuresis, sleep paralysis, sleep apnea, bruxism during sleep,
and hypnagogic hallucinations. Broughton (1968) suggested that these
be called disorders of arousal, since it may be the arousal mechanism
rather than the preceding stage of deep sleep that contributes to the
abnormality.

Narcolepsy

Although narcolepsy and the narcoleptic syndrome (narcolepsy,
catalepsy, sleep paralysis, and hypnagogic hallucinations) involve excessive sleep, they differ from hypersomnia, which appears to be extended normal sleep (Rechtschaffen and Roth, 1969). In narcolepsy,
dreams are associated with sleep-onset REM periods, omitting the
usual NREM phase preceding the first dream. It may be that narcolepsy is associated with a dysfunction of the REM mechanisms;
hypersomnia may be a disorder of synchronous sleep, with preservation of normal REM functioning. It has been suggested that the early
appearance of dreaming in the sleep of narcoleptics may have
psychodynamic meaning, the patient essentially sleeping in order to
dream (Vogel, 1960). Narcoleptic dreams may be more vivid and ter-
rifying than usual dreams, particularly when catalepsy is a part of the
syndrome (Roth and Brůhová, 1969). Blood glucose levels have not
been found to change with the sleep stages of narcoleptics (Dement,
1974). In normal subjects, sleep-onset REM is rare, although it may be
more frequent in spontaneous napping than in laboratory napping.

Night Terrors

In psychoanalytic literature the classic study of the nightmare was
carried out by Jones in 1911. He emphasized repressed sexuality and
oedipal dynamics in his formulation. Fisher and associates (1973) differentiated the nightmare or the severe anxiety dream occurring in
REM sleep from the night terrors (pavor nocturnus) that occur especially in children. With few exceptions, night terrors arise out of deep,
delta-wave sleep; the severity of the episode correlates with the
amount of preceding delta activity. The episode usually occurs in the
early part of the night and is more common in boys; episodes decrease
in incidence in adulthood; one-third of cases are associated with somnambulism (Fisher and associates, 1973).

Sleep Talking

In the older literature it was generally believed that sleep talking occurred in relation to dreams. This was not the experience of my own family in childhood, as my sister and I realized at an early age that it was possible to converse with our father during his sleep. He would give clear answers, although his speech was somewhat slow; he did not at all appear to be describing dream states. It has now been established that sleep talking usually occurs in synchronized, NREM sleep (Murray, 1965), although this is not invariable. This NREM sleep has little affect, is rarely recalled, and (like the sleep speech of my father) generally concerns ordinary events or the actual setting. When REM sleep has been chemically suppressed, the amount of sleep speech of those who exhibit the phenomenon is increased during REM sleep recovery nights (Arkin and associates, 1968). Some studies have shown sleep talking to be randomly distributed throughout the night rather than concentrated in NREM sleep (Rechtschaffen and associates, 1962), although the amount of affect was greater in that from REM sleep, and references to the experimental situation were greater in NREM samples.

Somnambulism

Somnambulism or sleepwalking occurs frequently in males and in children, and it has some tendency toward a family incidence (Kales and Kales, 1974). Several authors have reported that it can be produced by lifting susceptible subjects into a standing position when they are in stage 4 sleep (Fisher and associates, 1973).

Bruxism

When bruxism (tooth-grinding) occurs during sleep, it tends to be associated with REM periods. Reding and associates (1964) suggested this as evidence that during REM sleep EEG spikes originating in the pons might lead to stimulation of the nearby motor nucleus of the trigeminal nerve, the innervation of the masseter muscles.

BIOLOGIC THEORIES

Biologic theories of dreaming center about neurohumoral and protein-synthesis models. In animal experimentation, increases in brain serotonin appear to be associated with a shorter sleep-dream

cycle, while a longer cycle is associated with depleted levels of serotonin in the central nervous system (Hartmann, 1967). Hartmann has also
suggested that REM sleep may play a role in restoring brain
catecholamine systems, most likely at their cortical endings, where
they may play a modulating role rather than exert a direct synaptic
effect (Hartmann, 1967, p. 149). Torda (1968) suggested that dreaming
is the result of interaction between a serotonin process promoting sleep
and an arousal system mediated by norepinephrine.

Because of the increased gastric motility and secretion of gastric
acid during REM sleep, it has been suggested that REM sleep plays a
role in nutritional reactions (Mandell and Mandell, 1969). Many authors have concluded that REM sleep is related to the development and
maintenance of visual perception, perhaps to depth perception
(Berggren, 1970).

What Rossi (1973) called the dream protein hypothesis maintains
that REM sleep is necessary for the consolidation of new behavior, and
this may be dependent on changes in proteins in the brain. Animal
studies in cats (Drucker-Colin and Spanis, 1975) have provided some
support for this view: perfusates from the midbrain reticular formation
had higher protein levels during REM sleep than during wakefulness,
usually twice as much. Using the dream protein hypothesis, the need
for sleep can be pictured as the need to allow for the reversal of conformational changes that have occurred in brain proteins during the
waking state. Kleinschmidt (1974) pictured this return to a free energy
level as producing the "reversed thoughts" of dreams. Although this is
attractive in some respects, such a theory does not allow for the exquis-
ite and meaningful connections between dreams and waking consciousness that can be observed in the psychoanalytic process. However, it is consistent with the evidence that dreaming sleep is needed
for reprogramming, or new learning (Greenberg and Dewan, 1968).

Laborit (1972) linked serotonin release to the regulation of protein
synthesis, which in turn accompanies learning during REM sleep. He
considered the balance between serotonin and catecholamines to be
involved both in dreaming and in the regulation of sexual response,
suggesting a nonrepressive analogy to Freud's sexual emphasis in
dream formation.

FREUD AND LABORATORY DREAM STUDIES

In this introductory review it is not possible to make a thorough
correlation between the considerable literature on psychoanalytic
dream studies and the literature on laboratory studies of dreaming.

Indeed, such a correlation would be premature. However, there are a few basic observations that appear as repeated themes in the literature. The staggering contributions of Freud to the understanding of psychological processes are scarcely diminished because he did not correctly foresee, long before laboratory dream studies, the true nature of sleep and dreaming. The utility and relevance of psychoanalysis, Freudian or otherwise, are based on other grounds as well.

The nature of NREM mentation, which varies from dreamlike to a state much like waking mentation, suggests the distinction that Freud made between preconscious day residue (similar to NREM thought) and dream (the REM state). The fact that a NREM period characteristically precedes a REM dream seems at first glance to support Freud's formulation. Rechtschaffen and associates (1963) noted that elements from NREM periods may at times be identified in REM dreams, suggesting that NREM mentation may function as a preconscious stimulus to the dream, much as in the model of a day residue activating a complex. They concluded that such elements were not perseverations from previous REM reports of the same sampling night.

Kramer (1970), among many others, found that manifest dream significant. Although the sex of the person collecting dreams that are remembered from nonlaboratory settings seems to have no effect on the contents of the dreams, the sex of the technician in laboratory dream studies appears to have an affect on the type of manifest dream reported. Perhaps this is because the subject wishes to maintain a persona role vis-à-vis the technician in the experimental setting. Differences in the dreams of the sexes have been reported. Although findings conflict, some studies have found that schizophrenic patients have dreams that are more unrealistic, that are more neutral in affect, that involve more strangers, and that have hostility (when present) directed at the dream ego. Dreams of depressed patients tend to be more realistic than those of schizophrenics but not as realistic as those of normals, and themes of escape are common. The dream reports of depressed patients may be "barren," and those of patients with organic brain syndrome have the fewest number of dream elements (Kramer, 1970).

Many other studies have dealt with manifest dream reports and have defined differences (e.g., as between hypertensives and normotensives). However, no such findings have had sufficient replication that they can be considered invariable. Nevertheless, it is increasingly clear that the manifest dream itself is a significant carrier of many factors that in Freudian theory would be attributable to the hidden latent dream. The theory still can allow for the meaningfulness of the manifest dream by postulating an incomplete disguise of the latent

dream through an inadequacy in the dream work, but such a postulation seems effectively to discard any evidence that might disprove the
theory. It is possible that the time-honored construction of latent
dream versus manifest dream is simply an impediment, but before it
can be discarded it is necessary to consider other ways of explaining
the obvious discrepancy between dream images and the waking events
of the dreamer's life. Such discrepancies can alternatively be explained
as functions of the nature of emotionally toned complexes and as functions of the action of the individuation process as seen in dreams.
Abandonment of the distinction between latent and manifest levels of
the dream would free researchers to consider the actual and demons-
trable referents of dream symbols. Open scientific observations could
replace restricted reconstructions from the couch, while the clinical
processes of analysis would remain invaluable, even indispensable, in
the delivery of insight about dreams to the individual patient.

Although Freud's contention that dreams can occur almost simultaneously seems not to be the case, there is some evidence for what has
been called telescoping in dreams (Roffwarg and associates, 1962). In
telescoping, some events of the dramatic sequence are simply indicated
or abbreviated, much as in cinematographic technique. In any case, the
question of dreams being prepared beforehand and then presented in
much less time than the experienced dream action is a minor point in
Freud's position.

Freud's concept of day residue has received support from experiments on incorporation of predreaming and dreaming stimulation, as
well as from field study of dreams. Foulkes (1964) interpreted the finding of mentation in both REM sleep and NREM sleep as supporting the
concept of day residue and its distortion by dream work. However, this
is not a necessary conclusion from the observations that Foulkes cited;
one might as easily argue that the observations support the position of
Ullman, Bonime, and others that the processes of problem-solving
continue during all stages of sleep as they do in the waking state.
Foulkes (1964) concluded that the data did not support Freud's contention that there is a sudden "attraction" of consciousness to mental
processes at the onset of dreaming, and he challenged both Freud and
Adler concerning the instigation of dreaming by repressed traumatic
affective experiences.

The model in Chapter 7 of Freud's *Interpretation of Dreams* based
on a reflex arc, shows inhibition of the motor limb of response during
dreaming. Energy that would in the waking state lead to action is
deflected back and supposedly reactivates a series of mnemonic traces
until vivification occurs in dreaming. Sleep and dream studies do indi-

cate an inhibition of motor movement at the time of dream onset. The inhibition does not lead to complete suspension of motor activity, and it is somewhat selective. For example, small wrist movements may continue (Wolpert, 1960), while neck and facial tone is decreased more. However, the muscle inhibition does not validate Freud's reflex model of dreaming. There is no evidence that muscle inhibition frees energy to pursue another pathway through the memory traces.

It has been found that when environmental stimuli presented during sleep are incorporated into a dream, the threshold of arousal from the dream is higher (Bradley and Meddis, 1974). This is consistent with Freud's belief that the dream has the role of protecting sleep. It does not, obviously, speak to the crucial question whether the same incorporation of repressed material pushing for discharge also preserves sleep. In fact, the sleep-protection hypothesis, a major component of Freud's dream model, is largely unsupported by the laboratory studies, which reveal a need for dreaming sleep in itself.

The association of penile erection with dreaming has been cited by some authors as evidence of the repressed infantile sexual wish that Freud considered to be the prime mover of the dream. This conclusion is highly questionable because of the occurrence of erections in both REM sleep and other states in the neonate boy, where they are likely to represent generalized arousal of the autonomic nervous system rather than indicate specifically sexual mental content, whether conscious or unconscious. The related observation that erections are fewer on the first nights of laboratory sleep (Jovanović, 1969), presumably because of greater anxiety, does not strengthen the repressed sexuality hypothesis; nor does the observation that erections are often lost with the onset of anxiety situations in the dream offer support for the theory. Exactly the same observation is possible in the waking state: anxiety interferes with penile erection. In fact, anxiety is probably the greatest cause of secondary impotence, wherein conscious worry over not having an erection interferes with the autonomic processes. To infer a sexual origin of dreams because of inhibition of erection by dream anxiety would be equivalent to inferring a light-source origin for automobiles because of the observation that they tend to stop at traffic lights.

Hartmann (1968) considered it tempting to attribute the observed 90-min dream cycle to the id, because it appears early in life, does not alter significantly with age, and is associated with dreaming. Such an attribution might support the theory that dreams arise from discharge of instinctual pressure from the id. However, Hartmann concluded that the diurnal cycle of waking and sleeping should, in psychoanalytic terms, be attributed to the ego, since it appeared to be an adaptation to the 24-hour day. Attribution of the 90-min dream cycle to the id, however, is a disturbing mixture of psychological and physiological systems, although the integration of these systems is an important question, a form of the perennial mind–brain problem. The regularity of the dream cycle can equally well be taken as evidence that it is more controlled and structured than the drives that are pictured as the contents of the id.

Foulkes (1969) commented on the greater occurrence of ego-alien motives in dreams than in waking life or in NREM sleep. Although this is true, it does not discriminate between the model of the unconscious as simply a reservoir of instinctual and repressed impulses and the model of the unconscious as the ground of consciousness from which opposites arise: both the impulse and the counterimpulse.

Observed relationships between different dreams on the same night suggest that during sleep there is an ongoing process that deals with conflicting issues, or at least with issues that are not neutral to the subject (Hawkins, 1966). This finding does not necessarily support the defensive model of the dream; rather, it suggests that dreaming is a purposive activity, as suggested by Jung, Ullman, Erikson, Fromm, French, Bonime, and others.

A frontier of dreaming that has yet to be explored is the manner in which new material is assimilated to existing complexes. In the past this has been considered in the old defensive model, picturing the ego as defending itself against a stimulus by transferring the stimulus to another figure in the dream. Such an interpretation assumes that the dream ego is somehow the same as the waking ego, an assumption that we will soon discuss in much greater detail.

Comparison of current sleep research with the dream theory that Freud proposed at the beginning of this century is not meant to detract from his amazing pioneering achievements. Nor does it seem profitable to attempt to distinguish among the approaches of Freud, Jung, Adler, and others on the basis of whether their models are supported well or poorly by laboratory dream studies. The distance from the laboratory to the consulting room is too great for simple answers. However, it must be admitted that the great respect accorded Freud's theory has perhaps been an impediment to experimental research (F.H.L., 1971). A view of the personality as a series of superimposed inner communications systems may be more valuable than Freud's model of layers (Rochschild, 1964). We are emerging from a period when waking and sleeping were considered polar opposites (Aserinsky, 1969) into a more complicated but more exciting era in which we must ask again the important questions in the light of a nonunitary conception of sleep that itself may be a precursor to deeper understanding of waking life as being composed of interacting psychological and neurological motives. It is hoped that this discussion, rather than invoking resumption of the sterile conflict between Freud and others, will help to open doors of communication so that psychoanalysis, as broadly conceived, can consider the stimulating questions that are now being posed in the scientific study of dreaming.

REFERENCES

Adelman S, Hartmann E: Psychological effects of amitriptyline-induced dream reduction. Psychophysiology 5:249, 1968

Agnew HW Jr, Webb WB, Williams RL: The effects of stage four sleep deprivation. Electroencephalogr Clin Neurophysiol 17:68–70, 1964

Altshuler KZ, Barad M. Goldfarb AI: A survey of dreams in the aged: II. Noninstitutionalized subjects. Arch Gen Psychiatry 8:33–37, 1963

Altshuler KZ, Brebbia DR: Sleep patterns and EEG recordings in twin idiot savants. Psychophysiology 5:244, 1968

Aristotle: De divinatione per somnum (on prophesying by dreams), in McKeon R (ed): The Basic Works of Aristotle. New York, Randon House, 1941, pp 626–630

Arkin AM, Antrobus JS, Toth MF, et al: The effects of chemically induced REMP deprivation on sleep vocalization and NREM mentation: An initial exploration. Psychophysiology 5:217, 1968'

Arkin AM, Lutsky H, Toth MF: Congenital nystagmus and sleep: A replication. Psychophysiology 9:210–217, 1972

Aserinsky E: Drugs and dreams, a synthesis. Exp Med Surg 27:237–244, 1969

Aserinsky E: Rapid eye movement density and pattern in the sleep of normal young adults. Psychophysiology 8:361–375, 1971

Baekeland F: Effects of presleep procedures and cognitive style on dream content. Percept Mot Skills 32:63–69, 1971

Baldridge BJ, Whitman RM, Kramer M, et al: The effect of induced eye movements on dreaming. Psychophysiology 5:230, 1968

Barad M, Altshuler KZ, Goldfarb AI: A survey of dreams in aged persons. Arch Gen Psychiatry 4:419–424, 1961

Barber TX: Dream deprivation. Science 132:1417–1418, 1960

Berger RJ: When is a dream is a dream is a dream? Exp Neurol 4:15–27, 1967

Berger RJ: REM sleep and the oculomotor system. Psychophysiology 5:202, 1968

Berger RJ, Oswald I: Effects of sleep deprivation on behaviour, subsequent sleep, and dreaming. Br J Psychiatry 108:457–465, 1962

Berger RJ, Walker JM, Scott TD et al: Diurnal and nocturnal sleep stage patterns following sleep deprivation. Psychonomic Sci 23:273–275, 1971

Berggren RJ Jr: The function of REM sleep for the oculomotor system. Unpublished doctoral dissertation, Tufts University, Medford, Mass, 1970

Bloch V: Claparede and the psychophysiology of sleep. Psychologie: Sweizerische Zeitschrift für Psychologie und ihre Andwendungen 33:268–273, 1974

Bradley D, Meddis R: Arousal threshold in dreaming sleep. Physiological Psychol 2:109–110, 1974

Brenneis CB: Developmental aspects of aging in women: A comparative study of dreams. Arch Gen Psychiatry 32:429–435, 1975

Broughton RJ: Sleep disorders: Disorders of arousal? Science 159:1070–1078, 1968

Buscaino GA, Spadetta V, Carella A, et al: Studio del contenuto visuo-motorio del sogno in soggetti con disturbi dells motilita oculare (A study of the visuomotor components of dreaming in subjects with impaired ocular motility). Acta Neurol 26:1–6, 1971 (English summary)

Cartwright RD: Problem solving: Waking and dreaming. J Abnorm Psychol 83:451–455, 1974

Cartwright RD, Bernick N, Borowitz G, et al: Effect of an erotic movie on the sleep and dreams of young men. Arch Gen Psychiatry 20:262–271, 1969

Castaldo V, Shevrin H: Different effect of an auditory stimulus as a function of REM and NREM sleep. Psychophysiology 5:219, 1968

Corcoran DWJ: Changes in heart rate and performance as a result of loss of sleep. Br J Psychol 55:307–314, 1964

de Konick J-M, Koulak D: Dream content and adaptation to a stressful situation. J Abnorm Psychol 84:250–260, 1975

Dement W: The effect of dream deprivation. Science 131: 1705–1707, 1960

Dement W, Kleitman N: Cyclic variations in the EEG during sleep and their relation to eye movements, body motility, and dreaming. Electroencephalogr Clin Neurophysiol 9:673–690, 1957

Dement W, Wolpert EA: The relation of eye movements, body motility, and external stimuli to dream content. J Exp Psychol 55:543–553, 1958

Dement WC: Some Must Watch while Some Must Sleep. San Francisco, WH Freeman, 1974

Dement WC, Kahn E, Roffwarg HP: The influence of the laboratory situation on the dreams of the experimental subject. J Nerv Ment Dis 140:119–131, 1965

Domhoff B, Kamiya J: Problems in dream content study with objective indicators. I. A comparison of home and laboratory dream reports. II. Appearance of experimental situation in laboratory dream narratives. Arch Gen Psychiatry 11:519–524, 525–528, 1964

Drew WG, Batt J: A contribution to the evolutionary theory of dreaming: An hypothesis on the role of the pineal in species and specimen protection. Biol Psychiatry 4:131–145, 1972

Drucker-Colin RR, Spanis CW: Neurohumoral correlates of sleep: Increase of proteins during rapid eye movement sleep. Experientia 31:551–552, 1975

Ephron HS, Carrington P: On the homeostatic regulation of cortical activation during sleep. J Am Soc Psychosom Dent Med 16:23–29, 1969

Fahrion SL: The relationship of heart rate and dream content in heart-rate responders. Unpublished doctoral dissertation, University of Oregon, Eugene, 1966

Feinberg I: Onteogenesis of sleep in the aged. Compr Psychiatry 9:138–147, 1968

Feinberg I, Carlson VR: Sleep variables as a function of age in man. Arch Gen Psychiatry 18:239–250, 1968

Feinberg I, Koresko RL, Gottlied G: Further observations on electrophysiological sleep patterns in schizophrenia. Compr Psychiatry 6:21–24, 1965

Feldman R, Dement W: Possible relationships between REM sleep and memory consolidation. Psychophysiology 5:243, 1968

Firth H: Sleeping pills and dream content. Br J Psychiatry 124:547–553, 1974

Fisher C, Dement WC: Studies on the psychopathology of sleep and dreams. Am J Psychiatry 119:1160–1168, 1963

Fisher C, Kahn E, Edwards A, et al: A psychophysiological study of nightmares and night terrors. I. Physiological aspects of the stage 4 night terror. J Nerv Ment Dis 157:75–96, 1973

Fleiss AN: Psychotic symptoms, a disturbance in the sleep mechanism. Psychiatr Q 36:727–733, 1962

Flemenbaum A: Pavor nocturnus: A complication of single daily tricyclic or neuroleptic dosage. Am J Psychiatry 133:570–572, 1976

Foulkes D: Theories of dream formation and recent studies of sleep consciousness. Psychol Bull 62:236–247, 1964

Foulkes D: Drug research and the meaning of dreams. Exp Med Surg 27:39–52, 1969

Frank G, Chase J: Sleep rhythms in premature infants. Psychophysiology 5:227, 1968

FHL: New directions in dream psychology research (editorial). Can Psychiatr Assoc J 16:279–281, 1971

Gardner R, Grossman WI, Roffwarg HP, et al: The relationship of small limb movements during REM sleep to dreamed limb action. Psychosom Med 37:147–159, 1975

Gillin JC, Buchsbaum MS, Jacobs LS, et al: Partial REM sleep deprivation, schizophrenia, and field articulation. Arch Gen Psychiatry 30:653–662, 1974

Giora Z: The function of the dream: A reappraisal. Am J Psychiatry 128:1067–1073, 1972

Globus BS: A syndrome associated with sleeping late. Psychsom Med 31:528–535, 1969

Goodenough DR, Lewis H, Shapiro LJ, et al: Dream reporting following abrupt and gradual awakenings from different types of sleep. J Pers Soc Psychol 2:170–179, 1965

Goodenough DR, Lewis HB, Shapiro A, et al: Some correlates of dream reporting following laboratory awakenings. J Nerv Ment Dis 140:365–373, 1965

Gottschalk·LA, Stone WN, Gleser GC. et al: Anxiety levels in dreams: Relation to changes in plasma free fatty acids. Science 153:1282–1289, 1966

Green WJ: LSD and the sleep-dream cycle. Exp Med Surg 27:138–144, 1969

Green WJ, Stajduhar PP: The effect of ECT and the sleep-dream cycle in a psychotic depression. J Nerv Ment Dis 143:123–134, 1966

Greenburg R, Dewan E: Aphasia and dreaming: A test of the P-hypothesis. Psychophysiology 5:203–204, 1968

Greenberg R, Pearlman C: Cutting the REM nerve: An approach to the adaptive role of REM sleep. Perspect Biol Med 17:513–521, 1974

Greenberg R, Pearlman C, Brooks R, et al: Dreaming and Korsakoff's psychosis. Arch Gen Psychiatry 18:203–209, 1968

Gresham SC: The effect of ethyl alcohol on inferred visual dreaming. Exp Med Surg 27:121–123, 1969

Greham SC, Webb WB, Williams RL: Alcohol and caffeine: Effect on inferred visual dreaming. Science 140:1226–1227, 1963

Hall CS: Representation of the laboratory setting in dreams. J Nerv Dis 144:198–206, 1967

Hartmann E: Mechanisms underlying the sleep-dream cycle. Nature 212:648–650, 1966

Hartmann E: The sleep-dream cycle and brain serotonin. Psychonomic Sci 8:295–306, 1967

Hartmann E: The 90-minute dream cycle. Arch Gen Psychiatry 18:280–286, 1968a

Hartmann E: Dauerschlaf: A polygraphic study. Arch Gen Psychiatry 18:99–111, 1968b

Hartmann E: The biochemistry and pharmacology of the D-state (dreaming sleep). Exp Med Surg 27:105–120, 1969

Hartmann E, Baekeland F, Zwilling G, et al: Sleep need: How much sleep and what kind? Am J Psychiatry 127:1001–1008, 1971

Hartmann EL: The Functions of Sleep. New Haven, Yale University Press, 1973

Hawkins DR: A review of psychoanalytic dream theory in the light of recent psycho-physiological studies of sleep and dreaming. Br J Med Psychol 39:85–104, 1966

Hord DJ, Lubin A, Johnson LC: The evoked heart rate response during sleep. Psychophysiology 3:46–54, 1966

Jacobs L, Feldman M, Bender MB: Are eye movements of dreaming sleep related to visual images of dreams? Psychophysiology 9:393–400, 1972

Johnson LC, Naitoh P: The operational consequences of sleep deprivation and sleep deficit. Neuilly sur Seine, France, NATO Advisory Group for Aerospace Research and Development, AGARDograph No 193, 1974

Jones E: On the Nightmare. New York, Grove Press, 1959

Jovanović UJ: Der effekt der ersten Untersuchungsnacht auf die Erektionen im Schlaf (Effect of the first examination night on erections during sleep). Psychother Psychosom 17:295–308, 1969

Kahn E, Fisher C: Dream recall in the aged. Psychophysiology 5:222, 1968

Kales A, Kales JD: Sleep disorders: Recent findings in the diagnosis and treatment of disturbed sleep. N Engl J Med 290:487–499, 1974

Kamiya J: A fourth dimension of consciousness. J Exp Med Surg 27:13–18, 1969

Karacan I, Salis PJ, Williams RL: Clinical disorders of sleep. Psychosomatics 14:77–88, 1973

Karacan I, Wolff SM, Williams RL, et al: The effects of fever on sleep and dream patterns. Psychosomatics 9:331–339, 1968

Kleitman N, Aserinsky E: Two types of ocular motility during sleep. J Appl Physiol 8:1–10, 1955

Kleinschmidt WJL: The nature of sleep, dreams, and aging: A theory involving conformational changes of biopolymers. Perspect Biol Med 17:371–378, 1974

Kollar EJ, Slater GR, Palmer JO, et al: Stress in subjects undergoing sleep deprivation. Psychosom Med 28:101–113, 1966

Korner AF: REM organization in neonates: Theoretical implications for development and biological function of REM. Arch Gen Psychiatry 19:330–340, 1968

Koulack D: Effects of somatosensory stimulation on dream content. Arch Gen Psychiatry 20: 718–725, 1969

Kramer M: Manifest dream content in normal and psychopathologic states. Arch Gen Psychiatry 22:149–159, 1970

Kramer M, Whitman RM, Baldridge B, et al: Drugs and Drams. III: The effects of imipramine on the dreams of depressed patients. Am J Psychiatry 124:1385–1392, 1968

Kramer M, Whitman RM, Baldridge B, et al: Drugs and Dreams, III: The effects biology of dreaming. Springfield, Ill, Charles C Thomas, 1969

Kupfer DJ, Foster FG, Detre TP: Sleep continuity changes in depression. Dis Nerv Syst 34:192–195, 1973

Kupfer DJ, Foster FG, Detre TP: Sleep continuity changes in depression. Dis depression. Am J Psychiatry 133:622–626, 1976

Kupfer DJ, Heninger GR: REM activity as a correlate of mood changes throughout the night. Arch Gen Psychiatry 27:368–373, 1972

Laborit H: Correlations between protein and serotonin synthesis during various activities of the central nervous system. Res Commun Chem Pathol Pharmacol 3:51–81, 1972

Larson JD, Foulkes D: Electromyogram suppression during sleep, dream recall, and orientation time. Psychophysiology 5:548–555, 1969

Lewis SA: Learning while asleep. Bull Br Psychol Soc 21:23–26, 1968

Luce GG: Current research on sleep and dreams. Public Health Service Publication 1389, Washington DC, US Department of Health, Education and Welfare

McGhie A, Russel SM: The subjective assessment of normal sleep patterns. J Ment Sci 108:642–654, 1962

Mandell AJ, Chaffey B, Brill P, et al: Dreaming sleep in man: Changes in urine volume and osmolarity. Science 151:1558–1560, 1966

Mandell AJ, Mandell MP: Peripheral hormonal and metabolic correlations of rapid eye movement sleep. Exp Med Surg 27:224–236, 1969

Maron L, Rechtschaffen A, Wolpert EA: Sleep cycle during napping. Arch Gen Psychiatry 11:503–508, 1964

Martin GJ: Drugs and dreams, perspective. Exp Med Surg 27:1–2, 1969

Morgan H, Scott DF, Joyce CRB: The effects of four hypnotic drugs and placebo on normal subjects' sleeping and dreaming at home. Br J Psychiatry 117:649–652, 1970

Moskowitz E, Berger RJ: Rapid eye movements and dream imagery—are they related? Nature 224:613–614, 1969

Murray EJ: Sleep, Dreams, and Arousal. New York, Appleton, 1965

Ornstein PH, Whitman RM, Kramer M, et al: Drugs and dreams. IV: Tranquilizers and their effects upon dreams and dreaming in schizophrenic patients. Exp Med Surg 27:145–156, 1969

Orr WF, Dozier E, Green L, et al: Self-induced waking: Changes in dreams and sleep patterns. Compr Psychiatry 9:499–506, 1968

Pasnau RO, Naitoh P, Stier S, et al: The psychological effects of 205 hours of sleep deprivation. Arch Gen Psychiatry 18:496–505, 1968

Pierce CM, Mathis JL, Jabbour JT: Dream patterns in narcoleptic patients. Am J Psychiatry 122:402–404, 1965

Pivik T, Foulkes D: Dream deprivation: Effects on dream content. Science 153:654–657, 1966

Pivik T, Foulkes D: NREM mentation: Relation to personality, orientation time, and time of night. J Consult Clin Psychol 32:144–151, 1968

Portnoff G, Baekeland F, Goodenough DR, et al: Retention of verbal materials perceived immediately prior to onset of non-REM sleep. Percept Mot Skills 22:751–758, 1966

Rechtschaffen A, Foulkes D: Effect on visual stimuli on dream content. Percept Mot Skills 20:1149–1160, 1965

Rechtschaffen A, Goodenough DR, Shapiro A: Patterns of sleep talking. Arch Gen Psychiatry 7:418–426, 1962

Rechtschaffen A, Hauri P, Zeitlin M: Auditory awakening thresholds in REM and NREM sleep stages. Percept Mot Skills 22:927–942, 1966

Rechtschaffen A, Maron L: The effect of amphetamine on the sleep cycle. Electroencephalogr Clin Neurophysiol 16:438–445, 1964

Rechtschaffen A, Roth B: Nocturnal sleep of hypersomniacs. Act Nerv Super (Praha) 11:229–233, 1969

Rechtschaffen A, Vogel G, Shaikun G: Interrelatedness of mental activity during sleep. Arch Gen Psychiatry 9:536–547, 1963

Reding GR, Rubright WC, Rechtsshaffen A, et al: Sleep patterns of toothgrinding: Its relationship to dreaming. Science 145:725–726, 1964

Ritvo ER, Ornitz EM, La Franchi S, et al: Effects of imipramine on the sleep-dream cycle: An EEG study in boys. Electroencephalogr Clin Neurophysiol 22:465–468, 1967

Riva A, Vitali S: Le differenze biolettriche e comportamentali fra il sonno di bambini di un anno normalmente ambientati e ospiti di brefotrofio. Archivio de Psicologia Neurologia Psychiatria 31:32–50, 1970 (English summary)

Roffwarg HP, Dement WC, Muzio JN, et al: Dream imagery: Relationship to rapid eye movements of sleep. Arch Gen Psychiatry 7:235–258, 1962

Rosenblatt G, Hartmann E, Zwilling GR: Cardiac irritability during sleep and dreaming. J Psychosom Res 17:129–134, 1973

Ross JJ: Neurological findings after prolonged sleep deprivation. Arch Neurol 12:399, 1965

Rossi EL: The dream-protein hypothesis. Am J Psychaitry 130:1094–1097, 1973

Roth B, Brůhová S: A clinical and polygraphic study of dreams in narcolepsy and hypersomnia. Nerv Super (Praha) 11:223–228, 1969

Roth B, Sona B: Dreams in narcolepsy, hypersomnia, and dissociated sleep disorders. Exp Med Surg 27:187–209, 1969

Rothschild FS: Uvdot veteoriot hadashot al hahalom (New facts and theories on dream). Harefuah 66:285–288, 1964 (English summary)

Rubin RT, Gouin PR, Kales A, et al: Luteinizing hormone, follicle stimulating hormone, and growth hormone secretion in normal adult men during sleep and dreaming. Psychosom Med 35:309–321, 1973

Saint-Laurent J: Contributions to psychiatry of recent studies on sleep. Can Psychiatr Assoc J 16:327–336, 1971

Saletu B: Is the subjectively experienced quality of sleep related to objective sleep parameters? Behav Biol 13:433–444, 1975

Snyder F: The new biology of dreaming. Arch Gen Psychiatry 8:381–391, 1963

Taub JM, Globus GG, Phoebus E, et al: Extended sleep and performance. Nature 233:142–143, 1971

Tebbs RB, Foulkes D: Strength of grip following different stages of sleep. Percept Mot Skills 23:827–834, 1966

Torda C: Contribution to serotonin theory of dreaming (LSD infusion). NY State J Med 68:1135–1138, 1968

Tune GS: The human sleep debt. Science Journal 4:67–71, 1968

Ullman M; The dream scene. J. Am Soc Psychosom Dent Med 16:4–6, 1969

Verdone P: Sleep satiation: Extended sleep in normal subjects. Electroencephalogr Clin Neurophysiol 24:417–423, 1968

Vogel G: Studies in psychophysiology of dreams. III. The dream of narcolepsy. Arch Gen Psychiatry 3:421–428, 1960

Vogel GW: REM deprivation. III. Dreaming and psychosis. Arch Gen Psychiatry 18:312–329, 1968

Vogel GW, Barrowclough B, Giesler DD: Limited discriminability of REM and sleep onset reports and its psychiatric implications. Arch Gen Psychiatry 26:449–455, 1972

Vogel GW, Traub AC: REM deprivation. I. The effect on schizophrenic patients. Arch Gen Psychiatry 18:287–300, 1968

Vogel GW, Traub AC, Ben-Horin P, et al: REM deprivation. II. The effects on depressed patients. Arch Gen Psychiatry 18:301–329, 1968

Vojtěchovský M, Březinová V, Simáně Z, et al: An experimental approach to sleep and aging. Hum Dev 12:64–72, 1969

Waldhorn HF: The place of the dream in clinical psychoanalysis, in Joseph ED (ed): Monograph II: Monograph Series of the Kris Study Group of the New York Psychoanalytic Institute. New York, International Universities Press, 1967

Webb WB, Agnew HW Jr: Sleep stage characteristics of long and short sleepers. Science 168:146–147, 1970

Whitman RM, Kramer M, Ornstein P, et al: The physiology, psychology, and utilization of dreams. Am J Psychiatry 124:43–58, 1967

Whitman RM, Kramer M, Ornstein PH, et al: Drugs and dream content. Exp Med Surg 27:210–223, 1969

Wilkinson RT: After-effect of sleep deprivation. J Exp Psychol 66:439–442, 1963

Williams RL: Sleep and dream studies: Current state of the art. Psychosomatics 10:209, 213, 1969

Williams RL, Agnew HW: The effects of drugs on the EEG sleep patterns of normal humans. Exp Med Surg 27:53–64, 1969

Williams RL, Agnew HW Jr, Webb WB: Effects of prolonged stage four and 1-REM sleep deprivation: EEG, task performance, and psychological responses. USAF SAM technical report 67-59, 1967

Wilson WP, Zung WWK: Attention, discrimination, and arousal during sleep. Arch Gen Psychiatry 15:523–528, 1966

Winget C, Kramer M, Whitman RM: Dreams and demography. Can Psychiatr Assoc J 17[Suppl 2]:203–208, 1972

Witkin HA, Lewis HB: The relation of experimentally induced presleep experiences to dreams. J Am Psychoanal Assoc 13:819–849, 1965

Wolpert ED, Trosman H: Studies in psychophysiology of dreams. AMA Arch Neurol Psychiatry 79:603–606, 1958

Wolpert EA: Studies in psychophysiology of dreams. II. An electroencephalographic study of dreaming. Arch Gen Psychiatry 2:231–241, 1960

Zimmerman WB: Sleep mentation and auditory awakening thresholds. Psychophysiology 6:540–549, 1970

Zukhar VP, Kaplan EY, Maksimov YA, et al: Opyt provedeniya kollektivnoĭ gipnopedii (An experiment in group instructions during sleep). Voprosy Psikhologii 1:143–148, 1965; English summary in Psychol Abst vol 39, no 9265

Zung WWK: Effect of antidepressant drugs on sleeping and dreaming: III. On the depressed patient. Biol Psychiatry 1:238–287, 1969

Zung WWK: Antidepressant drugs and sleep. Exp Med Surg 27:124–137, 1969

PART II

Jungian Dream Interpretation

To reinterpret a dream means to reinterpret the dreamer.

Erikson, *The Dream Specimen of Psychoanalysis*

4
Clinical Concepts

Jung often wrote using the abstract language of complex psychology, but he also wrote clinically using a language that better conveys the flavor of immediate emotional experience, using such concepts as *persona, shadow, anima, animus,* and *Self.* These terms have been expounded in many writings by Jung and others, and only a brief description will be offered here for those readers needing a basic acquaintance with these terms. A more detailed exposition is readily available in Whitmont's section on Jung in *Comprehensive Textbook of Psychiatry* (Freedman and Kaplan, 1967) or in *The Symbolic Quest* (Whitmont, 1969).

Jung did not elaborate these new terms a priori; he chose them to describe those phenomena encountered in a vast amount of clinical observation. They are terms to fit clinically useful entities, not theoretical concepts created by fiat. Thus their usefulness is more readily evident than their preciseness, although any clinician familiar with a significant amount of dream and fantasy material, even the clinician from another theoretical orientation, will be able to identify and use these Jungian concepts appropriately.

At the beginning of the infant's life there is no division into ego, shadow, etc. The world is experienced in a unitary fashion, although it may be experienced through opposites: good world and bad world correspond to sensations of gratification and sensations of displeasure or pain. Gradually, objects begin to be identified, with the personal face of the mother being differentiated from the archetypal smiling

113

response somewhere toward the end of the first 6 months of life. It is likely that good objects (mother, breast, etc.) are distinguished by the infant from bad objects, and these are then fused during the first year of life into ambivalent objects. This development is reflected in the child's ambivalent attitude toward conflicting impulses in himself. The ego as a knowable entity arose with the first sense of continuity of consciousness, the ability to remember oneself, to picture oneself reflexively to oneself, to know oneself, to have an ego image. The ego images then begin to be sorted into good images and bad images. Those that are reinforced by the nurturing person tend to be identified as dominant ego images, while those that are negatively reinforced or that elicit displeasure are dissociated from the centrum of the ego and tend to cluster in an alter ego image that Jung called the *shadow*. The *shadow* carries some of the sense of negative valuation that the ego gives to it, although to an outside objective observer the shadow of a person may actually carry important, meaningful, and life-supporting qualities that were dissociated in infancy and childhood because of an aberrant family situation. A mother, for example, who for her own neurotic reasons cannot tolerate normal aggressive activity in a child can influence that child to repress qualities that are of value in the adult ego. A famous literary example of ego shadow split is provided in Robert Louis Stevenson's *Dr. Jekyl and Mr. Hyde*. Because material in the shadow has been dissociated from the ego to prevent pain, the potential return of such material causes anxiety in the ego because it threatens the current dominant ego image.

Soon after the shadow begins to be disssociated from the ego image, the child learns that it is possible to pretend various roles. This is the beginning of *persona* formation. The persona is an outer layer of the personality. Its more adult forms are studied in sociology as role theory. The persona is always a compromise between what the ego wishes and what society permits as a functioning social role. There is always, it seems to me, some anger associated with elaboration of the persona, since the child always experiences his fitting into a social role as a limitation on his initial freedom, when he was accepted simply because he existed and his acceptance was not dependent on his fulfilling any social expectation. The persona allows duplicity, lying, and misrepresentation, but in its normal functioning it also facilitates social interactions that require people to relate only through their roles, without personal feelings being involved. The persona of the physician facilitates his examination of the body of the patient, while the patient contributes to the examination by adopting the persona of a patient. When such roles fit the actual abilities of the ego, the persona promotes easy social interchange. But if the persona becomes too "thick," or if the ego identifies itself with the persona role, a pathology of the persona can occur, with the ego feeling that it is nothing more than the role it fulfills. While the persona is often considered in negative terms, as something to be discarded in psychotherapy or in close relationships, it has a definite function. There are many persons who suffer from inadequate separation of the persona from the ego, so that there is no personal "space," and every encounter with another touches the sensitive ego, perhaps with injury.

Both persona qualities and shadow attributes can to a large degree be integrated into ego functioning. This is the task of most psychotherapy that does not go to the depth of psychoanalysis. The ego experiences such integration as an enlargement of its freedom and capabilities, but it is only reclaiming what it originally repudiated. In both the persona and the shadow there is an archetypal core that in all complexes cannot be assimilated to the ego image, but that is scarcely a problem in most psychotherapeutic experiences. Guggenbuhl-Craig (1968) carefully outlined the danger of the psychotherapist falling into his own shadow and becoming a "quack" or false prophet.

"Below" the shadow there is the boundary between the shadow and the inner world; it is analogous to the persona boundary with the outer world. Jung called this the *anima* in the psychology of a man and the *animus* in the psychology of a woman. In a man's unconscious productions, such as dreams and fantasies, there appears a feminine figure, the anima. The corresponding figure in a woman's unconscious material is the masculine animus. The anima and animus can be referred to in the neuter as the *syzygy,* a term that is seldom used. It is convenient to think of the anima and animus images as being partially formed (as is the shadow) by disssociation of elements that are considered by society to be contrary to the assigned sexual identity of the ego. Thus they fluctuate, although less readily than the shadow, with changes in the cultural norms of masculinity and femininity. It is their structure that is archetypal; their actual content is determined by personal, family, and cultural considerations.

The function of the anima appears largely in projected form. When the anima image is unconsciously identified with an actual woman, the ego may "fall in love." Use of the term *fall* is appropriate; it conveys the suddenness and involuntary nature of the anima projection. If the man relates to the woman on whom his anima is projected, eventually he is able to distinguish her real qualities from those he has projected on her. He can then form a personal relationship with her, withdrawing some of the projected qualities into himself; or he can decide that she is not the person he though she was and depart to project the anima anew on another woman. The anima thus pulls a man out of his usual mode of functioning, enlarging his ego in the external world. The same function is served by the anima in the inner world, where the function, if developed, enlarges the ego inwardly. It is possible to say that the true function of the anima is to enlarge the ego beyond the integration of the shadow and the persona. Exactly the same process occurs in feminine psychology through the functioning of the animus.

Some writers have accused Jung of a one-sided psychology, with a negative valuation of the animus and a positive valuation of the anima. It is true that Jung wrote largely from the view of the man, which is proper for him, but the concepts *anima* and *animus* are not culturally bound. They are equivalent in their functioning. Because of the society in which he observed the dreams of patients, Jung found that the phenomenology of the animus was such that it tended to represent the underdeveloped thinking function of the woman, while the phenomenology of the anima tended to contain a man's underdeveloped feeling discriminations. But these distinctions are patently culturally determined. It is my own impression that as the roles of male and female become more diversified, as is now happening, the phenomenologies of the animus and the anima will undergo similar change consistent with their functional role in the psyche.

The anima or the animus can be considered the inner boundary between the personal unconscious and the objective psyche. Often these personified inner figures become guides to deeper layers of the objective psyche in active imagination or in dreams.

The most profound contents of the objective psyche are the archetypal images, the archetypes themselves not being observable in their unimaged state. The archetypes constitute the contents of the objective psyche, in the same manner as the personal unconscious is inhabited by complexes. These layers are actually inseparable, and the core of each complex is archetypal. There is no fixed number of archetypes, since any recurrent human experience can be archetypally represented. It is perhaps more nearly correct to speak of an archetypal field, with the observable archetypal images indicating nodal points in which the field is particularly dense. Archetypes are not inherited images; they are part of the tendency to structure experience in certain ways. For example, there is no inherited image of the mother, but there is a universal tendency to form an image of mother from the experiences of the child. The most profound images are archetypal (e.g., the queen), moving toward more personal images of the actual mother and those associated with the mothering role.

Among archetypes, the most central is the Self, also called the central archetype.* When appearing in images, it tends to take on motifs that have been associated in mythological and religious systems with images of deity, although any image of sufficient affective numinosity is capable of being a representative of the Self.

The phenomenology of the Self presents difficulties because it carries several meanings. It is the totality of the whole psyche, the source of dream images, the archetypal core of the ego, and the center of the psyche as experienced by the ego. The images of the Self are not the Self. The Self as central archetype bears no relationship to such ordinary usages as self-aware, self-assured, etc., which in this system might more properly be called ego-aware, ego-assured, etc. As an image of the unification of opposites, the Self may appear in mandala form, often a square enclosing or enclosed by a circle; but the Self may also be represented by any object of high value (Abenheimer, 1968). It is possible to imagine a vector leading from the ego toward something of greater comprehension and value than the ego; that image would carry some of the numinosity of the Self, although it could later also become relative to another image of still higher value. Self-images also appear in schizophrenia (where they seem to function as impulses toward order) and in childhood (where they seem to be stimuli toward ego formation). Jung (CW 8:137), as well as others, referred to the Self as the central archetype, a term that has fewer confusions with ordinary terminology.

Fordham (1973) cautioned that in order to talk of the ego as separate from but related to the Self, it is necessary to keep in mind that the ego is also part of the Self taken as totality of the psyche. In the same essay, Fordham clearly distinguished between the Self and images of the Self. In a number of writings, Fordham put forward a concept that the Self as the totality of the psyche deintegrates (not disintegrates) to form both the ego and the other components of the psyche. The periodic integration and deintegration of the Self and the ego allow for psychic growth and promote accessibility to new integrations for the total organism. Fordham (1960) concluded that any comprehensive view of mental health must allow for periods of relative maladaptation during phases of deintegration. He realized that although the truly healthy personality contains elements of disorder, it is truer to itself

---

*Note: Throughout this book, I have chosen to capitalize *Self* when it is used in the sense of "central archetype" in order to differentiate it clearly from the ordinary uses of the word as "self-image" and "self-esteem," etc., that actually refer to ego images.

than the personality that by excessive effort toward stability adapts to social requirements at the expense of its inner development. Gordon (1968) asserted much the same position when she pictured our most basic needs as fusion and union on the one hand and separateness and differentiation on the other. Pratt (1967), in explaining the ordeal the caterpillar undergoes in the cocoon, suggested that the process, "whether of the body alone or of body and psyche both," is a series of deaths of achieved adaptations that must be gone beyond.

Edinger (1960) called the relationship of the ego and the Self a paradox, a position to which Fordham (1960) took exception. In Edinger's model, which I find appealing, the identity of ego and Self leads to an inflated act (the ego acting as if it were the Self), which produces rejection, separation, and damage to the ego–Self axis, followed by repentance, acceptance, and restoration of the ego–Self relationship. From the point of view of the ego, which is the only point of view we have, the realization of this process seems paradoxical. If the ego acts as if it is autonomous, it falls into inflated attitudes and is wounded. If it simply identifies with the Self, it remains immature and the Self then frequently seems to produce negative images to drive the ego into individuation and interaction with the world.

The Self or central archetype remains a borderline concept; it is less amenable to empirical verification than ego, shadow, and persona (which can be demonstrated by psychometric testing) or anima-animus (which can be verified clinically in interpersonal data). The Self is a valuable part of Jungian theory, however, and it is indispensable to our understanding of the unfolding of the individuation process over a period of time, as well as our understanding of the psyche as having personality, our understanding of the phenomena of synchronicity, and our understanding of many religious phenomena.

REFERENCES

Abenheimer KM: The ego as subject, in Wheelwright JB (ed): The Reality of the Psyche. New York, Putnam, 1968
Edinger EF: The ego-self paradox. J Anal Psychol 5:3–18, 1960
Fordham M: Ego, self, and mental health. Br J Med Psychol 33:249–253, 1960
Fordham M: The empirical foundation and theories of the self in Jung's works, in Fordham M,, Gordon R, Hubback J, et al (eds): Analytical Psychology. London, Heinemann, 1973
Freedman AM, Kaplan HI: Comprehensive Textbook of Psychiatry. Baltimore, Williams & Wilkins, 1967

Gordon R: Symbols: Content and process, in Wheelwright JB (ed): The Reality of the Psyche. New York, Putnam, 1968

Guggenbuhl-Craig A: The psychotherapist's shadow, in Wheelwright JB (ed): The Reality of the Psyche. New York, Putnam, 1968

Pratt JA: Consciousness and sacrifice: an interpretation of two episodes in the Indian myth of Manu. New York, Analytical Psychology Club of New York, 1967

Whitmont EC: The Symbolic Quest: Basic Concepts of Analytical Psychology. New York, Putnam, 1969

5
The Dream in Jungian Theory

Jung came to view the dream in a very different way than did Freud, although in Jung's earliest psychoanalytic writings one may find constructions that are still under the influence of the Freudian model. Jung did not see the reported dream as the façade of a hidden, latent dream. The dream was the dream. Nor did dream images seem to be inferior forms of thinking that could be made clear and logical in waking life. Instead, dream images were symbolic; Jung used the term *symbol* in its true sense of that which indicates what is not yet fully known. For Freud, the images in the dream were what Jung would call *signs*: things that stood for other things in a fixed way (tree = penis, cave = vagina, etc.), although Freud used (mistakenly) the term *symbol* to indicate these relationships. The increasingly impressive body of literature in which the dream as reported correlates with other parameters argues for Jung's position, as opposed to Freud's position of neglect of the importance of the manifest dream. There is an analogy that is frequently cited: If Freud and Jung came upon an inscribed stone memorial in the desert, Freud would assume that it was a disguised version of a consciously known language such as English or German, while Jung would approach it as would an archeologist—it has a meaning, but because it is in an unknown language, the meaning must be pursued. Jung (CW 7:100) stated that we should not accuse the dream of "a deliberate manoeuvre, calculated to deceive," because "nature is often obscure or impenetrable, but she is not, like man, deceitful." In this same writing, Jung also suggested that the Freudian doctrine of the latent dream could be used to avoid the problems of understanding the dream itself in its manifest form.

Mahl (1974) pointed out that Freud himself relied on the manifest dream as one of the empirical bases of the oedipus complex. In discussing typical dreams (those that were similar in many people), Freud (SE 4–5) found that free association was rarely helpful in understanding them. One such typical dream form was a dream of the death of a near relative. Freud noted that men more often dreamed of the death of a male relative, while women more often dreamed of the death of a female relative. Both observations are clearly made on the manifest content of the dreams. He interpreted this as evidence in support of his formulation of the oedipus complex.

Pontalis (1974) incisively concluded that Freud "concentrated on the dream itself and neglected the capacity to dream," so that he emphasized the construction of dreams rather than the "conditions of their creation" and the "creative power that they are testimony to." In similar manner, it would appear that all the data on REM dreaming only establish a physiological basis for dreaming; they by no means provide adequate explanation for the content of the dreams (Snyder, 1971). Emphasis on the creative aspects of dreaming (as opposed to its suggested defensive function) has not been the work of Jung alone. Assagioli echoed this same theme, and it was propounded at least as early as 1929 by Nunberg (1931) as the "synthetic function" of the ego.

The position of Jung has been largely ignored, however, outside the school of Jungian psychoanalysis. In an anonymous letter to the editor of *Manas*, a college student in psychology reported that when he asked his professors about Jung he was told by one that Jung is "hard to read," and by another that "Jung is not always scientific" (*Manas* editors, 1971, p. 455). I had a similar experience when I asked an internationally known speaker at a national meeting of the American Psychiatric Association why he had omitted any mention of Jung in a presentation in which all of the ideas had antecessory equivalents in Jung's writings. He shrugged off the question: "When you mention Jung it gets so complex." There have even been articles purporting to critique the theories of Jung, but with no writings by Jung mentioned in the bibliography (Giora, 1972). There are exceptions to this neglect (Dallett, 1973; Maduro and Martinez, 1974), but more often than not there is little awareness of the actual theories of Jung, even when such knowledge would offer support to the position being presented. For example, the possibility that REM sleep is involved in psychological adaptation to life events (Pearlman and Greenberg, 1970) is quite consistent with Jung's theory of the compensatory function of dreams.

COMPENSATION: THE FUNCTION OF DREAMS

In contrast to Freud's view that the dream occurs in order to preserve sleep, Jung assigned a psychological function to dreaming: The dream compensates the conscious attitude of the dreamer. Although all dreams are compensatory to the content of consciousness, this cannot always be clearly demonstrated (CW 8:250). The compensatory nature of the dream process is consistent with the nature of biologic processes in general (CW 8:250), where various reflexes maintain the internal state of the body within narrow ranges of temperature, oxygen tension, blood pressure, etc., the ranges necessary for life. Freud, too, had this basic idea of the compensatory nature of dreams, but he drew the process too narrowly, limiting it to the preservation of sleep (CW 8:252). Such simple dreams as a dream of food by a hungry sleeper can fit either the compensatory view of Jung or the wish-fulfillment model of Freud, but more complicated dreams that are related to the conscious psychological situation of the dreamer are not adequately articulated by the wish-fulfillment hypothesis.

An example may help to clarify what Jung meant by compensation, although the range of that function is so great that it is not exhausted by such examples. A person who restricts his own horizons in life because of neurotic comparison with the achievements of his father, which achievements he feels he can never equal, may dream of his father as being worse than the father really is; here the dream images exaggerate the father's attributes, but in the opposite direction to his conscious overvaluation of his father. Exactly the same sort of compensation may appear in any aspect of the dreamer's life, as will be shown in many clinical examples in subsequent chapters.

When the conscious attitude of the dreamer is more or less appropriate to his outer adaptation and to the degree of realization of his personality development, the dream will usually appear more gently compensatory, offering slight corrections and enlargements to his conscious position. In such normal situations the compensatory function of the dream may appear as mild *complementation* to his conscious view of his ego. But if his conscious attitude is notably ill-adapted to his objective situation or his subjective needs or both, his dreams may appear to have a "guiding, prospective function," still acting under the general principle of compensation (CW 8:257). Such dreams are capable of leading the ego into a new direction in life, as in the biblical example of the dream of Nebuchadnezzar. This *prospective* function of dreaming is in contrast to the reductive emphasis of Freud, which would reduce the significance of dream images to repressed, although previously experienced, conscious wishes.

According to Jung, the conscious attitude of the dreamer exists in dynamic relationship to the constellated form of the unconscious. Neither consciousness nor the unconscious simply follows the other. Not only is the unconscious compensatory to the conscious state; the contents of consciousness are relative to the active images in the unconscious (CW 8:254). The process of *individuation* involves cooperative interplay of the conscious and unconscious forms of the mind, with neither predominating to the detriment of the other. In fact, the unconscious mind, in Jung's view, functions satisfactorily only when the conscious ego fulfills its own tasks, giving the dreams a framework against which to exert influence (CW 8:296). If the unconscious were given a superior place (a view often mistakenly attributed to Jung), there would be no way to inquire as to why consciousness should emerge at all in the course of biologic evolution (CW 8:296).

It is possible to consider the principle of the compensatory nature of dreams as being congruent with the continuation, during sleep, of concern with the problems dealt with in consciousness—the dream motifs supplying additional material that was relatively unconscious during the waking state (CW 8:245). For this reason it is necessary to know the conscious attitude of the dreamer in order to understand his dreams (CW 8:260). However, the principle of compensation has broader application than merely the continuation of conscious problem-solving. Jung (CW 6:419) noted that Adler's view of the dream was also one of compensatory function, but Adler unnecessarily restricted the compensation to feelings of inferiority. Actually, the compensation may even correct conscious attitudes about the inferiority of another person, as in Jung's case (CW 7:179) of a man who consciously devalued his younger brother but kept dreaming of him as being an important figure, such as Bismarck, Napoleon, and Julius Caesar. The course of the analysis brought forth additional evidence in support of what had been seen in the dreams.

Jung distinguished the principle of compensation, implying balancing, from complementation, with its emphasis on two things merely supplementing each other. The dynamic activity of the process of compensation varies according to the conscious attitude. If the conscious view of the life situation is one-sided, the dream images may take the opposite side; if the conscious attitude is near the individuation needs, the dreams may add supplementary material; if the conscious attitude is "correct," the dream may further emphasize the conscious attitude without "forgetting its peculiar autonomy" (CW 8:287). It is also possible for the compensatory function of the dream to relate the ego to the ongoing individuation process rather than respond to immediate conscious situations. The compensatory nature of dreams may also relate not to the conscious attitude of the dreamer but to other aspects of his situation, e.g., the dreams of a child relating to the family constellation instead of to the child's conscious state. Dreams are also capable of compensating the cultural situation of the dreamer, in which case their personal meaning can be overshadowed. However, such cases of dreams compensating something other than the immediate life situation of the dreamer are somewhat rare.

What would appear in reductive (Freudian) analysis as the tracing of dream motifs to past life events can also be seen as the dream compensating the ego's image of itself as unrealistically independent of such factors. This form of compensation by dreams was "brilliantly investigated by Freud" (Jacobi, 1942, p. 78). A positive form of compensation is the production by the dream of a "guiding image" that can present to the ego the possibilities of its future achievements or dangers (Jacobi, 1942).

Compensation normally aims at establishing psychological balance and appears as a self-regulatory function of the psyche (CW 8:288–289). Self-regulation does not imply teleology (CW 7:294), but it does emphasize that a point of view of finality may be valid—things happening as if there were a fixed, final goal. Jung (CW 7:294, footnote 19) decried equally an absolute belief in causality and an absolute belief in teleology.

The movement toward a greater unification and wholeness, which seems to be the "intent" of dreams, is part of the individuation process. It is quite different from the regressive pull "backward" to a sense of unity of consciousness prior to the development of the ego. Rather, the movement toward wholeness (always a direction, never an achieved goal) is one in which conflicting forces can be tolerated as an essential part of being more fully human (Abenheimer, 1968). It includes the social demands of life that are a large part of the individual's existence (Seidenberg and Cochrane, 1964). Individuation (becoming more what one potentially can be) is quite different from individualism, which is an often excessive emphasis on individual (ego) concerns; these two terms can be confused in superficial reading.

The principle of the compensatory nature of dreams has some place in classic Freudian psychoanalytic literature, although it is not elevated to a prominent place nor called by the name compensation. Sharpe (1937, p. 93) discussed a patient whose desolation in waking life seemed to be compensated by gratifications during dreams. Although some effects of dream deprivation on projective psychological tests (the Rorschach and Holtzmann tests) appear to be consistent with the model of dreams inhibiting drive discharge, which then appears in pro-jected form on the tests, there are other aspects of dream deprivation that are not easily explained by the drive model (Greenberg and as-sociates, 1970). In the literature of laboratory dream studies, it has been noted that adults with effective daily functioning have less bizarre and less emotional dreams, which is consistent with the compensation model (Foulkes, 1969). In a study of aging women (Brenneis, 1975), it was found that as interpersonal interests narrowed and the women lost a sense of themselves as pivotal, their dreams showed more "robust and locomotor activity"—compensation?

If the compensation hypothesis is correct, it will offer a psycholog-ical equivalent to the recurrent observation that dreaming is important for adaptation to stress (Greenberg and associates, 1968).

SELF-REGULATION

The compensatory nature of dreams is part of the self-regulation of the psyche. Self-regulation is quite similar to what Hartmann (1973) called "self-guidance over time." Jung's concept, however, places self-regulation at the very core of archetypal processes themselves. Hillman (1968) distinguished between *prohibition,* a negative com-mand, and *inhibition,* an innate regulation against excess. Much of psychotherapy and psychoanalysis consists of helping the analysand distinguish between what seem to be imposed prohibitions (the superego in Freudian terms) and what are actual desires. When freed of neurotic complications, the person is able to realize that the feared excesses, as well as the overly rigid prohibitions against them, change into ego choices. In the process of such choice, the ego must bear the tension of opposite desires, but this tension itself promotes transforma-tion through the experience of symbolic forms that express both oppo-sites.

Jung borrowed the term *enantiodromia* from the philosophy of Heraclitus and used it to designate the tendency of any extreme posi-tion to turn into its opposite, revealing the hidden connection between a pair of opposites. Enantiodromia can be seen in the compensatory nature of dreams. If the conscious position is excessively distorted in one direction, the unconscious may express in dreams an equally exaggerated but opposite tendency. If the positions are switched (con-sciousness identifying with the previously unconscious opposite), nothing really progresses. But if the unconscious position is admitted to consciousness without consciousness relinquishing its former attitude, there can result an increase in conscious tension but also the potential for reconciliation of the opposites in a new position that allows for both of them.

It is a common phenomenon for the conscious ego identity to align itself with one of a pair of opposites, with the other being unconsciously projected onto another person or group; since that projected by the unconscious is usually considered inferior or undesirable, the situation is frequently a projection of the shadow, although the shadow may also contain positive qualities. Kettner (1968) discussed the problem of opposites in relation to masculine identity. Some societies tend to idealize one form of masculine identity, usually either a spiritual or a physical form, although for completeness it is necessary to develop both forms. Abenheimer (1968) showed how Christian emphasis on love may devalue chthonian, earthy powers; at the opposite extreme, the Nazis reversed the process, emphasizing power and ridiculing love. Cultures, like individuals, have their problems of shadow projection.

SYMBOLS IN DREAMS

Jung (1968, p. 92) criticized Freud's assumption that dream images were disguises as an "anthropormophic idea" that the dream wanted to conceal something. The value of dreams is that they present images that are not consciously constructed but arise spontaneously. Therefore, the dream has an objectivity in the same sense that a laboratory blood specimen has objectivity: it comes from the patient and reflects the internal state of his functioning but is not created by his conscious activity. The dream is a "natural product of the psyche" (CW 7:131). Jung (CW 8:263) once defined the dream as "a spontaneous self-portrayal, in symbolic form, of the actual situation in the unconscious." He pointed out the similarity of his view to those of Alphonse Maeder and Silberer.

The symbolic nature of dream images means that they provide the most adequate representation of the state of the mind at that time, its self-portrait. They are symbolic in that they stand for further contents that are not explicitly given but are involved in the representations of the dream. This symbolic view is in direct contrast to the view that dream images are disguised versions of potentially knowable but repressed thoughts. By way of analogy, the cross on the steeple of a church may convey, for a practicing Christian, a wide range of meanings, all of which are not immediately present in consciousness but none of which is repressed. To that person, the cross on the steeple is a symbol. Another observer of the same cross, having no such symbolic orientation, might use his perception of the cross merely to infer that the structure to which it is attached is a church building. The question of whether a perceived form is symbolic depends on the mind of the person perceiving it.

Jung (CW 7) referred to this symbol-making function of the mind as the *transcendent function*. He did not mean transcendental in a metaphysical sense; rather, it is called transcendent because it is able, through symbol formation, to transcend the tension of opposites that cannot be solved in the conscious terms in which their opposition is experienced before the symbol is evoked. By analogy, simultaneous contraction of both the agonist and antagonist muscle groups of an arm or leg, as may occur in grand mal epilepsy, produces paralysis rather than an effective and purposeful movement of the limb in the service of conscious goals. The supporting structures of the muscles, the bones, may even be fractured, rendering the muscular power impotent. But when these opposing groups of muscles function normally, they do not function in opposition but under the control of a guiding intent from consciousness, a symbol, as it were, that coordinates their opposition into a useful function with meaningful purpose. On a nonphysical basis, the symbolic image coordinates the opposing forces of conflicting impulses so that a useful action or thought results.

What Jung called the transcendent function is closely related to the Self or central archetype, which will be discussed further when we consider the process of individuation in more detail (Fordham, 1973). Paulsen (1968) related the transformative activity of the psyche to the alchemical image of Mercurius, an archetypal image of the spirit that acts so as to restore wholeness. In this process, as in dreams, the pressure of the symbol may be at one time directed toward further ego development and at another time directed toward giving up ego aims—both processes in the service of individuation, the continuing approximation of wholeness. The opposites united by the symbol may lie both in consciousness and in the unconscious (Fordham, 1973).

IMPORTANCE OF THE ACTUAL DREAM

Because the Jungian approach to dreams considers dreams to be in the same category as laboratory observations or x-rays in medical practice, the accuracy of reporting the remembered dream is of great importance. There will obviously be reporting errors, and at times missing portions of the dream will be remembered in the process of telling it;

but making an effort to stay with the dream itself is important. In discussing the word-association experiment, Jung said that it reveals the complexes active in the patient's mind at the time of sampling. The dream, in contrast, reveals what the unconscious mind of the patient is doing with those complexes. This latter information from the dream is of much greater interest and value in understanding the clinical situation. There are, of course, legitimate uses of dream material that do not require such adherence to the actual form of the dream, and some of these uses will be discussed later. However, such secondary uses are not equivalent to dream interpretation, and a distinction should always be made in the therapist's mind between actual interpretation and other uses of dreams. In obtaining a clear dream report (as clear as the patient can give), it is important to rule out, as far as possible, any ambiguity. If the dream ego turns to enter a room, for example, does it turn right or left into the room? If there is a setting for the dream, ask whether it is indoors or outside, day or night, summer or winter, etc. Nothing in the dream is arbitrary, and clear undistorted observation is as important as in the physical sciences.

AMPLIFICATION

The Jungian approach to dream images is· one of amplification. This is quite different from the Freudian free-association technique, and it leads to different results. Jung (1968) remarked that the technique of free association will indeed lead to whatever complexes are activated in the person's mind, but the list of stimulus words in the word-association experiment is as effective for that purpose as are the images of a dream. In fact, any relatively neutral stimulus will eventually elicit whatever is pressing for discharge into consciousness. It is on this projective hypothesis that much of psychological testing is constructed. Free association is a well-known technique. It consists of associating to the dream motif, then associating to that association, then associating to the association of the association, etc., thus permitting all mental contents to be spoken without censorship and leading, presumably, to the thought behind the disguised dream image with which the free association began. In contrast, Jung (1968, p. 91) did not ask what complexes were present; instead, he wished to know "what a man's unconscious is doing *with* his complexes." That people have complexes is already known, and one may even know with some degree of accuracy what the complexes are in a neurotic patient. The important and useful information is how the mind itself is already attempting to heal the divisions caused by the complexes. Conscious attention can then be brought as an aid to the unconscious healing process, in the same way that the physician tries to understand not only the disease but the state of the body's healing response, so that rational medical intervention can come to the aid of the natural healing activity.

Amplification consists of eliciting from the patient his associations to each dream motif. The associational process is not permitted to extend too far from the original images. Instead, the dreamer is brought back repeatedly to the actual image, so that one elicits understanding of what images, thoughts, memories, and affects lie in the immediate vicinity of the dream image.

Amplification can take place on different levels. The most immediate level produces material from the personal unconscious of the analysand, from his own memories and feelings. The second level is of cultural material assimilated to the image. The third and most abstract level consists of archetypal images; it brings in associations from folklore, mythology, religious traditions, and other systems of imagery that may not be known consciously to the dreamer. There is a clear order for amplification: personal material takes precedence over cultural material, and cultural amplifications take precedence over archetypal amplifications. Thus one does not move toward the less personal areas of cultural and archetypal amplification unless the meaning of the dream does not become clear within the range of personal amplification. At times, however, it is possible to understand the meaning of the dream only through archetypal amplification, although it is possible to provide perfectly adequate psychotherapy without even considering the archetypal level. The archetypal level of amplification raises many interesting theoretical questions about the nature of the psyche, but it is not usually essential in clinical work with dreams, although it is an advantage if skillfully used.

In amplification through these three layers, one is considering the various layers of the complex. Each complex rests on an archetypal core, since archetypes are simply the ordering structure of the mind. The archetypal core of the complex may be thought of as similar to a magnetic field; it has no physical structure, but it determines the order and relationships of images susceptible to its influence. Jung considered the archetype like a dry river bed—empty, but capable of determining the flow of libido when there is activation of a psychic process. The images in constellation around the archetypal core of the complex may be personal, cultural, or archetypal. In contrast to the archetype in itself, archetypal images are general, nonpersonal images: e.g., the Virgin Mary, the queen, the princess. Since one many always find personal historical images in a complex, it is easy to mistake the personal image as the origin of the complex itself. But other observations, particularly archetypal images in dreams, reveal the more detailed structure to involve nonpersonal elements as well.

Jung (CW 8:240–241) said that a dream image "results from the competition of several causes," so that the discovery of a single personal motif does not explain the image. However, it should be emphasized that he was not speaking of the same mechanism of condensation and displacement that Freud used to discuss the multiple meanings carried by a single dream image. Rather, Jung was speaking of the dream image in a symbolic way. The manner in which multiple contents can be symbolized in a single dream image will be clarified by the application of Polanyi's theory of focal and tacit knowing, which will be introduced after a detailed discussion of the relationship between the dream ego and the waking ego.

Amplification is not to proceed indefinitely, but only so far as "absolutely necessary in order to understand the dream's meaning" (CW 8:241). Such a stopping point is always a matter of judgment, and it is a common experience to find deeper levels of meaning in a dream that was once thought to be understood, although both levels of meaning may be valid. In her Zurich lectures in 1967, von Franz likened the amplification process to pulling up a blade of grass in a field where all the grass is connected under the surface of the ground, as all complexes are connected through the archetypal structure of the objective psyche ("collective unconscious" in the older terminology). If one insists on pulling hard enough, one gets the whole crop of grass attached to the single blade. This is not advisable, since it distorts the true field nature of the unconscious, and we should not think that we have found the "real nature" of the unconscious mind (CW 7:176).

In the process of amplification of dream motifs, emotional and affective responses frequently may be elicited. Dreams, like an artist's productions, are not simply conscious problems; they touch us in the core of our being, and they can be profoundly emotional (CW 7:183). The uncovering of emotional reactions in the process of amplification may aid in reconnecting the ego to the structure of the complex out of which the affect emerged. It is then possible for choices and insights of the ego to modify the structure itself.

OBJECTIVE AND SUBJECTIVE LEVELS

Since the images attached to complexes in the mind have relationships to the outer person, to objects, and to events on which those images are partially based, a problem arises whether a particular image in a dream refers to the complex to which it is attached or to the outer referent of the image. Referring the dream image to the complex structure of the dreamer's mind is called interpretation on the subjective level; referring the dream image to the outer referent is called interpretation on the objective level. The language of subjective and objective should not confuse the fact that both modes of interpretation are objective in the sense that the psychic complexes do exist, they can be demonstrated by the word-association test and other laboratory procedures, and they exert a profound influence on the person's perceptions, his affective responses, his ego image, and the manner in which he experiences life. The Jungian view keeps a delicate balance between the personal and the collective, both inwardly between the ego and the complexes and outwardly between the individual personality and the collective social and material world in which it exists.

In general, persons appearing in a dream who are currently involved with the dreamer and his problems in waking life are likely to be interpreted more usefully on the objective level. If persons appearing in the dream are unknown persons, or if they are known in waking life but are not currently of concern to the dreamer, they may appear in the dream a representatives of the subjective content of the dreamer's mind; then they can be interpreted more usefully on the subjective level. Judgment is necessary; it is not always easy to choose between the subjective and objective modes of dream interpretation (CW 8:276). The most practical stance is always to consider each dream from both points of view, although if an emphasis is needed toward one or the other, it is perhaps best to lean toward the subjective. This difficulty of distinguishing objective and subjective dream images was mentioned in the fourth century writings of the desert monk Evagrius Ponticus (1970, p. 41), who concluded that ill-defined dream images are symbols of former affective experiences, while those that are clearly seen indicate "wounds that are still fresh."

REFERENCES

Abenheimer KM: The ego as subject, in Wheelwright JB (ed): The Reality of the Psyche. New York, Putnam, 1968
Berry P: An Approach to the Dream. Spring 1974. New York, Spring Publications, 1974, pp. 48–79
Bonime W: The Clinical Use of Dreams. New York, Basic Books, 1962
Brenneis CB: Developmental aspects of aging in women. Arch Gen Psychiatry 32:429–435, 1975

Cirlot JE: A Dictionary of Symbols. New York, Philosophical Library, 1962

Dallett J: Theories of dream function. Psychol Bull 79:408–416, 1973

Evagrius Ponticus: The Praktikos (chapters on prayer). (Trans: JE Bamberger) Spencer, Mass: Cistercian Publications, 1970

Fordham M: The empirical foundation and theories of the self in Jung's works, in Fordham M, Gordon R, Hubback J, et al (eds): Analytical Psychology. London, Heinemann, 1973

Foulkes D: Drug research and the meaning of dreams. Exp Med Surg 27:39–52, 1969

Giora Z: The function of the dream: A reappraisal. Am J Psychiatry 128:1067–1073, 1972

Greenberg R, Pearlman C, Fingar R, et al: Effects of dream deprivation: Implications for a theory of the psychologic function of dreaming. Br J Med Psychol 43:1–11, 1970

Greenberg R, Pillard R, Pearlman C: Dream deprivation and adaptation to stress. Psychophysiology 5:238, 1968

Hartmann EL: The Functions of Sleep. New Haven, Yale University Press, 1973

Heuscher JE: Psychological effects of fairy tales. Confin Psychiatr 3:146–157, 1960

Heuscher JE: An introduction to the understanding of myths and fairy tales. Exist Psychiatr 1:196–206, 1966

Hillman J: Toward an archetypal model for the masturbation inhibition, in Wheelwright JB (ed): The Reality of the Psyche. New York, Putnam, 1968

Hobson R: The archetypes of the collective unconscious, in Fordham M, Gordon R. Hubback J. et al (eds): Analytical Psychology. London, Heinemann, 1973, pp. 66–75

Iandelli CL: The serpent symbol, in Wheelwright JB (ed): The Reality of the Psyche. New York, Putnam, 1968

Jacobi J: The Psychology of C.G. Jung. New Haven, Yale University Press, 1942

Jung CG: Analytical Psychology: Its Theory and Practice (The Tavistock Lectures). London, Routledge & Kegan Paul, 1968

Keeler CE: Secrets of the Cuña Earthmother: A Comparative Study of Ancient Religions. New York, Exposition Press, 1960

Kettner MG: Patterns of masculine identity, in Wheelwright JB (ed): The Reality of the Psyche. New York, Putnam, 1968

Kluger YH: Personal communication, 1968

McCully RS: Rorschach Theory and Symbolism: A Jungian Approach to Clinical Material. Baltimore, Williams & Wilkins, 1971

Maduro R, Martinez C: Latino dream analysis: Opportunities for confrontation. Social Casework 55:461–469, 1974

Mahl GF: Fathers and sons source material, vol 2. Journal abstract service of the American Psychological Association, no. 623. Abstract available in JSAS Catalogue of Selected Documents in Psychology, 1974

Manas editors (not named): The Manas Reader. New York, Grossman, 1971

Mendelsohn J: The fantasy of the "white child," in Wheelwright JB (ed): The Reality of the Psyche. New York, Putnam, 1968

Nagara H (ed): Basic Psychoanalytic Concepts on the Theory of Dreams. New York, Basic Books, 1969

Nunberg H: The synthetic function of the ego. Int J Psychoanal 12:123–140, 1931

Paulsen A: The spirit mercury as related to the individuation process. In Wheelwright JB (ed): The Reality of the Psyche. New York: Putnam's Sons, 1968, pp. 74–84

Pearlman CA, Greenberg R: Medical-psychological implications of recent sleep research. Psychiatry Med 1:261–276, 1970

Pontalis JB: Dreams as an object. Int Rev Psychoanal 1:125–133, 1974

Pratt JA: Consciousness and Sacrifice: An Interpretation of Two Episodes in the Indian Myth of Manu. New York, Analytical Psychology Club of New York, 1967

Sadler AW: Dream and folktale: A cognitive venture. J Individ Psychol 25:89–100, 1969

Seidenberg R, Cochrane H: Mind and destiny: A social approach to psychoanalytic theory. Syracuse NY: Syracuse U Press, 1964

Sharpe EF: Dream Analysis. London, Hogarth, 1937

Snyder F: The physiology of dreaming. Behav Sci 16:31–44, 1971

von Franz ML: The problem of evil in fairy tales, in Curatorium of the CG Jung Institute (eds): Evil. Evanston, Northwestern University Press, 1967, pp 83–120

Waldhorn HF (ed): The Place of the Dream in Clinical Psychoanalysis. New York, International Universities Press, 1967

6
Technique of Dream Interpretation

In order to be a Jungian psychoanalyst in the truest sense, one need not subscribe to a defined technique of dream interpretation or any other aspect of the analytic endeavor; it does not even involve a fixed and invariable descriptive language. All questions of technique were thoroughly relativized by Jung's repeated assertion: the wrong technique in the hands of the right person will achieve the desired result; the right technique in the hands of the wrong person will fail. Although this maxim does not free us from concern with the many techniques that are of value in psychotherapy and analysis, it clearly pinpoints the person of the analyst as the most crucial factor, rather than some set of principles that can be superficially applied but that do not govern the life of the analyst. The personal equation of analyst–analysand interaction is always more crucial than the type of technique applied, a position that is expressed by such old terms as *rapport* and by such modern terms as *therapeutic alliance*.

Jung's relativistic statement about technique may be a derivative of that quoted by Wilhelm from the ancient Chinese *Book of the Elixir:* "When the right man makes use of wrong means, the wrong means work in the right way" (Wilhelm and Jung, 1962, p. 63).

If one were to attempt a basic statement of Jungian dream technique, it might be to use the dream to help the analysand understand the direction of individuation that his central archetypal process is suggesting to his current ego. This statement is sufficiently general for a variety of purposes: to permit noninterpretative use of dreams, if that is appropriate; to allow for affective impact being most important with some dreams; to permit changing emphasis between the personal and archetypal levels of amplification, as well as between the objective and subjective modes, but keeping clearly in mind the underlying importance of individuation and its uniqueness in each individual so that the error of rote comparison to a collective norm will be minimized.

Jung (CW 8:247) estimated that he investigated some 2000 dreams each year, and he did find typical motifs. Instead of using the typical motifs to suggest some common denominator of fixed significance (such as an oedipal complex), he believed that the proper use of such typical motifs was to allow comparison to other material of the same order, such as mythological motifs that suggest a phylogenetically older mode of thought. In the individual dreamer, however, he believed that the typical motif might have a more personal application; thus investigation should not stop with the identification of the motif as typical. The causal, reductive method of interpretation tends toward uniformity of meaning, but from the final or prospective view the dream symbol often has a value more like that of a parable, teaching rather than concealing (CW 8:246). Stein (1973) likened dream interpretation to the process of helping toward symbolic completion, somewhat as suggested by the early experiments of Poetzl in subliminal perception. Association and amplification aid this process.

Jung frequently emphasized that there is no ground for assuming that the activity of the dream is in any way inferior to the conscious thought processes (CW 8:285). They may actually be more comprehensive than conscious processes, although they are revealed in a symbolic and nonverbal manner that makes direct comparison difficult. Whenever conscious awareness is present, the entire unconscious process underlies it, although it is not visible except in fantasy or parapraxia or by use of projective techniques and other intentional or unintentional integrations. It is perhaps not too much to assume that while one is dreaming, all the potential material of consciousness is also present, but in a less visible form.

The separation of the psyche into parts is an arbitrary device to aid our understanding. Freud (1943) said that "for any vital purpose, the separation of the ego from the id would be a hopeless undertaking." Williams (1973) confirmed, from the Jungian position, the indivisibility of the personal unconscious and the collective unconscious. She suggested that nothing in personal experience is repressed unless the ego is threatened by the archetypal power of the event; conversely, archetypal activity is dependent on the material of the personal unconscious to provide form and effect. The integration of the personality in the individuation process requires both archetypal activity and personal activity.

REDUCTIVE AND PROSPECTIVE ANALYSIS

Jung never repudiated the value of reductive Freudian psychoanalysis in uncovering past events that hinder a person's growth because of the formation of excessively charged complexes. A reductive approach to dream symbols does lead to such understanding, although dreams are not necessarily the most advantageous approach. What Jung did deny was that the past traumatic events uncovered by this process necessarily have explanatory value for those problems of life that occur at the growing edge of the personality. A hypothetical patient free of regressions or fixations would still encounter the conflict of opposites and the need to choose from among many competing possibilities in life. This growing edge of the personality experiences existential problems and becomes aware of its freedom of choice and its concomitant historical and personal limitations. The inner world also has its fixed form, which Jung referred to as *objective psyche* (Fordham, 1958) to indicate that the ego must face it as a given, over against the ego, in the same way that the ego finds itself thrown into historical existence in the outer world.

Later life is not just an "epiphenomenon of childhood events" (Jacobi, 1967), and dreams may be interpreted to show the way forward in ego development as well as the way in which growth is inhibited by a clinging to past ego states and their external representations. The deepest and most compelling images of such movement are archetypal, but the process often must begin with an understanding of the persona and shadow problems, which leads to an enlarged ego more capable of autonomy.

A situation frequently encountered at the beginning of analysis is that in which the outer adaptation has progressed beyond inward development of the personality. The collective social role, and the ego's dominant image of itself, may contain far more maturity than is warranted. This discrepancy between the appearance and the reality of the personality, between the persona and ego image on the one hand and the demands of individuation on the other, creates a stress to which dreams may respond with a negatively compensating or reductive function (CW 8:257). In such cases, which are frequent, a reductive movement in analysis is indicated, with exploration of past events, hidden guilts, and childhood history. This is not the whole of the process, but it is a prodrome to the deeper process of movement forward. Forward must not be construed as supporting the mistaken notion that positive emphases on "growth," "progress," "self-actualization," etc., are the essence of the individuation process. Individuation is a process that involves becoming more what one potentially is, and it is by no means an exclusively positive process. The pathway is meandering, convoluted—anything but straight movement toward "success." What may appear to be success from the ego's point of view may be, from the point of view of the central archetype, a hindrance to needed development. The reductive analysis may uncover the infantile sexual wishes that impressed Freud, as well as the infantile power claims emphasized by Adler (CW 8:258). The discovery of such reductive complexes facilitates a realistic appraisal of the person's actual situation, which can then permit him to move forward to significant life choices with more awareness of his true purposes. The negatively compensating or reductive function of the unconscious was elaborated largely in the work of Freud (CW 8:258).

Regarded from the causal point of view, any psychic structure appears to have been produced by events of the past; but it can as easily be seen from Jung's final standpoint as revealing its contribution to the forward movement of psychic processes (CW 8:239–240). The "final" or "finality" standpoint implies looking at the content in relation to movement toward a goal, having a sense of purpose (CW 8:241). The final approach is essentially identical with the prospective vector toward future conscious activity (CW 8:255). Polanyi's (1974) distinction between *causes* and *reasons* parallels Jung's distinction between the reductive and prospective modes of approaching dream images.

UNINTERPRETABLE DREAMS

One of the most useful of Jung's maxims regarding dream interpretation is that when one sits down with the actual patient and the actual dream, it is important to try to forget all theoretical considerations and approach the dream directly. It may even be helpful to say to oneself "I do not know what this dream means," in order to prevent a too-ready assimilation of the dream to what one already knows about the patient and his condition. If we accept seriously the compensatory function of the dream, a valid dream interpretation will evoke some element of surprise, something not known or not fully appreciated by the conscious mind of the dreamer. For several years, as I was preparing lectures on dream interpretation for the psychiatry residents at South-western Medical School, I had a recurring experience that reminded me of my own fallibility in dream interpretation. It seemed that every time I was in the process of preparing my talk on the techniques of dream interpretation, one or more of my patients would bring dreams that, despite my best efforts, failed to yield the usual sense of under-standing. This was a practical lesson in accepting Jung's maxim.

It is equally important to realize that not all dreams will give us a sense of understanding, although this says more about our limitations of understanding than it does about the nature of dreams. There are many similar medical situations in which understanding of the process in the body is not achieved, even by postmortem examination by the pathologist. At times, a dream that has not been understood will be-come clear in the light of subsequent dreams in the same series.

In presuming to approach the meaning of dreams, we embark on a complex and mysterious process. An attitude of humility is not just wise, it is mandatory. Even old Artemidorus (1975), the oneirocrit of antiquity, cautioned that "there are some dreams that cannot be inter-preted before their actual fulfillment."

REFERENCES

Artemidorus: The Interpretation of Dreams: Oneirocritica. (Trans: RJ White) Park Ridge, NJ, Noyes Press, 1975
Fordham M: The Objective Psyche. London, Routledge & Kegan Paul, 1958
Freud S: Some additional notes on dream-interpretation as a whole (1925). Int J Psychoanal 24:71–75, 1943
Jacobi J: The Way of Individuation. (Trans: RFC Hull) London, Hodder & Stoughton, 1967
Polanyi M: Scientific thought and social reality, in Schwartz F (ed): Psycholog-ical Issues 8(4), monograph 32. New York, International Universities Press, 1974
Stein L: What is a symbol supposed to be? in Fordham M, Gordon R, Hubback J, et al (eds): Analytical Psychology. London, Heinemann, 1973
Wilhelm R, Jung CG: The Secret of the Golden Flower: A Chinese Book of Life. (Trans: CF Baynes) New York, Harcourt, Brace 1962
Williams M: The indivisibility of the personal and collective unconscious, in Fordham M, Gordon R, Hubback J, et al (eds): Analytical Psychology. London, Heinemann, 1973

7

The Relationship between Dream Ego and Waking Ego

RELATIVITY OF THE EGO

Perhaps the most significant achievement of analytical psychology is its appreciation of the relativity of the ego. Jung, more thoroughly than any other medical psychologist, discussed the vicissitudes and changes experienced by the ego, describing them from a neutral standpoint (in the language of the complex theory) and in more experiential and existential terms (in the language of persona, shadow, animus-anima, and Self). Even in his doctoral dissertation, published in 1902, Jung (CW 1) described how the mediumistic personalities of a patient seemed to foreshadow potentials of future development in her own ego. In "The Psychology of the Transference" (CW 16) he pioneered the concept of an analytical relationship in which the analyst and analysand are joint participants in a process that, if successful, can only result in growth for both of them.

Some of the most illuminating of Jung's writings on the relativity of the ego are found in his autobiographical *Memories, Dreams, Reflections* (Jung, 1961). Three of his own dreams stand out as examples of the manner in which this insight was presented to Jung himself. First, his childhood dream of the underground phallus (Jung, 1961): He vividly describes sitting on "his" rock between the ages of 7 and 9 years, wondering "Am I the one who is sitting on the stone, or am I the stone on which *he* is sitting?" Second, one of the dreams that occurred toward the closing years of his life, after he had written on flying

saucers (CW 10), startled Jung into wakefulness with the sudden realization that the saucer might be "projecting" *him,* turning topsy-turvy
his conclusion that flying saucers could themselves be projections of
the dynamic center of the unconscious, experienced by the ego in the
imagery of the Self (Jung, 1961, p. 323). The third example is Jung's
dream of entering a small chapel and finding, in front of the altar, a yogi
in meditation (Jung, 1961, p. 323). Again reacting with a start, Jung felt
that the yogi in trance was somehow meditating Jung himself, who felt
that he would vanish if the figure "woke up."

Relativity of the ego may be experienced in an inner fashion, as the
childlikeness of the ego in relation to the unconscious, whose limits
cannot be known. Realization of the smallness and inadequacy of the
ego as compared to the vastness of the unconscious may give rise to
different emotional responses. If the ego still perceives itself as the
center of the personality, the recognition of its smallness can only be
frightening, representing the threat of annihilation of its world. If the
ego has already begun to experience its relationship to the self in a
conscious image, or conversely if it is still "unborn," the unconscious
may be affectively experienced as a protecting and sheltering matrix
that generates and sustains the ego itself. These two modes of perceiving the same relationship may be analogous to the opposites that appear whenever something of deeply unconscious or archetypal content
approaches consciousness.

Two faces of the archetypal image of the great mother, for example, reflect "her" role in both the life-giving and life-threatening functions of the unconscious. This is illustrated in the first dream of an
analysand, a professional man in his thirties:

I was descending a stairway, with several landings, down into what
seemed to be the boiler or heating room of a large building. Instead of walking
down the last flight of steps, I swung over the bannister and dropped a distance
of maybe 14 feet. Then I realized it was also a slaughterhouse, and the mistress
of it was angry that I had invaded her domain. She was a tall, thin woman in her
forties, dressed in black; she seemed sinister. There were animal carcasses on
hooks, and even large cans that contained entire animals—pigs and calves and
even dogs. She became more angry and threatened to harpoon me with a
trident. There was no place to hide. She threw the trident and missed my head
by only a few inches. But then I realized that by doing this she had also given
me a weapon to oppose her. I seized the trident and hurled it back, hitting her.
She fell behind a large boiler, apparently dead. Immediately the carcasses
began to come back to life. The cans opened and the animals emerged, alive
and well.

The question of the relativity of the ego relates directly to the most persistent and most paradoxical question asked by patients encountered in clinical practice: "What can I *do* to change?" Any answer to this question is somewhat unsatisfactory. Questions of psychological growth simply are not answerable in how-to-do-it terms. Consider the situation of the 10-year-old boy: "What can I do to grow up?" "I feel my life will be entirely unhappy until I can grow up and be my own boss." What can one say to him? Everyone "knows" how to grow up, but the question is unanswerable in specific terms, at least to the 10-year-old boy. It is unanswerable partly because he cannot incorporate the answers into his 10-year-old ego structure. Tell him that part of growing up is to be economically self-sufficient; how is he to make practical use of that knowledge? Tell him that part of becoming an adult is to be able to have a close, loving emotional and physical relationship with a respected person of the opposite sex; he may well despair.

In fact, no specifiable "knowledge" can be imparted that is likely to relieve the press of his question. It is only by actually growing up that it will be answered, and that is a process of transformation of the ego itself, only partially taking place in consciousness. To be sure, the process can be aided by an understanding parent, mentor, or peer, but only when the general problem of growing up has crystallized as a more specific problem: how to pass algebra, how to get along with a particular friend, how to keep a part-time job when it interferes with the desire to play, how to bear humiliation and shame and still retain a core of self-esteem, how to accept success without losing a sense of proportion and balance in one's image of oneself.

In one sense, the 10-year-old boy's ego is the parent of his future ego. But in another sense, it *is* his future ego still unfolding. When he has achieved maturity, the situation will not be that there is his adult ego and also, somewhere in the unconscious, outgrown and put away, the same ego that asked how to grow up. Somehow the child ego participates in the ego of the man, just as the adult ego was foreshadowed in the unconscious of the child.

This gradual transformation of the current ego into the future ego is that part of the individuation process that can be experienced by consciousness. It is indeed paradoxical, for there is nothing that consciousness can *do* that is sufficiently potent to bring about its own transformation. At the same time, growth does seem to require the participation of the conscious ego for the individuation process to result in its natural product: a wider, more comprehensive personality.

A patient, a young man in his early twenties, worked about a year before circumstances interrupted his analysis. This was his final dream:

> I was standing on a newly constructed boat dock on a river. There were some machines on the dock near the bank, but I didn't know what they were for or how they worked. I was fiddling with them, trying to understand them. I was trying to figure a way to get across the river, because there was a village I wanted to go to just downstream on the other side.

During the amplification of the dream, he further described that a large tree had been growing from the opposite bank of the river. It had grown quite low over the water, and its trunk had come to within a few feet of the boat dock, so that it would have been possible to step from the dock to the tree trunk and thus easily cross the river.

In the language of the dream, I believe that the machinery represented a constructed part of his personality, which he did not yet know how to organize. Its function was not clear to him. From his associations, it seemed that the boat dock represented the work that we had been able to do together in analysis. It was preparation for crossing the river, a dock where a boat could be moored, and the boat could take him across.

The lysis of this dream was only indicated; it did not take place within the dream itself. Only on awakening and writing it down did he realize that the tree represented an alternative route across the river, a way that had not occurred to the part of him that may have participated in building the boat dock. Nor did the symbol of the tree suggest that it grew in that particular direction in response to the building of the dock. Symbolically, it must have been growing in that fashion for many years. Neither did the dream indicate that the boat dock was built so as to take advantage of the position of the tree.

This coincidence of the boat dock and tree suggests Jung's concept of synchronicity. There were independent causes, potentially specifiable, behind the building of the dock and the growth of the tree. It is their meaningful coincidence that is striking. Of course we must remember that this is a dream, while synchronicity refers to a meaningful noncausal coincidence of an inner event and an outer event. It would be a specialized use of the term to apply it, without discussion, to the meaningful coincidence illustrated within the dream itself. Although I believe that the "synchronistic" events in dreams are of theoretical importance, their consideration is not appropriate to the present discussion. The image of the coincidence of the tree and dock shows an unconstructed and unexpected way toward solving a problem, one that comes through no direct effort of the ego, but seemingly in a meaningful coincidence with the efforts of the ego. This might suggest to a religious mind the concept of grace.

How does the dream ego on the boat dock relate to the waking ego? Are they identical? There is some temptation to think so, since the part of the dream image dealing with (1) the dock, (2) the "dream I," and (3) the machinery seems very parallel to (1) the basis for new action that had been built in analytical work, (2) the patient, who had not yet "crossed the river," and (3) his obsessive involvement with complex structures whose functions were not clear to him.

The tree and the river are another matter. Tree and river are natural phenomena of the world, not artifacts of man. The river and the tree seem to be outside the dream I; are they also outside the waking I? In the dream they are taken to be symbols of a natural boundary, the river, and a naturally produced way across the boundary, the tree growing low over the water. They are not, in the dream, part of the dream I. What is their relationship, in the waking state, to the waking I? They would be taken, I believe, as representatives of the deeper part of his personality, the transpersonal not-I of the objective psyche. Thus, in both the dreaming and waking states, the river and the tree would appear as not-I, but they are specifically that part of the not-I that is intimately related to the ego (whether waking or dreaming) as his own area of contact with the transpersonal world.

What of the relationship of the waking I to the dream I? Are they identical? Does not the dream indicate, in symbolic form, the relationship of the waking I to the deeper layers of his total personality? Can it not be a symbolic picture of his actual state as he was aware of it before the dream itself? His predream waking state is best described by the image of the dream I working on the unknown machinery on the newly built dock.

And what of the waking I *after* the dream? Is it the same as the waking I prior to the dream? After all, the postdream I contains, in addition to the state represented by the dream, the predream waking I plus the remembered knowledge of the dream itself. This becomes even more conscious when the dream is discussed with an analyst, but I suggest that it would exist to some degree, or at some level, even if the dream were forgotten. The dream adds something to consciousness, something that compensates and in some measure corrects the previous limitations of consciousness. That this is a relative process, never leading to "full" consciousness, does not detract from the progressive tendency of dreams.

The importance of the relationship between the dream I and the waking I lies in the fact that we are totally dependent on the ego itself (our sense of I) as a point of reference for everything we know of ourselves, of others, and of our world. We may to some extent choose whether we wish to approach outer phenomena by means of intuition, thinking, sensation, or feeling, although our predispositions place severe limits on our choice. We may to some extent choose our instruments for outer observation: we may approach the stars in a poetic and feeling way by constructing a poem, or in a more objective scientific fashion (emphasizing thinking and sensation) with a telescope, or as an exercise in intuition guided by unspecifiable rules, as in astrology. But all methods of observation are ultimately referred to the ego of the observer.

And the ego, we know, is realtive. This unavoidable reliance on an unspecifiable ego is the great problem of human knowledge.

OBSERVING THE RELATIVITY OF THE EGO

Two universal relationships are important in conceptualizing the relativity of the ego. Their familiarity, or their closenss to the ego itself, makes them seem commonplace and obscures their true mystery. The first is the relationship of past ego states to the present ego. The second is the relationship of potential future ego states to the current ego structure. A discussion of this area leads inevitably to a consideration of the process of individuation.

While the individuation process is of the greatest importance in analytical psychology, there are great difficulties inherent in discussing it; thus it is often exemplified in various symbolic ways: by alchemical transformation processes, by the group of mythological images that have been called "the night sea journey," and occasionally by lengthy compilation of personal material, such as Jung (CW 5) published in *Symbols of Transformation,* the book that made his break with Freud inevitable by contradicting Freud's concept of the sexual nature of libido. As with literary criticism, discussion of the individuation process in terms of personal material allows critics to take alternative views. The scope of the material is so vast and the alternatives of interpretation are so numerous that much reliance must be placed on the skill of the interpreter in finding Ariadne's thread.

Individuation, like the Self or central archetype, is one of the most important and most difficult of Jungian conceptions. It is a universal process, since anything that exists has its own individual form and development, and even inanimate objects can be said to individuate, to undergo the changes of fate; but it is particularly complex in living creatures. Individuation and the Self are related in that the activity of the Self, the regulating center of the entire psyche, profoundly influences the ego, the regulating center of consciousness. Although it is non-ego in a sense, the Self is in other ways the very core of the ego. This relationship between ego and Self was called an axis by Neumann and a paradox by Edinger (1960). Hofstadter (1968) referred to a similar paradox of consciousness, in that ego-awareness and nonego-awareness always arise at the same moment and in essential relationship; but Hofstadter was speaking as an existential psychologist and did not place the same emphasis on the non-ego center of subjectivity that seems to be part of the essential nature of the Self. Still, the phenomenologists are in general close to the Jungian outlook (Abenheimer, 1968).

Dreams seem to be a natural part of the individuation process in man, which may account for some of our difficulty in understanding them—they are natural occurrences, not something offered in terms of human (ego) expectation (CW 8:294). The neurotic probably has the best opportunity to become aware of the individuation process in himself (CW 8:271), since his neurosis impedes him from simply projecting and living out the processes of his unconscious. Fordham (1973) pointed out that while many Jungian psychoanalysts are concerned primarily with the individuation process in the second half of life, when the relativization of the ego in favor of the Self generally predominates, the term individuation also covers the same process in childhood, where ego development is the goal. Jung (CW 8:289) described how the compensatory function of dreams, which may appear to consist of many momentary adjustments, can with deeper insight over a period of time reveal the process as a series of planned, orderly developments: individuation. Individuation is always to some degree opposed to the collective norms of the person because it involves the very particular development of that person's life. However, individuation is not simply opposed to the collective norms, else it would only be another, although opposite, collective attitude. The individual way can never be a norm; it remains always individual (CW 6:449). It is striking that the psychology of Jung, which starts from transpersonal archetypal factors, leads to greater emphasis on the personal individuation process than does the theory of Freud, which begins with a personalistic psychology based on specific life experiences (Neumann, 1959). This life of individuation seems to be the "intimate intention of Western humanity," as exemplified by such personages as Leonardo and Goethe (Neumann, 1959, p. 4). In the process of individuation there is no single creative or heroic act, but rather a succession of transformations over a lifetime, each straining and testing the ego anew—a series of what Neumann (1959, p. 131) referred to as calvaries. Psychosis, too, has a process of individuation, but one that may proceed autonomously, without resistance from or effect on the ego, like "an ouroboros in the unconscious" (Jacobi, 1967, p. 32).

Although Jung first used the term *individuation process* in 1921, the idea can be found in his writings as early as 1902 (Jacobi, 1967, p. 12). Jung's 1902 essay "On the Psychology and Pathology of So-called Occult Phenomena" (CW 1) shows that he was quite early aware of the possible connection of individuation with processes that appear on the surface to be pathological.

Jung offered (CW 7:303) a clear presentation of what is involved in the production of individuality. It is what is unique in the person, although components may be chosen from the collective. It makes possible differentiation from the merely collective view of man. It is a developmental tendency toward the unique, although the person is still a link in his society. Development of individuality is also a simultaneous developement of society. Society is probably dependent for its own life on the personal growth of specific individuals who can influence society in return. Not only is suppression of the individual tragic for the individual, it weakens the ability of society to withstand disintegration. Perhaps most important, Jung stated that the development of individuality requires not only personal outer relationships but also contact with the objective psyche within (CW 7:303).

The individuation process can be seen in its richness only by taking into consideration a wide range of material from an individual life, either over an extended time, as in psychological autobiography, or by making up in depth what is omitted in time, as with analytical cases presented in detail, with both personal and collective amplifications. A third possibility is to present the individuation process in symbolic form, often in alchemical or mythological language.

The relativity of the ego may be seen at close range in dream material when that material is related to the conscious ego. The chosen focus is then on a microscopic section of the individuation process— that small sample that is exemplified in the dreams studied.

I hope to show how the relativity of the ego may be exemplified in the particular question of the relationship between the dream ego and the waking ego and how an epistemology based on the more traditional physical sciences (Polanyi's analysis of focal and tacit knowing) can be applied to our problem.

The second common illustration of the relativity of the ego is found in the problem posed by the mutual interpenetration of the dream ego and the waking ego. The classic statement of this dilemma is the dream of Chuang-tzu, a disciple of Lao-tzu (De Becker, 1968, pp. 405–406).

> Chuang-tzu dreamed that he was a butterfly, but then he awoke and was Chuang-tzu again. He did not know whether he was Chuang-tzu who had dreamed he was a butterfly or whether he was a butterfly dreaming that he was Chuang-tzu.

This relativity was first brought to my attention by the dream of an army officer. He had had a successful military career for 18 years, rising steadily in rank and responsibility. Although he was quite intelligent, diligent, and imaginative, he relied to an excessive degree on his persona image. Typical of this persona reliance was his habit of keeping a freshly ironed uniform in the closet of his office. If his superior officer called for him, he would quickly dress in the fresh uniform, standing on a chair to put on his trousers for fear of getting a crease in them at the knee. He would put on a fresh blouse with newly polished insignia and a special pair of shoes that were always "spit-shined." Then he would casually present himself before his commander, looking the classic picture of the perfectly dressed officer. It should be said that the same elements of persona reliance characterized his personal relations to a lesser degree.

This officer came into treatment as a result of severe and prolonged depression (which he had at first attempted to hide) following the death of his father, whom he had known only slightly in childhood. His parents had been divorced when he was small. He had requested leave to return to the United States to attend the funeral of his father, but his request was denied. His depression followed.

At the time I first saw him, he had already been hospitalized briefly in two other military installations, but each time he had used his persona facility to convince the physicians that he was well. The depression had continued to simmer beneath the surface.

It was the intial dream of this man that first made me acutely aware of the problem of the relativity of the ego, and of the dilemma posed by the dream of Chuang-tzu. His dream was as follows:

> There had been a theatrical performance, a play, on an outdoor stage in the center of a town or village. It was over, and the people were leaving the stage to go to their homes or their jobs. I was lying in the gutter at the foot of the stage. I was dead.

He used this dream to point out to me how hopeless he thought his situation actually was. "I'm already dead," he insisted, "just as in the dream, and there's no hope and no point in therapy.'' But after we discussed the dream, he was able to appreciate that it seemed to say that other people were alive both on stage and off—in persona roles and without them—while he seemed to be dead the moment he stepped off stage.

I questioned him further: "From position did you view yourself lying in the gutter?" In other words, the ego that was represented as dead was seen by another ego that he had forgotten to notice, since it was so abstract and so easily identified with the observing function of the ego. The dream seemed to say that the persona role identification was dead, or was a dead-end pathway. But there remained an ego that observed. This offered him some hope, and he entered an extended period of therapy, achieving some improvement and making a successful transition from military to civilian life.

THE DREAM I

Marjasch (1966) made the clearest statement, to my knowledge, of the problem of relating the dream ego to the waking ego. She divided dreams into two large categories: those that contain an I and those that do not. She then demonstrated, by example, that an apparently I-less dream may involve unrecognized attitudes of the dreamer, although in each case it is necessary to make an independent judgment whether the dream situation represents a conflict for which the dreamer has been avoiding responsibility or whether it represents the spontaneous eruption into his individual awareness of a more universal problem.

The larger group of dreams, those that contain a reference point of I-ness, are treated in the present discussion, although I agree with Marjasch that most I-less dreams may be shown, when analyzed, to have some importance for the dreamer's situation. Also, there seem to be some dreams, particularly those studied in cases of precognition, in which no direct reference to the dreamer's life is evident, although here, too, the compensatory function of the dream may be discovered, as the precognitive aspect of the dream may compensate the ego's usual sense of being time-bound and limited.

Among the dreams containing an I, Marjasch dealt with two specific types: (1) dreams of self-reflection, in which an image of the self is presented to the dream I, and (2) dreams of searching for the self. The present inquiry intends to address, instead, the general question of the relationship between the dream ego and the waking ego.

There is also a difference in the use of terms. Marjasch, if I understand her correctly, proposes to make a distinction as to whether the representation of the dreamer in the dream is (1) roughly equivalent to the waking ego or represents inferior parts of the ego or (2) transcends the level of consciousness of the waking ego. In the first case, she finds it useful to speak of the I or the ego in the dream; in the second she speaks of a dream I. These proposed distinctions are apparently put forward on clinical grounds and are meant to minimize the twin dangers of depression and inflation.

However useful her distinction between the I and the dream I may be on clinical grounds, the use of these terms in the present discussion does not follow her suggested pattern. Instead, the term dream ego is used in a phenomenological way to designate the point of view from which the dream is perceived, just as the unmodified term ego is used (as are waking ego and waking I) for that sense of I-ness that a person experiences when awake. No distinction is implied as to whether the dream I represents inferior, superior, or equivalent contents when compared to the ego or waking I. Such value judgments give excessive weight to the existing conscious attitude, the very attitude the dream may be altering. The most difficult part of the problem is, as Marjasch appreciated, the relationship of the dream I and the ego (or waking I), since both these states of awareness, at the time they are experienced, carry the feeling of I-ness.

It is obvious, of course, that we must continually deal only with the remembered manifest dream, which is the representation of the dream in the conscious memory of the wakened dreamer. Thus our access to the dream state is always through the conscious ego, and the dream I is subject to the distortions of waking memory. This does not seem to me to be a major difficulty, as the experience of both dreaming and waking consciousness is so universal that each person may judge somewhat for himself the relationship of these two states of being. It is unlikely that anyone acquainted with depth psychology would propose simply to relegate the dream I experience to the status of a delusion of the waking mind.

COMPENSATORY FUNCTION OF THE
UNREMEMBERED DREAM

It is now established beyond doubt that everyone dreams several times each night. Furthermore, if a person is deprived, under laboratory conditions, of his dream time, he often becomes tense, irritable, and even measureably impaired in his functioning. When allowed to

sleep without interruption, following several days of dream deprivation, subjects increase the amount of REM sleep, or dreaming time,
apparently to compensate for the missed dreaming.

It therefore has become increasingly clear that dreaming is a
natural part of psychological life and that deprivation of dreaming tends
to a progressive disorganization of the waking ego. Such a finding
seems clearly to contradict Freud's theory that dreams are a means of
preserving sleep. If such were the case, laboratory subjects deprived of
dreaming, but not of NREM sleep, should show no ill effects. Of
course, Freud also postulated that dreams give a disguised outlet to
repressed infantile wishes, often of a sexual nature, and it could be
argued that it is the deprivation of this outlet that leads to increased
pressure of id drives and to the observed disorganization of conscious
life. Some Freudians have argued that the high percentage of dreams in
which penile erection occurs is evidence of the sexual nature of
dreams, although it is more likely that penile erection is part of a
generalized autonomic arousal (as it seems to be in male infants who
are crying) rather than sexual arousal in any discrete sense. Such penile
erections occur in subhuman organisms, such as the opposum, where
their psychological meaning, if any, must remain obscure.

The now well-documented universality of dreaming in man raises
an important question for analytical psychology. The research data
suggest that dreams are somehow necessary as compensation to waking life, for deprivation of dreams interferes with the conscious mind's
functioning in a balanced manner. But many persons do not remember
dreaming at all, and scarcely anyone recalls having as many dreams
each night as the laboratory studies suggest are actually occurring. This
must mean that unremembered dreams are also somehow compensatory to consciousness. How is this to be conceptualized?

When we think of dreams as compensatory, we usually think of
them as being remembered and as representing to the conscious mind
some attitude, previously unrecognized or undervalued, that needs to
be added to consciousness for completeness. Often we think of this as
occurring during a formal analytical process, or in self-reflective moments in those who have learned, through guidance, something of their
own dream life and its meaning.

But the findings of the REM studies strongly suggest that the
dream automatically functions in a way that enhances the stability of
consciousness. Is this, too, to be called compensation? If so, how does
it differ (if it does) from the compensation that occurs following a
conscious understanding of dreams? The unremembered dream certainly cannot function in the same way as the remembered dream.

And what of the somewhat rare but admirable person who is

"naturally" individuated? People can be found who seem to have actualized their innate potentialities, but without any formal analytical process and without being able to express their unique individuality in the language of psychological insight (Jacobi, 1967). Almost everyone has met such persons.

One of my own early contacts with such a person was with an old cabinetmaker who seemed to have achieved such integration, although I did not know it in those terms at the time. Long hours of commerce with the woods he worked had given an air of ritual absorption in his work. I remember as a boy watching him smoke a home-rolled cigarette, exhaling his breath in a half-whistle, while lining up by eye, occasionally with the help of a rule, the angles he was about to cut. We didn't talk much. I did not know much about him in words, but he remains in my memory, and it seems I knew him well.

But Jung spoke of another "natural" individuation, one that leads to a different outcome. In his essay on "The Soul and Death," Jung (CW 8) told of an elderly female patient who broke off analysis just as she seemed to be getting to the center core of her neurosis. Later, she became terminally ill and lapsed into a semicomatose state. During this state, while oblivious to the persons around her, she seemed to resume, in her mumblings, the same problem she had avoided in analysis. Jung had the impression that before she died she worked through her problem without ever regaining clear consciousness. It seemed as if her unconscious was interested in her dying a more nearly whole person.

In the case of Jung's patient, the unconscious pressure toward individuation was unable to overcome her resistances, at least until her terminal state. In the case of the cabinetmaker, it seemed to me that the unconscious had achieved its goal, although not in the same fashion as in someone who has been formally analyzed and can tell others, in words, some of the process he has undergone.

One might generalize and suggest that natural individuation may occur at a more conscious level, if the ego participates, leading to a more integrated and coherent personality. If the ego does not cooperate, the process nevertheless goes on, but at a more unconscious level, still striving for a more total personality, but one in which the ego may perhaps be somewhat isolated from the orderliness of the deeper layers of the personality. In analysis itself, of course, the ego does participate; and if the process is successful, it leads to something like natural individuation plus conscious ego participation and memory.

I would suggest that the natural individuation process is analogous to the natural functioning of the unremembered dream, while that individuation process that is stimulated by analysis is analogous to the changes that take place when the dream is remembered and given some place in consciousness. If this supposition be allowed, it can be used to suggest possible relationships between the dream ego and the waking ego.

Perhaps several examples of dreams will make things clearer at this point. The first is that of a young man 19 years old. The second is the dream of a successful businessman in his middle forties suffering from an almost classic problem of trying to find time during the second half of his life for more introverted thoughts and an inner world of values. A third example is the dream of a man with a recurrent problem of pathological jealousy.

The younger man came to analysis for severe inhibitions. Still dependent on his parents, he was unable to bring himself to get a job and was miserable when around girls. He had an immense amount of repressed anger, which at times would burst out, usually directed at churches or at such religious leaders as Billy Graham, whom he saw as denying any sensuality or enjoyment in life.

The initial analysis revealed that as a child he had frequently been left in the care of a woman who filled him with exaggerated fundamentalist prohibitions. He believed that she had poisoned his mind and caused his inhibitions.

This young man frequently masturbated, and he observed a curious change in his feelings during the course of masturbation. When the desire to masturbate came to him, he frequently gave in to it, usually fantasying a seductive female pictured in one of the magazines such as *Playboy*. He found this enjoyable, but the moment he ejaculated his guilt feelings increased, and he would be unable to relax until he had partially dressed himself. It is this sudden, discrete change of feelings, occurring with ejaculations, to which I wish to direct attention. It is as if the personality that begins the masturbation suddenly changes, at the point of ejaculation, into a different form of personality, one that feels guilt and must make some symbolic undoing gesture, such as partially dressing.

During the course of his therapy, he was finally able to begin dating, although he felt constrained not to touch the girl in a sexual manner. At that point in his treatment he had a very revealing dream.

In the dream, he was with a very attractive unknown girl. They were having intercourse, and he found it very enjoyable. Just before he reached climax, however, her face suddenly became that of Billy Graham. His own position suddenly changed, and he was seeing "her" face as if from a distance of several yards. He then immediately awoke with a feeling of agitation.

If we put these dream images side by side with his waking experiences, they will be as follows:

Dream	Masturbatory Experience	Date with Girl
With attractive girl	Fantasy of girl	With attractive girl
Sexual intercourse	Fantasy of intercourse	Inhibited desire to approach her sexually
Sudden change of her face to Billy Graham's near point of climax	Sudden guilt feelings after ejaculation	Sudden anger with friends "having fun" while he is inhibited
Increasing distance from girl	Partial dressing-psychological distance	Increased feeling of estrangement in his relationship with the girl
Waking up agitated	Return to usual emotion state of tension	Usual emotional state of tension

This chart makes several comparisons obvious. His interpersonal relationship with the girl, which seems simply to hang in a prolonged state of anxiety, has many of the features that can be seen in an temporal way in his typical masturbatory experience. While his feelings about the girl seem to be paralyzed by ambivalence, in the masturbatory experience the warring feelings are seen in a temporal sequence: first the desire, then the guilt and magical repair.

The dream would seem to make the same statement, in a more symbolic way. Instead of changes in his feelings (in the I experience), he perceives changes taking place in the girl herself and in the relative distance between them.

If the dream were to be described in the language of the complex theory, it would be something like this: His dream ego is in relationship with (having intercourse with) an unknown female figure (who might represent the complex of the anima) when that complex is suddenly contaminated by another complex of ideas, represented by Billy Graham. The image of Billy Graham seems to be part of a complex of ideas to which also belong his childhood experiences of the repressive woman babysitter. It functions much as the Freudian superego in its more archaic form. The lysis of the dream is that his dream I is removed spatially from this complex. He wakes up feeling frightened by the experience and is once more in his usual state of estrangement from feeling relationships.

It is possible, when this dream is discussed, to view it as a compensation for his conscious feeling of being excessively inhibited in his emotional life. The dream presents in a rather stark form the way that his sexual desires are interrupted by his guilt feelings. This is almost precisely parallel to what he experienced emotionally during and after masturbation.

But if the dream had not been remembered and discussed in analysis, what would have been its function in his life? Here we are immediately faced with one of the most basic problems of psychology, one that makes its task so tremendously complicated, for, as Jung demonstrated, it is only in psychology that the psyche is caught in the dilemma of trying to understand itself. We cannot observe ourselves without in the process changing that which is observed, just as Heisenberg showed that it is not possible to observe a physical system without distorting the system by the effects of observation.

We can only speculate that had the dream not been remembered, it would still have been an abortive attempt to face the dreamer with a symbolic situation that exactly paralleled his waking experiences during masturbation and in relating to women. We can only guess that this would have had the "purpose" of giving him an opportunity to work through, in the inner structure of his complexes and his ego, a problem that he had not been able to face in an effective way in his outer everyday life.

If one chooses to deny the prospective, forward-looking activity of the psyche, as some reductive theorists do, the dream might appear simply as the inner model of relationships between the dream I and the other complexes. This inner structure would, by projection, tend to determine his relationship to outer events, leading to ambivalence, as with his actual girlfriend, or to erratic, overstressed emotions, as in his severe anger at anything suggesting a rigid morality. Such theorists could deny that this dream had any intent, even aborted, to change the dreamer's ego structure.

To meet such an objection, it would be necessary to show that a dream coincided with a change in outer life prior to the time that the dream was interpreted in analysis; that is, a change in the state of the waking ego occurred coincident with the dream but before the time the dream interpretation was added to consciousness.

Examples of such changes are not rare, although they are seldom called on to stand as evidence for the point in question. I, myself, prior to entering psychiatry, was once startled at the sudden change in my psychological state coincident with a brief dream, which was unfortunately not remembered even at the time. As a medical intern, I was on emergency room call many nights, often getting less than 2 hours sleep or no sleep at all. On one such occasion I had been in the hospital all day, had been up most of the night in the emergency room, and had worked all the next day. On the afternoon of the second day, after leaving the hospital, I attended a class in oil painting with a group of close friends. I came into the lecture late and took the only available seat, near the front. Although I was interested in the subject matter, my fatigue was great, and I found myself about to drift into sleep. I fought to stay awake, trying to listen to each sentence.

Suddenly I was aware that I had briefly been asleep and had dreamed, although I could not recall the content of the dream. I could remember the last sentence I heard before falling asleep, and the sentence I heard on awakening was on the same subject—either the end of the same sentence or a sentence in the same paragraph of thought. To my embarassment, the speaker made some remark about my having dozed. I would estimate that the time I was actually asleep and dreaming could not have been more than a minute. And yet a tranformation had taken place. I found, on awakening, that my mind was clear and fresh, as if I had slept deeply for hours. For the rest of the afternoon I had no difficulty in staying awake, no problem in following the interesting lecture. The time I had been asleep was too short for me to believe that the refreshed feeling was caused by some metabolic brain process taking place during sleep. Instead, it seemed that the change in my state of consciousness was due to the dream. Being with close friends, I was not really embarrased at having fallen asleep, and the speaker's remark did not jolt me to the point of releasing adrenalin or provoking a strong desire to preserve my persona, which could have been an alternative explanation for the fresh, alert feeling.

It seemed to me as if some psychological change had been pushing for actualization and had been able to accomplish its purpose during the brief dream, altering my whole state of consciousness for hours. Perhaps it was a dream that was denied the previous night because of my work in the emergency room.

A second example, which is illustrative of changes occurring apparently at the time of a signficant dream, comes from the man in his forties. Perhaps it meets some of the objections of our hypothetical critic. The man had at one time had almost a year of analysis, but he had not been in analysis for several years before coming for consultation. He was notably successful in business, as well as in his active social life, but he had increasingly found little emotional satisfaction in these activities. In this respect, he resembled the young man 18 years old, although the older man had none of the younger man's inhibitions.

After several months of analysis, he came for an hour after a hiatus of several weeks, occasioned by his being away on business. As was customary, he had typed all his remembered dreams; he brought a copy for me and a copy for himself. Since the time available was obviously not sufficient to deal with all his dream material in a responsible way, I asked him to choose the dream that interested him most. After a moment's hesitation, he chose the following dream:

I was sitting at a table in a coffeehouse with my father. I was about 22, and he was about my age now, about the age he was when he died. He got up from the table and sat at the end of the bar. He had his guitar, and he played a song. Nobody noticed. He played another song, and still nobody noticed. Then he played a third song and sang also. Everyone stopped and listened. When he was finished, they all applauded and my father immediately became blind. He groped his way back to the table, and as I got up to help him to a seat, I thought to myself that now I wouldn't be able to marry because I would have to spend my life taking care of my blind father.

His associations to the dream motifs are given below, as nearly as possible in the words he used:

Father: He was a very ambitious, unemotional man, stubborn in a way. He was president of a civic club and other business and social clubs, taking his position quite seriously and doing a good job. I wasn't emotionally close to him. He did play the guitar and sing, but never in a coffeehouse, and never ballads—more college fight songs, that sort of thing. He had no eye trouble. He died when he was about the age I am now.

Coffeehouse: Never been in one, but I think of them as a place for companionship and being together with people. Not like a bar, where everyone is getting drunk and is on the make.

Applause: Approval for a performance.

Blindness: Unable to see. Maybe being unconscious of something.

What are you blind to? I don't know, maybe my emotions. I would like to have a better integration of the anima side of my life.

Unable to marry: That's strange, since I am married. But in the dream, I seem to be younger, maybe about 22—before I married.

While we were amplifying the dream, the man suddenly thought of how the dream might apply to his present life. He had been thinking for several weeks, he said, about how unsatisfying it was to do administrative work. He had arranged his business so as to minimize the amount of administration he was required to do, but in his civic activities he seemed to go though a repetitive pattern that had just begun to become clear to him. In any civic activity he joined, he seemed to be led inexorably to seek control of the organization. He at first thought that this might be a power drive, but when asked to examine his feelings more closely, he realized that it was the climb toward the presidency of any organization that most excited him, the climax of his involvement coming when he was finally elected and installed, when he received the applause of the other members. But after election, he found the actual administration required to fulfill his duties a chore, often boring and tedious. He was usually glad when his term of office ended, but he seemed always to be taking on similar responsibilities in one civic group after another. His compulsive seeking of responsible positions, largely for the applause of winning the race, always faced him with a long and tedious term of office, during which he had to take care of the position that his ambition had won for him. His energies were drained by such caretaking, so that he had few resources of time and energy left for his deeper emotional needs.

After he had begun to understand the dream in this light (his blind father representing his own compulsive seeking of applause), he recalled that a few days after the dream, but before the dream was understood by him consciously, he had for the first time turned down a position of responsibility in a worthwhile civic organization. He had done this even after having previously agreed to accept the position, and his action was the more significant because the organization was one whose function he considered important to the community.

Thus it would seem that the change in his characteristic behavior pattern had begun to take place after the dream but before the dream was subjected to analysis. Would it be too much to suggest that the dream had produced an immediate effect on his ego, an effect that led to a change in his emotional choices, an effect illustrative of the natural course of individuation and growth? If so, the example refutes the criticisms that dreams may simply reflect the unconscious relationships of various complexes in contact with the ego, without having a purposive and constructive goal.

The analysis of the dream had an additional impact, permitting him to form in consciousness a clear conception of some of the forces behind his behavior in declining the position. Such a conscious thought is an added safeguard against his falling into a similar pattern in the future. Also, it permits the waking ego to participate more fully in decision-making.

Another example of a clear change occurring at about the time of a significant dream, but before the dream was consciously studied, occurred in the treatment of a businessman in his early forties. He was markedly identified with his urbane and cultured persona image, behind which he felt himself to be almost empty. He had married only a year before entering treatment. At the time he came for treatment, his most striking symptom was jealousy about his wife. He did not suspect her of any current infidelity, but he believed that she might have lied about the extent of her sexual involvements between her prior marriage, which ended in divorce, and their own dating.

This jealousy erupted in a most regular way, leading to a fit of rage approximately every 2 weeks. In fact, the regularity of his upset suggested strongly that it might be based on some organic factor, as seems operative in some cases of manic–depressive psychosis. Although the contents of his delusions were clearly dependent on a psychodynamic structure, the timing of the outbursts, the periodic release of the continuing conflict, seemed too regular and too precise to correlate with events in his outer life. In many instances his rage was turned against himself, and at times he had suicidal impulses.

After one weekend in which it was expected that the 2-week rage would probably occur, he came for a consultation in an exceptionally good mood, having had no jealousy or rage at the expected time. However, he did remember having had one of his very rare dreams. In the dream he was watching the approach of a bomber, which he feared would entirely wipe out a large city glowing in the night. As he watched, a fighter plane flew up from the vicinity of the city and shot down the bomber before it could destroy the city. The fighter plane then landed, and the pilot deplaned. The dreamer was startled to see that the pilot looked exactly like himself.

It was as if this dream occurred instead of the expected outburst of rage and jealousy. Also, it semed to show the autonomous nature of his destructive rages (the bomber) and the danger of its destroying a center of civilization (the city, perhaps his conscious personality). The protective fighter plan was equally autonomous, the dream ego experiencing the scene as a passive observer, as if the very dramatic situation were entirely outside the ego.

In the amplification process, the patient happened to mention something that had caused him little notice—the fighter plane was of unusual design, like a round wafer, with a cockpit in the center, and with no visible means of propulsion. Without employing the term, he exactly described the usual conception of a flying saucer. As Jung (CW 10) suggested, some flying saucer reports may represent the projection into external reality of the image of wholeness of the Self, represented as a mandala. If this were the case in this patient, the dream would suggest that some alliance between the Self and a portion of his ego was successful in interrupting on this occasion the destructive and recurrent complex that periodically possessed his consciousness.

The departure from his expected behavior was as startling to the patient's wife as it was to me, and she had no explanation for it, since their relationship had gone on much as usual, only lacking the antici- pated rage episode. This change seemed to be correlated clearly with the dream, which occurred within the 48-hour period when the rage was expected. The dreamer himself paid scant attention to his dreams, recording them only at my request. He had not seen any particular importance in the dream prior to our discussion of it.

As in the dream of the businessman that was previously discussed, this would seem to be an example of unanalyzed dream material lead- ing to a clear change in the ego state of the waking person, even before analysis of the dream was undertaken. In this respect, it may help to clarify again the hypothetical function of the naturally occurring dream that has not been subjected to any analytical process.

Examples have been presented to illustrate how the dream ego or dream I may participate in the same situations, expressed symboli- cally, as the waking ego, the I of ordinary waking consciousness. It has been suggested that the dream may function in a compensatory man- ner, even though it is not remembered and is not subjected to formal analysis. Indeed, it is hypothesized that the dream may be the natural vehicle by which the psyche as a whole, presumably through the cent- ral archetype of the Self, exerts pressures on the ego toward enlarging its scope (as is characteristic in the first half of life) and later relativiz- ing its own sense of dominance and deferring to a more comprehensive center, the Self.

It is a well-known experience for anyone who remembers a number of his dreams that sometimes the dream I behaves either in a manner more primitive than the waking I (shadow identification?) or in a manner more mature and more effective than the waking I (identifica- tion with the bright shadow? with the Self?).

It now remains to discuss, in terms compatible with Jungian com- plex theory, a way of conceptualizing the relationship between the dream ego and the waking ego.

REFERENCES

Abenheimer KM: The ego as subject, in Wheelwright JB (ed): The Reality of the Psyche. New York, Putnam, 1968
De Becker R: The Understanding of Dreams, or The Machinations of the Night. (Trans: M Heron) London, Allen & Unwin, 1968
Edinger EF: The ego-self paradox. J Anal Psychol 5:3–18, 1960

Fordham M: The empirical foundation and theories of the self in Jung's work, in Fordham M, Gordon R, Hubback, J, et al (eds): Analytical Psychology. London, Heinemann, 1973

Hofstadter A: The vocation of consciousness. Rev Existential Psychol Psychiatr 9:64–77, 1968

Jacobi J: The Way of Individuation. (Trans: RFC Hull) London, Hodder & Stoughton, 1967

Jung CG: Memories, Dreams, and Reflections. (Ed: A Jaffe) New York, Vintage Books, 1961

Marjasch S: The 'I' in dreams. Spring. New York: Analytical Psychology Club of New York, 1966, pp. 60–75.

Neumann E: Art and the Creative Unconscious. Princeton, Princeton University Press, 1959

8
Polanyi's Tacit Knowing

The analysis of knowing on which I will rely in dealing with the relationship of the dream ego and the waking ego was developed by Polanyi* and presented by him a number of publications, most notably his book *Personal Knowledge* (1951) and a later, smaller volume, *The Tacit Dimension* (1967).

Polanyi wrote as a philosopher of science, although his original professional training was in medicine and the bulk of his scientific career, until his later years, was devoted to physical chemistry. His work in chemistry led to his election to the Royal Society.

Polanyi wrote of two types of knowing: focal and tacit. In using these terms, he specifically stated that by tacit knowing he did not mean unconscious knowing, since tacit refers to the way in which knowledge is used, not to the state of consciousness in which it occurs. However, he did not *exclude* the possibility that tacit knowledge could be unconscious.

Before progressing further, a brief outline of the main points of Polanyi's analysis of focal and tacit knowing is necessary.

---

*Prior to his death, Polanyi read the original draft of this discussion of his work and told me that it was an accurate reflection of his thought. However, he did not wish to comment on the application of his concepts to dreams. In his youth, Polanyi had been a classmate of both Franz Alexander, later a Freudian psychoanalyst, and Jolande Jacobi, the distinguished Jungian, but he himself had not studied either Jungian or Freudian theory.

Polanyi's writings deal primarily with a reconsideration of the way in which scientific knowledge is held. He opposed the currently popular myth about science in which it is believed that scientific investigation is an emotionally detached search for objective data. In this myth, the personal passion of the investigator regarding his subject of study is considered to be either negligible or, if present, a regrettable imperfection in his work.

Polanyi (1951, pp. 135–136) said that there are actually three contributing factors on which an affirmation will be judged worthy of the attention of the scientific community, and deficiency in one may be balanced by excellence in another: (1) certainty (accuracy), (2) systematic relevance (profundity), and (3) intrinsic interest. Only the first two factors function in a strictly scientific way. For example, certainty is quite high in the measurements made in physics, thus compensating to some degree for the lack of intrinsic interest in nonliving matter. Systematic relevance might cause great interest in a discovery, even though the observations might not be repeatable or recurrent. Should the Loch Ness monster be identified as a living creature previously thought to be extinct, the discovery would have great systematic interest because of its contribution to the theory of evolution of species. Such systematic relevance would attach, also, to an unquestionably demonstrated case of extrasensory perception, even though it might not be strictly repeatable.

Biology relies quite heavily on the third factor, a nonscientific criterion, compensating by virtue of our intrinsic interest in living creatures for its lack of exactitude in observation. Another example Polanyi gave of a system relying heavily on the intrinsic interest of the subject matter is Freudian psychoanalysis. The broader sweep of analytical psychology would in similar fashion seem to be dependent on intrinsic interest, since it has a low order of repeatability because of personal, unique characteristics of each analysand.

Contrary to the current myth about science, the quest of the scientist is actually guided by an intimation of some meaning not clearly specifiable in terms of what is consciously known. Stated in psychological terms, Polanyi seemed to consider scientific theories as intuitions about possible meaningful insights that, if realized, will lead forward indefinitely into the future, revealing further "true" implications not suspected in the original insight. Of course, such an intuition may be mistaken, and the comprehensive entity to which it leads may be false. This is simply to say that something is risked, that the striving toward more comprehensive meaning may miscarry. This is quite similar to the search for understanding in psychoanalytic work. There, too, the process may miscarry, and the insight arrived at may be (as in the case of paranoid schizophrenia) an autistic system of thought that is overcomprehensive, pulling into its web of meaning facts that do not have the implications mistakenly assigned to them.

This passionate striving toward fuller ranges of meaning, toward more comprehensive entities, underlies not only scientific endeavor; it was seen by Polanyi as intrinsic to the fashion in which man develops as a human being. Rudimentary forms of the same ability can be cited even in other species of life. An earthworm, for example, may be trained in a laboratory, by means of mild electric shocks, to always take the right-hand turning in a maze. Assume that it takes an average of 100 trials for the worm to learn the situation, so that it almost invariably takes the turning toward the right; suppose now that the situation is reversed, and the worm receives a shock when it turns to the right, but not to the left. Af first it tries to repeat the turning toward the right that had been learned, only to be shocked each time the previously correct choice is made. It will relearn the situation, so that the majority of choices are toward the left, and it will learn the new choice in fewer trials than were required in the original situation.

A worm analyst might be tempted to say that his patient had an "increase in consciousness" during the first training period, which produced a more coherent and conscious model of the overall situation in which the worm existed: reversal of right–left choice within the terms of this model was a simpler and more easily learned response than the original construction of the model itself.

Of more interest is the fashion in which human infants acquire by gradual stages the abilities that fit them into society. Principal among these skills is language. In learning to speak, the child seems first to show an awareness of the meaningfulness of adult speech, which he cannot as yet comprehend in any focal and specifiable way, although he may respond to emotional tones of the adult voice. He then seems to discover the meaning of speech, first as names and vocabulary, which he later enriches by subjecting his vocabulary to a higher form of control in the formation of grammatical sentences.

Polanyi examined carefully one part of the myth about science— that scientists hold various theoretical positions only for convenience and are prepared to discard a theory the moment evidence inconsistent with the theory is produced. As a case in point, he discussed the supposed relationship of the Michelson-Morley experiment, performed in Cleveland in 1887, to the formulation by Einstein of the theory of relativity, conceived in 1905. The accepted textbook account states that the failure of the Michelson-Morley experiment to demonstrate ether drift led Einstein to abandon the Newtonian conception of space as being at absolute rest, substituting a language of relativity in which only the motion of bodies relative to each other would be expressed.

There are two facts showing that in this case the actual progress of science did not follow the mechanistic view of prevailing scientific dogma, based on an artificial separation of subjectivity and objectivity and seeking to eliminate from science "passionate, personal, human appraisals of theories, or at least to minimize their function to that of a negligible by-play" (Polanyi, 1951, pp. 15–16). First, the Michelson-Morley experiment did not show negative results, as is usually stated; actually it produced evidence of the relative motion of the supposed ether as not exceeding a quarter of the earth's orbital velocity, an effect of the same magnitude as that being found by Miller and his collaborators in a long series of experiments undertaken between 1902 and 1926. These supposed effects of ether drift, it now seems, may have been due to statistical fluctuations and temperature effects. Second, Polanyi offered Einstein's own testimony that the discovery of relativity dates from a paradox that occurred to Einstein at 16 years of age.

Scientific discovery, like other skillful human performances, is achieved by an intuitive appraisal of potential orderliness in observed data. In a more routine skill, or in a progressive series of discoveries, the performer seems to be relying on rules that he is not consciously capable of specifying: "By watching the master and emulating his efforts in the presence of his example, the apprentice unconsciously picks up the rules of the art, including those which are not explicitly known to the master himself" (Polanyi, 1951, p. 53).

Polanyi wrote of awareness as being both focal and subsidiary. This can be illustrated by considering the way that the common act of driving a nail with a hammer utilizes both a *focal* awareness of the task of hammering and a *subsidiary* awareness of the impact of the hammer handle against the palm. The skill in hammering can be afected, as can any skilled performance, if the performer redirects his focal awareness toward that part of the feat that is usually relied on in a subsidiary way in order that the performer may attend to the focal aspect. The subsidiary elements participate in sustaining the whole, and they derive their meaning, within the whole, from this function: "While focal awareness is necessarily conscious, subsidiary awareness may vary over all degrees of consciousness" (Polanyi, 1951, p. 92). Paying too much focal awareness to the impact of the hammer handle on the palm will cause the head of the hammer to miss the nail.

In *The Tacit Dimension,* Polanyi (1967) succinctly presented his further thinking about the structure of tacit knowing. Thinking is presented as having a *from–to* structure, the subject relying on some knowledge in a *tacit* fashion in order to have *focal* knowledge of other contents of his awareness. In the introduction to this volume, Polanyi stated: ''I shall show, for example, that when originality breeds new values, it breeds them tacitly, by implicaton; we cannot choose explicitly a set of new values, but must submit to them by the very act of creating or adopting them.'' This statement seems to echo Jung's use of the term *symbol* as that which most clearly apprehends a psychic content that cannot, at that time, be further reduced and specified. Polanyi stated: ''I have shown that any attempt to avoid responsibility for shaping the beliefs which we accept as true is absurd; but the existentialist claim of choosing our beliefs from zero is now proved absurd too. Thought can live only on grounds which we adopt in the service of a reality to which we submit.'' If Polanyi had been speaking in terms of the unconscious rather than in terms of the poles of focal and tacit knowing, this last statement could be taken as referring to the way in which the ego participates in (or sufers) the judgments of the unconscious, often met as outer projections. The ego must accept responsibility for its beliefs, although it is not sufficiently powerful or extensive to enforce its will on other parts of the personality. In fact, the claim to be able to choose our beliefs from zero, which Polanyi saw as characteristic of an existentialist view, would in a psychological language seem to indicate a state of inflation.

Having knowledge of a comprehensive entity must inevitably involve, in Polanyi's conception, a tacit component and a focal component. The way that we know our bodies, for example, is by tacitly dwelling in them in order to attend *to* the outside world. In normal health, and when the mind is alert, our nervous systems appear as ''transparent''—we assume their functions as our own, in a tacit way, and direct our conscious attention toward focal knowledge of some external entity. The same tacit–focal relationship may be thought of as obtaining even in the brain. One might say that the neural processes are tacitly relied on in order to attend to the world of phenomena that is beyond the nervous system but that impinges on it from the external world.

If tacit knowing is a part of all knowledge, as Polanyi believed, the implied goal of science to minimize or eliminate any subjectivism is impossible and may indeed lead to fallacies. This may seem analogous to that state often seen in individuals in which one psychological function is hypertrophied to a point that the personality as a whole becomes disorganized. Perfection of one function of the personality produces a compensatory movement in the unconscious portion of the psyche, which awaits only a decrease in consciousness in order to correct, perhaps abruptly and forcibly, the onesidedness of the conscious position. Such a psychological theme underlies numerous fairy tales of the type in which the old king seeks to decide his successor, frequently through a contest to determine which of his sons can find the most suitable wife. And an unconscious balancing compensation might underlie, it would seem, even Freud's (SE 6) view of slips of the tongue.

Polanyi believed he had shown that the goal of formalizing knowledge to the exclusion of any tacit knowing is self-defeating. In an analogous manner, it is understood in analytical psychology that any attempt to thoroughly reduce the personality to specifiable causes, as Freud suggested, is not possible, since the psyche seems to contain a progressive, synthetic force as well.

In his analysis of comprehensive entities, Polanyi defined higher and lower strata of organization. These strata are related in such a manner that each succeeding higher ordering depends on the reliable working of those levels of organization beneath it. In fact, the higher ordering imposes its configuration on the lower order only in those properties left indeterminate by the laws governing the lower order. "We may call this control exercised by the organizational principle of a higher level on the particulars forming its lower level *the principle of marginal control*" (Polanyi, 1951, p. 40).

From this it follows that the properties of a lower organization may destroy a higher organizational system that is dependent on their functioning, but they cannot explain the occurrence of the higher level of organization. Thus arises the problem of *emergence* — how it is possible for a more complex organization to arise at all.

The design of machines, for example, illustrates the embodiment of the laws of mechanics in those boundary conditions left indeterminate by the laws of physics and chemistry. If a lever in a complicated machine changes it structure or breaks because of metal fatigue, which *is* explainable in the language of chemistry and physics, the complex machine may cease to perform its designated function. Thus a change governed by the laws of physics and chemistry is sufficient to explain the breakdown of the mechanical function. But there is nothing in the language of physics and chemistry that can explain, on a chemical or physical basis, the design of the complex machine. This can be linked to evolutionary thought by pointing out, as Polanyi did, that excessive emphasis on the survival of species leaves relatively untouched the more important question of how any one individual of an advanced species can arise in the first place.

In the psychological sphere, the similar question of the emergence of higher levels of personality organization was at first ignored because of the emphasis on drives during the early years of psychoanalysis. However, it came to occupy a place of central importance in Jung's analytical psychology, being embodied most notably in his concept of the *Self* as an organizing center of the entire psyche. The problem of the ego in attempting to transcend the current level of organization—the tale of the old king and his sons—focuses on what Polanyi described as the inability of any one level to gain control over its own boundary conditions and thereby bring into existence a level higher than itself. The emergence of the higher level comes from something that is not organized at the current level—that is, something that is left indeterminate in the organization of the currently existing highest level. In the fairy tale, this may be the missing feminine side of existence. In the individual personality stuck at a certain stage of life, it may be the undeveloped inferior function.

WORD-ASSOCIATION EXPERIMENT AND TACIT KNOWING

If the universe is conceived as a hierarchy of ascending levels of complexity, with each level imposing control on those boundary conditions and possibilities left indeterminate by the level below it, how may we understand the function of consciousness in such a universe? The situation may be exemplified by an area familiar to analytical psychologists—the word-association experiment, which first convinced Jung (CW 2) of the possible validity of Freud's work and which made him aware that there was something happening unconsciously that interfered with normal word associations, either in the form of the response, as with the clang associations, or in their production, as with a delayed reaction time or complete blocking of response.

Wundt and others had used this experiment to study those ways in which words and ideas were paired together in the mind. A stimulus word was presented, and the subject's immediate association was recorded. Generally, words seemed to be paired by similarity, by differences, or by some past association.

However, in some cases the subject was slow in responding; in other cases the subject blocked completely and was unable to give a response to a particular word. For the purposes of studying word association, such responses were meaningless, a failed response giving no data for investigation.

Jung's remarkable insight about this situation was the the failed responses were themselves important, a prima materia that could, with a different focus, yield startling information about the emotional workings of the unconscious mind (CW 2, especially sections VII and X). By relying on the failed responses of the subject's conscious mind in order to attend to the workings of his unconscious mind, Jung began to elaborate his concept of the emotionally toned complex, a group of ideas and images related by a common emotional tone. Examples are familiar to everyone: father complex, mother complex, power complex, inferiority complex. Indeed, the success of his insight led to ubiquitous use of the term *complex* far outside the bounds of its original meaning in analytical psychology and produced banalization of the term.

Jung's primary observation about the word-association experiment was that something interferes with the subject's conscious mind and keeps it from doing what it intends. Something produces an unexplainable failure. His investigations of the subject's associations to the crucial stimulus words allowed him to infer the presence of an unconscious complex of ideas to which the stimulus word is also assimilated. The stimulus word activates a complex, which then behaves in such a manner as to alter the state of consciousness of the subject. And all this happens without the subject himself being aware of what causes his "failure." Even if he intellectually knows of the theory of complexes, he is not consciously, one might say focally, aware of which particular complexes are constellated by a certain stimulus word.

The subject, like the experimenter himself, can become focally aware of the constellated complex only by relying on his own associations to the stimulus word in order to attend to the complex. Both the subject and the experimenter, to become aware of the complex, attend *from* the associations *to* the complex. In the initial set of the experiment, the subject tries to attend to the stimulus word, for which he must rely, in a tacit way, on his own mind, including whatever complexes are constellated at that moment.

It is then possible to state that the failure, the subject's inability to execute successfully the initial instructions of the experiment, can be explained by the innate behavior of those complexes on which his consciousness must rely in order to attend to the task of the experiment. This is analogous to Polanyi's description of the failure of a machine. The laws of physics and chemistry leave open certain boundary conditions, those of mechanics, which can be shaped by the mind of the inventor so as to form a machine, whose principles are imposed upon the boundary conditions left open by physical and chemical laws.

Thus the laws of physics and chemistry cannot explain the presence of the machine, for they do not contain principles of the machine. However, they can explain a failure of the machine, since the mechanics embodied in the machine rely on the orderly working of levels below them, and these lower levels are explainable by physics and chemistry. In a similar manner, the conscious mind of the subject in a word-association experiment is relying on the orderly behavior of his mind, which can partially be described as a structure of complexes, in order to perform a task at a higher level—attending to the instructions of the experiment. The presence of complexes cannot account for his successfuly performing the task of the experiment, but they can explain his failure to do so.

It is significant that the word-association experiment, as used in analytical psychology, is divided into two parts. In the first, responses are elicited to a list of stimulus words, the time taken for responding being noted, as well as the response itself. In the second part of the experiment, those responses that have shown some indicator of complex activity during the initial session are further explored by asking for personal amplifications—ideas associated in the subject's mind with the words. Then the experimenter, in a rather creative leap, tries to make sense of the various indicators, postulating the presence of constellated unconscious complexes. This information may then be used in a psychotherapeutic way to help the subject understand the workings of his own unconscious mind.

Using the language of tacit knowing, the word-association experiment would appear as a situation in which:

1. The subject relies on his mind, composed partially of constellated psychological complexes, in order to attend to the task of the experiment.
2. His performance of the task is impaired by the presence of activated complexes.
3. While the subject is attempting to complete the formal task of giving his most rapid word associations, the tester is relying in a tacit way on the "mistakes," the atypical responses of the subject, in order to attend to an entirely different comprehensive entity— the unconscious complexes constellated in the subject's mind.
4. In the second phase of the experiment, both tester and subject rely on the subject's previous responses in order to understand a postulated entity, the constellated unconscious complexes. In this phase, both tester and subject attempt to comprehend the complexes that only the tester was able to observe in step three.

It is understood, of course, that the tester himself must rely on his own unconscious complexes in a tacit way while attending to the performance of the subject. His own complexes may distort his perception of the subject, either in the testing situation or in an analytical relationship. This consideration led to the basic maxim that the analyst must himself be analyzed. In mythical language, it is expressed in the image of the wounded healer.

This analysis of the interaction of subject and tester in the word-association experiment may be taken as a paradigm for much that takes place in analysis, particularly in reductive phases, when an attempt is made to apprehend and take an attitude toward those contents of a complex nature that are active in the analysand's unconscious. To this extent, the work of analysis parallels, at least for the analyst, the recognition of a gestalt, which Polanyi (1951, p. 57) investigated in his analysis of cognition.

DREAM EGO AND I

It is now possible to apply the concept of focal and tacit knowing, as developed by Polanyi, to the problem of the relationship between the dream ego and the waking ego, the sense of I-ness in dreams and the same sense of I-ness during the ordinary waking state. Jung himself (CW 8:256) suggested that dreams might rely on subliminal memory traces that are no longer able to influence consciousness directly. To facilitate discussion, it may be helpful to introduce a preliminary distinction between two sources of the feeling of I-ness, although these two wellsprings are mixed in actual experience.

The first is the Self, as the archetypal core of the ego, the template of a sense of centered orderliness and continuity that seems to be the very unique feeling of the ego complex. The second, of a less archetypal nature, is the sense of continuity and identity that comes from a continual reliance (I would suggest that this is in the sense of a tacit reliance) on certain complexes that are accepted as the content of the ego image. Ego image is chosen instead of self image because self image could easily become confused with the common way the word self is employed: self-esteem, self-reliance, etc. It should be remembered that Self and central archetype are equivalent.

There is an almost universal and perhaps unavoidable tendency to confuse these two sources of the sense of I. The usual situation is a feeling that the I-ness is dependent *only* on the stability of the complex structure associated with the ego, and on those outer objects that are identified with this complex structure through projection. But such stability derived from a persistent association of complexes is more properly conceived as the stability of the ego image. There are actually a number of ego images, one of which tends to predominate. I call this the dominant ego image (doegi).

This unconscious confusion of the two hypothesized sources of continuity leads to a sense of anxiety when the tacit components of the ego image are threatened. Such threats may arise either from without, in interpersonal relations, or from within, from the dissociative pressure of autonomous complexes or from the constant centering pressure of the Self tending to move the ego toward a greater inclusiveness and wholeness. Even though the pressure of the Self on the ego seems to have the purpose of enlarging the ego, it may be experienced as a threat of dissolution by an ego too firmly identified with its dominant ego image. Viewed from the standpoint of an ego partially free from identification with a changing dominant ego image, such pressure might appear as the compensatory function of the unconscious. To an individuating ego, whose primacy has been relinquished to the more comprehensive center of the Self, such pressure would probably seem to be more complementary in nature. To a hypothetical "transparent" ego, no longer resisting Self pressures, it might seem to be the strange sensation, described by Jung, of being the object of a superordinate subject (Jung, 1961, p. 323). An ego too weak to maintain some structure through which the Self may act could be overwhelmed, of course, by a flood of unconscious material, in which case it would appear psychotic.

Those unconscious complexes that are tacitly assumed by the ego to constitute the contents of the ego image with which it identifies may be strengthened by social reinforcement. In childhood, this takes the form of approval or disapproval by the parents or other dominant adults. The spontaneous activities of the child that are positively reinforced tend to become incorporated into the ego (and, at a slightly later age, into the persona), while those that are negatively reinforced tend to be repressed and tend to cluster in the image of the shadow.

Individuation might be described in terms of the complex theory as the gradual reshaping of the ego, under the pressure of the Self, so that it becomes more inclusive and more comprehensive. There is a loosening of the ego's transient identification with any particular ego image, so that it becomes increasingly able to reflect, with decreasing distortion, those contents of the total psyche that are focused and coordinated by the Self and given expression, to the extent that a time sequence allows, in the growth of the individuating ego.

In such an individuation process, the contents of the ego continually shift, gradually incorporating certain non-ego complexes, such as the shadow and persona, and perhaps parts originally associated with the animus-anima. Each new expansion of the structure of the ego complex makes untenable some particular form of a previous ego image, which must be left behind as an outgrown shell. Such changes may be pictured as the connection of complexes to the ego, or the incorporation of a complex into the ego. I would suggest that the language of focal and tacit knowing is of particular usefulness in conceptualizing this process. Instead of repression *by* an ego, or *connection* of a complex to the ego, it should be possible to speak of an active process of change in which the specific complexes on which the ego tacitly relies are altered. Thus, while the archetypal core of the ego assures a sense of continuity of existence in spite of shifting contents, the reworking of the specific contents on which the ego tacitly relies constitutes the point at which the unfolding of the Self, through the time-bound ego, generates the observable individuation process.

The point at which this process can be most clearly observed is in dreams, which may be thought of as the metabolism of the ego. Contents come into association with the ego or pass away from such association, often in response to the attitude the ego takes toward them when they are constellated in a dream or in the nexus of waking reality. The ego is like a gatekeeper who can permit or deny entrance into the boundaries he guards but who is helpless to command the appearance of a particular entrant (content), however much he might desire it.

For illustration, let us reexamine the dream of the man who had compulsively sought the presidency of a number of socially important clubs, only to be recurrently dissatisfied with the actual duties of the offices. His dream, in précis, was of being in a coffeehouse with his father. The father left their table and went to the bar, where he played two songs on the guitar, while being ignored by the other patrons. For his third song, the father sang, accompanying himself on the guitar. The clients of the coffeehouse listened attentively; when the father finished, they showered him with applause. At the sound of the applause, the father became blind; he groped his way back to the table where the dreamer was seated. As he helped his blind father to a chair, the dreamer thought to himself that he would never be able to marry, since he would have to devote myself to caring for his blind father.

Let us consider the entire dream as if it were a snapshot of a particular complex structure, or connection of complexes, on which the dreamer's waking ego had been tacitly relying as a part of his unexamined dominant ego image. It will be necessary to think of the entire structure as existing in the unconscious in a simultaneous way, although it is presented in the dream as a pictorial sequence. The dream can be paraphrased thus:

1. The dream I is related to (sitting at a table with) a complex that is based on the experience of the father.
2. This connection is easily dissociable (the father gets up).
3. The activity of the dissociated father complex is to seek public approval (applause) for a performance. This is sought from unknown people, the patrons of the coffeehouse, who are not in personal relationship with either the dream I or the father complex.
4. The approval of this collective mass of unknown people blinds the father complex (i.e., leads to unconsciousness).
5. The dream I has a feeling change and experiences the real cost of caring for the blinded father, whose activities leading to the blindness had not been opposed in the past. He will be "unable to marry"—unable to form a genuine transformative relationship with the anima. This can impede relating to a real woman.

This dream, even before it was discussed, coincided with a change in the emotional attitude of the dreamer, a change that led him to alter for the first time a long-established pattern of compulsive behavior. This could be thought of as a change in the construction of those complexes on which the ego had tacitly relied without there being a focal awareness of the pattern.

The original situation before the dream can be pictured as in Figure 1. The change in structure following the dream, but before it was interpreted, might appear as in Figure 2. In this figure there has been a split, the ego dissociating itself from the entire dominant ego image previously based on the complex structure presented in the dream.

I

Conscious	Focal awareness:	repetitively experienced neurotic pattern in the outer world
Unconscious	Tacit knowledge:	constellated complex structure of father–son relationship; dominant ego image (doegi) unconsciously (tacitly) based on father complex

Fig. 1. Dreamer's original situation

I plus emotional change

Conscious	Focal awareness:	emotional change
Unconscious	Tacit knowledge:	change in complex structure

Fig. 2. Change in dreamer's situation after the dream, but before dream interpretation

This is experienced as a change in feeling, not yet as a conscious idea. Figure 3 shows the further change occurring after the dream is formally interpreted in analysis. Here the ego not only dissociates from the previous complex structure but also forms an image of the complex structure that persists in consciousness and allows the ego more opportunity to identify similar structures should they present in slightly different imagery.

I am aware, of course, that there are other possible ways of presenting such a change, as by discussing a change in libido. In the libido metaphor, the change would appear to be one in which a quantity of energy was freed from the father complex and made available for the uses of the ego, simultaneously raising the level of consciousness. Although I have no basic quarrel with such language, it seems more meaningful to present the primary change in structural terms, which in themselves make the libido change more evident and allow a more precise relationship to the crucial area of ego image change.

To summarize, the analysis of focal and tacit knowing can help to conceptualize what might be termed the metabolism of those complex structures on which the ego tacitly relies for its sense of a persistent ego image, which can be distinguished from the sense of I-ness derived from the Self as the archetypal core of the ego complex itself. The concept of tacit knowing, when thus extended to intrapsychic events, permits a useful description of many dream processes and links the concepts of analytical psychology more closely to the general procedures of science as described by Polanyi. Applied to the problems of describing the individuation process as reflected in dreams, the con-

I plus conscious awareness

	Focal awareness:	interpreted dream in relation to
Conscious		life pattern
Unconscious	Tacit knowledge:	change in complex structure

Fig. 3. Further change following dream interpretation

cept of tacit knowing introduces a shift in emphasis from the topographical (and the mechanism of repression) to the structural (the contents of a personified complex). This shift in emphasis more clearly highlights the importance of the *choices* of the ego in influencing, although not strictly determining, its own tacit structure.

TACIT KNOWING AND ANALYTICAL PRACTICE

Several other aspects of psychoanalytic practice can be usefully conceptualized in terms of focal and tacit knowing. Three of the most important are (1) the forgetting of previously analyzed material, (2) changes in levels of consciousness, and (3) experiences of transcendence.

Forgetting Analytical Material

During the course of the analytic process, many memories may be uncovered, and there may be many dreams that for times of varying length exert profound effects on the consciousness of the analysand. Many times, however, such material is later forgotten and cannot be recalled to focal awareness by an act of will, although the effect of the material on the growth of the analysand's ego is clear. In such instances, it would seem that the material is first brought to focal awareness, then is again allowed to sink into the unconscious tacit state, where it continues to participate in the ego consciousness but only as a tacit substrate on which the ego relies for awareness. Such a change is essentially similar to that described in the preceding example of the father-complex dream. In that example the change in the ego occurring before the formal analysis of the dream would resemble a change in which material had been brought to a state of conscious perception by the ego (in the dream state) and then relied on in a tacit way (although differently than before the dream) to produce a change in the emotional state of the waking ego.

Forgetting dreams: The classic psychoanalytic theory of Freud ascribes the forgetting of dreams to a re-repression of material that was allowed to reach consciousness in a disguised form only during the sleep state, when the vigilance of the "censor" was relaxed. In Freud's view, the remembering of dreams would seem to be due to either (1) a failure of re-repression or (2) a success of the dream in so disguising the repressed infantile sexual wish that it could not be discerned even by the awake ego fully conscious of the remembered dream.

The focal–tacit structure of ego consciousness permits a more general and less defensive interpretation of the forgetting of dreams. The typical dream, involving a subjective sense of ego participation (Marjasch's second type) presents the dream I with a focal awareness of its relationship to other complexes. These complexes, when the dreamer is awake, may well constitute part of the tacitly held material, whether conscious or unconscious, on which the ego relies for its sense of consistent ego image. The dream, in this view, represents a situation in which the ego can look into its own inner complex structure. When the dreamer awakens, however, all this ego structure is then relied on in a tacit way in order to turn focal attention toward the outside world. Since it is difficult for material to be simultaneously in both focal and tacit compartments, the dream is difficult to recall. In an analogous way, it is impossible to simultaneously maintain a given part of a drawing as both figure and ground, although during the time it is perceived as ground it is possible to remember that it was previously seen as figure, and vice versa.

Changes in Levels of Consciousness

It is not uncommon to find that during the course of a successful analysis some change occurs in the attitude of the analysand toward certain crucial past events in his life. Often this does not involve any remembering of material that was previously repressed, and in that sense it does not fit well into a topographical model emphasizing repression. Instead, it seems to be the meaning of the past that is altered, not the memories themselves. Such change could be discussed, I believe, in terms of changes in the focal–tacit relationship of certain complexes comprising the ego, although the state of consciousness of such material might remain unaltered.

Experiences of Transcendence

During the height of the interest in psychedelic drugs, it was frequently reported that users of major hallucinogenic drugs sometimes experienced a sense of transcendence of the ordinary ego state. In a review of several hundred users of hallucinogenic drugs, I found only a few such peak experiences; thus they appear to be rare occurrences in the population studied. That they do occur, however, is not disputed. It may be useful to consider such experiences as transient awareness of the archetypal core of the ego, independent of the ego image. They appear to be very similar to nondrug peak experiences. The authentic experience is easily distinguished from the experience of inflation, which is rather more common with the psychedelic drugs.

A NOTE ON THE HIGHEST LEVEL

It would be comforting if we could agree with Polanyi (1967) that psychologically the highest level accessible to man is his moral sense. With some reservations, such agreement is possible, if the term *moral* is taken in a very personalistic way, realizing that an individual, in being moral to his own deeper nature, may at times find himself at variance with conventional morality or with other parts of himself.

But there are even more complex objections to a man's morality as the highest level of organization of comprehensive entities. This is the strange experience that seems to be part of the emotional state of individuation. Jung described it as the ego feeling that is the object of some superordinate subject. In his own material, it is represented by the dreams of the flying saucer and the yogi in meditation (Jung, 1961).

It is difficult to read Jung's remarks about these dreams except in such a way that it would seem that some agency other than his ego was relying on something other than his ego complex in order to be focally aware of his ego.

A patient, during the most critical episode of his life, once described feeling "as if I were filled with an inner cosmos of planets, suns, and stars, all whirling in their orbits, and there was no one there, but *I* was in all of it." Perhaps this was a fleeting perception of the inner cosmos, of which the ego, the I, is the representative in the outer world.

REFERENCES

Jung CG: Memories, Dreams, and Reflections. New York, Vintage Books, 1961
Polanyi M: Personal Knowledge. Chicago, University of Chicago Press, 1951
Polanyi M: The Tacit Dimension. London, Routledge & Kegan Paul, 1967

PART III

Clinical Dreams

We need a dream-world in order to discover the features of the real world we think we inhabit (and which may actually be just another dream-world)

Feyerabend, *Against Method*

9
Neglected Clinical Uses of Dreams

The interpretation of dreams for their classic psychoanalytic use is not the only value that dreams can have in clinical practice. Dreams can aid in diagnosis and prognosis, in deciding questions of medication, and in choosing between different modes of therapy; they can serve as indicators of past material to be explored and as a point of departure for the discussion of current problems. Nevertheless, interpretation of dreams in reference to the unconscious structure of the mind remains the primary focus in Jungian psychoanalysis. The Freudian writer Sharpe (1937) listed other uses that dreams can have: the dream can be used to placate the analyst; the dream can serve as a symbol of power, as fantasied control of a fecal product, as control of the analyst, and as a love gift.

There have been earlier attempts to employ the dream in a diagnostic way (Karpman, 1946). Kramer and associates (1967) suggested that the early memory of a patient better reflects the long-range characterologic traits of the personality, while dreams reflect the current situation of the mind.

DREAMS IN DIAGNOSIS AND PROGNOSIS

Dreams are frequently helpful in gaining a rapid impression of the likely prognosis in a new psychotherapeutic situation. While the ego may be obscured by dramatic symptoms, the dream is more likely to show the deeper movement of the psychic process. For example, a woman in her middle thirties, uncertain about whether to have a hysterectomy, dreamed that she found a peaceful, happy cow and led her home to a safe barn. The dream aided her analyst in concluding that the hysterectomy was not likely to evoke a sense of lost femininity, a conclusion that was proved correct by her smooth postoperative psychological course.

A young man in his late twenties, unable to establish close ties with a woman and afraid of his homosexual impulses, dreamed the following dream early in his analysis:

I got into a semi-kayak and was paddling alternately on both sides. I was going along the rim of a lake, but as I paddled northward, I could see that eventually I would be in the middle of the lake where the water was rougher. I stayed along the edge of the lake and came to a point where the lake met the ocean. Only a glass shield separated them. The waves of the lake were getting larger. I figured the depth of the lake to be 20 feet. I got to the mouth of the river. The current was very strong, so I paddled hard into the river. Gradually the river was less rapid and was narrowing. I realized the direction of the water flow had reversed. Pretty soon it was just a trickle.

The dream continued, but this portion is sufficient to illustrate that the fearful symptoms (waves) subside with the ego's effort, and a change in the flow of the water (libido) takes place. This same lake image was repeated in another of this man's dreams after a period of several weeks. In the subsequent dream, his boat actually turned over, but he then realized that the water was no more than 3 feet deep. Both dreams indicate a hopeful prognosis, in spite of surface symptoms.

A woman suffering from a turbulent marriage dreamed that she saw Noah's ark at a distance. It continued to change shape. She realized that the people who were on deck had to hold their breath when it changed shape, for they were temporarily under water. She was afraid that she would be unable to hold her breath a sufficient length of time. Within 2 weeks of the dream, she found that she could relate more directly to her husband, and she had a sense of her marriage enduring, although much work remained to be done.

PROGRESS

When the therapist is sufficiently aware of the dream life of a patient, it is sometimes possible to follow changes in the progress of the patient in dream motifs. A yound schizophrenic man had a series of dreams in which his car would begin to roll backward out of control. Each dream seemed to be followed by several days of regression in his level of functioning. Finally, he himself learned to watch for this motif and to ask for an increase in medication when the image suggested he might begin to have more symptoms. The same image of a car rolling backward might have a different meaning for another patient, although a particular image in a series of dreams from a given patient is often a reliable indicator. Before a period of marked improvement, this same young man dreamed that a minotaur lived behind his own home. A young woman matador (an anima figure?) protected him from the bull-man with capework. As the minotaur charged again, he took the cape himself and skillfully eluded the attack. The ego taking over and assimilating strength and skill that had previously been functioning in the ego's behalf, but separate from it, can be seen in this image.

ENCOURAGEMENT OF THERAPIST

It sometimes happens that no improvement can be seen clinically, and the outcome of a therapy endeavor becomes unclear in the mind of the therapist. The sensitive interaction between patient and therapist makes discouragement of the therapist a potentially decisive factor. If the patient is producing dreams, it is possible in many instances to get a reliable impression of the nature of the unconscious processes, which may indicate more possibility for health than the patient is able to verbalize. One woman looked very withdrawn and impassive for almost a year, but her dream images showed great activity and healthy interactions. The dreams appeared to indicate more health than the patient demonstrated. Although she claimed not to understand many of her dreams, they provided reassurance to the therapist that healthier personality factors were being prepared in her unconscious. Through a combination of group therapy and individual psychotherapy, she eventually actualized in her conscious personality the previously dissociated and healthy attributes in her shadow. Her initial feeling was that her life would be meaningless if she did not have a child (she had had numerous miscarriages); subsequently she successfully carried two pregnancies to term, and she depended less on the role of mother for her self-esteem. Furman (1962) reported a similar case in which the dreams showed that the ego was capable of functioning at a higher level than was clinically apparent.

CHANGES IN
TRANSFERENCE–COUNTERTRANSFERENCE

Dreams are clues to the way in which the unconscious mind of the patient views the relationship with the analyst. It is important, of course, that the analyst be sensitive to any dreams of his own in which unrecognized attitudes toward patients may appear. One woman who had resisted bringing her central problem to group therapy dreamed that she fell off a ship into the ocean in an attempt to rescue her (dream) baby. She was rescued, and as she went into the interior of the rescue ship, she found all the members of her therapy group sitting in a circle, waiting to begin. Because of the dream, she decided to tell the group of her most hidden problem, and she achieved both emotional relief and insight into her neurotic patterns.

CHANGES IN RELATIONSHIPS

Important changes in one's relationships with friends and family, as well as one's situation at work and elsewhere, may be foreshadowed in dreams. In one instance, two persons who had troubled relationships with a third person dreamed within 2 days of each other similar dreams that the third person had died. Objectively the third person remained in good health, but both dreamers felt free of what had been a difficult relationship for them both prior to their independent dreams.

UNDERSTANDING SPONTANEOUS CHANGES

An important affective change may occur without the person knowing the meaning of the change. In such situations, the dream material may offer a clue as to what complexes are involved and what change has taken place. The dream of the man taking care of his blind father, as previously discussed, is such an example.

DREAMS IN DEPRESSION

Depression has long been known to interfere with sleep because of the accompanying insomnia and early awakening. Although they are awake more often during the night, depressed patients appear to have a normal ratio between dream time and the amount of time spent in deep sleep (Murray, 1965). Hartmann (1973) suggested that depression is characterized by a need for more dream time. An increase in dreaming has been reported to coincide with clinical improvement in depression (Baer and associates, 1967). Baer and associates (1967) also found that depressed patients had few dreams relating to loss of self-esteem, and many had pleasant dreams, in contrast to their waking depression. The depressed person's dreams characteristically show him in a plausible situation with a family member, with hostility being shown either from or toward the dream ego in one-half of cases (Kramer and associates, 1968). A control series of dreams of paranoid schizophrenics included more strangers, more implausible situations, and a higher frequency of the dream ego being the victim of hostility. Dream recall, but not the frequency of dreaming, is decreased in depression; the manifest dreams of depressed patients contain more themes of "escape and helplessness-hopelessness" (Kramer and associates, 1968). In depressed patients there is some suggestion that decreases in dreaming, possibly due to medications, may be associated with suicidal tendencies (Detre, 1966). Clinical improvement of depression may occur before changes are seen in the dreams, which may show both escape themes and helplessness-hopelessness themes (Kramer and associates, 1965). Dreams of deeply depressed patients may be pleasant (Miller, 1969), which is consistent with the compensatory function of dreaming. Dreams of the same patients may become troubled at the time that clinical improvement occurs (Miller, 1969), which again is consistent with a change in the needed compensation. Miller (1969) noted that the dream ego of the depressed patient tends to be the recipient of hurt rather than the source. This observation suggests the relevance of such psychoanalytic constructs as Fairbairn's "internal saboteur" and Wisdom's "orbiting introject"—terms for a complex that behaves toward the dream ego as a persecutory internal object. These studies of manifest dreams seem to be consistent with the psychoanalytic formula of depression representing hostility directed toward the ego. Additional evidence is presented by Beck and Ward (1961), who found masochistic images (hostility toward the dream ego) in the manifest dreams of moderately to severely depressed patients. In a related psychoanalytic study of a single case, Volkan (1971) found that a man unable to end a prolonged state of grief after the death of his father had a series of dreams that the father was not dead, but he began dreaming of the father as dead as the problem was worked through.

The fine structure of dreams may help to follow the course of depression. A man in his late thirties had three clinical depressions of a severe nature, each precipitated by his receiving well-deserved promotion at work. The neurotic nature of the depression was clearly understood, but emotional insight had not been obtained. As his depression began to improve, he had the following dream:

> A bird was helping her young ones out of the nest so they could fly. Next it was a snake helping its young ones out of a nest. The last young snake said he could get out of the nest on his own.

Note the images of a new beginning (the young birds and snakes), help from the parental bird and snake, and autonomy in the last young snake. But both birds and snakes are far from human realm. Here, a knowledge of folktales is helpful, for birds and snakes are recurring images for a pair of opposites—the birds above and the snakes below, sky and earth. An Irish folktale, "The Battle of the Birds," begins with interaction between a bird and a snake and proceeds to images of human development. The Mexican emblem of a bird with a snake on a rock has some of the same import of a bringing together of extreme opposites.

As his improvement continued, his dreams took a more ordinary form and tended to show him in water, often an image of the unconscious mind. They thus could indicate his ego being effectively integrated into the unconscious. Two examples follow:

> I played in a hot spring, like at home in Arkansas, with my son.
> I played volleyball in a pool of water with friends from high school.

Note that the son may have some connection to the same complex as the young snakes and birds, but in a more "outer" human layer. Also note the temporal regression ("friends from high school") to a time when there was no depression and the ego felt secure.

ANXIETY

Anxiety is a frequent psychiatric complaint, ranging from mild anxiety to severe anxiety neurosis. Phobias have anxiety attached to specific objects or situations. The classic anxiety dream is that of traumatic neurosis. Dreams are of help in showing the symbolic source of anxiety and frequently in indicating compensatory responses.

One severe anxiety situation is that of the candidate about to take his psychiatry board examinations. Stone and associates (1972) collected a number of dreams from persons about to undergo this rite of passage; they showed a variety of responses and defenses involved.

One candidate dreamed that he was naked, but he tied a model of the brain stem in front of his genitals. I, myself, although recalling no dream, remember the anxiety of the night before the board exam. I fell asleep at midnight, despondent about my inadequacy, and awoke at 2:00 A. M. knowing that everything would be fine. Although I recalled no dream, there must have been one in that initial 2 hours of sleep, a dream that reconstituted my self-image and sense of adequacy. I awoke again 7:00 A. M., took the exams, and enjoyed the day.

Levitan (1974) described the dreams of a phobic patient that were unusual in that they contained orgasm in nonsexual situations, the same situations that were associated with phobic reactions in waking life. Many of the patient's dreams were of the examination type. Levitan interpreted these data as showing the classic Freudian displacement and disguise, but it is possible to consider that the same complex pattern is involved both in the anxiety dreams and in the phobia. One dream showed orgasm associated with facing obstacles, which could be taken as compensatory to a possible conscious desire to avoid difficult growth processes.

A young man suffering from marked anxiety reported these three typical anxiety dreams on three successive nights:

I couldn't perform as well as everyone else. I can't remember details. I remember thinking:"This is just like always, even going back to early school years."

I couldn't perform well and became very discouraged and upset.

I took a math test and flunked it.

These are sketchy dreams. The first two might even represent non-dream thoughts during sleep, but they were reported as dreams. As he improved, his dreams became more detailed. One of the transition dreams showed that an accident was not necessarily a cause of injury:

I was throwing a football with several people, mainly with a man I know at work. I was upset because I can't throw a football well. A bus in the vicinity turned over, but no one was hurt.

PSYCHOSIS

Jung and others suggested that psychosis may be conceptualized as dream life breaking through into waking consciousness. This clinical intuition is still viable, but it is unsupported by many research findings (Rechtschaffen and associates, 1964). It may be that any definitive study of dream life in relation to waking psychosis will have to consider fluctuations in ego stability and in the effectiveness of normally compensatory dream mechanisms. In 1937 Trapp and Lyons studied 37 hallucinating patients during various stages of psychosis and after recovery. Alcholic hallucinosis seemed to be associated with similarity between dreaming and waking content. They concluded that in 16 of 37 patients dream material and waking hallucinations were similar.

Kramer and associates (1970) found that male schizophrenics had less hostility in their dreams when they were improving clinically. With improvement, there also were fewer strangers as compared to known and familiar persons in the dreams. This could be taken as increased activation of the personal unconscious layer of those complexes personified in the dream. They also described increases in numbers of male figures and figures of undetermined sex in the dreams as the patients improved, speculating that this change might show the heterosexual distancing necessary for clinical improvement in these schizophrenic males. But if dream figures other than the dream ego are considered to represent possible complexes in the tacit structure of the waking ego, such increases in male figures could be a sign of increased normal sexual identity for the waking ego. The authors made the usual unwarranted assumption that the dream ego is equivalent to the waking ego.

Fifty male inpatient schizophrenics were compared with a control group by means of dreams presented to independent judges (Richardson and Moore, 1963). The judges were able to discriminate the dreams of the two groups with statistically significant results, although not with high accuracy. The judges' expectations of the schizophrenic dreams containing more unrepressed sexual and aggressive material were not substantiated, but they seemed able to identify schizophrenic dreams by their bizarreness. This bizarreness was attributed theoretically to a deficiency in secondary revision, but it can equally well reflect a more archetypal level of the constellated complexes in schizophrenic dreams. Leppo (1966) was also able to discriminate dreams of schizophrenics and those of controls.

Eleven schizophrenic subjects were studied by Kramer and associates (1972). Schizophrenic dreams showed more withdrawal and avoidance of personal relationships, as well as more strangers, more persons of undetermined sex, more unusual settings, more food items, and more verbal behavior. With improvement, changes in dream content could not be clearly demonstrated, although clinical improvement seemed to correlate with increased ego activity in dreams.

Boss (1959) described schizophrenic dreams as showing immediate impulse gratification, with the environment and scenery being treated as vague and unimportant. He contrasted that characterization of schizophrenic dreams with an emphasis on detail in the dreams of persons with organic brain syndrome.

Several investigators have found no consistent differences between schizophrenic dreams and those of normals (Onheimer and associates, 1965). Noble (1950) claimed that there are no dreams characteristic of schizophrenics, although he cited evidence that as schizophrenics improve their dreams become more complicated. He believed that interpretation of symbols was of little value with schizophrenics, perhaps neglecting the ego-manifesting reparative character of many schizophrenic dreams. A similar view was voiced by Kant (1952). The dream of the minotaur, as previously discussed, showed a coincidence between an increased ability of the dream ego to defend itself and an increased sense of reality and stability in the waking ego.

Katan (1960) described the dream as an intermediate level for the normal person and the psychotic, with the psychotic functioning in the dream better than in waking life and the normal person functioning less well. This observation is consistent with the compensatory function of dreaming. Katan also gave an unusual example of a man whose depressive delusions seemed to be triggered by a dream of his grandson's death; they were not prevented by the obvious reality that his grandson was alive and healthy. This autonomous function of the unconscious was described by Jung, but it is seldom considered in clinical discussions. Severe anxiety, depression, and other psychopathological states may be caused by the unconscious insisting on an ego development that is resisted by the dominant ego image.

Carrington (1969) found some consistency between the personality traits of schizophrenics in waking life and the traits in their dreams, although this may have been no more than the continuity of basic personality. Schizophrenic women had more dreams of hostility and of threatening environments, as well as more dreams of mutilation, loss of control, bizarre dreams, and dreams with paranoid ideation. Among nonschizophrenic controls, a small amount of bizarre imagery seemed to correlate with normal adjustment, while an extreme was considered maladjustment by MMPI measurements. She postulated a relationship between the dream ego and the waking ego in suggesting that the strength of the waking ego determines the effectiveness with which emotional problems are handled in dream sequences.

Rechtschaffen and associates (1964) found no similarity between waking electroencephalographic, electromyographic, and eye-movement responses of 5 schizophrenic subjects and those patterns characteristic of REM dreaming. Perhaps this waking measurement was too gross for success to be anticipated. Zarcone and associates (1968) held that the onset of acute psychotic symptoms is accompanied by a decrease in the baseline amount of REM sleep and that actively ill schizophrenics do not compensate for lost REM sleep. These findings are not consistently replicated, but the hypothesis of a relationship between schizophrenia and sleep changes is kept alive by such sleep research.

The many observations that Jung made on psychotic patients in the Burghölzli sensitized his thinking early in his career to the problems of psychosis. Jung was thus able to see much of psychotic process as reparative, showing the activity of the archetypes of the objective psyche, the basic structural components of both the normal and abnormal personality. The very abstract image of order, the mandala, is a representative of the central archetype, and it may be manifested in severe decompensating psychotic states, apparently in an attempt to bring needed structure to the disturbed personality. In contrast to the traditional use of mandala forms as meditation images in Tibetan Buddhism, this autonomous appearance of the mandala form is apparently part of the self-regulating function of the psyche, although it may, in pure form, represent a major emergency defense to prevent dissolution of the ego structure.

Several years ago at Duke University there occurred a psychiatric grand rounds presentation of the finger paintings of a woman who was hospitalized with an acute psychotic episode. Although they cannot be equated with dreams, these finger paintings seemed to show some of the same function, at least during her most disturbed periods. There was essentially an inverse relationship between the structured, mandalalike order of the paintings and her psychotic state. When she was most disturbed on the ward, her paintings were most like mandalas. As she improved clinically, the paintings became more free, more disordered. The compensatory function of the psyche was evident in this art material, as it frequently is in a series of dreams.

Fordham (1973) carefully discussed the empirical foundations of Jung's concept of the Self or central archetype. Perry (1957) described the action of mandalas and other archetypal symbols in the process of schizophrenic repair. Metman (1958) described four different forms of the ego in schizophrenia, relating them to the image of the trickster, a figure in Winnebago Indian mythology.

Even though there is much that remains obscure about the differences between normal and schizophrenic dreams when compared in pooled groups, it is still possible in a clinical situation to have a distinct impression as to the progress or regression of a particular patient if the clinician has sufficient acquaintance with an ongoing series of that patient's dreams.

PHYSICAL PROBLEMS

It is difficult to correlate dream imagery precisely with physical conditions, but many clinicians have the impression that the condition of the body is reflected in dreams. Jung (CW 7:115) considered the possibility of psychic factors causing injury in some cases, and he referred to "a remarkable inner symbolical connection between an undoubted physical illness and a definite psychic problem," suggesting that the physical problem may be a "mimetic expression" of the psychological situation (CW 8:261).

Major physical changes have been reflected in dreams. Newton (1969) found that in paralysis patients the amount of movement in dreams is greatest immediately after onset of paralysis, decreasing the longer the person experiences paralysis. This was particularly true of activity initiated by the dream ego, but it was also true of physical activity by all characters in the dreams. Onset of paralysis was not associated with a marked increase in movement in the dreams of 27 paraplegics and quadriplegics compared to the dreams of 29 controls, which would argue against the findings being simply an acute compensatory dream response. However, the long-range decline in dream movement perhaps parallels an increasing conscious acceptance of the paralysis, so that Newton's conclusions may support the compensatory nature of dreams. He suggested a two-factor theory: under ordinary conditions dreams replicate conscious behavior; under abnormal conditions they show a reversal of behavior. This is similar to Jung's view that in ordinary balanced life dreams may complement the conscious position, becoming clearly compensatory, however, when the conscious position requires modification.

De Becker (1968) cited Professor Y. N. Kassatkin of Leningrad as observing that dream changes can be seen before the diagnosis of physical illness, but he did not give details. Sharpe (1937, pp. 171, 175) gave two examples of dreams that preceded organic problems. In one of these cases a woman dreamed that she was clinging to a window ledge, but finally became exhausted and fell. Two days later she fainted for the first time in her life. An examination revealed a chronic infection that required 3 months of convalescence.

Statistically significant differences in the hostility content of manifest dreams were found in groups of hypertensive patients and normotensive controls (Saul and associates, 1954). Waldhorn (1967) believed that dreams may be particularly applicable to the study of psychosomatic illness. As further knowledge is gained in the area of what Scott (1948) called the *body scheme,* it may be possible to find more detailed correlations between the dreams of an individual patient and changes in his physical condition. Such dramatic anecdotal reports as a dream of "something exploding inside" prior to the diagnosis of an aortic aneurysm serve to keep research interest alive in what may prove to be a vital area of psychosomatic medicine.

Saul (1940) reported four cases of hypertension in males with similar nuclear conflicts. Their dreams carried a theme of being caught in a sexual situation with a woman by another man, with no means of escape. Dreams ending with escape tended to occur in the same subjects at times when blood pressure was lower.

Migraine was associated in one case report with a dream in which the dream ego escaped from a male drill instructor into a woman's quarters where he had a number of flirtatious exchanges (Tarachow, 1946). The author suggested that migraine is a disorder of excessive vascular relaxation in order to avoid tension.

Hamburger (1958) presented an impressive study of three cases of women with problems of excessive food intake. Over the course of psychoanalysis, the percentage of dreams dealing with food and eating declined dramatically. He noted the similarity of the manifest contents of the dreams of the 3 patients.

Wadeson (1966) was able to correlate anxiety in the manifest dreams of a neurosurgical patient with the course of his hospitalization and surgical procedures. Although a surge of dream anxiety was evident before each procedure, the overall curve was toward a lowering of anxiety throughout the hospital course, with the least amount of dream anxiety occurring just prior to discharge.

Body image alterations in the dreams of an epileptic patient were discussed by Epstein (1967), who concluded that brain pathophysiology may influence dream content. The patient in his study experienced dreams of altered body position prior to seizures, which he found to be similar to reports of sensations of falling, colliding, and dying in other reports in the literature. One of the dreams cited was of two trains that were in danger of colliding. All of the 17 dreams involved body images or bodily sensations, and 7 dreams referred to paired parts of the body, such as breasts, hands, and legs. Part of the epileptic aura seemed to be a desire for the left foot to touch the floor, with some force opposing that movement.

If epilepsy is pictured as a spreading of abnormal excitation of the cerebral cortex, it can equally be viewed as a decrease in normal resistance to such spreading excitation. The two opposing forces of the epileptic aura in Epstein's patient could conceivably represent the opposition of excitation by the epileptic focus and inhibition from the normal brain tissue surrounding it. Consider the similar possibility in the following dream of an epileptic girl in her early twenties:

> I woke up [in the dream] and there was a lot of noise coming from the TV set. It seemed that it was between two channels, because there were different voices, and I couldn't tell what was being said. I went back to sleep [within the dream] and woke up [in the dream] several more times. I finally decided to get up and turn off the television. I got out of the bed backwards, and I started falling backwards. I blacked out, and I seemed to be falling head over heels several times. I thought to myself that I was going to have a seizure or that I was already having one. This scared me, and I woke up [in reality].

It is possible that the waking may have served to abort an incipient seizure. This is certainly the implication the patient drew, but it is not possible to know what would have occurred had she remained asleep. Could the "two channels" of the TV image reflect competing brain functions of epileptic discharge and control?

Disorders of cerebral function in chronic brain syndrome seem to be reflected in dream content (Kramer, 1973). The patients with more severe chronic brain syndrome had more persons in their dreams, possibly a compensation to feeling more restricted in interpersonal relations in waking life. Dreams of "good fortune" and warm social interactions predominated, again a possible compensation. There seemed to be a deficiency of emotional content as compared to the dreams of a control group.

A difference between males and females in "barrier imagery" has been found in dreams, the males having signficantly higher scores. However, the differences in dreams are no more marked than the differences in daydreams and fantasies.

Although enuresis seems to be a disorder of nondreaming sleep (Waldhorn, 1967), there are suggestions that the dreams of enuretics contain more images of aggression and fires (Pierce and associates, 1961). In the treatment of urinary retention, Abenson and Findling (1972) reported an interesting technique of instructing 2 patients in the waking state to have a dream that night so that they would feel ready to pass urine when they awoke in the morning. One dreamed of the physician standing on a high rock in the middle of a stormy ocean that gradually calmed. The other dreamed of two balloons full of water (kidneys?) that burst simultaneously. Both voided without difficulty on awakening and were discharged from the hospital.

A young man with spells of momentary difficulty in speaking, which at that time were thought to be possibly organic, began to date a number of interesting women as he recovered from a period of depression. He had previously had an important dream in which he ate "one of mother's cookies" and was able to fly through the air, but was afraid he would fall to the earth and be injured when the effect of the cookie wore off. This had been taken to mean a sense of power from identification with the maternal image. As he was recovering from the depression (and the speech problem was improving), he dreamed:

> I am flying on some kind of cardboard with an appealing young woman on my left. It is an attractive 1920s scene. We take off and land five or six times.

Although there are several motifs of interest in the dream, the crucial comparison seems to be between the magical cookie flight of the earlier dream and the equally magical, but less solitary and more controlled, flight in this dream. Such comparisons of related motifs in dreams in a series are very sensitive indicators of psychological change.

A woman in her early fifties came for hypnotic treatment for her cigarette addiction (Hall and Crasilneck, 1970), which had continued in spite of severe emphysema. Her initial response to hypnotherapy was excellent, but during the course of the treatment she smoked several cigarettes after a notable period of abstinence. When I inquired into her dreams, it seemed that the night before she smoked the cigarettes she had dreamed of being "about to have intercourse with my ex-husband." Her association to her ex-husband was that he was "too easygoing." She concluded: "I must assert myself more!" She broke her smoking habit.

DIFFICULTIES IN INTERPRETING THE MEDICAL CONTENT OF DREAMS

In the files of the Texas Society for Psychical Research is an unpublished essay by Mary Kugler, a former president of the society, regarding her attempt to predict, through her own dreams, some of the difficulties encountered in the course of her physical illness. On February 27, 1972, she dreamed:

> Someone (me?) had been fatally ill, but seemed to have been healed. It was a miracle, and a number of people were discussing it.

At the time of this dream, there were no symptoms of physical illness in the dreamer. Later, on April 19, 1972, she dreamed:

Someone gave me an early gift, a square box with different-shaped boxes inside. It was from Mrs. Mitchell, Colleen, and Mrs. Robb. Written across the card was "I love you, Mary Helen" (my double name used by longtime friends).

On may 8, 1972, this dream was recorded:

I was traveling with my husband and my friend Dottie. Up ahead was a ravine with icy water in it. We had to cross this stream to reach some beautiful poinsettias on a hill on the other side.

On June 5, 1972, Mrs. Kugler dreamed:

I had on a white blouse, and as I looked down I saw a purple stain over the breast area on the left.

On September 20, 1972, a very specific dream occurred:

I was going to have an operation and was told that I'd need a good surgeon that could do two operations in one, for there would be two separate physical problems to be dealt with at the same time.

On October 22, 1972:

Two women were sharing a hospital room, and they had both had surgery. They were quite congenial. One woman had a breast removed and had bandages up to her neck, but seemed fairly cheerful. I asked her how the man in her life had reacted, and she indicated that he'd reacted pretty well.

Several other possibly relevant dreams have been omitted from this selected series, but these show sufficiently that there were dreams over a period of time that gave more or less specific indications about possible physical problems. Their sequence appears more coherent in retrospect, since the many intervening dreams unrelated to this question of physical health have been omitted.

Associations to the dreams were important, according to Mrs. Kugler. In her associations, Mrs. Mitchell and Mrs. Robb had both recovered from gallbladder surgery. Colleen had recovered from a near-fatal auto accident. Poinsettias were taken to indicate Christmas time. Dottie, too, had undergone surgical removal of her gallbladder. A dream of September 16 also suggested gallbladder problems: "I dreamed that I vomited bile from eating too many greasy French fries."

There were several reassuring dreams. As part of a dream on November 5, 1972, a psychic of international reputation, Ann Jenson, was placing her hands around the dream ego's rib cage with an intent to heal. The next night there was a dream that although the dream ego was in deep water and could not swim, a man was helping her to stay afloat. On December 16 she dreamed that she was naked from the waist up and noted that she had both breasts intact. On December 28 she dreamed that a woman was examining her breast and was deciding that it was healthy.

Some of these dreams in December followed a physical examination. On December 9, Mrs. Kugler became suddenly ill, and on December 18 her problem was diagnosed as gallstones, with speedy surgery recommended. Then a lump was also discovered in her left breast, and it was thought that biopsy might be necessary. On January 2, 1973, the gallbladder surgery was successfully completed. One week later the breast was rechecked, but the suspicious lump had disappeared, and there was no need for a second surgical procedure.

Coming as they did among many other dreams, it would have been difficult, according to the author, to have known ahead of time that these particular dreams were to be taken on the objective level, although they seem retrospectively to form a rather clear, consistent pattern, particularly when the personal amplifications are added to the manifest dream images. It is entirely possible that they represented foreknowledge in the dreams of bodily conditions that were not known to the conscious mind.

MARRIAGE PROBLEMS

In recent years it seemed to me that an increasing number of people come to analysis with concerns about marriage. As the social restrictions concerning marriage become less rigid, largely because of decreasing stigmatization of divorce, people are becoming more aware of marriage as a psychological relationship that is dependent on mutual maturity. Although this trend is basically healthy, it necessitates an increasingly deeper understanding of the place of marriage or other close relationship in the process of individuation. Jung (CW 7:299) showed that if the ego identifies with the persona, there is a tendency for this to be compensated by a projection of the anima, drawing the person into a love relationship that may help to restore the personal form of the ego.

A woman and her husband were in group therapy together to work on communication and marriage difficulties. She twice dreamed that he was seeing his secretary privately. Although she had no conscious suspicions of this particular other woman, she drove by the secretary's home, found her husband's car parked there, and left a note on his windshield. This event precipitated frank communication between the woman and her husband, with the result that he terminated the affair and is working toward a deepened marriage relationship. He is taking this position because his wife's understanding and nonjudgmental response (she had also been involved extramaritally, which he knew) allowed him to open himself to her in a manner that had not been possible previously.

A divorced woman who was still at times visiting with her ex-husband was trying to decide whether to attempt a reconciliation. She had the following dream:

> I went to visit Joe in Washington, D.C., where he works. He was surrounded by cobwebs. As I tried to approach him, I became entangled in these cobwebs. I then realized that to him the cobwebs made interesting ladders that he climbed to find things that he enjoyed doing and knowing. I then seemed to realize that if I stood perfectly still the cobwebs would drop away, which they did.

The dream led her to realize that if she wished to relate to her ex-husband again, she must understand that he saw things from a different perspective. If she did not struggle against his viewpoint, it did not blind her. With this understanding, they began to move toward a renewed life together.

After several years of analysis, a woman was considering whether to divorce her husband, with whom she had found the same problems that she sought to escape in divorcing her first husband. At that point she dreamed:

> I was lying on a couch (association: psychoanalysis) talking to a Mr. X, although I wanted to talk to Mr. Y (association: my former high school principal, a great man who could relate to kids, he seemed always to know where you were). I was pleading with Mr. X not to punish my 13-year-old son [by the first marriage]. Suddenly I heard a deep male voice that said, seriously, "Was it good?" And then the voice said "Are you about to destroy something in you that is good?"

She associated the voice in the dream to a dream 6 months previously in which her father, who was deceased, said to her in a dream: "Don't destroy this marriage, it's the best thing you'll ever have."

This dream and the remembered dream both compensated in a dramatic fashion her conscious desire to end the marriage. Although the marriage is still troubled, some 2 years later she is still working toward improving the relationship, with some evidence of success.

Dreams may serve to make the dreamer more aware of feelings that are consciously known but not sufficiently expressed. A young

woman with two children, angry that her husband was not communicative, dreamed:

> The outside of the house was on fire. A neighbor and her children were
> there. I calmly sent them all outside. I wrapped my own children in whatever
> was handy—a towel, a gown. Then I started gathering things, a change of
> clothes and food. The fire was really fierce at all of the windows. My husband,
> however, was asleep. When I got everything together the fire went out. My
> husband came walking sleepily through the den and asked what I was doing. I
> told him I was getting a few things together because of the fire. "What fire?" he
> said.

Things did not improve, despite her efforts to obtain more response
from her husband. Several months later she dreamed a similar motif:

> I was at an old supermarket looking for a certain kind of soft drink. They
> had racks and racks of drinks, but not the kind I was looking for. Then I went
> over and picked up a sack of crackers, and a roach ran up my arm. I put the
> crackers back and was leaving when my husband came up the aisle. I told him
> what had happened, but he insisted that we buy what necessities we needed
> anyway. We did. When we walked out of the store our car was covered with
> foam. The fire department had sprayed it to put out the fire. Someone had put a
> bomb in our car, and it had exploded.

Shortly after, her conscious despair about the relationship seemed to
be corrected by this dream:

> I'm in a car with my girlfriend and another couple. She's finding out names
> of lawyers for me to contact about my divorce. I say, "This is wrong—I don't
> want a divorce."

The image of the girlfriend may have indicated a splitting off of the
desire for divorce from her dominant ego identity. Later, her husband
agreed to enter therapy, but he stayed only a short time. Still, the
marriage endured and somewhat improved.

Another woman in her thirties was considering divorce, which she
often saw as the only solution to a difficult marriage that she blamed
alternately on her husband's domiannce and on her own excessive
feelings of guilt and responsibility. She had a graphic dream that reminded her of her own shadow activity in the relationship:

> I am in a bathtub with my husband, and there are lots of bubbles. I'm
> behind him in the tub. I feel like having a bowel movement and do so. He is not
> even aware of what I have done, and I don't tell him. Later he sees the mess,
> but he doesn't get mad at me.

This dream gave her courage to show to her husband parts of her own
angry reaction that she felt he could not accept. His willingness to care
for her in spite of these revelations aided their communication.

Marriage problems that appear in dreams may at times foreshadow actual developments in a marriage. When negative material can be identified in dreams, corrective measures can often be initiated in psychotherapy to avoid serious developments in the marriage itself. A successful businessman in middle life had difficulty dealing with the aggression of his wife, which he took to be competitive and often hostile. After a day in bed ill, he dreamed:

> My wife and I are on a flat-bed train car taking a group to a party. I had been at another party, and she was questioning me about it. She became very angry when I could not tell her if it had been snowing or not. I said that I frequently didn't pay attention to such things. She became sarcastic and cutting in her remarks. She asked me a question. When I did not know the answer, she told me in a low voice how stupid I was. I tried to get off the car when it slowed and tried to walk away from her, but she followed me. Finally I stopped, and she caught up with me and began beating me. I turned on her with a fury and began hitting her as hard as I could. We fought and I was surprised at how strong she was.

Several years after this dream, after the dreamer had interrupted analysis for a long period, he and his wife had an actual fight similar to the dream fight, leading to their separation. Both are now in analysis, working on their own growth as well as the marriage. The wife more recently dreamed:

> I am making space at my home office for a woman who is a neighbor and who is getting a divorce, but I am taking the space away from a former secretary who was obstructive and passive-aggressive.

Although the general tone of the dream is positive (change from the secretary to a more suitable woman), there is the tension implied in the woman planning to divorce. A more hopeful scene concludes the dream:

> I have a large, beautiful old Indian basket like I bought in Santa Fe (association: she had gone there in preference to a business trip—it was an assertion of more personal needs). Someone is telling me how it can be preserved by adding honey to it.

The personal association to honey was sweetness, and the dream inquiry was stopped at that level, although there are archetypal amplifications of honey that might also yield different views of the image.

Several months before a difficult marriage ended in separation, followed by divorce, a middle-aged man dreamed that his wife was leaving him and also leaving the city:

I didn't like her going and tried to dissuade her, but I was not using the "emotional pyrotechnics" I would have used in the past. My car was parked at an intersection facing south, and I knew that if she left she would go toward the east. I had some things stacked on the sidewalk near my car, and she began to "trash" them—to stumble over them. I was more concerned about her state of mind than about my stuff. She seemed more uncaring than angry.

In his associations to the dream motifs, he said the following:

I feel uncomfortable unless I know where north is.

You used to have a toy with two magnets in the waiting room, something like a compass. My wife and I aren't like magnets, we neither attract nor repel. If we part, it will have to be a conscious decision, not an emotional choice.

If you go east or west, you're not really moving. It's a time-marking move. West is a dying move; east is a borning move.

South, here in Texas, means moving where life is easier and you can be lazier, and not so much is expected of you.

Although many uncertainties followed this dream (they divorced, remarried, then divorced again), the dream seemed to have prognostic significance. After the second divorce, his ex-wife made a healthy change in her life, finding a sense of her own worth apart from the marriage. As in the dream, he moved "south" toward decreased tension and responsibility. His wife also had dreams foreshadowing the dissolution of the marriage.

Dreams can be of great importance in understanding the complexity of marriage relationships. Observations of dreams of both partners, although not always possible, often show the direction in which the relationship is developing and can yield valuable clues for the conscious growth of both persons, whether the marriage itself improves or declines.

SEXUAL PROBLEMS

Dreams often help in differentiating various unconscious causes of sexual difficulties, and dreams can act as sensitive indicators of change during the treatment of sexual disorders. In the differential diagnosis of sexual problems, dreams and such imaginal data as masturbation fantasies may give clues to the underlying structure of the mind. In assessing such data, however, it is important to be aware of the symbolic meanings of sexuality; otherwise there is risk of identifying the conscious position with what is merely a symbolic expression in the dream material.

A 45-year-old divorced man came to analysis for symptoms of depression and secondary impotence. There were clear oedipal psychodynamics, but discussion of these produced little improvement. He dreamed:

> On my mother's bed I saw a "crab monster." It had many legs, all movable like an octopus, not like a crab. I was afraid of it. There was nothing to hit it with. Finally, I hit it with my bare fist. It turned inside out and became a ten-in-one tool—a tool that can be used for a lot of different purposes. Then that turned inside out again, and I saw that it was my own billfold, in which I keep money, credit cards, and identification—my identity.

Overemphasis on reductive analysis could doubtless produce from this dream elements of the vagina dentata, castration anxiety, and other manifestations of the admitted oedipal complex. Looked at from the prospective view, however, the dream clearly says that when the dreamer relates to what he fears, it loses its fearfulness and becomes what it truly is—a useful tool and his own basic identity.

Neumann (1959) described in Jungian terms why sexuality is such an important and problematical area. It is the one area where the normal individual experiences the unity of the personal and the archetypal, where "the bodily, psychic, and spiritual are momentarily, at least, experienced as a unity." This is a unity experienced in nonsexual ways by the child and by the creative person. Thus there is a momentary bridging of the personal life in its unique (but perishable) form and the archetypal, which is eternally numinous but devoid of direct expression without embodiment in the individual.

In dealing with homosexual problems it is also important to realize that dream images, or even overt sexual acts, may serve primarily a symbolic function (Kettner, 1968). An archetypal model of the integration of masculinity through sexual imagery occurs in the Gilgamesh epic, in the relation of Gilgamesh to his shadow counterpart Enkidu. Some homosexuals elaborate a hypermasculine persona that alternately may hide the nonmasculine ego or, if analytically understood, may carry elements of masculinity that can be integrated into the dominant ego image.

Kinsey and associates (1959) investigated the content and incidence of women's nocturnal sexual dreams. Two-thirds of the women had clearly sexual dreams, and 20% of them had sexual dreams to the point of orgasm, usually every 3–4 months (median). Of the women having sexual dreams, with or without orgasm, 85%–90% had heterosexual dreams, closely matching the incidence of waking heterosexual activity. The sexual partners in the dreams were most often unidentifiable and therefore from a Jungian view more likely to be subjective. Of these women, 8%–10% dreamed of homosexual experiences, this being approximately the same number who had actually had such experiences. In the dreams, however, pregnancy sometimes resulted from the homosexual contacts, a very symbolic theme suggesting that the dream homosexual contact may have been in the service of integration of the shadow (a figure of the same sex as the dreamer) in order to bring to consciousness ("birth") new potentialities, represented by the pregnancy. There is not sufficient information in Kinsey's report to verify or refute such possibilities, although such meaning of homosexual involvement in dreams is not uncommon. There was no relation between age of menarche and nocturnal sexual dreams. Religious women who had not had sexual experiences in waking life tended to have fewer sex experiences in their dreams, although once a woman had become sexually active there was no difference in sexual dreams between religious and nonreligious persons. There was some evidence of compensatory sexual dreams in women who were denied orgasm, but the frequency of sex in dreams did not equal the number of missed heterosexual contacts in waking life. Considering the variability of dream reporting, no conclusion can be drawn, although the possibility of a compensatory theory is favored. Kinsey noted that 13% of the women dreamed of sexual activities that they had not experienced in waking life, suggesting a prospective or rehearsal function of the dreams.

In laboratory sleep studies it has been observed that men frequently have erections when dreaming. Karacan and associates (1966) found erections to occur in 80% of the REM periods of 16 young adult male paid volunteers. Dreams with high anxiety tended to be associated with variable or absent penile erection. Waldhorn (1967) applied this type of observation to a consideration of castration anxiety and drive pressures, although it is just as applicable to a discussion of the dreams attempting to overcome such problems, again the distinction being between the reductive and prospective views. The traditional psychoanalytic attribution of sexual meaning to many symbols (such as ship, oven, and room) has not necessarily been confirmed by semantic differential investigation of sexually symbolic concepts (Worthy and Craddick, 1969). The whole question of symbolism, as well as the distinction between a true symbol and a sign, is in need of clarification.

If there are sexual problems involved, dreams immediately after intercourse may be revealing (Eisenstein, 1949), although other dreams as well may relate to the problem. Porach (1970) showed that the dreams of women vary with the stage of the menstrual cycle. Deep stage 4 sleep decreases in late pregnancy and increases after delivery, reaching normal levels by the second postpartum week (Karacan and associates, 1968). Dreams from 1399 men and 1418 women were found by Hall and Domhoff (1963) to show a consistent sex difference: men dream more about other men; women about men and women equally. They related this finding to differences in oedipal situations for men and women.

Both men and women who are paraplegic or quadriplegic have continued to have vivid orgasm in dreams as a phantom phenomenon, although they usually have been unable to consciously experience orgasm in waking life.

A woman in her fifties remembered having been sent to the grocery store when she was 5 years old. She had come back earlier than expected and found her mother in bed with a strange man. She remembered that she quietly went through the house to the backyard to ride her tricycle, but she could not hold the handlebars because her hands were so sweaty. One year before she had the dreams to be reported below, she had set a trap for her third husband, whom she believed had been unfaithful. To prove his lack of fidelity, she arranged for another woman to lure him to an apartment for intercourse. He was nude, with an erection, about to approach the strange woman, when his wife burst from the closet where she had been hiding and accused him. From that evening forward, he had a problem of secondary impotence. Although her husband improved in psychoanalysis, she found it difficult to give up her suspicions of him. Approximately 1 year after the entrapment incident, she had the following two dreams, the only dreams reported from the same night:

Dream 1: I saw my husband in the back room of our office kissing a woman employee [with whom she suspected he had had an affair]. I grabbed her and slapped her against the wall.

Dream 2: I saw a nude woman on a bed. Looked like mother. A man was on top of her. I could see her breasts. I started to tremble and perspire (association: the way I felt when hiding, waiting to accuse my husband with the other woman, and the way I felt on my tricycle when I was five). The scene changed, and I saw a woman in bed with my husband. I said to him, "What are you doing?" He answered, "I'm not doing anything because I can't even get a hard on."

Although the childhood event had been in consciousness prior to the dream, this dream seemed an affect bridge between her present situation with her husband and the childhood event of her mother with the unknown man. Such a dream is usually considered from a reductive standpoint, in which case it shows the childhood trauma behind the adult complex. It may equally as well be seen as a spontaneous attempt of the patient's mind to link her present difficulties with the childhood template on which they are patterned, allowing her ego to free itself from the persistent complex structure. This latter view is more consistent with the outcome of her therapy. She was able to see her own contribution to the difficulty and to take a more understanding stance with her husband.

The dream of a young physician shows how the events of the past, persisting in complex structures, can throw light on present difficulties. His marriage, particularly its sexual aspect, was stormy. Both he and his wife were in group therapy and in individual analysis.

My wife's group was meeting at our house. She was lying on the floor, and Dick, another group member, was lying on top of her. Both of them were dressed. I didn't want to interfere and was going to leave the house so they could work out whatever problem it was. I got in my car and started it up, but was unable to move because the rear of the car was held by a man who looked like he was 55 to 65, with a beard like a rabbi [the dreamer was not Jewish]. The man might have a gun. I was frightened!

His individual associations immediately linked the male rabbi figure to an event that had occurred when he was 11 years old and was visiting with his mother in Scotland. He had been playing in the street when a man with the rabbi's appearance had angrily shouted, "Go home, foreigner!" His aunt had come immediately and scolded the man, but the 11-year-old boy had been very frightened; he had thought that there might be something wrong with him that he did not know about. The physician and his wife had similar neurotic problems of insecurity and excessive self-criticism, accounting for the tight interlocking of their neurotic patterns.

A further example of the motif of a man lying on top of a woman, both of them clothed, occurred in group therapy and led to the dissolution of a persistent erotic transference. A woman who had been in treatment for several years was unable to relinquish an erotic transference on her male physician in spite of many interpretations. She had been placed in group therapy partially to dilute the transference feelings and to allow her to see the therapist in a more realistic setting. Nothing changed. Finally, she had the following dream:

I was in the therapy group. My doctor was lying on top of me on the floor. We were fully clothed. I made some sexual movements, but he did not respond. I realized [in the dream] that he was simply allowing this to demonstrate to me that a sexual relation between us was not possible.

Discussion of the dream, both individually and in the group, permitted her to give up the troublesome transference feelings.

Dreams have been used as indicators of sexual anxiety that is not expressed consciously. Volkan and Bhatti (1973) noted that the dreams of transsexuals awaiting sex-change surgery showed anxiety that could be used as a basis for discussion of conflict about the desire for surgery. Ann R. Race, M.D., and I interviewed a person who had successfully undergone male-to-female sex-change surgery. Prior to the surgery there had been many recurrent anxiety dreams of a persecutory nature, but these diminished almost to the vanishing point following the procedure.

Cheek (1969) implicated dreaming as a factor in producing premature onset of labor. He reported that his rate of premature deliveries had dropped from 6.5% to 2.8% since he began paying attention to the nocturnal fears of pregnant women.

Changes in one's attitude toward sexual problems can be initiated by dreams. A middle-aged man who was married continued to have clandestine homosexual contacts, connected with repressed oedipal psychodynamics. An increased dislike of this behavior was awakened in him by the following dream, which may have been the intent of the dream experience:

I was going into a rest room under construction in a large hotel. There were marble partitions between the urinals. As I was leaving, I saw a man and a woman engaged in fellatio. Since this was inappropriate, I left quickly, fearing the police would come. In another part of the rest room I saw many men engaged in all forms of homosexual activity, even balanced on the partitions between the toilets.

Winget and Farrell (1974) reported that homosexual men have as many heterosexual dreams as do heterosexual male controls, although they also have more sexual dreams and more homosexual dreams. Zajur (1974) was able to trace the movement from lesbian to heterosexual functioning in the dreams of a female patient.

A man in his middle twenties had difficulty in establishing and maintaining emotional and sexual relationships with women. He had secret fears that he was actually homosexual, but these seemed to be related to his hypermasculine ideal, based on his father. Although his father was in reality controlled by his mother, there was a family myth regarding the father's prodigious sexual ability. Several sisters had all "had to marry" because of premarital pregnancy, and the dreamer had once feared a fate similar to that of his brothers-in-law, suspecting women of being powerful, secretive, and entrapping. Several dreams occurring within the same 2-week period dealt with this sexual difficulty.

Dream 1: I heard Sherlock Holmes and Dr. Watson talking about their plans to marry each other. I wondered what my father would say about it. I went to church services with a couple [male and female] and talked with them later. I wondered if I could ever achieve that kind of loving companionship. Then there was a fat king with long curly white hair who was about to leave in a vehicle like a spaceship. He decided that there was a young lady he would like to marry and jumped from his throne and raced down the spiral staircase. I knew she would make him happy.

Dream 2: I was at my parents' home with my sister. We noticed two wolves prowling outside. One wolf approached a sleeping animal. I got the shotgun and went out quickly. I pointed the gun at the wolf's heart and fired. A small pellet rolled out of the gun, but the wolf was sucked into the barrel. It turned into a spider and crawled out. I killed it with the barrel. The second wolf turned into a spider and I also killed it. I went back into the house. The sleeping animal awoke and asked, "Was the wolf here?" I said "Yes." Then it said, "I thought so because I felt foam covering me." I thought that sounded right, since it was really a spider and used foam to paralyze its prey.

Dream 3: I was passionately kissing a young woman and wanted desperately to make love to her. Then I was in a locker room and noticed how other guys' penises were larger than mine. I was then embracing and hugging Muhammed Ali. I was getting turned on, but the embrace became crushing and I woke up.

These dreams show an attempt at repair of his damaged sense of masculinity in order to move toward normal heterosexual functioning. The image of the marriage of Holmes and Watson, images of investigative thinking, is followed by a desire to have a warm heterosexual relationship like his friends. On a more archetypal level, this is reflected by the old king having a sudden desire for a young woman who will make him happy. Thus the masculine integration of the positive shadow (Watson-Holmes) at a level close to the ego seems to invoke a heterosexual response (king-woman) at a deeper level that is not yet available to the ego for its own dominant identity. Some animal (sexual? animal nature?) is asleep and is endangered by two wolves, masculine animals. When the dream ego gives up passivity and acts by shooting, the wolves are unexpectedly turned into spiders, a frequent image of the devouring mother. The sleeping animal (new potentials for the ego?) can then awaken. Since the animal speaks to the dream ego, it resembles the many helpful, talking animals in fairy tales, invariably a positive prognostic sign. The doubling of wolves and spiders suggests a content that is approaching consciousness, since such contents frequently appear in twos prior to their entering consciousness.

Several weeks later, this same dreamer was anticipating a visit from a girl to whom he had been close. The day before her arrival he dreamed of having intercourse with another less attractive girl and being discovered by his former fraternity brothers, who made fun of him, although he continued coitus. When the real girl was actually visiting and staying with him, however, he dreamed of being almost caught by a shark. The continued instability of the personified complexes that are in touch with the ego is evident, but the movement of the dreams as a whole shows very hopeful development.

Hillman (1968) described an innate inhibition of masturbation, which he considered to be a part of the self-limited nature of instinct. He presented archetypal amlifications from Taoist and Tantric Yoga practices of withholding ejaculation. Bernstein (1962) used dream material to aid in understanding the masturbation of an adolescent boy. Manifest dream themes of motion, particularly riding, were considered masturbatory equivalents.

Many variations in dreams seem to be related to one or another element of what can be referred to as the oedipal pattern of object relations. The actual complexities are greater than outlined by Freud (Devereux, 1969); they must include the part of the mythical story that takes place after the self-blinding of Oedipus. In these latter parts of the story, Oedipus becomes a demigod, being swallowed up into the earth (the archetypal mother?) without passing through death, a theme similar in some respects to the biblical passing of Elijah and Enoch.

A successful man in his fifties, who had been unsuccessfully married several times, was living in a homosexual relationship with another man, although their sexual activity was a minor and infrequent aspect of the interaction. Years before the man had dreamed that he was homosexually sodomized by his father. This had always been considered by him symbolically to represent a real feeling that he had been "screwed" by his father. When he resumed analysis, however, one of his early dreams was that he had to go under a bridge, into a dark and possibly dangerous place, in order to be given a majordomo staff that he needed before he crossed over the bridge. He associated to the staff as a phallic symbol of authority, and suddenly he was able to reevaluate the previous homosexual dream of his father as being the same sort of message in a more graphic and body-image form: you must humble yourself in order to receive masculinity. A series of dreams then suggested, in retrospect, that they may have had to do with repair of injured masculinity rather than with a basically homosexual orientation.

Not all dream images lead to a positive outcome. A medical student was in therapy for passive–aggressive character defenses that were threatening his graduation, as he habitually missed important medical conferences. He was in therapy at the time that President Kennedy was assassinated. The violent, sudden, and tragic death of the president seemed to be assimilated by him to the sudden removal of the feared father in the oedipal complex pattern. The night of the assassination he drove an automobile recklessly and fast, feeling a sense of freedom and power. The same night he dreamed that he had "the biggest erection in the world," perhaps a symbol of his feeling the sudden removal of fears of castration, with subsequent overcompensation. Unfortunately, he tended to identify with the sense of inflated power; he did not integrate the dream material, and he soon died in a automobile accident, most likely caused by similar hypomanic behavior.

Goldhirsh (1961) published a valuable study of the dreams of convicted sex offenders. In many dreams there were uncamouflaged elements of sex crimes, usually involving sex acts with minors. In the sex criminal dreams, 53% contained one or more sexual elements, as compared to less than 10% in the dreams of controls. This high percentage of dreams resembling the offenses suggests that the waking egos of these offenders tacitly contain a large amount of deviant sexuality, which could be the basis for acting out the dream fantasies if the ego identifies itself with such complexes. This study, although in need of independent verification, also suggests that dreams could possibly be a useful way to judge when such offenders have actually changed their basic psychodynamics.

Manifest dreams, without any conjecture about repressed sexual wishes, are themselves important indicators of sexual dysfunction, sexual identity, and psychodynamics underlying sexuality.

ALCOHOLISM

Alcohol has been shown to interfere with the sleep–waking cycle and particularly to block REM sleep (Gross and associates, 1973). There have been suggestions that alcoholic hallucinosis and the more severe delerium tremens may be the breakthrough of suppressed dreaming into the waking state.

Skinner and associates (1974) found a number of factors clustered in eight personality types in alcoholics. In one study (Curlee and Stern, 1973) alcoholics showed a marked fear of heights, in contrast to normal controls. In the diagnosis of alcoholism it is particularly important not simply to identify the alcohol problem but to relate it to other levels of diagnosis, such as neurosis and character state, and to use the diagnostic process as a way to formulate an active treatment plan (Petrilowitsch, 1968).

Sharpe (1937), a classic psychoanalytic writer on dreams, observed that when patients who are "subject to alcoholic excess" begin to dream of drunkenness instead of actually getting drunk, there is hope for a solution to the problem being found. She applied the same logic to problems of fetishism and compulsive masturbation. Choi (1973) offered more recent support for this observation. I have observed a similar shift in a conscious problem appearing in dreams at the time of clinical improvement, pratically in dealing with depression. My own conceptualization of this shift has been that the compensatory unconscious images of repair, present during the clinical depression, have begun to be the tacit basis for dominant ego identity, while the depressed images (usually anger toward the ego) that previously were central to the dominant ego identity are dissociated from ego identity and appear in the dreams as personified complexes in object-relations patterns related to the dream ego. The phenomenon is not unlike the splitting of the transference into improving and pathological identities when a patient begins to improve in everyday life but appears just as ill in the therapy situation, or vice versa. In a sense, the appearance of the target symptom in dreams is the reverse of De Becker's "motor effect," where the dream image acts, when the ego identifies with it, as the basis for action. It may well be that when the ego *disidentifies* with the image (alternatively, when the complexes of that image are removed from the tacit component of the dominant ego identity) the dissociated images appear in the dream in relationship to a dream ego that is then based on other tacit complexes in a different object-relations pattern.

In matched groups of alcoholics and controls, Scott (1968) found that alcoholics dream more about their children, but perhaps with feelings of guilt. Controls experience more joy in their dreams than do alcoholics, while alcoholics experience more strangers and more views of themselves as passive victims, as well as more dreams of drinking. A difference was found between male and female alcoholics, the males dreaming more often of death.

Some investigators have reported up to 100% stage 1 sleep in alcoholics just prior to the onset of delirium tremens (Greenberg and Pearlman, 1967). Wolin and Mello (1973) did not find this same effect, but their results may have been influenced by different conventions for defining the onset of sleep.

It has at times been possible to find in the dreams of alcoholics indicators that the unconscious mind is pressing for a change in the pattern of excessive drinking. Many times it seems that alcoholics are persons interested in understanding levels of reality "deeper" than the persona-social, but lacking the courage or decision to approach non-persona relationships, they attempt to get beyond the persona level by chemically dampening the ego defenses with alcohol. Even when they are "dry," alcoholics frequently face the problem of misusing sedative medication to the same purpose as alcohol.

A woman in her late fifties, a self-defined nondrinking alcoholic for many years, suffered reprimands from her dreams whenever she used sleeping medication. In one night she dreamed two dreams related to the use of medication:

Dream 1: A monkeylike little man (association: "monkey on my back"—booze) was on a stage chasing, like a monkey, a young woman in blue jeans who was doing acrobatics. I was disgusted with him and did not like a roll of fat visible under his shirt.

Dream 2: Someone asked me if Dr. Hall knew I was taking so many sleeping pills.

The same woman disliked her work, but her dreams were consistently favorable to her job until she faced her reluctance to deal with people more openly, at which time her dreams supported a move to a job with more possibilities for autonomy.

REFERENCES

Abenheimer KM: The ego as subject, in Wheelwright JB (ed): The Reality of the Psyche. New York, Putnam, 1968

Abenson MH, Findling J: Dream treatment of urinary retention. Br J Psychiatry 120:225–226, 1972

Baer R, Ebtinger R, Israel L, et al: A propose des rêves de déprimés (Apropos of the depressive's dreams). Ann Med Psychol (Paris) 2:812, 1967; English abstract in Psychol Abst vol 42, no 10841

Beck AT, Ward CH: Dreams of depressed patients. Arch Gen Psychiatry 5:462–467, 1961

Bernstein I: Dreams and masturbation in an adolescent boy. J Am Psychoanal Assoc 10:289–302, 1962

Boss M: The psychopathology of dreams in schizophrenia and organic psychosis, in DeMartino MF (ed): Dreams and Personality Dynamics. Springfield, Ill, Charles C Thomas, 1959, pp 156–175

Buck LA, Barden M: Body image scores and varieties of consciousness. J Pers Assess 35:309–314, 1971

Carrington P: Dream reports of schizophrenic and nonschizophrenic women. Doctoral dissertation, Columbia University, 1969, abstract in Diss Abst Intern 30:4134A, 1970

Cheek DB: Significance of dreams in initiating premature labor. Am J Clin Hypn 12:5–15, 1969

Choi SY: Dreams as a prognostic factor in alcoholism. Am J Psychiatry 130:699–702, 1973

Curlee R, Stern H: The fear of heights among alcoholics. Bull Menninger Clin 37:615–623, 1973

De Becker R: The Understanding of Dreams (Trans: M Heron) London, Allen & Unwin, 1968

Detre T: On the psychodynamics and the ego psychology of the depressive illnesses: Sleep disorders and psychosis. Can Psychiatr Assoc J 11:S169–S177, 1966

Devereux G: Retaliatory homosexual triumph over the father. Int J Psychonal 41:157–161, 1969

Eisenstein VW: Dreams following intercourse. Psychoanal Q 18:154–172, 1949

Epstein AW: Body image alterations during seizures and dreams of epileptics. Arch Neurol 16:613–619, 1967

Fordham M: The empirical foundation and theories of the self in Jung's works, in Fordham M, Gordon R, Hubback J, et al (eds): Analytical Psychology. London, Heinemann, 1973

Furman E: Some features of the dream function of a severely disturbed young child. J Am Psychonal Assoc 10:258–270, 1962

Goldhirsh MI: Manifest content of dreams of convicted sex offenders. J Abnorm Soc Psychol 63:643–645, 1961

Greenberg R, Pearlman C: Delirium tremens and dreaming. Am J Psychiatry 124:133–142, 1967

Gross MM, Goodenough DR, Hastey J, et al: Experimental study of sleep in chronic alcholics before, during, and after four days of heavy drinking, with a nondrinking comparison. Ann NY Acad Sci 215:254–265, 1973

Hall C, Domhoff B: A ubiquitous sex difference in dreams. J Abnorm Soc Psychol 66:278–280, 1963

Hall C, Van de Castle RL: An empirical investigation of the castration complex in dreams. J Pers 33:20–29, 1965

Hall JA, Crasilneck HB: Development of a hypnotic technique for treating chronic cigarette smoking. Int J Clin Exp Hypn 18:283–289, 1970

Hamburger WM: The occurrence and meaning of dreams of food and eating. Psychosom Med 20:1–16, 1958

Harrison IB: Follow-up note on a patient who experienced hypomania following a dream. J Am Psychoanal Assoc 15:266–269, 1967

Hartmann EL:The Functions of Sleep. New Haven, Yale University Press, 1973

Hillman J: Toward the archetypal model for the masturbation inhibition, in Wheelwright JB (Ed): The Reality of the Psyche. New York, Putnam, 1968

Kant O: Dreams of schizophrenic patients. J Nerv Ment Dis 95:335–347, 1952

Karacan I, Goodenough DR, Shapiro A, et al: Erection cycle during sleep in relation to dream anxiety. Arch Gen Psychiatry 15:183–189, 1966

Karacan I, Heine W, Agnew HW Jr, et al: Characteristics of sleep patterns during late pregnancy and postpartum periods. Am J Obstet Gynecol 101:579–586, 1968

Karpman B: Dream analysis of a constitutional psychopath: Toward the problem of differential dream analysis. Psychoanal Rev 33:84–101, 1946

Katan M: Dream and psychosis: Their relationship to hallucinatory process. Int J Psychonal 41:341–351, 1960

Kettner MG: Patterns of masculine identity, in Wheelwright JB (ed): The Reality of the Psyche. New York, Putnam, 1968

Kinsey AC, Pomeroy WB, Martin CE, et al: Nocturnal sex dreams, in DeMartino MF (ed): Dreams and Personality Dynamics. Springfield, Ill, Charles C Thomas, 1959, pp 71–86

Kramer M: Dream data on CBS patients pinpoints emotional needs. Quoted in Reports from Meetings, Roche Reports: Frontiers of Psychiatry 3(15):3, 1973

Kramer M, Baldridge B, Whitman RM, et al: An exploration of the manifest dream in schizophrenic and depressed patients. Psychophysiology 5:221, 1968

Kramer M, Ornstein PH, Whitman RM, et al: The contribution of early memories and dreams to the diagnostic process. Compr Psychiatry 8:344–374, 1967

Kramer M, Trinder J, Roth T: Dream content analysis of male schizophrenic patients. Can Psychiatr Assoc J 17(Suppl 2):251–257, 1972

Kramer M, Whitman RM, Baldridge W, et al: Dreaming in the depressed. Can Psychiatr Assoc J 11:S178–S192, 1962

Kramer M, Whitman RM, Baldridge B, et al: Depression: Dreams and defenses. Am J Psychiatry 122:411–419, 1965

Kramer M, Whitman RM, Baldridge BJ, et al: Dream content in male schizophrenic patients. Dis Nerv Syst 31:51–58, 1970

Krippner S, Davidson R, Lenz G: The dreams of transsexuals, in Woods RL, Greenhouse HB (eds): The New World of Dreams. New York, Macmillan, 1974

Kugler M: Difficulties encountered in interpretation of medical content in dreams. Unpublished essay, Texas Society for Psychical Research files, 1976

Leppo L: Fenomenologia del sogno nella schizofrenia (Phenomenology of the dream in schizophrenia). Revista di Psichiatria 1:222–240, 1966 (English summary)

Levitan HL: The dreams of a phobic patient. Int Rev Psychonal 1:313–323, 1974

Mahl GF: Fathers and sons, source material, vol 1: Early memories, current daytime thoughts, and current dreams college men have of their fathers. Journal Supplement Abstract Service of the American Psychological Association, no 623

Metman P: The trickster figure in schizophrenia. J Anal Psychol 3:5–20, 1958

Miller JB: Dreams during varying stages of depression. Arch Gen Psychiatry 20:560–565, 1969

Money J: Phantom orgasm in the dreams of paraplegic men and women. Arch Gen Psychiatry 3:373–382, 1960

Murray EJ: Sleep, Dreams, and Arousal. New York, Appleton, 1965

Neumann E: Art and the Creative Unconscious. (Trans: R Manheim) Princeton, Princeton University Press, 1959

Newton PM: Recalled dream content and the maintenance of body image. Doctoral dissertation, Columbia University, 1969; abstract in Diss Abst Intern 30:2424B, 1970

Noble D: A study of schizophrenia and allied states. Am J Psychiatry 107:612–616, 1950

Onheimer P, White PT, De Myer MK, et al: Sleep and dream patterns of child schizophrenics. Arch Gen Psychiatry 12:568–571, 1965

Perry JW: The Self in Psychotic Process. Berkeley, University of California Press, 1957

Petrilowitsch N: A clash between psychiatric diagnosis and therapy? Psychiatria Clinicia 1:109–119, 1968

Pierce CM, Whitman RM, Maas JW, et al: Enuresis and dreaming: Experimental studies. Arch Gen Psychiatry 4:166–170, 1961

Porach LB: The relationship of masculine and feminine identification dream scores, and to menstrual reactions. Doctoral dissertation, University of Virginia, 1970; abstract in Diss Abst Intern 31:4558, 1971

Rechtschaffen A, Schulsinger F, Melnick SA: Schizophrenia and physiological indices of dreaming. Arch Gen Psychiatry 10:89–93, 1964

Richardson GA, Moore RA: On the manifest dream in schizophrenia. J Am Psychoanal Assoc 11:281–302, 1963

Saul LJ: Utilization of early current dreams in formulating psychoanalytic-cases. Psychoanal Q 9:453–469, 1940

Saul L, Sheppard E, Selby D, et al: The qualification of hostility in dreams with reference to essential hypertension. Science 119:382–383, 1954

Scott EM: Dreams of alcholics. Percept Mot Skills 26:1315–1318, 1968

Scott WCM: Some embryological, neurological, psychiatric and psychoanalytic implications in the body scheme. Int J Psychoanaly 29:141–155, 1948

Sharpe EF: Dream Analysis. London, Hogarth, 1937

Skinner HA, Jackson DN, Hoffman H: Alcoholic personality types: Identification and correlates. J Abnorm Psychol 83:658–666, 1974

Stone MH, Forrest D, Kestenbaum CJ, et al: The psychiatrist faces the board examination. Psychiatry 35:366–372, 1972

Tarachow S: The analysis of a dream occurring during a migraine attack. Psychoanal Rev 33:335–340, 1946

Trapp GW, Lyons RH: Dream studies in hallucinated patients. Psychiatr Q 11:253–266, 1937

Vogel GW, Traub AC: REM deprivation: I. The effect on schizophrenic patients. Arch Gen Psychiatry 18:287–299, 1968

Volkan V: A study of a patient's "re-grief work" through dreams, psychological tests and psychoanalysis. Psychiatr Q 45:255–273, 1971

Volkan VD, Bhatti TH: Dreams of transsexuals awaiting surgery. Compr Psychiatry 14:269–279, 1973

Wadeson RW: Anxiety in the dreams of a neurological patient. Arch Gen Psychiatry 14:249–252, 1966

Waldhorn HG:The place of the dream in clinical psychoanalysis. New York, International Universities Press, 1967

Winget C, Farrell RA: Homosexual dreams, in Woods R, Greenhouse HB (eds): The New World of Dreams. New York, Macmillan, 1974, p 22

Wolin SJ, Mello NK: The effects of alcohol on dreams and hallucinations in alcohol addicts. Ann NY Acad Sci 215:266–302, 1973

Worthy M, Craddick RA: Semantic differential investigation of sexually symbolic concepts. Journal of Projective Techniques and Personality Assessment 33:78–80, 1969

Zajur E: (A case of feminine pseudohomosexuality). Revista de Psychoanalisis, Psiquiatria y Psicologia 4:14–36, 1974; English summary in Psychol Abst 54:12369

Zarcone V, Bulevich G, Pivik T, et al: Partial REM phase deprivation and schizophrenia. Arch Gen Psychiatry 18:194–202, 1968

10
Dreams as Indicators

A noninterpretative use of dreams that is of much clinical importance is their use as indicators of areas for psychotherapeutic exploration. Four major examples are (1) the dream as an indicator of past conflicts that continue to influence current functioning through their incorporation into complexes and object-relations complex structures, (2) the dream as an indicator of unrecognized current causes of conflict, (3) the dream as an indicator of transference–countertransference problems, and (4) the dream as an indicator of troublesome family and social configurations.

Whitmont (1969, p.114) offered an exceptionally clear discussion of the relationships among archetypal potentiality, childhood experience, complex formation, and psychopathology later in life. Although the archetypal patterns available in the child's mind carry an extended range of life possibilities, their manifestation is immediately limited by the early formation of complexes in which personal images from actual experience (or from internal fantasy) evoke only a portion of the archetypal potentiality. Thereafter these personal images carry that archetype as the core of a complex based on the personal experience. Anything that subsequently activates the personal complex may penetrate to the core of the complex and also activate the archetypal meaning, so that the evoking stimulus can elicit more response than is proportionate to the merely personal layers of the complex. The widespread reaction to the death of a president or a king, noted respectively by myself and Fairbairn, revealed in the dreams of many analysands the archetypal core of the father complex to which the image of the ruling male figure had been unconsciously attached.

Since childhood experience actualizes only a part of the archetypal potentialities, there seems to be continuing pressure for enlargement of the original complex to include those potentialities that have not been sufficiently experienced. The activation of further archetypal possibilities seems especially to be stimulated when the ego is struggling with a problem that it is unable to solve within the terms currently available to conscious experience. The activity of dreams often appears to be a spontaneous attempt of the psyche to actualize further unrealized archetypal patterns as models for ego change in the process of individuation.

Whitmont (1969) explained that identical environmental factors may evoke differing archetypal responses, while diverse environmental factors can evoke the same archetypal response. Thus growth of personality is always an interaction between the environment and the ego, while the ego is also related to varied archetypal processes that are not determined by the environment.

DREAMS AS INDICATORS OF PAST CONFLICTS

The importance of recognizing the relationship between past conflicts and current difficulties cannot be overemphasized, although emotional insight frequently follows rather than initiates such connections. The importance of recognizing relationships between past and current object-relations patterns is not necessarily simply to gain an understanding of the "causes" of current difficulties. To imply that past events are simple causes of current problems would be to overlook the participation of past ego choices in the initiation and continuation of the problems. Without ego participation in the problem, which implies a level of responsibility, although not necessarily guilt, there would be no immediately available action by which the ego might begin to move its unconscious tacit identity structure in the direction of a more desired form.

Recognition of the past, and acceptance of some responsibility for it, allows abandonment of repression, facilitates transvaluation of past experiences, and frees libido for more desired purposes (Sharpe, 1937). Dream reporting may lead directly to recognition of relevant past experiences (Bach, 1954). The early psychoanalytic literature is a rich source of stories of discovery of forgotten past events. Fenichel (1926) presented a typical example, although it suffers, as do many others, from interpretative inferences. Fromm (1965) reported the occurrence of spontaneous age regression in a dream following an unsuccessful attempt to induce age regression by hypnosis.

There may be objective indicators in dream research for the pressure of dreams in adaptive processes. Greenberg and Pearlman (1976) found that prediction of successful use of psychotherapy required knowledge of dream material as well as measures of REM latency (time from sleep onset to first REM period) and the amount of REM time during sleep. In an interesting integrative statement, they suggested that decreased REM latency showed the need for the type of adaptational work that takes place in dreams, while the amount of REM time shows an ability for such work. However, it was also necessary to review the content of dreams, since some psychological defenses interfered with the use of the dreaming ability to meet the need. Since dream content is the only one of the three measures readily available to the clinician, further studies are needed to refine such indicators in manifest dream content. It is likely that the effectiveness of dealing with dream images from the past could be such an indicator, although I know of no quantitative studies of this hypothesis at the present time.

In subjects who have lost memory of recent events as a result of encephalitis, dreams become more simple. Instead of being symbolically concerned with current difficulties, they tend to contain memories of events prior to the illness. Torda (1969), who observed these findings in 6 patients, was able to link the remembered dream event with the satisfaction of a need from the past that was similar to a current need. Her finding is an excellent demonstration of the function of complexes in dreams being linked to the past, but not simply representing the past.

Robbins (1966) used motifs from the dreams of subjects to elicit their personal amplifications of similar past events. This identified areas of tension that had begun in the past and had not yet been resolved. His method suggests the Jungian word-association experiment, but starting from the subject's own dream images rather than from the list of stimulus words. His method certainly leads to the identification of active complexes, but as with free association it would need to be demonstrated that the dream images are superior to other stimulus words for this purpose.

Dream images may associate through images of earlier dreams toward childhood events that it is important to explore in psychotherapy. A man in middle life had an earliest childhood memory of attempting intercourse with a young neighbor girl when both were preschool age. He remembered no punishment, although he consciously assumed that there may have been punishment, since they were caught by her mother. A later dream of a polar bear breathing fire had been associated, through analytic work, with the childhood event. Some time after the bear dream, he dreamed that he found a mandala-shaped garden that had not been tended by the couple who lived there. As he began to work the garden, a symbol of his own neglected whole-ness, he discovered three white guinea pigs (experimental animals?) that could strike fire from their noses. The similarity between the guinea pig's nose and the polar bear's flaming breath served to link the mandala dream with the childhood event through the previous bear dream. His dreams soon produced more active and revealing develop-ments of the mandala garden.

A young widow was having difficulty in recovering emotionally from the suicide of her husband. A number of her dreams seemed to encourage her to detach herself from his memory, complete the mourn-ing process (which included a great deal of anger toward him), and live a more normal life. One such dream showed the need to continue analytic concern with his meaning in her life. At the same time, the dream itself furthered the separation process.

My husband was leading me, my parents, my brother, and my children to the ocean. We came immediately to a beach like I remembered at my grand-father's summer house. My husband said the ocean was farther on, although my grandfather's house had been on the ocean. He led us into a mountain, and we climed through a passageway. Finally we crawled through a small hole, and my husband said we were at the ocean at last. But what I saw was a deep black pool of water, completely inside the mountain. My husband gave me a present, and I knew he wanted to please me, but I wanted to go on to the real ocean that I knew must be somewhere on the other side of the mountain.

The dream suggests the need to make a discrimination between the mistaken "ocean," actually a subterranean lake suggesting the mythological river Styx, and the real ocean in the outer world. Other dreams showed that there was not room for her to be buried beside her husband, again seeming to urge her toward life.

A woman with a severe mother fixation, although her mother was deceased, had transferred many of the old feelings for her mother to her husband, who was older than herself. She dreamed:

I seemed to be in British Honduras or some place like that. I chose to die with my mother rather than escape. It was to be a slow, torturous death. I had chances to get away, but I didn't take them. They took my mother away, and later I was told she had come back. Someone told me she had blood all over her arms. I was told to put stockings over her arms so that I would not see the blood.

This dream contains no lysis of the problem, but it does present the patient's clinging so tenaciously to an identity pattern based on her mother that it had been impossible for her to arouse a desire for a new identity. The dream may have contributed to her beginning to relinquish this old pattern.

A woman who had been married four times had the following dream that seemed to link together several past relationships with her current marriage problems.

I had a Cadillac that needed repair (association: it does, a day residue). I turned into the dealer's lot and then realized it was a Chevrolet dealer's lot. When I tried to drive away, the car vanished. Dr. Hall and my third husband were there. I had some kind of injury and bled more than Dr. Hall thought I would. I think I was dying, but I had a sense of "calm panic." There was no longer any use to be frantic.

She associated the Cadillac with her second husband, who had "class," was refined and rational—qualities that she saw in her current husband, although she was beginning to realize that there were deeper problems. Her third husband, whom she associated to the Chevrolet, had more negative associations. Therefore, as she began to repair her current marriage, she could expect to find problems resembling those of the preceding "Chevrolet" marriage rather than those of the "Cadillac" marriage she would have preferred to have. The bleeding could suggest either that she was more willing to suffer this change than I thought she would be or that it would be more of an injury to her than expected. Her death, as with most instances of the death of the dreamer in the dream, was taken as an indication of her need to revise her current self-image completely.

Although she agreed with these meanings in her dream, she declined to continue therapy, feeling that her current marriage was unable to continue except through her sacrificing her own wishes to her husband's neurotic demands. Fortunately, she later returned briefly to therapy; she had dreams indicating more hope, and she seemed to make some progress toward confronting those aspects of her husband that she found unacceptable.

DREAMS AS INDICATORS OF FAMILY AND SOCIAL FACTORS

Manifest dream content can reveal information about the way a particular group, such as black people, are seen in dreams. Nichols (1967) sensitively discussed this aspect of cultural myth in America.

Dreams are also important in understanding family patterns, and they can be used as a focus in family therapy for discussion of material that the family might otherwise ignore (Markowitz and associates, 1968). There is some evidence that birth order in the family may relate to the number of dreams recalled and possibly to the amount of affiliative and dependent elements in the dreams (Ward and associates, 1973). Firstborns remembered significantly fewer dreams, a prediction that the authors had based on the Adlerian theory that firstborns are more socialized; since dreaming in Adlerian theory compensates for a sense of inferiority, they would have less need for dreams.

Unusual situations sometimes permit the observation of dream material from both husband and wife. In such cases, dreams seem consistently to offer corrections to the way the relationship is viewed consciously by each dreamer. Although this is useful in therapy situations, free discussion of dream material between spouses, particularly if both have not been analyzed, is a potentially upsetting procedure, since the spouse hearing the dream may project into it the "secret" intention of the dreamer, although the dream may appear quite different to an objective interpreter. Usually it is best for the ego of the dreamer to deal directly with the meaning of the dream and then, with that added understanding, make whatever modifications are appropriate toward the person who appeared in the dream. Directly telling another person a dream about that person is somewhat like suggesting that you secretly have read the person's palm or that your own secret thoughts about the relationship are expressed in the dream, which the person may not see as you do. Both possibilities can often be unsettling to the relationship.

Dreams may indicate family difficulties and their possible mode of resolution. A middle-aged man whose family was of Hungarian descent had great difficulty with his consanguineous family when growing up. His marriage had ended unhappily, and he felt acutely the absence of his children (who had returned with their mother to another country). He had emotional and sexual difficulties in relating closely to women. A dream concerning Adlai Stevenson, who had died before the time of the dream, aided him in understanding his family situation as it continued to exist in his unconscious mind:

> Adlai Stevenson visited our home, my parents' home where I grew up (association: Adlai Stevenson was in the American social hierarchy, where my parents never made it, but he understood relating to Hungary, Russia, and Eastern Europe, where they came from—he could bridge those things). The time is the present. I feel my mother is alive, but I don't see her in the dream. She's around somewhere. I feel overawed by Stevenson and am afraid of a

face-to-face meeting. Now the house seems to be where I lived with my wife before the divorce. My son is playing hi-fi music and I am afraid he will wake Stevenson, who is sleeping in a bedroom. I stop my son rather sadistically by grabbing his arm and squeezing. Now I'm in bed, in a large bed; Stevenson is sleeping in another bed in an alcove. I'm in bed with my whole family: brothers, mother, maybe my children, too—all except my father, who is in the same room but, like Stevenson, is in a different bed. I wake up [in the dream] during the night and sense that some of the people in my bed have left, including my mother. The scene changes, and I know I am about to depart for military service, as if to Vietnam. Stevenson is going along to negotiate with the enemy. Outside a military mess hall I see Stevenson, who has become a Hungarian officer with the name of a scientist who was barred from visiting the United States and put in a hospital as if he were schizophrenic (association: my own depression). He was only released because of the pressure of other scientists. The scene changes, and I am being bitten on the left hand by a large cat that I am unable to shake off.

The figure of Stevenson represents someone able to bridge opposites that were not united in the patient's family, nor in his current unconscious mind. The similarity to problems with his father is shown in both Stevenson and his father being in separate beds, while in the same room the dream ego is in bed with a mixed group of family members, including most specifically his mother. A separation of the complexes represented by these family figures occurs autonomously, and the dream ego wakes up in the dream. There follows an increase in the level of conflict—it is to be military, but Stevenson is still expected to resolve the conflict. In the process, however, the complex personified in the image of Stevenson is taken over by the other side, the Hungarian uniform, where other forces (by association) are hostile to it. Only in this form is the dream ego able to approach the complex of Stevenson, part of the father complex, which it needs to integrate in order to resolve the warring sides of the personality. The attempted rapprochement on the "Hungarian" side fails, and the dream ends with an image of another autonomous action: the cat biting the left [unconscious] hand. The dreamer had no associations to cats, but the cat is often seen as a primitive feminine symbol, and therefore it is at times related to the anima grouping of complexes.

Although the reconciliation attempted by the dream failed, the dream shows the dream-making activity trying to produce affective ego states in which reconciliation can be attempted. This dream related more to the initial family stresses in childhood than to immediate environmental factors, so that those earlier relationships were pursued in the waking analysis.

A man who believed that a great deal of his anxiety and difficulty in being productive might have stemmed from early experiences with his father, who was strongly German in culture, had several dreams that seemed to show that the dream placed a higher value on this culture than did the waking ego. In one dream a German restaurant was placed high up in the dome of a church. Another dream was as follows:

> I'm in the house of my uncle and aunt. It is really quite nice-looking in the house. The outside of the house is the same as always, but the inside is new. Wood-beamed and vaulted ceilings, all beautifully done, have been added. I'm amazed that this could be done within the existing frame of the house.

The dream suggests that in regard to his troubled cultural background, as well as his severe father complex, much renovation has already taken place that is not visible on the outside (to the ego?). There is more spaciousness inside than appears from the unchanged traditional exterior.

Family constellations are often revealed in dreams. Significant discrimination between objective content and subjective content, which is more easily done in dreams of the past, can allow integration into the ego of strengths that were dissociated in childhood in order to deal with particular role expectations.

DREAMS AS INDICATORS OF TRANSFERENCE–COUNTERTRANSFERENCE

Jung was among the first psychoanalytic pioneers to emphasize the importance of the transference, although he clearly gave Freud precedence. Jung may have been the first of the early psychoanalysts to appreciate the transference phenomenon as a situation in which both analyst and patient can be caught in psychic constellations that diminish the conscious level for each. Jung was the first to understand that transference phenomena can have archetypal as well as personal forms of projection, that the analyst is also changed in the analytic process, and that there are parallels to the complicated projections of transference–countertransference in alchemical and religious literature. Fordham (1974) carefully detailed the position of Jung about transference–countertransference, which is perhaps best indicated in this linked form to acknowledge Jung's understanding of them as inevitably related phenomena. In the non-Jungian psychoanalytic literature, transference neurosis and its interpretation have come to occupy a position of importance, but the creative uses of the analyst's countertransference, particularly as it arises in dreams, have just begun to attract support (Whitman and associates, 1969).

Jung (Fordham, 1974) also found that in the evolution of the images in a transference, one can sometimes find a movement toward individuation in the patient. Jung's (CW 16) most detailed study of the transference was presented in images from an alchemical text, and they are somewhat difficult to comprehend if the reader is accustomed to considering the transference–countertransference situation in terms of clinical data alone. Nevertheless, the model that Jung presented is directly useful in clinical practice as a reminder of the several levels and vectors that are constellated between analyst and patient. In actual practice, of course, some aspects may be of greater weight than others, although all are present. In summary, these factors are the following:

1. The relationship between the ego of the analyst and that of the patient: the conscious relationship.
2. The relationship between the unconscious mind of the patient and the conscious personality of the analyst (and the reverse).
3. The relationship between the unconscious mind of the analyst and the unconscious mind of the patient.
4. The relationship between the conscious mind of the patient and his unconscious mind, with a similar constellation also occurring in the analyst.

For the term *unconscious* in these items it is usually correct to substitute *anima* or *animus,* depending on the sexual identity of the ego to whom one refers. One can imagine that the complexity of these interactions can be confusing. Both the dreams of the patient and the dreams of the analyst can offer important insight into the situation. In interpreting such dreams, great care is needed to discriminate the objective and the subjective levels. When the analyst appears in the dreams of the patient in a negative light, the analyst must seriously consider that the dream may be objective, showing some unrecognized shadow aspect of his actual interaction with the patient. Some patients, however, will cite such dreams as "proof" that the analyst is negative, while the dream may actually be more appropriate on the subjective level, where the negative figure of the analyst in the dream can show the complex in the patient's mind that is projected in the analytic situation onto the analyst. Ancillary evidence from a series of related dreams may help to resolve the question. If the image of the analyst in the dream is paralleled by other figures shown to be in somewhat the same relationship to the dream ego of the patient, the likelihood of the image being subjective is increased.

At times the analyst will dream of a patient, and he must then consider the same question of the objective or subjective nature of the dream image. It is a basic task of the analyst continually to reexamine his own dreams in the service of his ongoing self-analysis, which may require at times that he discuss troublesome dreams with another competent therapist. It is rarely of value for the analyst to disclose to the patient a dream about the patient, but such dreams should be considered carefully for any revelation of possible countertransference meanings that need to be understood and that should not be allowed to undermine the analysis.

An analyst-in-training reached an impasse with a severely neurotic control patient who was potentially borderline. The patient accused the analyst of being exactly like her actual parent, who had produced innumerable double-bind situations in her childhood. She claimed she no longer trusted the analyst and was considering terminating treatment. The analyst, in his control supervision, had become aware of taking the role of a positive parent figure, thinking of the patient somewhat as a favorite child. This came into his awareness through his own excessive pain at the patient's accusations, which he felt to be unfounded, although assertion of what he considered to be the reality of the situation had not led to any solution. Instead, it had simply produced a confrontation in which the patient said "You are like my parent" and the analyst continually asserted "I'm not."

A dream of the analyst helped to resolve the impasse, although the dream was not discussed at all with the patient. The analyst dreamed that he and the patient were about to enter an arena or a courtroom in which their confrontation was to be resolved. Just as they started up the stairs, it seemed that they mutually agreed not to go through with the process of deciding who was right and who was wrong. Instead, they sat by a small lake on the grass and talked in a friendly manner. As they sat there, both became aware of a dangerous white rhinoceros grazing nearby. They knew that it might attack, but both decided it would be safe to stay there together, since if the animal attacked it would be possible either (1) to knock it into the lake or (2) to jump into the lake and escape the beast. The analyst's associations to the rhinoceros were that it was a phallic animal, whose horn was used as an aphrodisiac (i.e., wanting to elicit affection). White was associated to death (an old association in the analyst's own personal material) and to an image of whiteness as being "not vitally alive," which had been noted in the past dreams of the patient. There were no particularly important cultural amplifications, and no archetypal amplifications arose spontaneously. Although some archetypal associations might be found, none were used in this instance, since the imagery of the dream itself seemed to show that the problem facing the analyst and the patient was a mutual problem that they were capable of handling without the analytic relationship being destroyed, so long as they dealt with the autonomous affective strength (the rhinoceros) and did not turn the process into a legal (thinking) dispute about who was right and who wrong. This level of interpretation of the dream allowed the analyst to feel secure that he was not unconsciously failing to respond to real aspects of the patient. Although the analyst's dream was not mentioned to the patient, his assurance, based on the dream image, allowed him to withstand several delusional distortions from the patient until the distortions lost emotional importance in the patient's mind (the rhinocerous fell into the lake?). A working relationship was again established, and the analysis progressed. It is important to note that the image of the rhinoceros in the language of this dream is like an autonomous content that can attack analyst or patient or both. It therefore resembles what can be pictured as an archetypal constellation that affects both analyst and patient (Meier, 1959, p. 28).

At times the patient's dream images of the analyst can immediately be seen as subjective and related to a content of the patient's unconscious that has been projected onto the analyst. A woman who suffered from depression because of unrealized creative potentials in herself dreamed that her male analyst had "bull's balls." This indicated, and the analysis subsequently showed, that the woman's own creativity, which needed a certain amount of bullish aggression, was attached to an animus image that tended to be projected outside on men rather than used as a guide to the development of her own personality. As she found her own creativity, the projection of such images of power on the analyst diminished, and he assumed his normal human dimensions in her mind. Overvaluation of the analyst can indicate a projection that can retard the patient's growth (CW 8:275).

In the Tavistock lectures Jung (1968) discussed the transference not as a way toward resolution of neurosis but as a hindrance in the analytic process, although Fordham (1974) showed reasons why Jung may have overstated this position at that time. Nevertheless, there is in Jungian analysis less emphasis on the importance of transference than in classic Freudian models. As a practical matter, no one consciously creates transference or countertransference phenomena, and when they occur they must be dealt with analytically, their resolution inevitably offering the chance for new insights in patient or analyst or both. But there is no reason to induce transference by any unnecessary regressive arrangement, such as the traditional use of the couch. If transference phenomena do not occur, there still is much else to be analyzed (Jung, 1968, p. 170). In all cases the restoration of projected material to the subject himself is needed, whether the projection occurs onto the analyst or elsewhere (CW 8:265–269). The natural termination of the transference–countertransference situation should be an increase in self-realization in both analyst and patient and a realistic relationship between them (Fordham, 1974). Sometimes when nothing seems to avail to resolve transference difficulties, the passage of time alone may be an aid, probably through shifting in the unconscious ego constellations in one or both parties of the dyad.

Jackson and Haley (1963) emphasized one of the conceptual problems in discussing transference–countertransference: the original emphasis on transference and the language associated with it did not take account of what has come to be seen as a dyadic relationship. The Jungian model allows for an understanding of dyadic interactions and even permits observation of transpersonal archetypal factors in the situation. Jackson and Haley (1963) offered a useful critique of regression as it occurs in classical Freudian analysis. Rhally (1968) spoke of the dyadic transference–countertransference situation as similar to the tension between Buber's I–It (the original transference model) and the more actual I–Thou form in which both parties are involved as persons. In this view, such conceptions as "feeling into" and "experiencing with" are meaningful.

Waldhorn (1967) suggested that dream interpretation may offer a relatively neutralized area, free of therapeutic split, where analyst and patient may converge efforts in the understanding of the patient's dream material. But even the apparently neutral ground of the sleep laboratory does not insulate dreams from transference content (Reding and associates, 1969; Keith, 1962).

The manifest dream of the patient may have clear relevance to the transference situation. Stewart (1973) described how a patient who dreamed that she saw things in a cinema or theatre had a sense of the analytic relationship as being also unreal. Although Stewart took a different approach to the observation, his data could suggest that the dream imagery reflected the object-relations patterns of complexes on which his patient's waking ego relied, and therefore the sense of unreality in the real situation. In Stewart's apt words: "The dreamer's experiencing of his dream, an intrapsychic function, mirrors the state of the transference, an interpersonal function."

Etchegoyen (1973) cautioned that if patient and analyst have similar qualities, the patient may attribute to the analyst a repressive ideological response when the analyst interprets the patient's defense.

The patient can then call his own side of the conflict an impulse, since he has assigned the defense (or control) to the ideology of the analyst. Such splittings are a troublesome but productive aspect of transference interpretation.

At times the anticipation of an interruption in treatment lowers resistance and permits the recall of "relatively little disguised dreams" (Peck, 1961). Omitting the theoretical statement of the dream as a disguised production, Peck's observation is correct, and it may parallel the way that many hypnotic subjects experience the "deepest" part of the hypnotic state immediately after the hypnotherapist has begun to bring them out of the trance (Crasilneck and Hall, 1975). Such interruption of treatment may produce some of the same reactions as anticipation of the end of analysis (Farrell, 1974).

A brilliant young student who had conscious feelings of competition with the analyst dreamed the following:

> My analyst, myself, and another person—I think a woman—are going along a stream. The third person goes along and may point something out, but she seems to drop out. Most of the action is between the analyst and myself. We are in the stream, heading in the direction of the current. He is worried about the edges of the bank. I tell him he doesn't need to worry, that we can find places to climb up on the bank and that I'll help him if he needs it. We follow a rivulet or tributary for a short way against the current. I am ahead of him and spot what I think is the source. Yes, it is the source! I see a columnar-like rush of a bright, almost luminous, watery substance coming up, probably from a spring. It comes from the ground which such force that it retains this columnar shape for a moment. It's like water, but less substantial. Then I am downstream from the source, and my analyst is up beside the source, a little way beyond it. It's where I originally spotted it, but there's also water beyond it and out to the side. Possibly it distributes water in directions other than downstream. I am trying to get up there, too. I am emotional—crying, I think. I call out that "I want to see it—in all its details!" The doctor understands exactly, and he may have originally finished my sentence with "in all its details" before I repeated the sentence. My saying this is a victory. I have gotten together simultaneously a very high pitch of emotion with spoken words. I've done it after failing many times in analytic sessions. Has my analyst noticed? [These last thoughts, too, are a part of the dream.]

Although there is archetypal imagery in the dream (the source here resembles perhaps the source of the four rivers of paradise in the center of the Garden of Eden), the main focus in the dream seems to be on the transference situation. Both patient and analyst can see the source of the stream they both explore, although the anima of the patient (the woman at the inception of the dream) may have had to start the process moving. Neurotic competitive questions about who is in charge are relativized. Both see the source, from different viewpoints at various times.

Often both poles of an ambivalent transference relationship can be seen in dreams, sometimes paralleling a split in parent images into a good and a bad. A scholar who was both angrily competitive with his analyst and concerned about the analyst dreamed this about the analyst:

> He had gone way overboard in an effort to come up with some sort of new way to deal with me therapeutically. He's read what I wrote [the patient's view of some difficulty with the analyst that arose in the patient's mind but that was not revealed by the patient at the time it occurred] and has decided to positively take my side and associate himself with my attitude in a way unexpected by me. I feel aghast, as though his behavior is rather sick, and a sad attempt to handle the situation. I feel really turned off.

Four weeks later, in the same dream series, he had another image of the analyst that related to his dislike of the concern in the preceding dream—it reminded him of a problematical potential relationship with a woman on whom his anima was projected.

> The analyst gives out Christmas cards [the dream was in December], and I am pleased to note that he has picked out a card that I would find pleasing. As I open the card, I find it is from Jane [the woman to whom he was attracted]. It is affectionate. There are many newspaper clippings [objective events?] as well. I am excited, surprised, and pleased by this turn of events.

Although the development and analysis of a transference neurosis is not an essential part of analysis in depth, the therapist must always be alert to dreams of the patient that indicate a transference situation, as well as dreams of his own that might bring to light unrecognized countertransference reactions. The transference–countertransference situation is an organic part of analysis, with both positive and negative potential, and it can lead to change in both analyst and patient. Dreams can be an important and at times indispensable aid in the resolution of a frozen transference–countertransference situation; if resolution does not come from the analyst's efforts, it sometimes comes from the autonomous activity of the patient's unconscious (CW 7:134).

DREAMS AS INDICATORS OF CURRENT CONFLICTS

In addition to the fact that they are one of the keys to the past, dreams always serve as indicators to the current situation. By seeing the way in which complex material is assimilated, the analyst can gain information about the nature of the complexes activated in the patient's unconscious mind in response to immediate problems. Judgment is important. To assume that recent events that appear in dreams are merely residues of the day, serving only to stir to visibility an old repressed wish, does not show sufficient appreciation of the intricate weaving together of past and present in dream images. The opposite extreme is equally to be avoided—some clinicians have suggested that everything that takes place in the session in which the dream is reported should be considered to be associations to the dream. Such an assumption of unconscious association between the dream and the material of the session may be quite therapeutic, but it is *not* dream interpretation. It is permissible, of course, to use dream material for purposes other than dream interpretation, but it should be done as a conscious therapeutic choice. To substitute such uses and consider them equivalent to dream interpretation blurs the framework of the analytic situation and opens a Pandora's box of intuitions without the firm corrective of the actual compensatory function of the dream.

Jones (1971) presented guidelines for use of the manifest dream during analysis. These include facilitation of the patient's memory and as symbolic counters for various achievements in the analysis. A number of laboratory investigators have studied the effect of stress on dreams, but these stresses were usually those easily controlled in the experimental situation. Freedman and associates (1970) used the stresses of a regular psychotherapy session to study in a patient the effects of the stresses on the patient's dreams the night before and the night following the therapy hour. The higher the patient rated such positive therapy session variables as self-satisfaction, wish fulfillment, elation, and control, the longer was the fourth REM dream period of the night after the session. But such long fourth REM periods were followed by therapy sessions in which the patient felt depressed, less controlled, less self-satisfied, and more anxious. The study was not sufficiently extended for general conclusions to be drawn. Kaplan (1973) succinctly reviewed other studies of dreams and social environment.

Breger and associates (1971) also studied the effects of an interpersonal stress situation (group psychotherapy sessions) on dreams. All 29 dreams of the experimental subjects incorporated elements of the theme of the group interaction the prior evening. Rossi (1972) has presented in detail a case example of the use of dreams, developed from a Jungian perspective.

Woltmann (1968) writing about resistance in psychotherapy, gave several striking examples of dreams attempting to bring to consciousness material that the dreamer might wish to avoid facing. One woman who had maintained a relationship with a man for 5 years, apparently hoping that it would develop further, dreamed that she came upon a garbage can with a shiny top. Her boyfriend's face was reflected in the top of the garbage can. The dream led her to make conscious some negative feelings that she had tried to suppress, and she decided to terminate the relationship with the tardy suitor.

The similarity of the material in a therapy session and that in a dream reported in that session has been emphasized by Fielding (1966). There is a great deal of clinical usefulness in his suggestion, particularly in noting the remarks that the patient makes after telling a dream and being aware of ego strengths that are shown in the dream. But the distinct meaning of the dream should be kept in mind, not reduced to simply another association in the therapy setting.

A young woman who was infatuated with a man she had known for a very short time was trying to decide whether to move to another state to be with him, although the future of the relationship was uncertain in her mind. When she had about decided to risk the move, she dreamed that she had caught from him a boil on her right thigh. In her associations, she assumed that this would have been contracted in the course of sexual congress, so that it might have come from his left thigh. If the frequent symbolic meaning of left (unconscious) and right (conscious) is allowed, the dream may have been saying that she had been infected with things that were unconscious in him, potential but not yet actualized. The dream caused her to consider the move more carefully.

REFERENCES

Bach GR: Intensive Group Psychotherapy. New York, Ronald Press, 1954
Breger L. Hunter I, Lane RW: The Effect of Stress on Dreams. New York, International Universities Press, 1971
Crasilneck HB, Hall JA: Clinical Hypnosis: Principles and Applications. New York, Grune & Stratton, 1975
Etchegoyen RH: A note on ideology and psychoanalytic technique. Int J Psychoanal 54:485–486, 1973
Farrell D: The prediction of terminability in analysis. Bull Menninger Clin 38:317–342, 1974

Fenichel O: The appearance in a dream of a lost memory. Int J Psychoanal 7:243–247, 1926

Fielding B: The dream and the session. Psychother Psychosom 14:298–312, 1966

Fordham M: Jung's conception of transference. J Anal Psychol 19:1–21, 1974

Freedman A, Luborsky L, Harvey RB: Dream time (REM) and psychotherapy: Correlates of REM time with a patient's behavior in psychotherapy. Arch Gen Psychiatry 22:33–39, 1970

Fromm E: Spontaneous autohypnotic age-regression in a nocturnal dream. Int J Clin Exp Hypn 13:119–131, 1965

Greenberg R, Pearlman CA: REM sleep and adaptation of psychiatric patients: An application of sleep studies. Am J Psychiatry 122:1147–1150, 1976

Hall CS: Dreams of being attacked, in DeMartino MF (ed): Dreams and Personality Dynamics. Springfield, Ill, Charles C Thomas, 1959, p 123

Jackson DD, Haley J: Transference revisited. J Nerv Ment Dis 137:363–371, 1963

Jones WL: Manifest dream content, an aid to communication during analysis. Am J Psychother 25:284–292, 1971

Jung CG: Analytical Psychology: Its Theory and Practice (The Tavistock Lectures). London, Routledge & Kegan Paul, 1968

Kaplan SR: Dreams of the social environment. Soc Sci Med 7:483–485, 1973

Keith CR: Some aspects of transference in dream research. Bull Menninger Clin 26:248–257, 1962

Markowitz I, Taylor G, Bokert E: Dream discussion as a means of reopening blocked familial communication. Psychother Psychosom 16:348–356, 1968

Meier CA: Projection, transference, and the subject-object relation in psychology. J Anal Psychol 4:21–34, 1959

Nichols CR: The Negro myth: A symbol in manifest dreams and its potential social implication. Presented at annual meeting, American Psychoanalytic Association, December 1967

Peck JS: Dreams and interruptions in the treatment. Psychoanal Q 30:209–220, 1961

Reding GR, Offenkrantz W, Daniels RS: Systematic transference interpretations in the sleep laboratory. J Nerv Ment Dis 149:152–185, 1969

Rhally M: Difficulties in the therapeutic encounter, in Wheelwright JB (ed): The Reality of the Psyche. New York, Putnam, 1968, pp 222–234

Robbins PR: An approach to measuring psychological tensions by means of dream associations. Psychol Rep 18:959–971, 1966

Rossi EL: Dreams and the Growth of Personality. New York, Pergamon, 1972

Sharpe EF: Dream Analysis. London, Hogarth, 1937

Stewart H: The experiencing of the dream and the transference. Int J Psychoanal 54:345–347, 1973

Torda C: Dreams of subjects with loss of memory for recent events. Psychophysiology 6:358–365, 1969

Waldhorn HF: The place of the dream in clinical psychoanalysis. New York, International Universities Press, 1967

Ward CD, Ward KM, Randers-Pehrson SB, et al: Birth order and dreams. J Soc Psychol 90:155–156, 1973

Whitman RM, Kramer M, Baldridge BJ: Dreams about the patient: An approach to the problem of countertransference. J Am Psychoanal Assoc 17:702–727, 1969

Whitmont EC: The Symbolic Quest: Basic Concepts of Analytical Psychology. New York, Putnam, 1969

Woltmann AG: Resistance and dreams. Psychoanal Rev 55:115–120, 1968

11
Dream Recall

Some patients dream readily, and in such cases it is necessary to try to select the most appropriate dreams for study in the analytic hours. Excessive dreams may even be used as a defense, inundating the analyst. Knowing when it is appropriate to pass up available dream material for other inquiries is a matter of clinical judgment and experience. Dreams are, of course, an aid to analysis, but dream analysis is not an isolated goal. The competent therapist should be able to treat psychological disturbances without the use of dream interpretation at all; thus if the patient either does not dream or resists telling dreams, analysis may still proceed by other means: examination of past psychological history; examination of current conflicts in the family, at work, or in social life; elucidation of transference–countertransference phenomena; examination of interactions with others in group psychotherapy. However, dreams remain a most valuable contribution to the psychoanalytic process because (1) they require less allowance for distortion through projection of complexes onto persons in the environment and (2) their symbolic nature spontaneously involves the patient's conscious mind and also points toward a deep range of meaning. The process of collecting dream specimens requires that the analysand remember dreams and that the analyst inquire carefully as to the actual remembered content of the dream before moving to the stage of the personal, cultural, or archetypal amplification. The exact form of the dream itself serves as a correction to projections into the reported dream by either the analyst or the patient.

BASIC INSTRUCTIONS FOR RECORDING DREAMS

The best way to "catch" dreams is to put pencil and paper, together with an available light, right beside the bed, where they can be reached without getting up. Then, the moment one awakens, the question should be asked: "Have I been dreaming?" Wait a moment for the response. Often a complete dream, or several, will quickly flash into memory. The dreams should be written down immediately. Additional details can be added later. Also, it is useful to write down one's associations to figures or events that occur in the dreams. For example, if a man dreams of his father, he might write, on the same page as the dream, "Father: 67 years old; was harsh when I was a child; feel close to him now; don't like his temper," and similar observations.

The dreams should be dated and kept in chronological order for easy reference. It is sometimes useful to do some reading about the symbols that come up in dreams, such as cats, crosses, horses, etc.

Trained psychotherapists can often find many important meanings in their own dreams, particularly a series of dreams; but it is by and large not a good idea to try to find a particular important meaning in one's dreams without conferring about them.

Garfield (1973) described her experiences in keeping a journal of her own dreams for 25 years. Various "interference" phenomena occurred, including distortions in penmanship, writing over lines during the night, pens running out of ink, etc. Because she was sleepy, she sometimes chose shorter words that were less exact. Sometimes the task of writing down a "flood" of dreams tempted her to quit the recording. Sometimes she dreamed that she had written the dream. Recording dreams became itself a theme in some of her dreams.

Even the simple intention to remember dreams can increase dream recall (Reed, 1973). Sometimes the placing of a pad and pen beside the bed of someone who allegedly never dreams leads to a sudden awareness of dreaming. Wallenstein (1971) suggested using an alarm clock rather than a clock-radio in order to ensure sudden rather than gradual awakening. He also advised not talking to anyone for a quarter of an hour after awakening—simply lying quietly in bed.

Tart (1965) predicted that eventually there will be techniques for influencing dreaming, so that it will no longer be such a private experience. It might be possible, he suggested, to train subjects to respond at various times during dreaming to cues from outside. This could represent "a new strategy in the study of private events" (Stoyva and Kamiya, 1960).

Barber (1969) found that both drive content and logical structure characterized the dreams of "reporters" as compared to "nonreporters" of dreams. Recallers have been found to dream about 22 min per night longer than nonrecallers (Antrobus, 1962). When the nonrecallers were simply asked to keep a daily record of dreaming, they recalled an average of 10 dreams per month (Antrobus, 1962).

Meier and associates (1968) in Zurich studied an adult male for 45 nights in a sleep laboratory. Repression did not seem to account for forgotten dreams, but such classic learning variables as recency, intensity, amount of material, etc., were found to be important. Most likely to be recalled were long and intense dreams occurring about an hour before awakening; short, neutral dreams from the early part of the night had a lesser chance of being remembered. Similar findings were reported by Trinder and Kramer (1971), who also found that dreams recalled in the morning were generally representative of the whole night's dreams.

Using a modification of Jung's word-association test, Emery (1971) identified words that were apparently associated with anxiety evoked by activated complexes. It was found that individuals who recalled more dreams 2 weeks after dreaming also were able to recall a greater number of words in the second presentation of the word-association test. Instead of using a standard word-association list, each subject's list was compiled from words that were changed between the first telling of his dreams on awakening and the retelling 2 weeks later.

In an attempt to use conscious purpose to increase the amount of dreaming, Rechtschaffen and Verdone (1964) offered money as an incentive for increased laboratory REM time. The increase was small and insignificant. They did report that the longer the sleep period before the first dream, the longer the dream. The attempt to remember dreams may have an impact on the dreams and on the dreamer. Any observed phenomenon is altered in the process of observation. When subjects were asked to awaken themselves at predetermined times, all the successful subjects awoke after a REM period, and about one-third of them reported having experienced a dream involved in meeting a time commitment or implying a definite time (Orr and associates, 1968). This was similar to my own experience in Meier's dream laboratory in Zurich, where I dreamed in order to change (it seemed in the dream) the physiological recordings to that the experimenter would awaken me. Dittborn (1963) trained himself to awaken after dreaming by using a tape recorder with a closed loop on which he had recorded the words "I am going to awaken while dreaming." During the experimental nights, as well as later, his number of spontaneous awakenings increased. During the experimental nights he would awaken when the recording was heard, even if the phrase about dreaming was replaced by a neutral phrase. After the experiment, he reported a greater ability to remember dreams.

DECREASED EMPHASIS ON REPRESSION

One result of the laboratory dream studies has been to indicate a number of factors involved in the lack of dream recall. The classic psychoanalytic explanation of repression of memory of the manifest dream because of anxiety associated with the latent dream must be considered only one factor in the forgetting of dreams. Cohen and Wolfe (1973) did not find repression to be a strongly supported formulation, but a psychodynamically neutral postsleep distraction had a strong inhibitory effect on dream recall. The concept of repression has been correlated with factors indicating cognitive control (Lachmann and associates, 1962).

Schonbar (1961) studied persons above and below the median in dream recall in a group of 45 graduate students. Dreams immediately preceding a waking period were better remembered. Dreams that awakened the dreamer contained more unpleasant affect than dreams that were followed by a period of sleep. Frequent recallers seemed to have more unpleasant dreams, with more affect in all dreams. The group low in recall remembered more dreams from the period just prior to awakening. The adaptive function of sleep was reaffirmed by Grieser and associates (1972), who found that subjects who slept after exposure recalled neutral material better than those who did not sleep, while those who both slept and experienced REM sleep recalled threatening material better than controls who slept but had no REM period.

Cohen (1970, 1974a) made many studies of dream recall, which he pictured as the result of factors of physiology, experimental methodology, and personality. Repression as a simple explanation of failure to recall dreams was not considered sufficient. Dream recall frequency determined by early morning telephone calls to the subjects correlated well with their own records of dreaming, but not with a questionnaire on dream recall frequency administered later (Cohen, 1968, 1969). Dream salience (subjective emotional impact of the dream) was higher for recallers than for nonrecallers (Cohen and MacNeilage, 1974). Comparisons of dream recall for monozygotic and dizygotic twins provided no evidence for a genetic factor in dream recall, but they did suggest that similar environmental living patterns correlated with levels of dream recall (Cohen, 1973b). Males high on "masculine" scores (California Psychological Inventory) more often had dreams with aggressive content than did women or men scoring high on the "female-ness" side of the scale (Cohen, 1973a). An interesting finding was that "masculine" subjects, most particularly males whose sex-role orientation was different from the cultural stereotype, had more unpleasant dreams than did those whose role orientations were congruent with cultural expectations. Sex-role orientation rather than genotype seemed to play a fundamental role in affecting dream content.

Further evidence of the adaptive function of dreaming came from Cohen's finding (1974a) that home dream recall was greater on mornings when the preceding night's mood ratings were more negative, particularly for infrequent recallers. Cohen interpreted this finding as supportive of the salience hypothesis of dream recall, but not supportive of the repression hypothesis. Similarly, infrequent dream recallers were more likely to remember dreams when their presleep self-confidence was lowest (Cohen, 1974b), a finding that was not duplicated for frequent recallers. Stress conditions produced greater recall of dreams for frequent recallers (the dream as adaptive?) and less recall for infrequent recallers, who may have used repression, according to Cohen (1972a).

PRESLEEP FACTORS

Presleep mentation can affect dream content, although it is by no means established that one can order a dream to deal with a specific problem, as some popularized dream books have suggested. The dreams of 27 subjects were found to be similar to their presleep associations during a tape-recorded hypnagogic association period (Baekeland and associates, 1968). Presleep stress increases affect in dream reports, and dreams with affect seem to be best recalled (Lewis and associates, 1974). Stress did not affect dream recall frequency in field-independent subjects, while field-dependent subjects reported less dreaming on nights with presleep stress. The lessened reporting was not simply a function of repression, the authors believed, since anxiety also interferes with attention at the moment of awakening, when dream recall can be disrupted.

An interesting experiment required subjects in presleep periods to wish to reduce discrepancy between self–ideal-self rankings (identified from Q sorts) during their dreams. While some dreams dealt with the ideal traits, these traits were seldom assigned to the dream ego, showing a differential between waking and dreaming intent. It is as if the intention to deal with a particular item may influence the occurrence of that item in dreams, but the dramatic use to which the trait is related varies according to the autonomous function of the dream. In Jungian terms, the trait might be shown by the dream to be attached to a part of the personality other than the ego, perhaps to the structures of the persona or shadow.

AWAKENING

Grotjahn (1942) discussed the process of awakening in terms of ego psychology, presenting a number of excellent phenomenological observations. During gradual awakening the person may become aware of "functional symbols" that do not show the content of the mind but rather symbolize in what manner the mind is functioning. *Functional symbols,* a term taken from Silberer's work, are much the same as what Jung would call the self-representation of the psyche. Grotjahn (1942, p. 17) also stated that the "kernel" of the ego is always present during sleep and "only the Ego boundaries change during different stages of sleep, dreaming and awakening." Again, this is an excellent phenomenological description, although I would prefer to say that the tacitly held complexes that comprise the contents of the ego change. The ego in its archetypal identity does not change, but its identification with various ego images is in constant flux. While relatively more stable than other ego images, the dominant ego image is also in a state of constant metabolism, awake or dreaming, under the individuation pressure of the central archetype. Grotjahn (1942) discussed several interesting dreams in which the dream ego realized that it was in a dream, although there may have been doubt, and that awakening was an option. Awakening may be produced by anxiety in the dream, and it is possible (as in my Zurich dream-laboratory dream) for the dream ego to initiate some activity for the purpose of inducing awakening.

Advice varies about the method of awakening most likely to preserve memory of dreaming. Experimentally, gradual awakening has led to more reports of dreaming than when subjects have been awakened abruptly (Shapiro and associates, 1963), a finding not consistent with Wallenstein's (1971) report of his own experience. Clinically, however, no generalization is possible at this stage of knowledge. Perhaps simply altering the patient's usual mode of awakening will increase recall of dreams. Gradual awakening that is produced by a neutral stimulus (natural awakening, as compared with that accomplished by a radio) often seems more conducive to dream recall than sudden awakening. Crucial in the process of remembering dreams is the manner in which the few minutes immediately following awakening are spent. Lying quietly in bed without attending to any external stimulus seems most likely to facilitate dream memories.

REGRESSION

Kalsched (1972) found that subjects who scored high on "adaptive regression" remembered more dreams. Also, their dreams were significantly longer and contained more bizarre, uncanny, and illogical material. An earlier study in the same direction (Zucker, 1958) showed that hospitalized paranoid schizophrenics had less firm ego boundaries but also less primary process material in their unconscious productions, while paranoid schizophrenics who were functioning outside a hospital had much stronger ego boundaries but also produced more primary process material and bizarre material. These findings seem relevant to the problems of creativity, where the creative person requires access to unconscious material together with ego strength sufficient to contain the unconscious pressure and weave it into a conscious form. Such findings also suggest that in most instances the unconscious pressure of dreaming may be tailored to the ability of the ego to tolerate stress, under the control of the central archetype process. The compensatory activity of the dreaming process is thus evidenced in another form.

AFFECT

It has been suggested that NREM sleep facilitates retention of nonemotional material and that REM sleep deals with material that has affective components (Grieser and associates, 1972). Frequent recallers of dreams tend to have dreams that are affectively charged rather than neutral (Schonbar, 1961). Frightening dreams seem to be more easily recalled (Desroches and Kaiman, 1964). Subjects who recall dreams usually have dreams of greater subjective impact (salience), according to Cohen and MacNeilage (1974).

EXTENDED SLEEP

Apparently, extended sleep may increase dream recall (Taub, 1970a, 1970b). This may be the effect of there being more time for repetition of the REM cycle during extended periods of sleep, but there are other factors at work as well. Clinically, patients sometimes seem to sleep for extended periods of time just prior to improvement, or when a new emotional stress is being accommodated. It is possible that such extended sleep is for the purpose of reworking complexes through increased dream time.

EFFECT OF CONTEXT ON DREAMING

The place and situation in which the dreamer sleeps seem to influence the content of dreams. Weisz and Foulkes (1968) found dreams reported when sleeping at home to contain more verbal aggression and physical aggression than dreams collected in a laboratory setting. There were no differences in percentages of recall, median dream word counts, and ratings of dreams for vivid fantasy, unpleasantness, active participation, and sex. Examining dreams obtained in the laboratory, Hall (1967) found that 14.2% of 559 laboratory dreams incorporated some aspect of the experimental situation. When only significantly influenced dreams were counted, however, the percentage fell to 6.2% of the dreams. Interestingly, he found no adaptation effects.

The person or group to whom the dream is to be told may influence the form of the reported dream (Whitman and associates, 1963; Winick and Holt, 1962), making it particularly important to inquire in such a way as to elicit the most reliable report of the remembered dream. The sex of the interviewer may influence the dreams reported (Ritter, 1963). Expectation of ability to recall may have more effect on NREM recall than on recall of dreams (Herman, 1971). The questionnaire technique of studying dream recall seems to give a reliable estimate of frequency, but estimates of sleep disturbance are more influenced by the form of the question (Howard and Orlinsky, 1965).

BODY EFFECTS

Popular belief accepts the theory of bodily influences on dreaming. A bad dream may be "just something I ate." Particular recurrent dreams, often of distortion in body size, may accompany fever. There is little experimental literature in the area of body effects on dreaming. Gross brain changes, such as prefrontal lobotomy, seem to interfere with dream recall, even when the subjects are awakened from REM periods (Jus and associates, 1972). Sheldrake and Cormack (1974) studied dream recall in convergers and divergers: convergers were individuals with high IQ scores but relatively low scores on tests requiring imaginativeness; divergers had the opposite test configuration. In female subjects an interesting finding was noted: the curve for dream recall for convergers paralleled the curve for progesterone secretion, and the curve for divergers paralleled that for estrogen secretion. The suggestion of physiological influence on dream recall is in need of further study.

MEMORY

It might be expected that memory variation could be a significant factor in the recall of dreams. A capacity for visual imagery may contribute to both the form of the dream and the dreamer's recall ability (Hiscock and Cohen, 1973). In one study memory variables (better memory for visual stimuli) distinguished those who recalled dreams from those who did not (Cory and associates, 1975). Problems of memory consolidation were thought by Giora (1973) to account for more forgetting of dreams than psychodynamic factors such as repression.

PERSONALITY

Personality factors may influence dream recall, in spite of some studies to the contrary. The mere fact of deciding to remember dreams may be crucial. When asked to record dreams, some nonrecallers suddenly can describe themselves as dream recallers (Domhoff and Gerson, 1967). If such easily transformed nonrecallers were moved into the recall grouping before personality measurements were undertaken, dream recall ability and personality factors might relate more consistently. A "positive attitude toward dreams," or a belief in their meaningfulness, may therefore be a major factor in recall ability (Cohen, 1974d). Among hospitalized schizophrenics, chronic schizophrenics were able to recall dreams as well as acute schizophrenics (Chang, 1964), although in the chronic patients dreams were shorter and tended to concern family members. Whatever factors influence sleep-talking seem to be correlated with ability to recall dreaming (MacNeilage and associates, 1972). It may be useful to differentiate various types of nonreporters in future research (Lewis and associates, 1966).

Rychlak and Brams (1963) related dream themes to personality variables. Their subjects who dreamed about having enjoyable interpersonal relationships were socially introverted, which suggests the compensatory function of their dreams. Baekeland and Lasky (1968) reported that those who remember dreams tend to be field-independent. Comparing reporters and nonreporters of dreams, Puryear (1963) found reporters to have a self-revealing tendency, showing more expressiveness and less ego strength and tending to be ruminative and ideational. Tart (1962) reviewed three studies relating dream recall to psychological test results. The relationship of dream recall to anxiety was positive, to repression or inhibition negative, to ego strength negative. There was no relationship to neuroticism or maladjustment. Tart commented that some measures of "anxiety" might better be considered as a tendency to introspection and rumination.

With field-dependent subjects, dreams were reported less frequently on stress-related nights (Goodenough and associates, 1974), but this may have been related to stress interfering with memory consolidation on awakening. No relationship was found between extraversion–introversion and neuroticism (Eysenck Personality Inventory) and self-reported frequency of dreaming (Farley and associates, 1971). Women reported a slightly higher frequency of dreaming than did men. A comparison of reporters and nonreporters of dreams with the MMPI scales *A, R,* and *ES* showed no relationship (Robbins and Tanck, 1971), although the number of dreams reported was small. No relationship between dream recall and MMPI scores was found by Redfering and Keller (1974).

Bone (1968) cautioned that future research in dream recall must consider the sex of the dreamer, since in his study extraversion (Eysenck's scale) correlated with recall for females ($p = 0.05$) but not for males, while grouped scores were insignificant. Cohen (1972a) reported that total sleep time was a predictor of dream recall for males only; results for women were in the same direction but did not achieve significance.

DREAM RECALL IN CLINICAL PRACTICE

Although Freud is frequently quoted to support the argument that repression is the only reason for forgetting dreams (Nagara, 1969, p. 70), Freud himself admitted the possibility of other causes (SE 6).

Factors other than repression include classic psychological concepts such as the time available for memory consolidation, the proximity of the consolidation to the end of the dream, the characteristics of the dream, and the situation at awakening (Wolpert, 1972). Awakening from a REM period may facilitate memory (Baekeland and Lasky, 1968). In clinical practice there are many other factors influencing whether a dream is reported (Klauber, 1967), not the least of which is conscious withholding because of transference distortions.

Our review of experimental literature relating to dream recall leads to one major clinical understanidng: repression cannot be assumed to be present when dreams are not recalled, since type of dream, motivation to recall, and interference with memory are prime factors (Cohen, 1974d). The illusion of being awake may even obscure dream memory (Calef, 1972). Both dreams and fantasy material appear to reflect a continual, ongoing stream of subliminal fantasy that underlies the everyday experience of the world (Cartwright, 1966).

In the clinical use of dreams, statistical correlations of personality characteristics associated with lack of dream recall are of little value. Dealing with persons individually or in therapy groups means that if dreams occur they can be employed, although any competent therapist should be able to carry forward analysis without the use of dreams at all. Changes in frequency of dreaming often have psychodynamic meanings, as when someone who allegedly never dreams suddenly recalls a dream, or a habitual dreamer encounters a period of no dream recall.

TECHNIQUES FOR FACILITATING DREAMING

A few techniques are sometimes of aid in eliciting dreams from analysands who do not habitually report dreams.

1. Keep a record of dreams, a diary.
2. Intend to remember dreams. Make a decision to remember dreams even when sleepy or when the dream appears meaningless at first appearance.
3. Have writing materials (or tape recorder) within reach of the bed, so that no major movement is necessary to record dreams.
4. When first awakening, lie quietly in bed with eyes closed for at least 10 min if no dream is recalled. Often a dream will suddenly return to memory.
5. Have recording materials available throughout the day, since events may stimulate memory of a forgotten dream.

Dreams should be recorded in as great detail as possible, since seemingly minor variations may alter the symbolic meaning of the dream images.

REFERENCES

Amann A: The dream as a diagnostic and therapeutic factor, in Wheelwright JB (ed): The Reality of the Psyche. New York, Putnam, 1968

Antrobus JS: Patterns of dreaming and dream recall. Doctoral dissertation, Columbia University, 1962; abstract in Psychol Abst Intern 38:829, 1963

Antrobus JS, Dement W, Fisher C: Patterns of dreaming and dream recall: An EEG study. J Abnorm Soc Psychol 69:341–344, 1964

Baekeland F, Lasky R: The morning recall of rapid eye movement period reports given earlier in the night. J Nerv Ment Dis 147:570–579, 1968

Baekeland F, Resch R, Katz D: Presleep mentation and dream reports. Arch Gen Psychiatry 19:300–311, 1968

Barber B: Factors underlying individual differences in rate of dream reporting. Doctoral dissertation, Yeshiva University, 1969

Bone RN: Extraversion, neuroticism and dream recall. Psychol Rep 23:922, 1968

Calef V: I am awake: Insomnia or dream? Psychoanal Q 41:161–171, 1972

Cartwright RD: Dream and drug-induced fantasy behavior. Arch Gen Psychiatry 15:7–15, 1966

Cartwright RD: The influence of a conscious wish on dreams: A methodological study of dream meaning and function. J Abnorm Psychol 83:387–393, 1974

Chang SC: Dream-recall and themes of hospitalized schizophrenics. Arch Gen Psychiatry 10:119–122, 1964

Cohen DB: Relation to anxiety level and defense style to frequency of dream recall estimated by different methods. Psychophysiology 5:224, 1968

Cohen DB: Frequency of dream estimated by three methods and related to defense preference and anxiety. J Consult Clin Psychol 33:661–667, 1969

Cohen DB: Current research on the frequency of dream recall. Psychol Bull 73:433–440, 1970

Cohen DB: Presleep experience and home dream reporting: An exploratory study. J Consult Clin Psychol 38:122–128, 1972a

Cohen DB: Dream recall and total sleep time. Percept Mot Skills 34:456–458, 1972b

Cohen DB: Sex role orientation and dream recall. J Abnorm Psychol 82:246–252, 1973a

Cohen DB: A comparison of genetic and social contributions to dream recall frequency. J Abnorm Psychol 82:368–371, 1973b

Cohen DB: Toward a theory of dream recall. Psychol Bull 81:138–154, 1974a

Cohen DB: Presleep mood and dream recall. J Abnorm Psychol 83:45–51, 1974b

Cohen DB: Effect of personality and presleep mood on dream recall. J Abnorm Psychol 83:151–156, 1974c

Cohen DB: To sleep, perchance to recall a dream: Repression is not the demon who conceals and hoards our forgotten dreams. Psychology Today 7:50–54, 1974d

Cohen DB, MacNeilage PF: A test of the salience hypothesis of dream recall. J Consult Clin Psychol 42:699–703, 1974

Cohen DB, Wolfe G: Dream recall and repression: Evidence for an alternative hypothesis. J Consult Clin Psychol 41:349–355, 1973

Cory T, Ormiston DW, Simmel E, et al: Predicting frequency of dream recall. J Abnorm Psychol 84:261–266, 1975

Desroches HF, Kaiman BD: The relationship between dream recall and symptoms of emotional instability. J Clin Psychol 20:350–352, 1964

Dittborn JM: Experimental recollections of dreams. J Psychol 55:39–41, 1963

Domhoff B, Gerson A: Replication and critique of three studies on personality correlates of dream recall. J Consult Psychol 31:431, 1967

Emery MP: The differential assimilation of dream content into waking consciousness. Doctoral dissertation, Columbia University, 1971; abstract in Diss Abst Intern 32:3632B

Farley FH, Schmuller J, Fischback TJ: Dream recall and individual differences. Percept Mot Skills 33:379–384, 1971

Garfield PL: Keeping a longitudinal dream record. Psychotherapy: Theory, Research and Practice. 10:223–228, 1973

Giora Z: Dream recall: Facts and perspectives. Compr Psychiatry 14:159–167, 1973

Goodenough DR, Witkin HA, Lewis HB et al: Repression, interference, and field dependence as factors in dream forgetting. J Abnorm Psychol 83:32–44, 1974

Grieser C, Greenberg R, Harrison RH: The adaptive function of sleep: The differential effects of sleep and dreaming on recall. J Abnorm Psychol 80:280–286, 1972

Grotjahn M: The process of awakening: Contribution to ego psychology and the problem of sleep and dream. Psychoanal Rev 29:1–19, 1942

Hall CS: Representation of the laboratory setting in dreams. J Nerv Ment Dis 144:198–206, 1967

Herman JH: Social variables influencing dream recall. Doctoral dissertation, Yeshiva University, 1971; abstract in Diss Abst Intern 32:6031–6032, 1972

Hiscock M, Cohen DB: Visual imagery and dream recall. J Res Pers 7:179–188, 1973

Howard KI, Orlinsky DE: Effects of suggested time perspective and order of presentation on responses to questions about dreaming. Percept Mot Skills 20:223–227, 1965

Jus A, Jus K, Villeneuve A, et al: Absence of dream recall in lobotomized patients. Lancet 1:955–956, 1972

Kalsched DE: Adaptive regression and primary process in dream reports. Doctoral dissertation, Fordham University, 1972

Klauber J: On the significance of reporting dreams in psycho-analysis. Int J Psychoanal 48:424–432, 1967

Lachmann FM, Lapkin B, Handelman NS: The recall of dreams: Its relation to repression and cognitive control. J Abnorm Soc Psychol 64:160–162, 1962

Lewis HB, Goodenough DR, Shapiro A, et al: Individual differences in dream recall. J Abnorm Psychol 71:52–59, 1966

Lewis HB, Koulack D, Cohen H: Repression, interference, and field dependence as factors in dream forgetting. J Abnorm Psychol 83:32–47, 1974

MacNeilage PF, Cohen DB, MacNeilage LA: Subject's estimation of sleep-talking propensity and dream-recall frequency. J Consult Clin Psychol 39:341, 1972

Meier CA, Ruef H, Ziegler A: Forgetting of dreams in the laboratory. Percept Mot Skills 26:551–557, 1968

Nagara H (ed): Basic Psychoanalytic Concepts on Theory of Dreams. New York, Basic Books, 1969

Orr WF, Dozier JE, Green L, et al: Self-induced waking: Changes in dreams and sleep patterns. Compr Psychiatry 9:499–506, 1968

Puryear HB: Personality characteristics of reporters and nonreporters of dreams. Doctoral dissertation, University of North Carolina at Chapel Hill, 1963; abstract in Diss Abst Intern 24:3425, 1964

Rechtschaffen A, Verdone P: Amount of dreaming: Effect of incentive, adaptation to laboratory, and individual differences. Percept Mot Skills 19:947–958, 1964

Redfering DL, Keller J: Comparison between dream reporters and low reporters as measured by MMPI. Social Behavior and Personality 2:201–203, 1974

Reed H: Learning to remember dreams. J Humanis Psychol 13:33–48, 1973

Ritter WP: Verbal conditioning and the recalled content of dreams. Doctoral dissertation, Columbia University, 1963; abstract in Diss Abst Intern 24:3840, 1964

Robbins PR, Tanck RH: MMPI scales and dream recall: A failure to confirm. Percept Mot Skills 33:473–474, 1971

Rychlak JF, Brams JM: Personality dimensions in recalled dream content. Journal of Projective Techniques and Personality Assessment 27:226–234, 1963

Schonbar RA: Temporal and emotional factors in the selective recall of dreams. J Consult Psychol 25:67–73, 1961

Shapiro A, Goodenough DR, Gryler RB: Dream recall as a function of method awakening. Psychosom Med 25:174–180, 1963

Skeldrake P, Cormack M: Dream recall and the menstrual cycle. J psychosom Res 18:347–350, 1974

Stoyva J, Kamiya J: Electrophysiological studies of dreaming as the protype of a new strategy in the study of consciousness. Psychol Rev 75:192–205, 1960

Tart CT: Frequency of dream recall and some personality measures. J Consult Psychol 26:467–470, 1962

Tart CT: Toward the experimental control of dreaming: A review of the literature. Psychol Bull 64:81–91, 1965

Taub JM: Dream recall and content following extended sleep. Percept Mot Skills 30:987–990, 1970a

Taub JM: Dream recall and content following various durations of sleep. Psychonom Sci 18:82, 1970b

Trindler J, Kramer M: Dream recall. Am J Psychiatry 128:296–301, 1971

Wallenstein HG: A method for recalling dreams. Am J Psychiatry 127:1421–1422, 1971

Weisz R, Foulkes D: A comparison of home and laboratory dreams collected under uniform sampling conditions. Psychophysiology 5:220, 1968

Whitman RM, Kramer M, Baldridge B: Which dream does the patient tell? Arch Gen Psychiatry 8:277–282, 1963

Winick C, Holt H: Differential recall of the dream as a function of audience perception. Psychoanal Rev 49:53–62, 1962

Wolpert EA: Two classes of factors affecting dream recall. J Am Psychoanal Assoc 20:45–58, 1972

Zucker LJ: Ego Structure in Paranoid Schizophrenia. Springfield, Ill, Charles C Thomas, 1958

12
Phenomena Related to Dreaming

It is by no means clear how nocturnal dreams differ from certain related phenomena. The dynamically oriented therapist will be able to employ any conscious or unconscious production for the purposes of analysis, but the importance assigned to the dream in Jungian theory makes it essential to form some judgment about whether the production is a dream (with implications of origin in the central archetype and relevance to individuation) or is formed by some more conscious process. The dream is a dialogue between waking ego and central archetype, through the induced experiences of the dream ego. Although all experiences may relate to individuation, the dream is most free of other contaminants. Whether an imaginal product is a dream or not must remain a question of clinical judgment. Simply keeping in mind that there are other dreamlike states of consciousness is usually sufficient for useful discriminations to be made.

ISAKOWER PHENOMENON

Isakower (1938) described a number of hypnagogic sensations associated with falling asleep. Although he indicated that they might differ, they have tended to be considered together as distortions of body image and to be referred to by his name. There may be a blurring of distinctions between different regions of the body and between what is internal sensation and what is external sensation. "Something" may be felt to be approaching, often experienced as a doughy mass that may be both outside the body and inside the mouth cavity. This something (breast?) may increase in size as it approaches and may or may not seem to threaten the ego with being crushed by it. Isakower cited the similarity of some of these experiences to the aura of epilepsy and to déjà vu, the sensation of having experienced before what is currently happening. He distinguished two basic processes in the phenomenon: disintegration of parts of the ego together with loss of differentiations. The "institution" of the ego that perceives, and which is usually closely identified with the body ego, becomes opposed to the body representation, and the boundaries of the latter blur and fuse with the external world. These sensations usually occur when going to sleep (hypnagogic) but may occur on awakening (hypnopompic).

HYPNAGOGIC HALLUCINATIONS

During the hypnagogic period between full wakefulness and the beginning of sleep, mental activity is almost always present (Foulkes and Vogel, 1965) and may vary from affectless visual imagery to hallucinatory dreamlike states. At times a dream state occurring in the hypnagogic period is particularly impressive to the subject. The reasons are immediately obvious: there is a sense of still being awake and in one's familiar surroundings, but then a dreamlike occurrence happens! The contrast can be startling. Two such experiences from a 30-year-old male analysand occurred a few days apart. Both indicated unassimilated ego content, in one instance "breaking in" and in the other a particular form of the "womb" of the unconscious:

I was lying in bed about to get drowsy, when I suddenly realized that the front door was opened by a large hairy arm, like the arm of a large monkey or ape. I awoke with a fright and realized I had not really been awake!

I was lying in bed [the same room as above] and did not intend to go to sleep. I was startled by seeing at the foot of the bed a large spider 16 feet tall! I saw it in cross section, and inside it was a womb, pink and egg-shaped, warm, moist. In the womb, facing away from me, a fully formed embryo was asleep. The spider had an elephant's trunk that it used to gently offer food to the baby. I was frightened!

Again the dreamer awoke, not knowing that he had been asleep until he experienced an abrupt transition to the waking state. Both of these hypnagogic hallucinations were psychodynamically very important, perhaps of more or deeper import than dreams of the same period of time. Theoretically, it seems as if a greater "pressure" for dreaming is required to invade the hypnagogic state with such formed dream images. Dittborn (1968) reported that taped suggestions played during sleep caused hypnopompic distortions on awakening in 2 of 5 subjects. Only one dream distortion was related to the taped suggestion. In one instance the awakening subject heard the tape in Portuguese, although it was in Spanish.

SLEEP PARALYSIS

The sensation of awakening and being unable to move is fairly frequent. In any group of a dozen people, one or more is likely to have experienced sleep paralysis at some time. Sleep paralysis is a disorder of arousal and is a component of the narcoleptic syndrome (the other components being narcolepsy, cataplexy, and hypnagogic hallucinations). Often the paralysis is accompanied by the hallucination of some threatening person standing over the sleeper. Liddon (1967) suggested sleep paralysis as the origin of the old folk belief that nightmares were caused by a demon crouching on the chest of the sleeper. An explanation of the nature of sleep paralysis often relieves the intense anxiety associated with it. There does not seem to be psychodynamically useful material associated with sleep paralysis, which may simply be a dysfunction of the reticular activating system.

DÉJÀ VU

The sensation of having previously experienced what is currently happening is fairly common. Both psychological and neurophysiological explanations have been offered for the phenomenon. Persons who do not remember dreaming also tend not to experience déjà vu, which suggests a similarity of the two stages (Zuger, 1966).

DAYDREAMING

In casually asking a new analysand about dreams, there is sometimes a spontaneous confusion of meaning between daydreaming or fantasy and night dreaming. Asking in several ways, or following with further clarifying questions, is sufficient to make the question precise. Daydreams do not have the profound implications of nocturnal dreams.

Most daydreams involve practical concerns and may be associated with an ability to tell stories effectively, with creativity, and with a greater similarity to the mother than to the father (Singer and McCraven, 1961). Daydreaming seems to decline in frequency with age.

HALLUCINATIONS

It is clear that hallucinations are different from dreaming, tending to be confused with the actual world. Even hallucinators maintain distinctions between dreams and hallucinations, but not between hallucinations and normal perceptions (Kass and associates, 1970). Hallucinations do not seem to invade the dreams of the hallucinating subject, although more study on this question is needed.

DREAM FANTASIES

Freud spoke of particularly well-constructed dreams as reflecting the particular clarity of some latent dream thoughts, and he considered a category of dreams whose elements were not subjected to condensation and displacement and were rather like fantasies occurring during sleep. He dropped this category, but later he was not certain he should have done so (Nagara, 1969, p. 52).

LUCID DREAMS

Dreams in which the dream ego realizes that it is dreaming have been called lucid dreams and have been studied particularly by Green (1968). A direct transition from waking to a lucid dream seems to occur only in those who attempt to make this transition. Ouspensky called such states half-dream states. The most common cause of lucidity arising in the dream is emotional stress in the dream, although noticing incongruities, initiating analytic thought, or noting the dreamlike quality of happenings may trigger the change (Green, 1968, pp. 30–36). Once the dream ego realizes that it is dreaming, it seems to have some control over the course of the dream (Green, 1968, p. 7). It seems likely that lucid dreams represent an intermediate state between dreaming and fantasy. There are also dreams within dreams of varying complexity, so that the realization that one is dreaming is a variable statement and may represent truthfulness but not necessarily truth (Malcolm, 1959).

HYPNOTIC DREAMS

The use of hypnosis to induce and explore dreams has a long history (Crasilneck and Hall, 1975, p. 229). Hypnosis has been used to implant chosen conflicts to determine in what manner they influence dreaming (Whitman and associates, 1964). Some such studies have been used as evidence to support a Freudian view of symbols, as in telling a hypnotic subject that he sees a female breast and later noting that he "dreams" of a "Mount Pleasant" that when drawn while under hypnosis somewhat resembles the profile of a breast (Farber and Fisher, 1943). Moss (1967, p. 70) found no evidence of Freudian dream work mechanisms in hypnotic dreams.

When a subject is instructed during hypnosis subsequently to dream of a specific lost memory, the dreams may refer to the memory indirectly (Crasilneck and Hall, 1975). By requesting dreams and then new versions of dreams, a form of free association can be used under hypnosis (Sacerdote, 1969) that can help bridge the gap between intellectual and emotional insight (Sacerdote, 1968a). Quoting Erickson, Sacerdote (1969, p. 137) suggested that having the hypnotic subject repeat a dream several times while in trance leads to less disguised versions of the dream. Dreams may reflect change in the clinical state of a patient undergoing hypnotherapy (Kampman and Ihalainen, 1974).

While there is no doubt about the clinical usefulness of "dreams" induced under hypnosis (Sacerdote, 1967a, 1967b, 1968a; Schneck, 1947, 1971), clinicians disagree about whether the dream produced in hypnosis is the same as a nocturnal dream (Schneck, 1966), is "equivalent" to a nocturnal dream (Sacerdote, 1969, p. 39), or is one of a large class of phenomena that will be produced by the hypnotic subject on command (Moss, 1967).

Dreams may more readily be recalled in the hypnotic state (Stross and Shevrin, 1967). The old question of whether dreams can compress subjectively extended events into a short amount of clock time (effectively settled negatively in REM studies) still arises with hypnotic dreams (Schjelderup, 1960). The suggestion of an unpleasant dream (without suggesting specific content) has been found to reproduce dreaming more closely related to current neurotic conflict than the suggestion of a pleasant dream (Horvai, 1969). Repetition of a hypnotic dream has been used to deepen the hypnotic trance (Wiseman and Reyher, 1962), although it is not clear that other, nondream repetitions might not have achieved the same result.

Induction of what Crasilneck and I (1959; 1975, pp. 16–17) have called neutral hypnosis does not produce changes in dreaming, but posthypnotic suggestions for decreased dreaming are effective in some persons, both subjectively and to a lesser extent objectively (Albert and Boone, 1975). In one subject, autosuggestion for increased dream recall brought dramatic results, but it produced some unpleasant side effects that may have been related to transference complications (Frenkel, 1971). Tart (1965, 1966a) was able to use posthypnotic suggestion to cause highly hypnotizable subjects to awaken at the beginning or the end of their dreams, but it could not change the amount of stage 1 REM time. Walker and Johnson (1974) found that hypnotic suggestion may influence the content of dreams to some degree, but they were not convinced that a hypnotic induction procedure is necessary. The effect of using subjects who are highly hypnotically suggestible must be considered in interpreting such results (King, 1971). In a study couched in Freudian theoretical terms, Wiseman and Reyher (1973) noted that the indication of a hypnotic dream in response to a chosen Rorschach card caused those subjects later to show more signs of adaptive regression in a subsequent administration of the Rorschach.

It is not clear at present how hypnotic dreams resemble or differ from nocturnal dreams (Domhoff, 1964). Weitzenhoffer (1971) reported eye movements in a hypnotic subject that seemed to follow the hallucinated (dream?) movements of a swinging watch. Finding that both slow and fast activity in the EEG may correlate with hypnotizability, Akpinar and associates (1971) increased speculation about the possibility that there may be a neurophysiological basis for hypnosis that may resemble REM sleep. Stoyva and Budzynski (1968) countered the theory that the hypnotic dream is a postwaking fabrication by pointing out that if such were the case, then long awakening latencies should yield long (fabricated) dream reports, whereas the opposite is observed, thus suggesting that the hypnotically suggested REM dream is a report of genuine experience in sleep.

Honorton (1969) carefully reviewed problems in conceptualizing the hypnotic dream. Stoyva's finding (1965) that posthypnotic suggestion to dream interfered with REM time suggests a real effect of hypnosis on dreaming. He also found that although the suggested dreams might contain a chosen motif, the context in which it was embedded varied. This can be taken as evidence for the hypnotic suggestion acting as a day residue rather than as a causative factor in the dreaming, or alternatively it can be seen from the Jungian view as evidence for the primarily autonomous function of dream production.

Tart (1965) discussed methodological problems in studying hypnotic dreams and produced a number of studies relating to this problem.

Different neurophysiological states in the same subjects when having hypnotic and nocturnal stage 1 REM dreams were reported (Tart, 1964b). During hypnotic dreams there was a waking EEG pattern and a lower basal skin resistance than in stage 1 REM sleep. Suggestions affected the hypnotic dreams more than the REM dreams. The equivalence of hypnotic and REM dreams was questioned. In response to Tart, Schneck (1969) stated that the crucial factor was the structure of the hypnotic dream, which might resemble a nocturnal dream or not. Tart (1964a) was aware of how factors other than the formal experimental intentions can influence the behavior of the subject, factors similar to what Orne (1959) called demand characteristics of the experimental situation. Tart (1966b) stated that the hypnotic suggestion to dream may elicit thinking, daydreaming, vivid hallucinations, or a feeling of being bodily in a dream world. Although formal induction of hypnosis did not correlate with a sense of dreaming, various measures of hypnotic "depth" did seem to be related.

In a study of inducing posthypnotic sleep-talking, Arkin and associates (1966) concluded that the achieved state resembled both sleep and the posthypnotic state. Increased talking during REM periods suggested that a useful technique might be developed for eliciting dream reports without full awakening. Hypnotic dreams have a greater amount of accompanying eye movement than imagined dreams, greater ocular activity occurring with increased resemblance to a nocturnal dream (Brady and Rosner, 1966). These hypnotic dreams were remembered more easily than ordinary nocturnal dreams.

Barber (1962) criticized some assumptions in the study of hypnotic dreams, the same considerations he raised in discussing the utility of the trance concept for hypnosis. Nevertheless, he found that hypnotic inductions increased the number of nocturnal thoughts that pertained to the stimulus topic (Barber and associates, 1973). Evans and associates (1967) found that subjects conditioned to respond to verbal commands during sleep might respond to the same cues after a marked passage of time, thus raising the possibility of finding a sleep model for posthypnotic suggestion.

While we must still question whether the hypnotic dream duplicates the nocturnal dream (Brenman, 1949), it is abundantly clear that hypnosis will be a useful tool in the investigation of dreaming (Schiff and associates, 1961). For the clinician, however, the question of the hypnotic dream is less crucial. It is perhaps wisest to place most clinical weight on the nocturnal dream, the more unconscious product, while using other imaginal productions, such as the hypnotic dream, to aid the analytic process, when indicated.

REFERENCES

Akpinar S, Ulett GA, Itil TM: Hypnotizability predicted by digital computer-analyzed EEG pattern. Biol Psychiatry 3:387–392, 1971

Albert IA, Boone D: Dream deprivation and facilitation with hypnosis. J Abnorm Psychol 84:267–271, 1975

Arkin AM, Hastey JM, Reiser MF: Post-hypnotically stimulated sleep-talking. J Nerv Ment Dis 142:293–309, 1966

Barber TX: Toward a theory of "hypnotic" behavior: The "hypnotically induced dream." J Nerv Ment Dis 135:206–221, 1962

Barber TX, Walker PC, Hawn KW: Effects of hypnotic induction and suggestions on nocturnal dreaming and thinking. J Abnorm Psychol 82:414–427, 1973

Brady JP, Rosner BS: Rapid eye movements in hypnotically induced dreams. J Nerv Ment Dis 143:28–35, 1966

Brenman M: Dreams and hypnosis. Psychoanal Q 18:455–465, 1949

Crasilneck HB, Hall JA: Physiological changes associated with hypnosis: A review of the literature since 1948. Int J Clin Exp Hypn 7:9–50, 1959

Crasilneck HB, Hall JA: Clinical Hypnosis: Principles and Applications. New York, Grune & Stratton, 1975

Dittborn J: Hypnopompic distortion of repeatedly heard verbal material. Psychophysiology 5:222, 1968

Domhoff B: Night dreams and hypnotic dreams: Is there evidence that they are different? Int J Clin Exp Hypn 12:159–168, 1964

Evans FJ, Gustafson LA, O'Connell DN, et al: Response during sleep with intervening waking amnesia. Science 152:666–667, 1967

Farber LH, Fisher C: An experimental approach to dream psychology through the use of hypnosis. Psychoanal Q 12:202–216, 1943

Foulkes D, Vogel G: Mental activity at sleep onset. J Abnorm Psychol 70:231–243, 1965

Frenkel RE: Remembering dreams through autosuggestion: Relationship of menstruation and ovulation to the autosuggestion dream recall cycle. Behav Neuropsychiatry 3:2–11, 1971

Green CE: Lucid Dreams. Oxford, Institute of Psychophysical Research, 1968

Honorton C: Some current perspectives on the hypnotic dream. J Am Soc Psychosom Med 16:88–92, 1969

Horvai L: Induced dreams during hypnotic sleep in neurotics. Act Nerv Super (Praha) 11:154–155, 1969

Isakower O: A contribution to the patho-psychology of phenomena associated with falling asleep. Int J Psychoanal 19:331–345, 1938

Kampman R, Ihalainen O: A changing dream in the hypnoanalytic treatment of torticollis patient. Am J Clin Hypn 16:206–209, 1974

Kass W, Preiser G, Jenkins AG: Interrelationship of hallucinations and dreams in spontaneously hallucinating patients. Psychiatr Q 44:488–499, 1970

King HH: An investigation of relationships between hypnotic susceptibility, manifest dream content, and personality characteristics. Doctoral dissertation, Louisiana State University, 1971

Liddon SC: Sleep paralysis and hypnogogic hallucinations: Their relationship to the nightmare. Arch Gen Psychiatry 17:88–96, 1967

Malcolm N: Dreaming. London, Routledge & Kegan Paul, 1959

Moss CS: The Hypnotic Investigation of Dreams. New York, Wiley, 1967

Nagara H (ed): Basic Psychoanalytic Concepts on the Theory of Dreams. New York, Basic Books, 1969

Orne MT: Nature of hypnosis: Artifact and essence. J Abnorm Soc Psychol 58:277, 1959

Sacerdote P: Therapeutic use of induced dreams. Am J Clin Hypn 10:1–9, 1967a

Sacerdote P: Induced Dreams. New York, Vantage Press, 1967b

Sacerdote P: Induced dreams: Additional contributions to the theory and therapeutic applications of dreams hypnotically induced. Am J Clin Hypn 10:167–173, 1968a

Sacerdote P: Induced dreams. Am J Clin Hypn 10:167–173, 1968b

Sacerdote P: Some projective techniques in hypnotherapy. Am J Clin Hypn 11:253–264, 1969

Schiff SK, Bunney WE, Freedman DX: A study of ocular movements in hypnotically induced dreams. J Nerv Ment Dis 133:59–68, 1961

Schjelderup HK: Time relations in dreams: A preliminary note. Scand J Psychol 1:62–64, 1960

Schneck JM: The role of a dream in treatment with hypnosis. Psychoanal Rev 34:485–491, 1947

Schneck JM: The structure and function of hypnotic dreams. Percept Mot Skills 23:490, 1966

Schneck JM: Comment on Tart's "approaches to the study of hypnotic dreams." Percept Mot Skills 28:982, 1969

Schneck JM: The hypnotic nightmare. Percept Mot Skills 33:582, 1971

Singer JL, McCraven VG: Some characteristics of adult daydreaming. J Psychol 51:151–164, 1961

Stoyva JM: Posthypnotically suggested dreams and the sleep cycle. Arch Gen Psychiatry 12:287–294, 1965

Stoyva J, Budzynski T: The nocturnal hypnotic dream: Fact or fabrication? Psychophysiology 5:218, 1968

Stross L, Shevrin H: A comparison of dream recall in wakefulness and hypnosis. Int J Clin Exp Hypn 15:63–71, 1967

Tart CT: The influence of the experimental situation in hypnosis and dream research: A case report. Am J Clin Hypn 7:163–170, 1964a

Tart CT: A comparison of suggested dreams occurring in hypnosis and sleep. Int J Clin Exp Hypn 12:263–289, 1964b

Tart CT: Effects of posthypnotic suggestion on the process of dreaming. Doctoral dissertation, University of North Carolina at Chapel Hill, 1963; abstract in Diss Abst 25:4820, 1965

Tart CT: The hypnotic dream: Methodological problems and a review of the literature. Psychol Bull 63:87–99, 1965

Tart CT: Some effects of posthypnotic suggestion on the process of dreaming. Int J Clin Exp Hypn 14:30–46, 1966a

Tart CT: Types of hypnotic dreams and their relation to hypnotic depth. J Abnorm Psychol 71:377–382, 1966b

Tart CT: The control of nocturnal dreaming by means of posthypnotic suggestion. Int J Parapsychology 9:184–189, 1967

Walker PC, Johnson RFQ: The influence of presleep suggestions on dream content. Psychol Bull 81:362–370, 1974

Weitzenhoffer AM: A case of pursuit-like eye movements directly reflecting dream content during hypnotic dreaming. Percept Mot Skills 32:701–702, 1971

Whitman R, Ornstein PH, Baldridge B: An experimental approach to the psychoanalytic theory of dreams and conflicts. Compr Psychiatry 5:349–363, 1964

Wiseman RJ, Reyher J: A procedure utilizing dreams for deepening the hypnotic trance. Am J Clin Hypn 5:105–110, 1962

Wiseman RJ, Reyher J: Hypnotically induced dreams using the Rorschach inkblots as stimuli: A test of Freud's theory of dreams. J Pers Soc Psychol 27:329–336, 1973

Zuger B: The time of dreaming and the déjà vu. Compr Psychiatry 7:191–196, 1966

13

The Actual Dream

The most frequent difficulty of the analyst learning dream interpretation is remembering to stay with the dream images themselves. Only by listening to the dream itself can the therapist avoid projecting his own thoughts about the patient into what is meant to be an objective interpretation of the dream (Day, 1949). If one stays with the dream images, particularly over a series of dreams, the internal structure of the dreams offers a corrective to unconscious projections.

The typological orientations of analyst and analysand also enter into the problem of dealing with the actual dream. Jung described not only the basic attitudinal orientations of introversion and extraversion but also four functions: thinking and feeling (the rational functions) and sensation and intuition (the so-called irrational functions). Thinking and feeling are considered rational because it is possible to order experience in terms of its logical form or according to the emotional value that it carries. Both the thinking and the feeling functions can produce order. The so-called irrational functions of sensation and intuition simply tell what is present, not its value. Sensation discloses the actual objects or events—the objects in a room, the events that impinge on the current situation, the thoughts that refer to a particular topic. Intuition tends to show the direction of a situation—what is likely to come out of it, what pregnant future possibilities it carries. Combination of introversion or extraversion with the four functional types produces eight possible personality configurations. In each person, one function will be developed to a greater extent than the others, while another function will tend to be largely unconscious (and therefore is able to repossess for consciousness contents that are in the unconscious).

The psychological type of the analyst affects his approach to dreams. If intuition is dominant, the analyst may tend to see in the dream what he intuitively feels is happening in the patient's life; alternatively, he may project what he thinks the patient's dream reveals, or focus more on the feeling and affective content of the dream. The most neglected function, in my experience with analytic trainees, appears to be sensation. Dream images are precise, even if man's memory is incomplete. By constantly maintaining an awareness of their preciseness, the analyst and dreamer may be prevented from straying into projections rather than dealing with the actual dream.

When I was in training in Zurich, a senior analyst who was in charge of a dream seminar objected when I asked the trainee who was reporting a client's dream about the size of a turtle in the dream. "A turtle is a turtle!" said the senior analyst, accusing me of nit-picking. He did not know that I had just had two dreams involving turtles. In one dream they appeared to be rocks about 10 feet in diameter, but they began to swim out to sea when I stepped on them. In another dream a small turtle no more than 2 inches in diameter had suddenly revealed itself to be a dragon. Turtles were not just turtles in my dreams. No dream image can lightly be assumed to be a constant without inquiry.

Berry (1974) offered a corrective to facile categorization of dream motifs without due regard for their particularity. The dream image not only reveals the value of what it symbolizes, but also it can be read so as to reveal to the waking ego the locus of the emotion that it experiences in the dream (Berry, 1974, p. 65). She disapproved of "heroic" approaches that dichotomize the dream in terms of friends–enemies, positive–negative, good–bad, all in the service of "notions of progression" (Berry, 1974, p. 70). As a corrective to using dreams for the ego's conscious purpose, her statements are important. However, she may have gone too far in the opposite direction in stating that "images are entirely reversible" and have "no fixed order or sequence" and in suggesting emphasis on "the imagistic" rather than the usual focus on narrative. Psychic objects, object-relations patterns, and complexes *are* potentially reversible, as she said; but if the dream presents itself in a sequence of particular images, then the movement of images (one need not say "progression") is a given form of the dream. Cocteau's statement comes to mind: "The dreamer must accept his dream." Berry's warning, however, like those of Jung himself, serves to remind us to approach the dream as a living entity, not something to be cannibalized for our ego purposes.

An important aspect of the phenomenology of a dream is whether the dream ego is an observer or whether the dream ego experiences its own image in the dream (Rossi, 1972). Marjasch (1966) made similar distinctions.

DREAM AS DRAMA

Not all dreams fit a dramatic construction, but many do. If the process is not overdone, it is useful to consider the dramatic construction of the dream as similar to consciously produced drama (Polri, 1954; Wilde, 1931). As Sharpe (1937) reflected, "drama is derived from the same material as the dream." Jung (1968, p. 100) suggested that when a scene changes in a dream, the representation of a thought has come to a climax. I would add an important observation: when one scene follows another in a dream, it is possible that the second scene can usefully be seen as a response to the attitude (or action) of the dream ego in the preceding scene. This usefulness of the dramatic process of the dream images is in direct contrast to the attitude of Berry (1974, p. 63), if I understand her position correctly. Her statement that "no part [of the dream] occurs before or leads to any other part" seems to impose dogma in place of careful observation of the changes in the dream images. It may be true, as she said, that dream images are layers of one another (layers of a complex?) and inseparable in time; *but* in a particular dream they are experienced by the *dream ego* in a sequence that may be dramatically structured and is not chosen by the dream ego itself. Any point of view from which the dream images could be considered "non progressive" would be an abstraction from outside the dream and not an experience of the dream ego. Again: "The dreamer must accept his dream."

Jung (CW 8:266) stated that "a dream is a theatre in which the dreamer is himself the scene, the player, the prompter, the producer, the author, the public, and the critic." Jung was describing the subjective interpretation of the dream, referring all aspects of the dream to personified parts of the dreamer's personality. He also allowed, of course, for the possibility that some figures in dreams may represent figures in the outer world. The bridge between the subjective and objective views of the dream images could be the complex; it can both act as a partially autonomous inner force and be the basis for perception of outer events. A dream often begins with a statement of place, introduces protagonists, and less frequently shows the time of action, all constituting the *exposition* (CW 8). The second phase is *development of plot,* followed by the *culmination* or *peripeteia* (CW 8:295). The last phase is the *lysis*—the solution or the result. This sequence can be abbreviated or modified, and not all dreams follow a dramatic form.

The usefulness of cinematic language in describing the phenomenology of dreams was noted by Pegge (1962). Koch (1973) suggested that there are parallels between various forms of communication about cinema and the process of psychotherapy.

In attempting to be true to the dream itself, it is important that both analyst and analysand allow for the distortions introduced by their own typologies, their relationship, and the danger that either may use the reported dream as an unstructured stimulus in which projections can be lodged. Careful attention to the exact image and dramatic construction (if any) of the dream are correctives, as is consideration of the dream within an ongoing series of dreams. If one does not fall into the trap of assimilating the dream to already existing ego purposes, it is useful in many cases to consider the dream as a dramatic production in which no image and no sequence is without meaning.

DREAMS IN SERIES

Over a series of dreams it is possible to follow psychological development in the dreamer (CW 5). Alexander (1925) early noted the relationship of dreams in pairs and series. Jung (1968, p. 86) cautioned that a single dream can be interpreted arbitrarily, while a series of dreams has internal correctives. This interrelationship of dreams of a single night has recently been confirmed (Kramer and associates, 1964). The similarity of concerns in waking life and dream motifs has also been noted (Offenkrantz and Rechtschaffen, 1963).

Trosman and associates (1960) studied 106 dreams of 2 subjects over 32 nights by REM monitoring techniques. Patterning of manifest content and the relationships of dreams in sequence were again confirmed. They also noted the relative autonomy of dreaming "as an ego functioning," which is consistent with the Jungian view of the autonomy of the dream process; but in Jungian theory dreaming is not, strictly speaking, an ego function.

AMPLIFICATION

When the dream has been reported in analysis, the next step is to obtain amplifications of the motifs of the dream. Motifs can be broken down in various ways, usually by the objects and persons in the dream, and then by sequences of action. Amplification differs from the Freudian technique of free association in that one does not continue associations to associations but rather comes back frequently to the dream image. Amplifications give information on the context of meaning in which each dream element exists in the mind of the dreamer.

Amplification can be personal, cultural, or archetypal. It is best to follow a sequence: the personal amplifications taking precedence over the cultural, and the cultural over the archetypal. This sequence prevents seeing archetypal amplifications at every turn. Making sure that each feature of the dream is understood in the dreamer's own associations was called by Jung (CW 8:285) "taking up the context." This taking up the context is not to be confused with Bonime's "contextual association," by which Bonime (1962) meant that a dream, once interpreted, comes back to memory in other, later contexts, which may serve to further illuminate the dream or to comment on the context in which it recurs.

Personal Amplifications

As early as the time of Artemidorus it was realized that the context of the dream images and the context of the dreamer's life were important in interpretation. Dung, for example, might indicate good luck in the dream of a farmer, said Artemidorus, but not for those with occupations where it could be put to no such use as fertilizer. Amplifications may change the meaning of a dream image. Artemidorus, for example, interpreted as positive a man's dream of beating his mother, since the man was a potter by occupation, and we call the earth that he beats into pots "mother" (White, 1975, p. 188).

The importance of personal associations makes it impossible to conceive of compiling a dictionary of dream symbols, for such a list would necessarily omit the personal level of association (Bonime, 1962), although Freud considered such a possibility (SE4-5). Waldhorn (1967) considered it possible to proceed without the patient's detailed associations if the patient is familiar to the analyst; he considered this another example of analyzing the patient and not the dream. But such a process would, as he admitted, not be dream interpretation.

Hartmann (1973) said that dreams seem to be lacking in subtle emotions that depend on feedback from the environment, but he apparently did not consider that emotions in dreams may appear directly or may be symbolized. What may be experienced in waking life as shading of emotion can appear in the dream as changes in scene or content.

In eliciting personal amplifications, it is sometimes of value to substitute the dreamer's given name for the pronoun I in recording the dream. For some analysands, this substitution makes the dream more objective and evokes new insights. For others, however, it may decrease the personal impact of recording it in the first person.

Cultural Amplifications

At times, personal amplifications give no information, and it is permissible to move to cultural levels of association. Most often it will simply be necessary to remind the dreamer of the cultural association to his dream motif, asking for his assent to the amplification. Often the dreamer will simply include cultural amplifications with his personal associations, with no specific instruction to do so. Artemidorus also recognized cultural symbols in dreams in Book 1, Part 8, of the *Oneirocritica*. Certain actions were considered universal, such as worship of gods, whereas others were varied from one culture to another. For example, the Thracians tattooed their children, while the Getae tattooed their slaves (White, 1975, p.21).

Archetypal Amplifications

Archetypal images appear in forms that have been passed through many minds over generations. Such images are therefore meaningful for many individual minds and across extended times. The use of archetypal amplification is a specifically Jungian technique in dream interpretation. The repositories of archetypal imagery are most often myths, folktales, systems of mythology, and religious imagery. Background studies in such symbol systems are important, although no person can hope to know an extensive field of such symbolism. Fortunately, even if the archetypal level of amplification is not extensively used, dream interpretation is still valid. But there are some dreams in which only an archetypal amplification seems sufficient for an understanding of the imagery.

Hobson (1973) quoted Jung (CW 9) as requiring four criteria to identify an archetypal theme: (1) the theme is a typical phenomenon in the material of different individuals, (2) it must be shown to occur in many parts of the world and in different times, (3) it must have a similar meaning whenever it occurs, and (4) the image must not have been acquired through education, tradition, language, or religious ideas. This fourth criterion is impossible of fulfillment as practical matter in clinical work. Indeed, it brings to light the competing theories to explain the occurrence of archetypal motifs that have not occurred in the past personal life of the dreamer. In brief, these theoretical possibilities are the following: (1) physical inheritance of imagery, which is *not* what Jung means by archetype; (2) some form of paranormal acquisition of the image, as by psi processes such as clairvoyance; or (3) a form of retention of memories of previous existences or reincarnations. However, the most usual explanation would be none of these, but rather simply cryptomnesia. In considering whether a motif is widespread, diffusion is an explanation always competing with archetypal origination (Pratt, 1967).

If the emphasis is placed, as I think it properly should be, on the use of the archetypal material in the dream, rather than on its being absent in past personal experience, the concept of archetypal amplification is more useful. In clinical situations one is not trying to prove the existence of archetypes but rather to use the concept for clinical understanding. In such cases Hobson's fourth point should not be overly stressed.

McCully (1971) cautioned that one must not think that because an archetypal image is ancient it is archaic. He stated (McCully, 1971, p. 53): "Just as evolution has developed within us a physiological isotonic seablood essential for life on dry land, the psyche contains the symbol projections and images that were necessary for the survival of consciousness and its development." Even if psychological concepts should eventually be reduced to "shorthand descriptions of complex brain events," as Hartmann (1973, p. 159) believed, the concept of archetype might still be valuable to point toward an ordering process prior to consciousness, and possibly prior to the growth of the brain.

We actually live in a sea of archetypal forms, but their commonplaceness renders us unaware of them. In the history of culture, particular archetypal forms are embodied and institutionalized in particular cultural forms. They then appear as simply the structure of the outer, social world. Since the living processes of the objective psyche are not static, there is always tension between the archetypal forms previously established in the world and those new images rising to conscious awareness. Neumann (1959) saw the individual as having inwardly to integrate the same materials that press for outward assimilation into world culture.

Myths are somewhat bound to particular cultures, and they tend to tell of supposed real persons in the early history of the culture. Fairy tales are closer to consciousness; they have fewer heroic qualities, less bound to particular cultures, and seem to form patterns of ego development that are somewhat in compensation to the dominant cultural forms. Mendelsohn (1968) traced this same process, on a less archetypal basis, to the literary form of the novel.

In amplification it is imperative that the tension between the particular and the general be maintained, allowing dream motifs to parallel mythic images without being reduced to the archetypal form (Berry, 1974). When an archetypal image appears in a dream, it manifests with a certain power, either a numinous affect or a compelling impetus to action (CW 7:70).

In contrast to the Freudian mode of reductive analysis, which reduces all images to personal experience (Nagara, 1969, p. 48), archetypal amplification reinforces and extends meaning (CW 7:81). Both methods have their uses. Archetypal activity can appear projected on the environment, usually noted in overvaluations or undervaluations (CW 7:95). One example that Jung (CW 7:99) used was the night sea journey, a form of myth collected by Frobenius early in this century. The story of Jonah and the whale is a typical account.The hero is swallowed by a sea monster; he travels eastward toward the rising sun; often he injures the monster internally and is disgorged at dawn in a newborn form. The same image may have a variety of archetypal meanings (Iandelli, 1968), and thus the context of its relationship to the ego is important. In fairy tales, which make visible fundamental archetypal structures (von Franz, 1967), there is no consistent morality. The wrong action in one tale may be the right action in another. Von Franz (1967, p. 102) suggested one exception: being kind to animals seems always to be the appropriate action in fairy tales, perhaps indicating the necessary presence of the animal soul in the process of individuation. Archetypal symbol systems vary from culture to culture, and thus any reduction of material to a particular archetypal form should be considered cautiously (Neumann, 1959). Collections of symbols, such as that published by Cirlot (1962), are useful, but they must be used with care. Fairy tales are a rich source of archetypal material, and they have aroused interest outside the Jungian field

(Heuscher, 1960, 1966; Sadler, 1969). Kluger (1968) demonstrated that archetypal themes appear more frequently in childhood dreams and in vivid dreams.

Several examples may illustrate how archetypal amplification can aid in dream interpretation. A number of years ago I had a vivid dream that contained an animal that was difficult to describe. In the dream this animal had two small cubs. I wanted to take one cub as a pet, but the mother animal was so angry that I felt it was dangerous, and I returned the cub to her. In my analysis we related this dream to a previous dream of two children; we believed that is showed a more archetypal form of a mother complex. In writing down the dream, I first described the large animal as an elephant, then as a mastodon, since it was more primitive than an elephant. I then decided that even more than a mastodon the dream animal resembled a giant tapir. Thus the most exact description of the dream image would be a giant tapir, an animal that does not exist. It was approximately a year later that I learned of Keeler's work with the Cuña Indians in Central America (Keeler, 1960). In their secret mythology there was an important figure called Achusimmutupalit, the "spirit of the Earth Mother's placenta," who was always pictured as a giant tapir! This is illustrated in Figure 1. So the image in the dream behaved appropriately to the Cuña mythological story—protecting the fruits of the tree of life, the cubs, from being taken. Even if I had seen Keeler's work prior to the dream, which I do not think was the case, it would still be an impressive cryptomnesia, and one would have to consider how the archetypal image of the dream was chosen in such close conformity to the unknown meaning of the giant tapir in the Cuña material.

Another impressive example of archetypal symbolism in a dream occurred with a patient who had a severe anxiety neurosis that prevented him from venturing more than eight blocks from his apartment. If he tried to cross this invisible barrier, he would develop an overpowering fear that his heart would stop. He supported himself by running a poker game in his apartment 2 nights a week. After 1 year of analysis, we understood quite well the origin of his fear (an oedipal situation in childhood), but his symptom was no better. Treatment was interrupted by my military service, but when I returned he was essentially unchanged, although electroconvulsive therapy given him by another psychiatrist had increased his range to 10 blocks from the apartment. Several months after he had resumed treatment, his girlfriend left him, saying that she was tired of being confined to the 10 block radius. At his own insistence I hospitalized him; he said he felt suicidal. The next

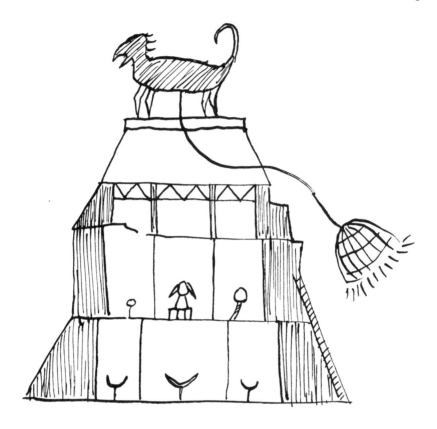

Figure 1. Image of Achusimmutupalit as a giant tapir standing on the Earthmother's house (womb) in which are images of the womb (lower three levels),
the Earthmother standing on a bed, and two "sprouts" formed by mixing of
male and female fluids. In Cuña mythology, Achusimmutupalit guarded the
plants, animals, and men produced by the Earthmother. (Composite drawing
by Donna Hall Lamb.) [With permission, from Keeler (1960, fig. 31, p. 40).]

morning he was better. Within 2 weeks he was able to drive a circular
route around Dallas without panic. He got a job and was discharged.
His improvement was dramatic, and it was too rapid to be attributed to
the medication I had placed him on when he entered the hospital.
Looking for a cause for this marked improvement that came suddenly
after years of treatment, I asked him about any dreams that he might
have had that first night in the hospital. He recalled only one dream:

I was standing on the deck of a ship that was in a canal. We could not move forward because a water monster in the canal blocked our path. Three young men in loincloths with spears went down to the canal to get the monster out. I was afraid they would be killed, but they succeeded.

I asked him, during the inquiry about the dream, to describe the water monster more carefully. "It was a large hippopotamuslike animal, but it had a pointed head." He had no personal associations to such a creature, nor did he or I have cultural associations. I did not immediately know of any archetypal amplification, but I went to a book on Egyptian mythology where I had remembered seeing a picture of a hippopotamus goddess of childbirth. Before I could find that picture, I found one even more striking. It was a representation of the judgment of the dead before Osiris. In the far corner of the picture was a large hippopotamus with a crocodile's pointed head, the "Swallower," the cosmic garbage can for those souls who did not pass the judgment of Osiris. It was a perfect representation, within the system of Egyptian mythology, for the threat of total annihilation that the patient had felt when trying to leave his apartment. The dream image of its being prodded out of the canal so that the ship could move forward coincided in time with his marked clinical improvement. It seemed as if the archetypal image shifted in the dream, and he simultaneously shifted his conscious orientation to the world. Further work was done with personal material after his improvement. He obtained good employment and soon married the girlfriend.

REFERENCES

Alexander F: Dreams in pairs and series. Int J Psychoanal 6:446–462, 1925
Berry P: An Approach to the Dream. *Spring* 1974. New York, Spring publications, 1974, pp 58–79
Bonime W: The Clinical Use of Dreams. New York, Basic Books, 1962
Cirlot JE: A Dictionary of Symbols. New York: Philosophical Library, 1962
Day D: Dream interpretation as a projective technique. J Consult Psychol 13: 416–420, 1949
Hartmann EL: The Functions of Sleep. New Haven and London: Yale University Press, 1973

Heuscher JE: Psychological effects of fairy tales. Confin Psychiat 3:146–157, 1960

Heuscher JE: An introduction to the understanding of myths and fairy tales Exist Psychiat 1:196–206, 1966

Hobson R: The archetypes of the collective unconscious. In Fordham, Gordon R, Hubback J, Lambert K, and Williams M (Eds): Analytical Psychology: A modern science. London: William Heinemann, 1973, 66–75

Iandelli CL: The serpent symbol. In Wheelwright JB (ed): The Reality of the Psyche. New York: Putnam's Sons, 1968

Jung CG: Analytical Psychology: Its theory and Practice. London, Routledge & Kegan Paul, 1968

Keeler CE: Secrets of the Cuña Earthmother: A comparative study of ancient religions. New York: Exposition Press, 1960

Kluger YH: Personal communication, 1968

Koch C: Cinema, discours, événément (Cinema, discourse, and event). Revue d'Esthétique nos 2–4 1973, pp 173–181; unpublished English translation by Mikel Dufrenne

Kramer M, Whitman RM, Baldridge BJ, et al: Patterns of dreaming: The interrelationship of the dreams of a night. J Nerv Ment Dis 139:426–439, 1964

McCully RS: Rorschach Theory and Symbolism: A Jungian approach to clinical material. Baltimore: Williams & Wilkins, 1971

Marjasch S: The "I" in dreams. Spring 1966. New York, Analytical Psychology Club of New York. 1966, pp 60–75

Mendelsohn J: The fantasy of the "white child." In Wheelwright JB (Ed): The Reality of the Psyche. New York: Putnam's Sons, 1968

Nagara H (Ed): Basic Psychoanalytic Concepts on the Theory of Dreams. New York: Basic Books, 1969

Neumann E: Art and the Creative Unconscious. Princeton, New Jersey: Princeton University Press, 1959

Offenkrantz W, Rechtschaffen A: Clinical studies of sequential dreams. Arch Gen Psychiat 8:497–508, 1963

Pegge CD: The mode of the dream. J Ment Sci 108:26–36, 1962

Polri G: The Thirty-Six Dramatic Situations. Boston, Writer, 1954

Pratt JA: Consciousness and sacrifice. New York: The Analytical Psychology Club of New York, 1967

Rossi EL: Dreams and the Growth of Personality. New York: Pergamon, 1972

Sadler AW: Dream and folktale: A cognitive venture. J Individ Psychol 25(1): 89–100, 1969

Sharpe F: Dream Analysis. London, Hogarth, 1937

Trosman H, Rechtschaffen A, Offenkrantz W, et al: Studies in psychophysiology of dreams. IV. Relations among dreams in sequence. Arch Gen Psychiatry 3:602–607, 1960

von Franz M-L: The problem of evil in fairy tales. In Curatorium of the C G Jung Institute (Eds): Evil. Evanston: Northwestern University Press, 1967, pp 83–120

Waldhorn HF (Ed): The place of the dream in clinical psychoanalysis. New York: International Universities Press, 1967

White RJ (Trans): The Interpretation of Dreams: Oneirocritica of Artemidorus. Park Ridge, New Jersey: Noyes Press, 1975

Wilde P: The Craftsmanship of the One-act Play. Boston, Little, Brown, 1931

14

Personal Drama: A Meaning of Dreams

Interpretation is not the only word for a Jungian approach to the dream. Interpretation implies putting something in a framework, but the Jungian approach tends more to open the dreamer to his dream. To interpret a dream could mean to know the dream, to know its origins and purpose, to own it as a possession rather than own it as part of oneself. Pure interpretation might attempt to steal the dream from the unconscious mind and lock it up in the storehouses of consciousness. But the dream is like an x-ray of the mind, a spontaneous picture. One may keep an x-ray film under lock and key, but it is not possible to own the living process that it reflects except as one can own up to something: one can say, "Yes, that's *my* x-ray picture of *me*."

In the Jungian use of the dream, the goal is not to reduce the dream to consciousness nor to a past event of consciousness, although it has relevance to current consciousness and often shows indications of past conscious states persisting in the unconscious part of the mind. In its unexamined state the dream is a natural compensatory process that attempts to maintain the health of the ego and move it forward on its path of individuation. When examined, the dream becomes a form of dialogue between the ego, which is the center of consciousness only, and the Self, which is the center of the entire psyche, the organizing template of the ego itself and the representation of the nucleus of the psyche appearing to consciousness in such images of totality as the mandala.

In addition to interpreting dreams, one can simply record dreams without interpretation. This is another use of dreams, and a valid one. Keeping the dream images closer to consciousness by such recording gives them a form in consciousness and seems to add energy to that part of the unconscious mind that is activated in the dream. Such recording seems to promote further unfolding of dreams.

The title of this chapter was chosen with some deliberation. Personal drama is intentionally parallel to the title of Polanyi's *Personal Knowledge*. Whereas Polanyi was speaking of how we *know*, Jungian dream theory speaks to how we *are* and how we are *becoming*, a process that is experienced as dramatic movement—personal drama. The subtitle emphasizes a meaning of dreams—one use among many. The unconscious is not exhausted by our interpretations.

In looking at the dream as a personal drama, some maxims are useful. One must remember that they are maxims in Polanyi's sense, and they serve only as aids to memory for those craftsmen who already know their trade. They are not rules that inevitably lead to the desired result.

Avoid presumptions about the meaning of the dream. Always begin with the expectation that the dream will reveal something unique, some new understanding of the dreamer as seen from the view of his potential wholeness. One meets an old acquaintance and asks "What's new?"—really expecting and wanting to know; this is near the correct approach. Unexpected new contents can be missed if one approaches an old friend with the attitude "He'll only tell me the same old story again."

What is the form and structure of the dream? Most dreams have a visual dramatic form that moves from the problem through development and climax to the outcome. Does the dream follow this form? Other dreams can be pure symbolic images.

Where is the dream ego in the dream? Some dreams seem simply to exist, with the dream ego resembling a spectator at a drama who loses a sense of himself in watching the dramatic action, forgetting the proscenium arch that defines the situation in an "as if" form. Does the ego take action in the dream? If one scene of the dream is followed by another, does the action (or inaction) of the dream ego in the first scene seem to initiate the response of the second scene? Sometimes the dream ego shifts identity within the dream or is assigned to several characters at once or in sequence.

Is each motif in the dream described as carefully as the memory of the dreamer permits? As with an x-ray, the slightest opacity, the smallest visible line, may be important in the total picture. There will always be a limit to the observability of dream images, as there are limits in waking observation, but the inquiry should push those limits to their natural boundaries. If "a woman" is reported, is she young or old, known or unknown, etc.? There is no absurdity in asking any question at all that could lead to a more complete description of the dream images. This process is essential to minimize projections onto the dream images by either the dreamer or the analyst.

What feelings does the dream ego experience? Would they seem appropriate to the waking ego if the dream situation happened in the everyday world? Is there an absence of feeling by the dream ego in a situation that would seem to require feeling? Does any change of scene follow the experiencing of an emotion by the dream ego?

Are the motifs of the dream, particularly persons in the dream who are known to the dreamer in waking life, better taken as objective or subjective figures? There is no clear answer to this question, but it should always be considered. Since personified unconscious complexes are often projected onto persons in the environment, a complex linked to a dream image that is taken subjectively can still influence the perception of the waking ego and therefore the relationships of the waking ego.

When it is felt that the dream itself is understood in as clear a fashion as possible, amplifications are obtained on the three concentric levels: personal, cultural, and archetypal, with the archetypal being the most "inner" layer of the complex. It is then important to relate the dream to material outside the immediate context of the dream images. It is to be related to other dreams of the dreamer, to his outer relationships, to his past, to his individuation process, and to his relationship to the analyst. Relating the dream to the individuation process seems to be close to what Hillman referred to as "the dream in the underworld," that is, the dream pointing not toward the obvious life of the ego but toward its relationship to more archetypal movements that may, in some phases of the individuation process, seem to be taking the waking ego "out of life" toward the "underworld." The individuation process can be seen as a whole only through symbolic forms. One can read the map, but one must still travel the road.

In relating the dream and its amplifications to the waking ego life of the dreamer, a number of considerations are important. Again, they are memory aids and not rules.

Where does the dream fit within the ongoing series of dreams from the dreamer? Is it an exactly recurrent dream? Are there familiar elements from other dreams? Does the dream introduce a new element in the dream series, or is it a reprise of older themes for reemphasis?

Is it a "big" dream or a "little" dream? Does it seem to the dreamer, or to the analyst, that the dream speaks about "surface" and rather immediate compensations, or is it a large dream from "deeper" in the personality, possibly foreshadowing a major new direction of movement in the psyche?

Don't treat the dream concretely or as direct advice. To simply take a dream figure as equivalent to a waking ego person or situation would be to totally ignore the subtle relationship between the subjective and objective views of the dream. To "ask" the dream what to do in an objective situation ignores the compensatory nature of the dream, abandons the responsibility of the waking ego, and gives no conscious standpoint for the dream process to compensate.

Don't reduce the dream to interpersonal terms alone. There is a tendency in some persons to reduce all dream images to interpersonal terms, as if the field of personal relationships were the total reality of the psyche. Although they are immensely important, it must be kept in mind that relationships are reflections of the intrapsychic state as well as causative factors in its formation. Dreams, in fact, offer a corrective to any tendency of the waking ego to simply identify itself with an extraverted "other-directed" evaluation of itself as reflected back from other persons in the world. It is equally undesirable, of course, to reduce the dream simply to inner "underworld" images.

Does the dreamer have any private unspoken interpretations that he has not subjected to the analytic process? Unless the analytic interpretation of the dream is open to both sides, analyst and patient, some unspoken assumption of the patient may undermine a valid interpretation. Inquire into the patient's feelings about the meanings that have been arrived at by apparently mutual work on the dream. A correct view of the dream may not "click" with the patient because of his defenses to seeing that meaning. But the patient is always "right," since it is only through the influence the dream has on him that dream interpretation can move into the ongoing process of individuation.

WHEN NOT TO INTERPRET A DREAM

Not all dreams should be interpreted. The observation of the dream, like the observation of any phenomenon, alters the object of study in the process of bringing it to an observable state. Since the dream is a natural function of the mind, it is in some instances more important to leave that function undisturbed than to gain the insight available through conscious reflection. For example, a woman with a severely negative mother complex once reported a dreamlike experience during mass. She felt that she "remembered" having been with the Virgin Mary, who had said "I love you very much." This was a meaningful experience to her, which she presented somewhat hesitatingly, unlike her usual approach to dreams and fantasy material. She was partially afraid that I would look down on her for her religious feelings, she said; and she also felt the vision was strange, not like a dream or ordinary waking life. If it had been some person she had known in real life, she said, it would have seemed as if she had suddenly remembered something she had forgotten.

I believed that the visionary experience, although relating to dreamlike processes, must have had extremely strong pressure behind it, since it had invaded waking life (although in a state of somewhat altered consciousness) even more than if it had been a hypnagogic hallucination. Also, it seemed to me that it was perhaps a spontaneous attempt of her mind to repair the damaged archetypal image of the mother by actualizing in her conscious experience a positive archetypal image of the mother to counteract the previous negative image of her personal mother. But to have discussed these psychological meanings with the patient at that time could have risked depotentiating the obviously numinous experience. I simply acknowledged the experience as meaningful and deferred any interpretation.

The general principle behind this example is that the function of the dream to repair the ego can in rare instances do more when uninterpreted, although the whole use of dreams in analysis is to aid the waking ego in taking a more effective stance toward its own process of individuation. The patient in the example above was not schizophrenic, but in treating some schizophrenics and persons in other psychotic states, one finds that symbolic discussion of dreams can at rare times work against the actual movement of the unconscious is attempting to restore adequate ego functioning. These are matters of developed clinical judgment.

In the following section, specimen dreams will be presented to illustrate some of the clinical uses of Jungian dream work. Because they have been chosen to emphasize various points, the dreams have been taken out of context, without the correctives, of (1) the series of dreams to which they belong and (2) the conscious situation of the dreamer. This should be remembered in case any reader notes a dream similar to one of his own. These specimens can in no way be taken as standard models; they must stand simply as examples.

INITIAL DREAMS

The first dream that occurs during analysis often reveals the state of the unconscious mind and may have prognostic and diagnostic value. The initial dream in a difficult and unfinished analysis of a very intellectual man was as follows:

> I'm talking to a man about the results of some tests and x-rays of my mother and me. He says it looks like there are brain lesions, indicating that a D&C (dilation and curettage, a treatment for uterine problems, such as excessive menstrual bleeding) of the brain will be necessary. The lesions result from too much abstract thinking, or working on one thing (only), or working overly hard. I ask whether this means it's the end of the line. He replies: "Oh, no, they can take care of that without any problem. It takes about a year of work—tough, hard work—but they can take care of it without any surgery or anything."

The dream seems to indicate(1) the presence of a problem, (2) that it is in the head (the mind), (3) that it may relate to a mother complex, (4) that treatment is indicated, and (5) that about a year may be required to see results. This man showed some improvement in analysis, more than he himself admitted, but largely through work on problems associated with his father (which his dreams also brought up). Had analysis been allowed to continue for the year indicated in this initial dream, the deeper problem might well have been found to be related to the mother; the excessive concern about the father was itself probably a symptom of "too much abstract thinking."

The initial dream of a young man upset by frequent use of LSD was as follows:

> I am standing on the seashore. A tidal wave is approaching the shore. It is so huge and so close that I know there is no place to run and nothing to do. I will be swept out to sea and drowned.

Although his conscious view of the situation was that the use of LSD had given him deep insights, the dream indicated the actual opinion of his own mind about the chemical: it produces a surge like a tidal wave that is capable of overwhelming the ego. If his ego centrum were to be overwhelmed by rising unconscious pressure, the man seen from outside would most likely be psychotic. After a very brief period of therapy, approximately 14 sessions, he had a related but different dream. During this brief therapy he had been able to understand his situation as one of danger. He had agreed to enter psychoanalysis, and arrangements for analysis had been made in his hometown, where he was to return. So this second dream may be considered an initial dream of the psychoanalysis that was about to begin:

I am the captain of a modern submarine that is going out to sea. The crew works well with me and I feel safe.

Put in contrast to the tidal wave dream, this shows that his mind accepts going into the unconscious rather than being swept into it. But the dream ego has allies—the other crew members and the hull of the submarine (the analysis?) that permits him to enter the sea of the unconscious but also to return. After this second dream, a much better prognosis could be anticipated.

PERSONA

An example of the importance of the persona in dreams was given previously in the dream of the army officer who dreamed he was lying dead in front of the stage—unable to live without his military role. This was an extreme example of persona identification. Reference to persona attitude is not uncommon in dreams; it is often shown in references to clothing, to performances on the stage, or to the cinema. A man who taught himself self-hypnosis and used it to overcome his natural shyness was successful for about 6 months in increasing his ability to motivate the sales force that worked for him. But after 6 months he became depressed and came for psychotherapy. His initial dream showed him at the national convention of the corporation for which he worked. He was to put a film strip about motivation on a movie projector and show it to the whole audience. The film strip broke. He rethreaded it into the projector. Again it broke. He realized that it would break each time and that he could no longer motivate the people (parts of himself?) with such a "canned" presentation. In therapy he rapidly improved, learning to rely on himself and to overcome his shyness rather than mask it behind a persona performance.

At times a dream can show that apparent improvement is only on the surface and not yet integrated. A man who had several relapses of depression had once again been improving. He dreamed the following:

People from my office are involved in a Sunday School play from about 12 years of age. It is pleasant and lighthearted and has lots of laughs.

His fear of not being good enough for the job, a factor in his depression, was again being masked by a Sunday School performance. The dream helped to keep both therapist and patient focused on his real growth needs, which lay behind the appearance of improvement.

A woman who looked and acted in a more mature fashion than she felt was unable to establish lasting relationships, largely because she felt empty inside, she felt that if she allowed herself to develop close friendships, she was sure of rejection if the friends discovered her inner vacuum. In her actual situation, a very adequate persona so effectively hid her problem that she made no progress in maturing. Her good qualities were assigned to the persona, with the ego image remaining impoverished. This state of affairs, and the need to face her fears, was shown in this dream:

I had made an elaborate meatloaf, taking great care to put in the right amounts of special ingredients so it would be my best meatloaf ever. After I got through, however, it didn't seem right. I finally realized what I had neglected to put in—the meat! I was thinking about this when there was a knock on the front door. I didn't want to answer, as I knew it must be a crippled salesman who had no legs and scooted around on a board with wheels. I didn't want to go through the agony of feeling sorry for him. Shortly thereafter, though, I was in a neighbor's carport, and the salesman approached. I decided to buy from the salesman the meat I needed for my meatloaf, since this would help him and I wouldn't feel so sad over his unfortunate situation.

Note that the dream salesman may represent some of her own under-developed animus function. She must face her feelings of actual inadequacy and give value (money) to them before she can get in return the ingredient needed to complete her own meatloaf, which may stand for both a food for herself and a food that can be offered to others in a relationship.

The night after a suicide attempt, a young male college student dreamed:

The lights went out in my apartment. I got a flashlight and looked for the fuse box. When I found it, it had a nameplate: "Kliegle Brothers."

The dream seemed unrelated to the suicide attempt until his personal association to "Kliegle Brothers" was added: "I don't know for sure, but I think they make klieg lights—spotlights and things that are used to light stage performances." The dream thus commented on his dramatic suicide gesture as a staged performance, which he admitted. He began to work on the underlying problems.

It is important to remember that the function of the persona is a natural part of the personality. Its underdevelopment can be as unbalancing as an identification with the persona.

SHADOW

Images of the shadow in dreams often appear frightening to the dream ego, but they may actually represent useful contents that can be integrated into ego functioning. It is important to know that the shadow is simply an alter ego image that is considered undesirable by the waking ego because of the dissociation involved in its formation. A great part of psychotherapy work is the identification and integration of shadow contents. Gestalt work on "polarities" is largely in this area of the personality.

A young man had felt isolated in high school in a small West Texas town because he was "neither a hood nor a cowboy." He identified his stepfather, a West Texas "cowboy" type, with a lot of the rough but reliable masculine qualities, particularly trustworthiness, that he needed in his own ego growth. Because these qualities were associated with the shadow, he saw himself as weak and ineffective, sometimes masking that sense of inadequacy with belligerent, noncaring attitudes. He dreamed:

> Ursula Andress and John Wayne are making love on the beach.

He considered Ursula Andress "the most desirable woman in the world," and his thought about John Wayne was that "he's the archetypal cowboy!" Thus his dream put a much higher value on "cowboy" than he did consciously, helping him to correct the dissociation of these qualities from his own ego identity into his shadow.

A 37-year-old married man had trouble with his wife and his 14-year-old son. The day before the dream, the son would not let his sister into the bathroom. That night the patient saw a TV show in which a young man and an old man robbed a bank. The young man was finally shot; the old man was also killed by going along with the young man in spite of his own judgment. The patient and his wife were in frequent conflict, the man wanting his son to be active in sports, the mother feeling the boy was being pushed. Between themselves, the parents had a conflict in which each felt the other was not warm and each felt "used" for the convenience of the other. The father had the following dream:

> We (association: not sure who) go out to someone's ranch. The owner of the ranch sends me out to a line camp not too far from his house to stay with his son. The son is trying to escape from the ranch for some reason, and he tells me about it, and I'm supposed to cover for him while he slips away during the night. I am to sleep inside a little shack by a big fireplace. He is outside on a

bedroll by a campfire. To escape he runs a rope up a tall tree, which is tall enough to get him over to the cliff where his horse is. The next morning the rancher and all the hands come looking for him. When they tell me he is gone, I say that he slept outside last night and I'm surprised that he is gone, but I'll help find him. Although he has gotten away on his horse, which is slow traveling, I figure he'll get away because no one will know which way he went. A bunch of people turn up at the camp to look, and we find only his dog is there. The father shows up in a big Cadillac, and several of us get in to go look. We look in a big garage-barn. The father says the horse will be there, but it is not. About this time, another big car pulls up, and a man says the son is in the back seat. When he gets out of the car, he is all roughed up. The man says they found him at a rodeo and identified him through his horse, which was killed at the rodeo, where he was a contestant. The boy looks tired, is not talking, and looks mad. In looking for the boy, I have passed several times through a shopping center. I see the office of "Dr. Love."

In this dream, the conflict between the ranch owner and his son can be seen as similar to the TV day residue, to the relationship of the waking ego and the actual son, or to different aspects of the dreamer's mind personified as the various characters. The conflict is one of masculine identity, between taking risk (the son, the rodeo) and fulfilling responsibility (the father). The dream ego does not choose between these, nor does the dream ego suffer sufficient tension to aid in reconciliation of the opposites. Perhaps the most interesting image of the dream is the office of "Dr. Love," which is merely seen, not involved in the action of the dream. This is an indication of the missing element that potentially could unify the opposites, whether they are seen in the intrapsychic or the interpersonal situation. When applied to the dreamer himself, he habitually identified more with the attitude of the father in the dream, having difficulty contacting the shadow "son" elements of play and risk that he befriended early in the dream. The dreamer's initial dream, for example, had shown him to be trying to pull a ship through waters infested with poisonous fish for the sake of his supervisor (father figure?) at the company where he was employed.

The shadow in the dream often shows negative parts that the dreamer has not faced in waking life. One man had a clear shadow dream but chose to deny the negative interpretation and to think of the appearance of shadow figures in his dream as "a definite manifestation of personal progress and development." Almost immediately another dream followed to correct that conscious position. In the new dream, 5 days later:

I am forcefully removed from my house out into the driveway, where a group of folks (males, as I remember, some of them people I know) are ready to attack me. I try to escape, as a couple of them are ready to burn me with cigarette butts.

On the strength of the second dream, the waking ego was willing to consider that the first shadow dream may have referred to negative qualities that needed attention.

The shadow has some similarity to the youngest son of fairy tales, often the despised fourth son who is considered unable to match his brothers, but who wins in the final accounting, often with the help of animals he has befriended. Also, the shadow, being more unconscious, seems to have greater access to the underdeveloped inferior or fourth function in Jung's concept of typology.

The waking ego of a woman felt that she was working long and hard to change her neurotic patterns. But in her dreams:

I was standing outside a ride at Disneyland watching people dare to get on and ride. A man controlling the ride was very gruff-looking, but I was not afraid of him. I wanted to ride, but was scared to. Then I realized that, scared or not, I had to get on the ride. But I never did. I just stood outside and watched.

This dream, showing the unadmitted passivity in her shadow, initiated a greater examination of her holding back from significant confrontations as well as from pleasures. She decided to become more active. Her marriage almost ended, but her action led to a better communication with her husband and to real growth in her personality.

A married man in his early thirties dreamed that his mother was accepting his mistress. Later, in waking life, he talked to his mother by telephone and realized for the first time that she seemed to enjoy talking to him about his sexual life. For the first time he realized that in his mother's mind he must either (1) be sleeping with a lot of women, or (2) be a homosexual. The dream aided him in seeing this unconscious theme that had driven him to excessive sexual involvements and to a secret fear of homosexuality. He was able to integrate in a more mature fashion ego-persona-shadow components, finding his own more secure identity that involved fewer compulsive sexual involvements together with lessened fear of homosexual tendencies.

A woman who was trying to rationalize her destructive marital situation as tolerable dreamed the following:

I am in a room, entirely surrounded by shit, wanting to get out but not knowing how.

The split between positive emotion in the shadow and fear of such emotion in the ego was revealed to a graduate student in a dream in which he, the dream ego, was cutting back ivy at the home of a professor whom he admired. Below in the house lived a young man who was a songwriter; he published folk songs that spoke with much feeling and played the guitar (association: the highest form of music). The dream ego also did work for the songwriter, because he liked him, but the songwriter did not respond. Neither did the professor, who was responsible, who worked and earned money, but who did not know the young songwriter who lived below in his own house. Obviously the integration of these identities in the dreamer's life was a goal of psychotherapy.

The shadow is a vital part of the personality that resists ego integration because of former value judgments that may not be consistent with current goals of the analysand. Both positive and negative qualities can exist in the shadow. Unintegrated, they tend to be projected and faced in the outer world, so that integration of the shadow often prevents recurrent complications in interpersonal situations.

ANIMA-ANIMUS

The anima (in the dreams of a man) and the animus (in the dreams of a woman) may have characteristics that are complementary to the persona (CW 6:468). The anima and animus are psychological functions that have retained a "personality" because they are autonomous and undeveloped (CW 8:210). The more the anima is developed, the less it appears in projected form, producing attraction or repulsion to persons in the outer world, usually of the opposite sex. In its undeveloped and personified form the anima can invade or possess the ego. When this occurs, a well-adapted man may suddenly find himself at the mercy of childish emotion. A woman who consciousness is taken over by her animus may find herself attracted to a man's impressive but ungrounded ideas, or she may find that she is putting forward as her own thoughts ideas that have not really been assimilated into her own mind but have been borrowed unconsciously from outside. These descriptions of anima-animus functioning are schematic and culturally influenced. In the individual case, the nuances soften and personalize such stereotypes. The functioning of the animus-anima cannot be as fully integrated into ego consciousness, since the anima-animus area of the psyche underlies the need for relationship with non-ego contents both internally and externally. But some functions of the anima-animus can be integrated, and the more progressed this integration is, the less the anima-animus appears in personified form. A man, for example, may cease to be helplessly fascinated by women or overtaken by moods, finding instead that he "knows" in a feeling way what he previously learned from the image of the anima.

A young man in his early thirties had difficulty getting into life professionally, socially, and emotionally. He dreamed:

> I was milling around with a lot of people where a boat was about to depart. There was a gangplank going up to the boat. All the people on the boat were dead, but among them I saw a girl that I had once been interested in. She was heading up the gangplank. I ran up the gangplank after her, thinking how nice it would be to see her again, when suddenly the gatekeeper stuck out his foot and said "Stop! You can't go on this ship now. Maybe you can next time if you insist on it."

When the dreamer reflected on the dream, he was somewhat frightened, since the boat seemed likely to represent the passage into death, while the gatekeeper, like Charon on the River Styx, admitted only those who had died. This dream came at a time when the man was trying to make a major decision: whether to enter a graduate program in clinical psychology or to study library science and, as he saw it, "hide out in a library and work with books instead of people." He recognized in the dream a strong pull toward the past and its security, but he also knew that direction was "death." He chose the more interpersonal and to him more challenging field of study.

A lack of developed feeling is shown in the dream of a younger man:

> There are two hills. On one of them my wife is being crucified. On the other hill a young woman is also being crucified. A gnomelike man is moving back and forth, untying them both (they are tied, not nailed to the crosses). He is getting water for them. I say to the gnome, "Don't you get bored doing that?" I have absolutely no feeling in the dream.

This example shows how a dream may indicate, through lack of response in the dream ego, something that is missing in the conscious adaptation. Apparently the feeling for the anima (wife and beautiful young woman) resides in a very primitive layer of the masculine identity in this man, in the gnome, who mythologically can be related to the archetypal image of the Great Mother. A development of feeling is indicated in a later dream from the same man:

> I go to the college where I am a student. I am dressed in a very dark green wizard suit with a pointed hat. The building is on fire, and people are running about. I am calm and simply go to the class that I am to teach as a student assistant. The class is waiting. I dismiss them, and they run quickly out of the burning building. The scene changes, and I am sitting on the ground where a fire has been (the fire having consumed the building?). A very human ape is

sitting in the same pose across from me. Between us is a small "survival fire." We seem to be in close communion. The scene again changes, and I am in a house that grandfather bought from two old "pioneer ladies" (actually true in the patient's past history). My wife and I are cooking a meal over a hearth fire.

This dream illustrates three kinds of fires (consuming and dangerous, survival fire, and family hearth fire), and it shows a progression toward more feeling for the wife, in contrast to the crucifixion dream.

The developing animus of a woman who had been overly compliant to a cold, autocratic husband for many years showed first in her dreams. The helping animus figure, itself in need of care, paralleled her waking experience of being able to care for other people in a useful way in her work long before she learned to care for her own needs effectively. The nascent animus function is indicated in this dream:

A young man was in the hospital following an accident. But he was the healthiest patient I ever saw. When I reached the hospital for the first visit, I found that he had talked the nurses into rolling his bed out where several halls came together. [We considered in discussing the dream whether "hall" was a dream pun on my name, but decided against that possibility.] He was comforting everyone in sight and all who passed. People were deliberately going to where he was to stay with him a while: little ones, lonely adults, hurt people. But he wasn't strong enough to leave the hospital or his bed just yet.

Often the developing anima-animus needs response from the dream ego to continue the development, and this is frequently indicated in dream imagery. A woman who had relied too heavily on a persona to hide her infantile and undeveloped ego had the following dream. Note the several different figures associated with the animus function. They seem to move from a more normal male figure to someone who suggests the archetypal image of the Old Wise Man.

I'm with an attractive man about my age, a girl about my age who is blonde and attractive, and a young boy of about twelve. The man explains that he has learned a secret of everlasting world peace. He begins to tell the boy that the boy is black and not a Christian, that I am a prostitute, and the other woman is a snobbish society babe. The boy objected that he was not black and that he was a Christian. I quickly realized the man's approach—that if we learn more about the lives of people different from ourselves we can develop empathy and understanding and thus a caring for all peoples. Next thing I know there is an assembly of people. I noticed an odd little man who was shorter than myself, bald, too heavy, and wearing nothing but a white loincloth. He spoke softly, but everyone strained to hear him. Somehow I felt he was a teacher of the first man. He talked about how things can change. He pointed to the dark sky, and I saw that the sun and the moon were there at the same time, moving overhead in a circle around each other. I noticed, too, that the hands of my watch were spinning round. Then some men in uniform came and arrested the man, saying he was a threat to the state. As he was taken away, a woman and man (association: like the sun and moon?) stood up and said they would not let his teaching die. They began to leave, but officers were waiting to arrest them also. Then we all went with them, thinking that they can't arrest the whole population. The scene changed, and I was with the first man and the woman again. He said we should know life. There was something wrong with the plumbing where we were, and we were about to check it out when I woke up.

This is clearly a very complicated dream that can be discussed only briefly here. In addition to the positive animus figures, female parts of the ego are indicated as well. A regression to archetypal imagery (sun and moon) occurs, which seems to add validity to "knowing life" as opposed to keeping intact the "state," the old collective rules under which the waking ego had been severely unhappy. The need to "fix the plumbing" at the end of the dream places action back into the real world where small changes are possible, leading toward a larger growth of the entire personality.

In dealing with anima-animus in dream images, it is well to consider carefully the relationships of the dream images to current and past interpersonal situations of the waking ego, since the anima-animus often manifests in relationships. The transference situation being a relationship, it, too, should be scanned for possible relationship to the dream images of the anima-animus.

EGO ACTIVITY OR PASSIVITY

It is very instructive to note whether the dream ego takes appropriate action in dreams. Most of the examples in this book will show such action as positive, although this is not always the case. In fairy tales, too, the correct choice of the hero is usually action, although passivity may sometimes be the better choice. Action may also include taking an attitude or having an emotional response. It is possible that the high value placed on the action of the dream ego is partially an artifact of these dreamers being relatively young and still involved in the task of establishing adequate identity in the outer world, the first phase of the individuation process. In those stages of life where the ego must defer to the Self, dreams might show ego action as less appropriate, although one would have to judge by the specific situation, since dream action could lead to a state of the waking ego being less aggressive.

A man in his fifties dreamed that he was in a store with his mother:

I saw that the women were stealing brightly colored stockings and wearing them out of the store. I strongly urged my mother to stop them from stealing, but she simply indicated that it was none of her business, as if to say, "Who, me?" The women then turned into three cats, one of whom began to defecate in a bowl that was meant to be used for food.

In associating to the dream, this man remembered a dream he had several years earlier when working with another analyst. In the earlier dream, his ex-wife was driving a car, with him in the passenger seat. Balanced on the hood of the car was a bowl in which bread dough was rising. It fell off the car. He also associated the dream with a past sexual involvement with an older woman, an affair in which he experienced the most exhilaration and energy of his life, but that soon left him in a state of helplessness and apathy.

Although the ego in this dream is active, it is active only toward asking the mother to take charge of the situation. The result is not effective; it leads to a regression in the complex toward the image of the cats, a more primitive form. The cat defecating in the bowl paralleled the bowl of food that was lost in the previous dream when he allowed himself simply to be a passenger, his ex-wife determining the course of the action, just as the mother made the decisions in the recent dream. The relationship with the older woman had shown the extreme amount of energy he derived from a connection to the image of the mother, but also the ineffectiveness of that connection in transforming his ego without the ego taking direct action. The opposite effect, a disturbing image turning into a less disturbing one, occurred in the dream of a woman with a very negative mother complex. A large frightening spider was trying to enter her window, but when she locked the screen to prevent its entering, it moved to the front yard and became a puppy.

Another woman who had trouble using her great energy in her own behalf dreamed the following:

There were two of me. One was patiently listening, but the other one was a stoic and would not talk. This passive woman acted as if there could be no solution; she just had to endure.

This motif was repeated in another dream of the same woman the next night:

I dreamed I was in a hospital as a patient. An intern cut down on a vein to give me a transfusion of packed red cells (association: for anemia?). Another of me was helping the intern.

In this second dream a night later, the woman who was "just listening" became more active, although the most direct action is taken through the intern, probably representing an animus image.

A month prior to these two dreams, the same woman had a dream that seemed to indicate that it was indeed possible for her to survive her many psychological problems. She had dreamed that she was in a lifeboat one-quarter of a mile long—certainly large enough to rescue all the parts of herself that she felt might be lost.

A sad dream that clearly shows the danger of ego passivity, as well as illustrating again the attribution of power to a mother image, is from a woman who had just begun to separate herself from a subtly domineering and controlling mother:

There was a "mothering contest." I wanted to enter, feeling I had mothered well enough during the last 2 years [i.e., had mothered her own young child]. Then I realized that I couldn't even enter the contest because I wasn't eligible, since I had not been mothered adequately. Any success with my own child might establish what I could do as a mother, but it did not change the fact that I had received inadequate mothering from my own mother. It was a sad realization, although not devastating, and it seemed very, very true.

This dream helped her to see the absurdity of always referring to the past instead of focusing ont he many strengths she was already able to use.

WATER IMAGES IN DREAMS

There is no way to make an invariable equivalence between any image, such as water, and its meaning in a particular dream. All that can usefully be said is that certain images tend to have recurrent meanings in the dreams of different people. It is absolutely necessary to examine each dream independently of any preconceived idea of fixed symbolic meanings. Water is a very basic image, for example, and it can have a wide range of meanings: the flow of energy, the surface of the unconscious, the ocean from which life originates, a cleansing or baptizing medium, etc. These few examples by no means cover the range of water imagery, but they can perhaps help the imaginative intuition of the therapist who is new to working with dreams.

A man whose former adaptation, based to a large extent on hypertrophied thinking function, was beginning to be inadequate to his life dreamed the following:

I'm at an old college campus. The campus is being abandoned, and I'm attending a farewell service. It had been a church-related institution. It is being abandoned because it is located on a promontory extending into a large lake or sea, and the waters are encroaching on the buildings. There is some new construction, though, including a rest room for handicapped women. I think they may have had to build this because of new federal regulations. This leads me to think that the place is being sold on rather short notice. At least the place had not been allowed to run down.

Another man who was having difficulty deciding whether he needed therapy or was simply a hopeless neurotic dreamed the following:

Flood waters cover much of a landscape. I move about in the air holding onto the end of a pole that is about 10 feet long. I seem to be floating through the air, and my only link to the earth and water is the pole.

He drew a picture of himself above the water, floating. The dream did not suggest he had reached the point of ending therapy; it suggested in the flood imagery the possibility of the mythic image of flood waters covering the earth before creation—a time before water and earth were separate, psychologically before the ego was established apart from the unconscious matrix of its origin.

Another man found his insecurity both expressed and reassured in a dream that showed him removed from the flooding:

I am on a mountain watching a flood below. A dike has broken, but it is not a disaster. It is more like the flooding of the Nile, which makes it possible to grow crops.

A woman dreamed that she was asleep in her bedroom and then awakened (in the dream). She went to a window:

I see that there is water up to the bottom of the window, black, like in a lagoon, with leaves floating on the surface of the water. I feel both fascinated and terrified. Would the house itself float? I look at a neighbor's yard and see that it is only wet, like after a rain, not flooded. I go to the front of the house [toward consciousness?], and there is no flooding at all. I realize it is Easter [which it was not at the time of the dream].

This differential flooding shows a rise in unconscious energy "at the back of the house"—in the personal unconscious. Because there is no way for the water to flow, it is stagnant. This is her own problem, since the dream does not show it affecting the neighbor. The Easter motif, which suddenly appears at the lysis of the dream, seems to suggest the possibility of resurrection, psychologically a time for change in her dominant ego image, a change that actually began to occur.

It is important in noting water symbolism to pay attention to such details as whether the dream ego travels upstream or down, whether it is a cosntructed lake (likely to indicate the personal unconscious) or the ocean (which may be the objective psyche). Sometimes it is important to compare the behavior of the water with how it would naturally behave:

> I dreamed I wanted to study a strange round fish under the waters of a lake. I went down a ladder and was just under the surface when I suddenly realized I was as deep under the water as the fish I had seen [this might indicate some identity of the dream ego and the round fish, which can, from alchemical archetypal amplifications, be a form of the Self image]. I knew that I was able to breathe under the water, but I was afraid that if I did so I might never get back to the surface. I held my breath and climbed back up the ladder to the air. There my analyst showed me how to let down a bucket on a rope, drawing one of the fish to the surface where it could be studied safely in an aquarium.

When water appears in flooding, it often seems to symbolize an increasing amount of libido in the unconscious, creating a relative deficit of energy in the waking ego. This may manifest clinically as the waking ego being lethargic, or it may seem that the waking ego has a great deal of energy but does not function with the usual amount of conscious discrimination. The image of the flood seems to have some relationship to such other natural images as earthquakes, but earthquakes seem to deal more with ego and character structure, less with energy flow.

DOUBLING OF IMAGES

It has been noted empirically that a content approaching consciousness may be represented in a dream in a doubled form. This is not invariable, and the explanation of two forms carrying the additional energy better is not entirely satisfactory. Yet the phenomenon can be seen in some dreams. Such images were so frequent in the dreams of one man that he coined the label *gemination* for them. In his case, the geminated images often consisted of two apparent halves that were actually chiral; that is, they appeared to be mirror images but could not be brought into congruence by rotation or change of plane. In his own clinical material, this seemed to relate to a tendency to see himself as inferior to idealized persons who represented, in actuality, his own strengths. The dream images of gemination might have been saying "separate and equal, not parts of a whole." Sometimes two figures of the dream ego appear, as in two dream specimens discussed in the section on ego passivity. In such instances they apparently show two divergent ego images that exist as competing potentials for the dominant ego image of personal identity.

FATHER COMPLEX

A man afraid of homosexuality (based on being unable to live up to an exaggerated masculine ideal) dreamed that he made a call to a woman he was interested in seeing:

I called her on the phone to ask her out. She said she couldn't go out Saturday, and after probing a bit she said she didn't want to go out with me at all. I felt rejected and hurt.

This was immediately followed by another short dream:

I was riding piggyback on my father. He was racing around a field. I hated the sexual feelings I was having in reference to him, and it disgusted me.

This second dream shows in almost immediate clarity the way in which the infantile dream ego, who is afraid of rejection by women, is carried by and gets pleasure from the father complex, shown in personified form in this dream. In actuality, when the waking ego called the woman the next day she was delighted. The first dream showed the extent of the patient's fear, which he had consciously tried to minimize.

CHANGING IMAGES IN DREAM SERIES

A woman had dreamed early in her analysis that all the life in a lake had been eaten by a giant prehistoric shrimp, an image of an archaic complex dominating the personal unconscious. As she improved, she dreamed that a large shrimplike creature "made of garbage" was chained to a tree. It was nauseating to see. She later dreamed that she was trying to eat a fossil fish, not realizing that it was fossilized. Her father was disturbed that she had broken off a fin. This same motif is seen in the dream below, which she reported several years after the initial prehistoric shrimp dream.

I was going to see Father B [a priest to whom she felt close]. He was in a hospital by the ocean. I saw his chart and realized that he had been married in the past for the same amount of time I had been married [before her husband's death]. I was upset to learn that he hadn't been "just a priest," that he had been married. When I went to see him he had an attractive woman about 50 with him. I wasn't jealous. As I was going to his room in the hospital, I found that there were shrimp all over the hallways, some still alive. Maybe the ocean had washed them in. They were ugly.

Note how over a period of time these recurrent images, related but different, show progressive modifications in the unconscious. The first prehistoric monster shrimp is a marked contrast to the shrimp in this later dream.

A man with a dominant mother and weak father had difficulty realizing his own considerable potential, both intellectually and personally. A change in the father image seemed to occur with this dream, reported after several years of psychoanalysis:

I see my father as a young, naive, and shy man in his twenties, before he married my mother. My mother, my younger brother, and I are talking with him. In the dream he is not my real father, and we are not his children. He doesn't know us very well, because he mixes up the names of my brother and myself. I am surprised when in a bold and confident manner he asks my mother to marry him.

This first dream goes "behind" the personal experience of the father to objectify what the dreamer may already have known in his waking life but not experienced with emotion: his father's problems that were similar to his own. In addition, the aggressive approach of the father may indicate a changing emphasis within the father complex. It may show consciously disregarded strengths of the father. In a purely object-relations model, it may indicate the beginning of a conjunction between the images of the father and the mother in the patient's unconscious—a union that often portends clinical improvement.

IMAGES OF KINGSHIP

It would seem that the considerable amount of imagery that mankind has devoted to kingship reflects archetypal processes in the unconscious structure of the mind. The same processes are also seen in fairy tales. Some dreams seem to be personal fairy tales, with many identifiable motifs. Images of royalty, of course, may also shade into other images of political or social personages (the president, the pope, etc.), which indicates that a more archetypal layer of the complex is being personified.

A ministerial student dreamed the following:

The kingdom has changed, and things are being shifted to the new capitol. I am there in what looks a lot like my actual house. Many kinds of people are there—all races. The king or leader has just arrived. I seem to be a sort of entrepreneur and am very busy with all the changes involved in moving the capitol. There is something about a tree that is to be used for compromising with enemies. I am heading back out of the new capitol on a mission. I think I speak another language in addition to the one used in the nation, and this allows me to move on the outskirts of the kingdom more safely, something like an undercover agent. I may carry the tree or a fruit or small plant with me, a representation of the new kingdom to which people are naturally attracted. Although confusion seems to be the order of the day, I have no doubt about the firm establishing of the new kingdom.

Although he was a theology student, and the dream spoke of a kingdom, this seems to have more meaning for his personal development than as a religious conception of the kingdom of God. Note that the ego goes to the new ruling center, but does not stay at that center, does not identify with the king, but acts for the king in outer regions. There is no inflation of an ego–Self identification. The fruit or tree shows a symbol of the living unity that is actualized in the ruling center of the kingdom. The ego carries such a symbol, but is distinct from the symbol, although responsibly related to that which the symbol represents.

An even more elaborate symbolism based on archetypal imagery of kingship occurred in a woman who was undergoing psychotherapy because of a deep sense of self-doubt and depression. Early in childhood she had felt rejected by several different families with whom she lived, and she had vowed never to be open to rejection again. She had developed a view of the world that relied heavily on differentiating right from wrong by somewhat inflexible standards. The dream occurred following the actual marriage, against her wishes, of her eldest daughter. This dream also illustrates with unusual clarity the unification of opposites, involving a recognition that they are somehow part of a more comprehensive whole. In her dream, this is shown in the image of good within evil and evil within good. She dreamed the following:

I was the chief wife of a Good King. Our daughter had just been married, and I was getting a suite ready for her. My daughter was already in bed and seemed to want me to go. The prince she had married was in the other room. I excused myself and left through two successive doors. I realized that they had left the key in the outer door; I fixed it so that it would lock and they would not be disturbed. I took the key back to the prince, who had begun to undress and was embarrassed.

Then I left and realized we were on a long train. The Good King had been wounded in a battle with the Bad King and had not fully recovered. Still, the

Bad King insisted on continuing the battle. The Good King, against the advice of his ministers, rode out to meet him, saying that it was a point of honor and that he must continue the fight even if it kills him.

I seem to see their meeting. The Good King praises the Bad King and tells him how much he admires his responsibility, his honor, and his trustworthiness—all of which is not true. The Good King asks the Bad King to take care of his family if he is killed in the battle. But this so confuses the Bad King that when they fight the Good King kills him. But now the Good King does not appear so good, since he used psychological trickery to defeat the Bad King.

As I go back farther on the long train, I realize that the Bad King had also had rooms on the same train. In his bed is a little white kitten. I realize that he could not have been all bad or he would not have cared for such a small, helpless creature. I take the kitten and decide I will give it to my daughter and the prince to raise. I wonder if the prince was the son of the Bad King.

This complex dream has a wealth of fairy tale motifs. The dream ego is identified with a past conjunctio—she is the chief wife of the Good King. But that relationship seems not to be active, and the real forward movement occurs in the marriage of the princess and the prince, which the dream ego facilitates. She is afraid that the Good King will die [a source of depression?] and can do nothing to help. But what actually happens is an enantiodromia: the good shows badness, and the badness shows a good side, both perhaps already in the process of reconciliation in the image of the prince and princess. The activity of the dream ego is largely one of increasing understanding in this dream, but perhaps the kitten is a symbol of rediscovered femininity and individuality. Jung (CW 7:182) reported a similar dream. In his patient's dream a white magician worked to a certain point and then said a black magician was needed. But when the black magician appeared he was dressed in a white robe.

DREAMS OF INTERPERSONAL SITUATIONS

At a time when she was afraid that an important relationship with a man she loved and hoped to marry might be in crisis because of his interest in another woman, a young divorced mother had the following reassuring dream:

I am in a house with Don [the man she loves] and a number of other people. We are waiting for Jean [the other woman], who never appears. I tell Don I am sick of being in competition with Jean, of having my emotional responses compared with hers. Prior to this I have done or said something that has caused Don to refuse to talk to me or to hear what I have to say. I tell him I want very much to talk *now* because I feel if we don't talk seriously and openly our relationship is lost. Don relents, smiles, and puts his arm around my shoulder. He says he is ready to talk. I feel like things will work out now.

She had other dreams that also repeated the motif that Don cared. These dreams helped her through the difficult period of time until in actuality he decided to not see Jean any more.

A woman who had improved greatly in psychoanalysis was concerned that her husband, who was also in treatment, would not work on anything of value for himself. She found a compensatory message to that attitude in the following dream:

A very valuable diamond had been entrusted to John [her husband] for safekeeping. He would have to be careful, for some clever crooks were seeking a way to obtain the diamond. Whenever they approached John with some trick for stealing the gem, John was always one step ahead of them, actually planning and executing his own plans in advance. I was really happy he showed this ability.

It seemed entirely possible that some of the "crooks" in the dream referred to animus problems of the dreamer herself that still tended to test out her husband and his stability. Diamond, of course, is a common symbol for something of high value, as in this dream of a young college student:

I was digging in a cellar and found some marvelous gems. But then I was told that although they were mine, I would have to come to the cellar to see them. I could not take them into the outside world or sell them.

This would seem to be an image of the treasures of imagery and potentiality in the unconscious (cellar) that belong to the dream ego but not in the sense of a disposable object in the everyday world.

DREAMS OF OBJECTS

A woman patient was fascinated by an object on my desk. It was a clever gift that consisted of a square glass toothpick holder on a round, black wood base, covered by a small glass dome. The friend who had given this to me had placed a round glass sphere in the top of the square holder, entirely changing the appearance. Instead of a toothpick holder, it now looked like a mysterious holder for a clear crystal sphere, a complex mandala form in three dimensions. The woman saw this and commented on it for several sessions before she asked me what it was.

I told her, and as she picked it up to examine it more closely she saw a small gummed label: "Made in Japan." "Oh," she said, putting it back abruptly onto my desk, "It's just some cheap thing!" But before her next visit she dreamed:

> I was inside a glass container, like the one on your desk but very large. I could see the clear ball floating in space above me but could not determine how it was supported. I backed up to get a better view and bumped into the wall of the glass container. It was then I realized I was inside it.

In a purely compensatory fashion, this dream can be taken to show the fascination that she had previously felt and that she had suddenly dismissed with the animus response to "Made in Japan." Her dreammaker apparently did not agree with that judgmental response and had her experience in a vivid way the strangeness of an apparently ordinary object, possibly because of the manadala form and its representation of order and stability.

These specimen dreams illustrate many ways in which dreaming constitutes a personal drama for the dream ego. The examples are illustrative only. Each, if placed in the context of the clinical situation, could be elaborated forward toward personality change and backward toward past conflicts, showing the influence of the dream in moving the dreamer along a serpentine path of individuation. Such a long series of dreams related to personality change was described by Jung (CW 5). These dream specimens do not at all cover the wide range of meaning that can be found in clinical dreams by the application of the principles of Jungian dream interpretation. They may, however, serve as suggestive examples.

15
Types of Dreams

There are certain recurrent types of dreams, some well known and others scarcely recognized. Several outstanding types are mentioned here, although this listing is not meant to be complete. Categories often overlap. This discussion is meant merely to alert the clinician to certain trends that may be of help in identifying aspects of dreams that could otherwise escape notice. One must always remember the caution not to place any actual dream in a category; each dream must be approached as a new mystery to be explored.

Gutheil (1951) listed various types of "universal (typical) dreams," such as tooth dreams, flying dreams, falling dreams, exhibition dreams, examination dreams, and dreams of coming too late. Ward and associates (1961) collected a great amount of literature about typical dreams among psychiatric patients, outlining 17 typical dreams and their "classic" and "modern" meanings. Their dream categories involve the following: an endangered object; falling through space; being chased or pursued; swimming or being in water; eating; finding money; being lost; fire; being naked or scantily clothed; having something happen to one's teeth; flying through the air, or being able to fly; taking a test or examination; losing objects; missing a train or similar conveyance; being rescued; passing through a narrow space; being in a cave. However, both their classic and modern interpretations were couched in Freudian theory, either of classic or ego psychology phase, and were far removed from the Jungian approach, although their listing of typical dreams is a useful reminder of types of dreams frequently seen clinically.

The title "Types of Dreams" was chosen rather than "Typical Dreams" because the term *typical dream* involves a technical distinction in Freudian theory. Freud apparently first believed that such dreams had invariable meanings, but he later adopted the more reasonable attitude that they can be understood only within the context of the individual dreamer's life (Ward and associates, 1961). In the Freudian literature, however, the original meaning is usually indicated by the term *typical dream*. Epstein (1973) studied typical dreams in four nonepileptic individuals and found that the feeling tone in all was painful. Three of the four indiviuals studied had abnormal waveforms in their all-night electroencephalograms. Epstein considered the possibility of neurological factors being involved in typical dreams.

TRAUMATIC DREAMS

Dreams often recapitulate a traumatic event that was overwhelming in waking life. This observation, particularly in regard to war neuroses, led Freud (SE 18:7–64) to consider a "death instinct." Keiser (1967) reviewed various nuances of the meaning of the term *trauma* in psychoanalytic theory. Grinker and Spiegel (1945) collected many examples of traumatic neurosis, with repetitive dreams of war trauma. Alliez and Antonelli (1968) considered battle dreams to be part of a severe poststress syndrome.

It now appears clear that the repetition in dreams of actual traumatic situations helps the ego overcome severe experiences of helplessness and passivity by reliving them in dreams until some form of mastery can be achieved by the dream ego. From a Freudian view, this process involves the defense mechanism of identification with the aggressor (Freud, 1946), which is a natural stage in the development of the superego. It may well be that resolution of the traumatic dream occurs when the ego is again able to experience itself as the subject instead of as the passive recipient of external stress. This return to a sense of subjectivity is similar to Whitmont's emphasis (1969) on the need for encounter between persons.

Lowenstein (1949) described a case in which the change from passive victim to aggressive actor in a dream occurred only one night after the dreamer was rescued from what seemed certain death in a boating accident. This dream did not have the exactly repetitive character of the traumatic dream, but Lowenstein argued persuasively that the mechanisms were similar. In the dream the waking ego's experience of "humiliating passivity" was transformed into the dream ego's "active exploit.'' The compensatory function of this transformation is apparent. Stewart (1967) reported "unusual dreams" in which traumatic childhood experiences appeared directly in the manifest content of the dreams. Such dreams are unusual only in contrast to the disguise hypothesis of Freudian dream theory. Kalter and associates (1968) were unable to correlate changes in excretion of urinary indoles with recurrent dreams, although their study was inconclusive.

Jung spoke (CW 8:260) of *reaction dreams* that exactly reproduce an affect-charged experience and that seem to be equivalent to the traumatic dream. He reminded us that it is possible for a past traumatic event to be reproduced in a dream for symbolic purposes. I have at times observed this effect—a traumatic event in waking life not appearing in the dreams of the patient until there occurs a later, second event of different content but equivalent symbolic meaning. The first event is then sometimes seen in a dream as a symbol of the problem area.

Although the normal course for a recurrent traumatic dream is to diminish over a period of time, this does not inevitably occur. I saw one case in which dreams of being beaten while in a Japanese prison camp in World War II did not change over a period of more than 30 years. The personal experiences of this man have been reported by his wife (Kellett, 1976).

There are doubtless minor forms of the classic traumatic dream, as Lowenstein suggested, but they shade toward the category of anxiety dreams. Close observation, however, will produce frequent examples. The night after a minor automobile accident, a man reported having several "small dreams involving the car wreck and problems in getting the car fixed." His dreams from later in the night, however, became more symbolic. Marshall (1975) proposed that some night terrors associated with posttraumatic syndrome are problems of arousal from stage 4 sleep and lack the psychodynamic meanings of dreams.

ANXIETY DREAMS

The forms of anxiety in dreams are virtually endless. Adler (1923) believed that both anxiety dreams and dreams of falling indicate exaggerated precautions because of fear of what might conceivably happen in waking life. Nagara (1969) pointed out that Freud considered anxiety in a dream to indicate a failure of the censorship function to prevent arousal caused by latent dream thoughts breaking into awareness. At times, said Nagara, the anxiety can be tolerated by introducing into the dream the thought that "it is only a dream" (Nagara, 1969, pp. 56–60), thereby converting the dream into what Green (1968) called a lucid dream. It is possible that the shift toward awareness of dreaming that Nagara and Green cite is simply the ending of the dream by shifting toward stage 4 thinking rather than toward the waking stage.

The content of anxiety in dreams generally parallels the waking fantasies that produce anxiety: anticipation of physical harm or anticipation of psychosocial trauma such as embarrassment (Beck and associates, 1974). It is reasonable to consider that dreams of nakedness, a form of embarrassment dream, may at times relate to a transference feeling of embarrassment in revealing intimate details to the analyst (Saul, 1966). It is also important to remember that some severe anxiety dreams, so-called, may really be night terrors of arousal from stage 4 sleep, with the dreamlike form being retrospective (Kahn and associates, 1973).

Theoretical considerations about failure of censorship in anxiety dreams are of questionable help in most clinical dream work. Nakedness, for example, often relates to an inadequacy of persona development that may or may not be shown in the dream to cause embarrassment. If it does not, the dream may still be saying to the dreamer that such persona development is necessary. Dreams of falling may compensate an inflated dominant ego image, rather than show failure of dream defenses.

It is entirely possible, for example, that the dream will deliberately produce anxiety to compensate for an ego feeling of well-being that is not adapted to the actual situation. An example that is too readily at hand occurred during the work on this book. I had overslept by an hour, delaying the time that I would be able to start work on a chapter, when I dreamed that I was in a vacation house but was told I would have to move. I first felt anxiety, then anger. Then, as I awoke, I realized that I did not really want another hour of "vacation" sleep but would prefer to get out of bed and write.

CHILDREN'S DREAMS

Dreams in early childhood were believed by Freud to be often simple wish-fulfillments, without disguise. Whether or not this is the case, they certainly appear to be less complicated than adult dreams. In very early childhood, children may confuse dreams with reality, only later internalizing them as what is called by adults a dream. Neumann (1959) described the child as living in a "prepersonal world," a world whose unity is not "split into an outward physical reality and an inward psychic reality." Foulkes and associates (1968) found that children (median age 4–6 years) had dreams that generally were realistic, that dealt with everyday events, and that seemed free of marked disturbance of affect. Frequently children dreamed of playing. Podolsky (1962) noted that children's dreams might express wishes. Night terrors (pavor nocturnus), which occurred most commonly between 4 and 7 years of age, tended to leave no memory, unlike nightmares, which began about 9 years of age. In analyzing a latency-age child, Harley (1962) found that dream material gradually faded in importance in the analysis, only to return again at the beginning of prepuberty tensions. Root (1962) suggested that latency-age children are simply less willing to bring anxiety dreams into the analytic situation. Markowitz and associates (1967) developed an interesting technique of asking parents to identify the dreams of their own children when those dreams were mixed with dreams of other children. They believed that this technique tended to demonstrate to the parents areas in which they were giving conflicting and disturbing messages to their children.

Elkan (1969) reported that a group of boys 4–5 years of age tended to dream of threatening monsters and fear of bodily injury; boys 8–9 years old dreamed of events in the community and cooperative enterprises; boys 14–15 years of age had dreams with political and religious concerns and attention to the body image. At all ages, some return of previous crises might be seen, which is consistent with Erikson's epigenetic model of development. Elkan discussed some drawbacks of the study: the homogeneous population and the fact that many dreams could not be scored.

An early report of dreams of children in analysis was made by Victor Tausk, but recent scholarship suggests that he may have been reporting the dreams of one of his own children (Kanzer, 1971). His identification with his son may be a significant factor in Tausk's own tragic suicide, according to Kanzer.

DeMartino (1955) reviewed characteristics of children's dreams reported in the literature. He found that children who become blind before the fifth year are unlikely to have visual dreams. If sight is lost after the seventh year, dreams are like those of a sighted person. In the dreams of blind children there are prominent representations of parties and family experiences, while deaf children frequently dream of hearing clearly. Blind children dream frequently of fires. Children who are institutionalized dream frequently of being at home, dreams that are compensatory in nature. Children's dreams often clearly relate to experiences of the day. Some sex differences are found in children's dreams, but they are not marked. From 8 to 14 years of age the incidence of animals is approximately the same in the dreams of boys and girls, but boys dream more of large animals such as lions, tigers, and bulls, while girls dream more of smaller animals such as dogs, rats, and snakes.

The childhood sleep disorders of somnambulism and pavor nocturnus were successfully treated by imipramine in 7 patients (Pesikoff and Davis, 1971). The sleep patterns of two autistic twins could not be differentiated from those of normal children of the same age (Ornitz and associates, 1965). Children who gave little response to the Children's Apperception Test could be induced to give further and relatively undisguised material when they were asked what a sleeping character in a story was dreaming (Cain, 1961).

At times one can see in relatively undisguised form changes in children's remembered dreams. Although this could be cited as evidence of repression, it could equally well reflect actual reworking of complexes in a child's mind. A girl 5 years of age dreamed that she was hiding under her bed because some "bad animals" in the woods were trying to break into the house to hurt her mother. She retold the dream in a few days, and it had changed to her father and herself going into the woods with guns to kill the bad animals. She later retold the dream in a still less threatening form and then ceased to have memory of it. There is a probable similarity to traumatic neurosis dreams, but with internal stresses as the origin.

ADOLESCENT DREAMS

Adolescence has been described as that strange stage of life consisting of "freedom under bondage" (Sharp, 1963). Kraft (1969) recommended the use of discussion of manifest dream content with adolescents to help establish an effective and logical approach to material that may seem irrational. Foulkes and associates (1968) compared the dreams of institutionalized and noninstitutionalized adolescents and found that the institutionalized subjects had dreams that were rated more imaginative and unpleasant and that in many cases contained more physical aggression. Amant (1974) noted that dreams of inpatient adolescents were more primitive and contained more cognitive disturbances than dreams of an outpatient control group. The outpatient adolescents had more elements of sexuality in their dreams. In a pilot study the manifest dreams of 15 adolescents were compared with those of a matched group of adults (Langs, 1967). Adolescents showed "more open id expression" of a destructive and aggressive form, more concern with masturbation, and more frequent occurrences of monsters and animals. There were fewer sexual themes than in the adult dream material. Adolescent dreams were judged to be more narcissistic and were thought to show more castration anxiety. It would seem that the adolescent must master the more advanced form of integrating affective and cognitive aspects of the unconscious, which Piaget (1973) described so well in childhood. This is done through the gradual formation of a dominant ego image, a process that may extend far beyond physiological attainment of maturity.

DREAMS OF FALLING

The dream of falling is a frequent type of dream; it occurs with a high incidence in the quite varied populations that have thus far been studied. Reviewing the literature of falling dreams, Saul and Curtis (1967) found the incidence of at least one such dream to vary from 52.3% to 88% in various groups. They found a common latent meaning: the impulse to give up, to let go, to regress, to escape from effort. They considered the dream of falling to be a special and extreme form of the dream of descent. Often, they concluded, it is combined with "hostility directed more or less against the self."* Judging the dream of falling from a Jungian perspective, Paulsen (1971) suggested that if it is seen as a "true symbol," one can detect in the dream of falling a purposive process that leads toward the theme of death/rebirth. The patients studied by Paulsen seemed involuntarily to seek thrills, and they manifested disequilibrium in their relationships, particularly with those to whom they were closest. Another Jungian psychoanalyst, Amann (1968), contributed useful counterpoint to the dream of falling by citing dreams in which the dreamer is off the earth, needing to get back down.

If the dream of falling is seen in a compensatory relationship to the dominant ego image of consciousness, it usually seems to be a corrective to the ego seeing itself as too secure, too much in control of the situation. To consider, as Saul and Curtis did, that it shows an "impulse to give up" is to identify inappropriately the waking ego with the dream ego. To attribute the compensatory action of the dream ego to an impulse of the waking ego leads to hopeless confusion and obscures

---

*The word *self* is used here in its ordinary meaning, not as a technical term in analytical psychology; therefore, it is not capitalized.

the compensatory function of the dream. The dreamed fall is a potentiality of the waking ego's inflated position, in most cases; it occurs in the dream as a warning before outer circumstances produce a more objective fall.

KOAN DREAMS

Over a number of years I have noted occasional dreams that seemed similar to the koan as used in Zen Buddhism. The koan is a question, unanswerable in rational terms, used to help the student realize enlightenment of his mind prior to the categories of discursive thought. A famous koan is "What is the sound of one hand clapping?" (Hoffmann, 1975). The first such dream I encountered occurred to a man who had actually practiced Zen meditation in Japan:

I was in Philadelphia, in the train station, desperately trying to find someone who could tell me which train to take to get to Philadelphia.

The dream seemed to be saying that the dreamer's question was foolish, since he was already where he desired to be, if only he could attain recognition of his true condition. Another such dream from another person:

I was in Germany. World War II was just over. I was trying to escape from a German prison camp.

Here, in different imagery, is the same message: There is no need to escape; you have already been liberated, if only you can realize your true state. Another woman dreamed a similar dream that she was a "volunteer prisoner of war," indicating that her neurosis was in some sense optional.

Another woman had a dream that showed her mirror responding to her almost as a Zen master might to a student trying to solve a koan:

I was standing in front of a mirror describing myself, saying "I am. . . ." Each time the mirror would respond that I had not given quite the correct answer, although I was observing myself in the mirror very carefully.

A man dreamed:

I was uncertain whether to take the freeway to Dallas to see Dr. Hall or to hike over the mountains to get to the appointment. I knew he would be disappointed if I missed the appointment, and I could not make up my mind. But Dr. Hall was standing just behind me in the dream.

Here, again, is the conflict of trying to achieve that which has already been attained. The essense of the koan is to give up the meaningless struggle and accept what is already present in the nature of the mind itself.

A related form of riddle dream is interpreted by Adelson (1966) in transference terms, the riddle being presented as a challenge to the therapist. Interpreted differently, these dreams may be koan dreams. Kirsch (1960) pointed out affinities between Zen and analytical psychology. It is clear that the self that is to be given up in Zen, or in the process of successful analysis, is not the self essential to the carrying on of daily life. Instead, it is the dominant ego image, in fact the search for any particular dominant ego image, that must be seen as entirely relative. It would seem to be an experience of the core of the ego, the Self or central archetype, which underlies the deepest sense of identity that only seems to come from the contents of the dominant ego image.

DREAMS OF DEATH

In his autobiography, Jung (1965) told of dreams he experienced before and at the time of his mother's death, as well as dreams he had when he was near death following a nonfatal heart attack. In most cases, dreams seem to treat the approach of death in a manner no different than they treat other major life changes, such as marriage or the beginning of a journey. When death is near, dreams are more likely to contain an image of the death of some symbol for the body, such as a horse or the personal mother who gave birth to the body (CW 8:404 – 415). The appearance in a dream of the death of the dreamer often foreshadows a change in the ego image, but it does not suggest impending physical death.

A woman in her mid-forties was approaching death because of a terminal illness. She was worried particularly that one of her two sons would return to his father's custody and that such an arrangement would be detrimental to him. Two nights before her death she dreamed:

I was with Billy [the son] at a very elegant treatment center that specialized in helping mothers with problem sons. The diagnostic procedure was for us to lie down side by side on a metal ottoman that was covered with something like Hindu carvings. It revolved and rose into the air. It suddenly dropped, and that meant that he would be all right.

With this dream she seemed consciously to relinquish worry about the welfare of this son. On her last night (she died early the following morning) she dreamed of a horse race that was about to begin, possibly an image of the last efforts of her body to counteract the breakdown of its processes. She died peacefully in her sleep.

The risk of death is sometimes shown as necessary to the continuation of life. A woman who had difficulty facing negative parts of herself dreamed that she was in an upper room overlooking a courtyard in which there were many people ill with a serious disease. Someone brought a baby [her own growth possibility?] from the courtyard into her room. She knew that for the baby to get well she would have to kiss it, but she would incur the disease in the process.

The images that dreams elaborate about death show us something of the way death is seen from the objective psyche. It frequently seems to be imaged as a separation of parts that were joined in life.

The night after his pet dog was accidentally killed by his wife, a man who greatly mourned the dog dreamed:

> In the main room of a house that seems to belong to my wife and myself there is a fish that is large, two and a half feet long. It swims through the air, and no one seems surprised. I feed the fish some food. It nibbles at my hand (association: as the dead dog had done in life). It seems to be becoming a pet. In the same room I see a gas cooking stove. Among the flames of a griddle on the stove I see a horned toad with a head resembling a rhinoceros. He seems to live in the flames comfortably, like a mythological salamander.

The dreamer noted that the fish swimming in air might represent the "elements" of water and air, while the salamander-toad might symbolize fire-earth. It was not possible to establish a subjective meaning for the dream. A woman whose female friend had committed suicide dreamed of "two circular things that had been together but had been divided off," which seemed to refer to the dead friend.

Whether such images suggest anything about the nature of an existence following death cannot be said with any certainty. What is psychologically true, however, is that the psyche seems to contain archetypal images of death being something other than annihilation.

At times the dreams of surviving relatives are important. After the death of his father, a man dreamed:

> I was working on the books of my father's estate. He came home with a suitcase, as if he had been on a trip, and greeted me casually but warmly, then went into another room to say hello to my mother and my sister.

The man's sister dreamed:

I saw my father sitting at a large round table with some people who were friendly to him. He seemed to be enjoying himself, and I kissed him lightly on the cheek.

The father himself, 3 months before his death, had told of a dream of visiting with an uncle who had taken him into his household when he was just out of high school and needed a place to stay. The father had never before told a dream to the family. Neither he nor the family seemed to be aware of his approaching unexpected and sudden death, but the dream may have been an unconscious compensation to death, reassuring him that once before he had found a safe home.

The whole question of the meaning of death awaits clearer definition of what constitutes the living personality. All that can be said at the present time is that the unconscious mind, as reflected in dreams, views death with much less concern than does the waking ego, which attaches much anxiety to the thought.

Unlike dreams of one's own death, dreams of the death of another person may at times foreshadow that person's death. Usually this is because the person is known to have a possibly fatal illness. Some such dreams, however, may be based on some form of psi ability, such as precognition. For example, a woman reconciled with her ex-husband, but they had been together only 3 days when he suddenly died with no warning signs. In looking back over her dreams, she found several that seemed to foreshadow his death. In one of these he was descending by a rope from an airplane to the top of a mountain where she was waiting for him. The rope broke and he fell into a deep chasm. Such a dream, of course, may have been the result of her unconsciously reading clues to his physical condition that were not known consciously to anyone, including the husband. Alternatively, the dream may have been symbolic of a probable failure of the attempt at reconciliation. Still, her dream may have been precognitive of his death. A woman who knew that her brother was about to die of a terminal illness dreamed that he reached for a potted plant, but accidentally pulled it up by the roots.

It is not surprising that in one study subjects over 65 years of age had the most dreams with death themes (Winget and associates, 1972). Sharpe (1937) told of a dream a woman experienced 3 days before the woman's death. The woman did not regain full consciousness after telling the dream. In the dream, her sicknesses were no longer illnesses, but were roses that she knew could be planted and would grow. Sharpe said in discussing this dream: "Eros alone . . . *knows* . . . the roses . . . will grow." Dreams seem to be a source of reconciliation for many persons approaching death.

DREAM WITHIN A DREAM

Ernest Jones's classic Freudian explanation for the dream within a dream was based on a supposed parallel to grammatical construction: Since in Freudian theory the dream was supposed to be a disguised version of an unacceptable thought, the dream *of* a dream was like a double negative in grammar, and it therefore presented the latent dream thought in an undisguised form. Jones suggested a literary parallel to the play within a play, as in *Hamlet,* where the drama within a drama revealed what had not been consciously known to Hamlet. The disguised disguise was considered to be the true face. This exlanation is not convincing to me, as it rests too heavily on theoretical assumptions. Also, movement within a dream from one form of dream ego to another can be very involved. There can, for example, be dreams of dreams of dreams, etc.

Green's discussion (1968) of lucid dreams approached the same problem in a different manner. If the dreamer knows he is dreaming, she would call the dream lucid. It seems possible, however, that such lucid dreams may represent a transition from stage 1 REM sleep to stage 4 mentation. They may also be dreams within dreams. I know of no laboratory data bearing directly on this question. Green (1968, p. 91) cited one difference between waking thought and the thought in lucid dreams: careful examination of the relationship between the dream world and the waking world is foregone, perhaps to avoid disturbing the lucid dream state. She also described "false awakening," in which the dreamer "awakens" within the dream. Freud's position was that when the thought "It's only a dream" occurs in a dream, it is a way of handling anxiety-laden material that has escaped censorship and entered the manifest dream. This has some merit, although it seems better to avoid the dichotomy of waking and dreaming and speak of the shift of ego image within the dream, which is often concerned with anxiety but may be the result of other dramatic developments.

A woman who always wore leg braces dreamed that she awoke (in the dream), got out of bed, walked to a chair, woke up (the second awakening within the dream), realized that she had walked without her braces, and wondered if it had hurt her. She then awoke into the actual world. This double awakening within the dream places the act of walking without braces into a dream within a dream. Could it have meant that her hope of being able to do without leg braces is a dream?

A man with many neurotic problems dreamed:

I am being held down by many hands, and I have to struggle to get free. I then wake up [in the dream] and realize that struggling against the hands was a dream [within the dream], but that it was still important for me to struggle. I then awakened "completely" [but again within the dream] and found two attractive women to the right of my bed. The nearest woman said to me that the dream of the hands had been one in which I was struggling against my unconscious. The other woman asked me to explain the nature of the ego, which I did in an abstract way. The scene changed, and I was at the apex of the intersection of two hallways, one to the right and the other to the left. To the left was a spot of light 1½ feet in diameter, source unknown. It gave the same feeling as my dream of Hamlet and Oedipus [his initial dream in analysis, in which he felt there would be a great explosion if the two met]. There seemed to be a shadowy form moving from the left. I became frightened and woke up [into the actual world].

This dream shows the dream ego working on the meaning of a dream within a dream while in the dreaming state; it also has reference to a previous dream that had been important in this man's analysis. The shifts from "dream" to "waking state" seem to have dynamic meanings. Another patient dreamed that he knew the meaning of a previous dream, one that had been recurrent for years, after which the recurrent dream seemed to fade.

In terms of focal and tacit knowing, the dream within a dream seems to be another instance of the shifting tacit component of the dream ego.

MIRROR DREAMS

A mirror is a metaphoric symbol for the mind (Shengold, 1974); there are similarities in Zen imagery (Hoffmann, 1975). A mirror in a dream may show the act of reflection, seeing oneself in a different way; or it may be an indicator of narcissism, as in the myth of Narcissus, who saw himself reflected in the mirror surface of still water and fell in love with his image. Shengold (1974) poetically referred to an "unsynthesized introject" in mirror dreams as "the devil behind the glass." Miller (1948) suggested that mirror dreams reveal elements that are just emerging into consciousness, thus linking this imagery with the doubling or gemination that sometimes accompanies the images of such contents. Eisnitz (1961) considered the mirror dream a form of the dream ego being in a dual role: observer and observed. This same mechanism may, of course, be seen in other ways—as a change in identity of the dream ego or a duplication of the dream ego. The process of self-reflection in dreams (Rossi, 1972) has some relationship to the imagery of the mirror.

A woman dreamed the following:

I saw a face trying to see its right side in a mirror. The right side (association: my worst view) of the face was old and wrinkled, as if it were about to sag. I was on the right of the face. Suddenly I realized it was my own face! I was concerned with the right side, since I am only 32 years old. I couldn't cover it with makeup. "It looks just like your mother," I thought, "and she's almost 70!" Suddenly I became the face looking in the mirror.

Before the dream, this woman had always thought that she resembled her father more than her mother, whom she considered as being unable to make decisions or to care for herself. The dream led her to consider real but undesirable similarities to her mother's way of living, which she then began to alter in her own life.

FOREIGN LANGUAGE DREAMS

There are unexplored meanings of polyglotism in neurology and psychiatry (Steyn, 1972), particularly the relationship to the elaborate "languages" developed by some schizophrenics, the coining of neologisms, and the frequent sense of anxiety when a new language is about to become readily available to a student (when it passes into a tacit form). There must naturally be some isolation between available languages in the mind. The occurrence of a foreign language in a dream has a meaning that depends on the personal associations of the dreamer to that language. Often one language is seen as more emotional or more sexual than another. The appearance in a dream of a foreign language that the dreamer does not consciously know may simply indicate a meaningful understanding that is not yet available in consciousness. In many cases, the person associates a particular foreign language in a dream with a certain period of his past life, as in the following example.

A woman in her early forties had come to the United States from France when she was 18 months of age. The family spoke French at home in her childhood and thought that she did not understand French, since she refused to speak that language with them. However, she had actually understood their communications, but she wished to preserve her sense of independence. When she grew up and entered college, she signed up for a course in French, thinking that her early exposure would make it an easy language to acquire. She found to her surprise that she had great difficulty learning French, apparently because of the emotional meaning she attached to the language. When she was struggling in analysis with problems of her marriage, she had the following dream, which seems to show a dissociated part of her mind connected with the French language:

I had gone to the airport to see "the wisest woman in the world" who was just arriving on a plane. There were a lot of other people gathered around her. She knew the answer to everything, but she did not understand me when I asked her a question in English, since she spoke French. Finally, I found an interpreter in the crowd, a man. The interpreter did not actually say a word, but in his presence she could understand my question, spoken in English, and she replied in English. Her reply was rapid and precise, like a computer, as if she had all the information and was telling it to me as fast as possible. I asked her if I should leave my husband, which I had decided to do, but she said this was not the time.

Although the marriage later ended, it seemed at that time that the right move was to stay, since further emotional working-through was needed. The role of the interpreter in this dream is related to that of the mediator (Walker, 1975).

SPOKEN WORDS IN DREAMS

Isakower (1954) suggested that spoken words in a dream are a direct contribution from the superego. However, in a detailed study of Isakower's thesis, Baudry (1974) found multiple meanings for spoken words in dreams, reflecting the various ways in which language participates in the acquisition of culture. One of the most dramatic forms of the spoken word in the dream is that form in which it seems to come as a voice without a speaker. Often such a voice seems to speak with great authority, much as the "wisest woman in the world" in the preceding dream illustrating foreign languages in dreams. When such voices occur, they give the impression of coming not from the superego but from the central archetype, or at least from an archetypal locus similar to the Old Wise Woman or the Old Wise Man when personified in a dream. This is a very different phenomenon than the voices that invade waking life in paranoid schizophrenia, where they often seem to come from dissociated complexes that relate to the ego as persecutory inner objects.

A man of forty had procrastinated making needed changes in his life. He awoke from a vivid dream that consisted simply of an authoritative male voice saying:

You are not living your true life!

The voice did not belong to anyone he recognized and it did not seem judgmental or threatening, but like "the wisest woman in the world" it simply spoke directly what was absolute knowledge. This dream was a great aid to the dreamer in determining the values of his various activities.

NUMBERS IN DREAMS

Numbers are among the most difficult of dream images to interpret. They often have great significance in dreams, but their abstractness can interfere with gaining a sense that they are correctly understood. Freud's fear of dying at a certain age (which he lived beyond) hinged on special attention paid to numbers. There was early psychoanalytic interest in numbers in dreams (Daly, 1921), where they sometimes associated with clearly personal material, as, for example, the room numbers of a hospital where the dreamer worked (Daly, 1921). Even mathematical equations can be found to have sexual meanings if sufficient interpretive latitude is permitted (Feldman, 1923). Sometimes a punning intention is attributed to numbers in dreams, as the number 180 being taken to mean "I ate nothing" (Sharpe, 1937).

Von Franz (1974), in her scholarly work *Number and Time,* began the complex investigation of the relationships between numbers and archetypes, a very promising but difficult approach to the possibility that numbers may represent a continuum lying behind both consciousness and the physical world. This deep significance of numbers is suggested by the striking way in which mathematical innovations, which come directly from the mind, seem frequently to parallel the structure of the physical world when it is sufficiently understood by scientific investigation. There is no immediately obvious reason why there should be this meaningful coincidence of the mind and the physical universe, except that they may both be manifestations of an underlying unitary reality.

Abstract speculations are of little use when one is faced with a dream containing particular numbers. The process of dealing with such dreams is the same as with other dream contents. Personal associations are taken first. A number may refer to an important date in the dreamer's history, for example. Then cultural associations are considered. For example, in current usage the number 69 has sexual meaning in the culture that is not dependent on a particular individual association. Similarly, the 11th hour culturally suggests the last possible time for action. Beyond cultural associations, one enters the area of archetypal amplifications.

Archetypal meanings of numbers are somewhat abstract, but they can at times be helpful. Numbers are important in the alchemical formula attributed to Maria the Prophetess: out of the one comes the two, out of the two comes the three, and out of the three comes the one *as* the four. Unity is thus indicated by both one and four; four can be considered a higher unity of one. Certain numbers seem to indicate the completion of a cycle, as 9 (in numerology) and 12 (in calendar and clock timing).

Related to dream images of numbers are those showing measure and proportional form:

My dream was about a measure of depression on a baseline. I was contented to have the dream; it was as satisfying as a complex identity in algebra. It looked like this:

	Together but not relating	Some relating, less remote	Relating well	
(−)				(+)
Withdrawn, not myself	Negative passivity	Positive passivity	Individuation	

Fodor (1951) offered an extended discussion of number symbolism and dreams for those who might wish to pursue the subject further.

Aside from the actual occurrence of numbers in dreams, it is useful to apply to dreams some of the same principles that are found important in the psychological understanding of fairy tales (von Franz, 1970). Attention to the number of characters, the proportion between male and female characters, and changes in the number of figures from the beginning to the end of the dream (or in a dream series) can be important. The dream of the Good King and the Bad King (p. 296) shows an imbalance in the feminine, for example, if one simply counts the initial figures: Good King, Bad King, and prince (three males); dream ego and princess (two females). After the death of the Bad King, the male/female ratio is reestablished at unity, with the possible exception of a slight appearance of an extra female figure if one considers the white kitten a character and considers it symbolically female.

DREAM MONSTERS AND THE DEAD

Not to be confused with dreams of the death of the ego are dreams in which persons who are actually dead appear alive in the dream, sometimes with the dream ego having knowledge that they are supposed to be dead. Such figures often represent the continuing pres-

ence in the dreamer's unconscious mind of active complexes to which
the images of the dead persons relate. A black nurse who had established herself well as a professional woman still dreamed that she was
back in her former town and that her father, who was actually dead,
kept coming out of his grave. This seemed to represent the family
culture in which she had grown. Although she had left that culture, it
still refused to transform itself in her mind. The actual family seemed to
reject her for her success, which was against the unspoken norm by
which they judged themselves. She finally moved to another country
where racial differences were less marked in order to try to find her
true personal identity and bury the past.

Such monsters as vampires, the Frankenstein monster, etc., may
appear in dreams. They take on specific meanings from the personal
associations of the dreamer or from cultural associations. Sometimes
the feeling tone in the dream adds a different dimension to the monster,
as in the case of a woman who dreamed that she was being chased by a
monster, but "a silly monster," not really serious. Vampires often
suggest some content that "should have died" but is maintaining its life
at the expense of the blood (libido) of the waking ego. The Frankenstein monster, in contrast, is a synthetic monster, composed of parts of
various "human" complexes. The minotaur (p. 185) seemed to be an
image of partially humanized energy that was not integrated into the
ego, although in the dream cited it was no difficulty for the anima figure
in the dream.

DREAMS OF REALITY

When a dream shows a situation exactly as it is in waking life, it
may be difficult to find a compensatory meaning. However, if such a
dream is examined carefully, there will often be found one revealing
detail that is different from the actual situation.

I dreamed that I got out of bed and found that a flowerpot had been
knocked off the window. I didn't want to clean it up. I noticed the new pretty
curtains in the bedroom, which my mother had made from sheets, and was
pleased with them.

When the woman awoke from the dream, she found that the curtains
were not real. Reflecting on this part of the dream, she realized a
change in herself: she had always loved to be alone, but now was realizing that she did not like an absence of people. She had at times been too
close to her neurotic mother, and this was another possible message in
the dream.

If no small detail reveals that the dream is actually different from the real situation, the dream may be compensatory to reality in an unusual way. It may be saying that the way the real world is seen is a dream. One must also consider that dreams of reality may be stage 4 mentation reported as dreams.

ALCHEMICAL DREAMS

Alchemy was a rich source of archetypal imagery for Jung, although its obscurities and multiple names for the same object bring confusion to any attempt to convert it into a logical process. The alchemical images of the king and queen, ending in the formation of the androgyne, a symbol of the unification of opposites, were used by Jung (CW 16) as a model for discussing transference–countertransference interaction. Even if one has only a slight acquaintance with the involved alchemical imagery, it is possible to see many parallels in the dream imagery of analysands. Sexual symbolism is often involved, as in Jung's discussion of transference. It appears in the following dream, which shows the unifications of opposites in a way that could not, in reality, occur:

I [a recently divorced woman] dreamed that I was pursued by my therapist, who kept trying to drive cars that I was in [a danger of forming an animus based on the therapist?]. Finally, to escape, I entered my home [not her actual home]. I realized that above my bed there was a cream-colored male cat that wished to mate with a white female cat. I carried it into another room where there was a female cat. They mated. The male cat had long hair and the female had short hair. During the intercourse of the cats, both became mottled in cream-and-white colors, and in addition their hair became a length intermediate between the two.

The mixing of the colors of the cats and their hair length seemed to show a change in her own psyche at a deep level.

On a more human level, the same motif occurred in the dream of another woman, whose concern was that an important relationship with a man should continue to be right for both of them. She thought, "between waking and sleeping," that the posts and crossbar at the foot of her bed were part of an irrigation system of a greenhouse. Returning to sleep, she dreamed:

There were two conjoined souls, male and female, that were as yet undifferentiated. For a moment it seemed that Bill [the man] and I were lying side by side, he on the left, I on the right. We seemed in some way to be growing into one another. We were very much a part of the soil of the flower bed on which we lay. Something flew upward from our conjoined selves. It seemed to me to be a "ray of darkness," and then I thought "syzygy" [she was familiar with Jung's work]. Two words came to me spontaneously: conjunction and putrefaction. After a while I could feel that a pillow was supporting our two heads, and it struck me as odd that there should be a pillow in a greenhouse bed.

She associated this dream to an earlier dream, also in a greenhouse, in which the man's mother became aware of their liaison but approved.

Prima materia in alchemical writings refers to the material with which the alchemical work is begun. It is described as "despised" and of no value, available everywhere; but it is also the origin of the philosopher's stone, an image of the most valuable of all things, the elixir of life, the lapis. This identity of highest and lowest is a complex of opposites. Psychologically, prima materia may simply mean one's ordinary life, always available. It is sometimes pictured symbolically as excrement, as in this dream of a woman in her mid-thirties, who felt as if her life was a series of difficult relationships:

> I had a long involved bowel movement that looked as if it had "knots" in it. It looked almost like jewelry.

In other dreams the image of prima materia occurs as an object of high value that is treated as if it were worthless dirt. One analysand dreamed that the parking lot of the shopping center was strewn with jewels that no one seemed to notice. Another dreamed that he saw bottle caps in shallow water and that among them were gold coins.

At times a dream of a kitchen has alchemical implications, since the kitchen is a place of transformation. A man dreamed that he was in the kitchen of his (female) analyst. She was cooking a meal for him and another man. Suddenly he heard a metallic crack and realized that one of the steak knives had broken in its case. As he picked up the knife, it was transformed into a large sword, so large that he could barely hold it above the floor by standing on his toes. There was defect near the hilt that could be repaired, but the other man said, "The official guardians may not let us repair it."

A very clear alchemical parallel occurred in this dream of a man familiar with such symbolism, although most of his dreams did not reflect alchemical images:

> I am making coffee according to my girlfriend's instructions. I am using my drip-model coffee maker to purify a liquid. The idea is to recirculate the dark liquid through the coffee maker. Each time it will be of a lighter color. Very likely this process will yield gold.

The idea of circulation (circulatio), often in a vessel called a pelican because of a curved neck that reentered the body of the flask, was a common alchemical image. The idea of circulation is found also in Chinese Taoist imagery as "the circulation of the light" (Wilhelm and Jung, 1962). Jung's (CW 12-13) works are a good starting point for the study of alchemical symbolism. It should be said, as with archetypal amplification, that perfectly good clinical interpretations of dreams can be accomplished with personal and cultural amplifications, although knowledge of archetypal or alchemical amplifications adds an additional depth to the view of some dreams.

TIME AND DREAMS

Dreams are able to show an intricate weaving of past and future, a fabric of importance to the present. Structurally, this often seems to indicate the interaction between various layers of a complex structure. At times it appears that the dream is moving toward some point in the past from which a fresh development can emerge, much as controlled regression can take place in hypnoanalytic age regression. It is important to know the time, or changes of time, in a dream. If any part of the described dream seems different from the current reality, such as the dreamer being smaller, this may represent an earlier time or a younger age. Often on inquiry the dreamer will be able to verify that in the dream he felt younger.

Dreams may also occur on special occasions, such as the anniversary date of an event important in the dreamer's life, or Christmas or Easter. It has not been infrequent for several analysands to come to their first hour in January and say, "Well, here's my New Year's dream!"

A minister who felt very ambivalent about his profession, so much so that many persons in his hometown did not know he was preaching, had this dream on Palm Sunday:

I ride to the other side of the parking lot on some army or construction company equipment. We go north. I come back with Joe [a senior minister in the same church] riding a donkey. I'm late for a meeting of the church board. There is an accident right outside the church, and people are killed. I stay at the board meeting and never go over to check the wreckage.

It is not difficult to see in the imagery of this dream a conflict between his official church position and a feeling that he is ignoring human need, quite possibly his own need. The donkey, of course, suggests Palm Sunday.

PSI DREAMS

Dreams are the most prominent form of spontaneous parapsychological events such as precognition (Rhine, 1961). While the findings of parapsychology are still questioned by many, admission of the Parapsychological Association into membership in the American Association for the Advancement of Science indicates that the field itself has become a valid area of scientific investigation. A most convincing description of the psi influence in dreaming was furnished by Ullman and associates (1973), reporting a large series of laboratory experiments on telepathy and dreaming.

Although it appears to me that the occurrence of psi effects in dreams (largely of telepathy and precognition) is established beyond reasonable doubt, most dreams that are presented in analysis as psi dreams are not convincing. Often the person wishes to compensate a weak ego identity by demonstrating to the analyst an unusual ability. Such claims are then best handled in a reductive analytic way.

At other times an analysand may bring what appear to be valid psi dreams. There is then a temptation to become fascinated with the psi content, which almost invariably makes the dreams of no value for therapy. The proper study of psi dreams as such is by a parapsychologist, while the psychoanalyst should be concerned with their relevance to psychological growth and individuation.

The rule that I have found useful with dreams of undoubted psi content is to ask why that particular material, even if relating to someone other than the dreamer, should have been appropriated by the dreamer's own unconscious psi process and used as material for the dream. Often there are striking parallels, for example, between the situations of the persons who are telepathically perceived and parts of the dreamer's own personality or life situation.

COLOR IN DREAMS

Color may be more frequent in dreams than is generally appreciated. With careful interrogation soon after awakening, Kahn and associates (1962) found color reported in 82.7% of dreams. Color may be present in some part of most dreams (Tauber and Green, 1962). Hall (1959) found a lower incidence of color (29%), with women reporting a slightly higher percentage of color dreams than did men (31% compared to 24%). Hall did not find any significant differences in other aspects of dreams between those who dreamed in color and those who did not, nor between colored and uncolored dreams of the same person. Kafka (1963) pointed out that colorless dreams appear as bleached or neutral, not as black, white, and gray. Dreams with color were more vividly recalled and had more intense affect and unpleasantness. Tauber and associates (1968) had subjects wear lenses that transmitted only red-orange-yellow and noted increases of those colors in their dreams that night. Their findings are offset by the observation of Padgham (1975) that 6 men with normal color vision had their most saturated dream colors in the red and orange areas, with notable absence of saturated purple, blue, and blue green. Padgham suggested that a minority of blue color areas may exist in the part of the visual cortex concerned with color perception.

Psychoanalytic writers have generally considered dream colors as representing affect or other contents in a defended form. Yazmajian (1964, 1968) thought that completely colored dreams showed interior representations of body organs or childhood memories of genitals. Woltmann (1965) regarded a recurrent color in black-and-white dreams as unconscious contents breaking past resistances. Suinn (1967) found that subjects with high test anxiety had less vivid colors in their dreams. He concluded that color in dreams may be expressed in ways other than the frequency with which it appears.

In laboratory sleep studies, Herman and associates (1968) found color in 68.5% of REM awakenings and 38.4% of arousals at sleep onset, but in only 5.3% of stage 2 arousals. They found that the percentage of dreams with color increased with the subsequent REM periods of a night. Also, the mean number of colored objects in dreams, the ratio of chromatic to achromatic objects, and the saturation of object colors increased as the night progressed.

Suinn (1966) compared color in dreams to Jungian type of the dreamer, basing his type classifications on the Myers-Briggs test. Introversive men had greater frequency of color dreaming, but greater vividness of color appeared in Sensation and Feeling types of individuals, with greater pervasiveness of color in Feeling types. Women showed greater proportions and frequencies of color dreaming in Feeling types of individuals, with greater vividness in Intuition subjects.

For persons who report all dreams in color, it is difficult to formulate a general psychodynamic meaning. However, for subjects who rarely dream in color, there may be meaning to those colors that do appear. Some subjects report specific times in their lives when color dreaming appeared, possibly related to increased organization of the visual cortex or to psychological changes that allow greater expression. One woman reported dreaming only in black and white until menarche, but in color since. It is best not to use any standard equation of translating various colors into psychological meanings, although many such charts are available; one should derive the meaning of the color in a dream as far as possible from the dreamer's own personal associations and preferences. If associations are not easily given, it is sometimes helpful to instruct the person to "be" a particular color: "Be red and describe your feelings."

We have by no means toured all types of dreams nor paid tribute to the many ways in which the phenomenology of dreaming can be explored. Perhaps we have made a beginning.

REFERENCES

Adelson J: The dream as a riddle. Psychiatry 29:306–309, 1966
Adler A: Individual Psychology. London, Routledge & Kegan Paul, 1923
Alliez J, Antonelli H: Les rêves de bataille (Battle dreams). Ann Med. Psychol (Paris) 1:505–538, 1968
Amann A: The dream as a diagnostic and therapeutic factor, in Wheelwright JB (ed): The Reality of the Psyche. New York, Putnam, 1968, pp 92–97
Amant E: Contents of day and night dreams of emotionally disturbed adolescents. Child Psychiatry Hum Dev 4:157–167, 1974
Baudry F: Remarks on spoken words in the dream. Psychoanal Q 43:581–605, 1974
Beck AT, Laude R, Bonhert M: Ideational components of anxiety neurosis. Arch Gen Psychiatry 31:319–325, 1974
Cain AC: A supplementary dream technique with the Children's Apperception. Test. J Clin Psychol 17:181–183, 1961
Daly CD: Numbers in dreams. Int J Psychoanal 2:68–70, 1921
DeMartino MF: A review of the literature on children's dreams. Psychiat Q Supp 29:90–101, 1955
Eisnitz AJ: Mirror dreams. J Am Psychoanal Assoc 9:461–479, 1961
Elkan BM: Developmental differences in the manifest content of children's reported dreams. Doctoral dissertation, Columbia University, 1969
Epstein AW: The typical dream: Case studies. J Nerv Ment Dis 156:47–56, 1973
Feldman S: Physics in dream symbolism. Int J Psychoanal 4:318–320, 1923
Fodor N: New Approaches to Dream Interpretation. New Hyde Park, NY, University Books, 1951
Foulkes D, Larson JD, Swanson EM: Dreams of institutionalized and noninstitutionalized adolescents. Psychophysiolgoy 5:222–223, 1968
Freud A: The Ego and the Mechanisms of Defense. New York, International Universities Press, 1946

Green C: Lucid Dreams. Oxford, Institute of Psychophysical Research, 1968

Grinker RR, Spiegel JP: Men under Stress. Philadelphia, Blakiston, 1945

Gutheil EA: The Handbook of Dream Analysis. New York, Grove Press, 1951

Hall CS: What people dream about, in DeMartino MF (ed): Dreams and Personality Dynamics. Springfield, Ill, Charles C Thomas, 1959, pp 55–63

Harley M: The role of the dream in the analysis of a latency child. J Am Psychoanal Assoc 10:271–288, 1962

Herman J, Roffwarg H, Tauber ES: Color and other perceptual qualities of REM and NREM sleep. Psychophysiology 5:223, 1968

Hoffmann Y: The Sound of the One Hand: 281 Zen Koans. New York, Basic Books, 1975

Isakower O: Spoken words in dreams. Psychoanal Q 23:1–6, 1954

Jung CG: Memories, Dreams, and Reflections. New York, Vintage Books, 1965

Kafka H: The use of color in projective tests and dreams in relation to the theory of ego autonomy. Doctoral dissertation, New York University, 1963

Kahn E, Dement W, Fisher C, et al: Incidence of color in immediately recalled dreams. Science 137:1054–1055, 1962

Kahn E, Fisher C, Edwards A, et al: Mental content of stage 4 night terrors. Proceedings, 81st Annual Convention, APA, 1973, pp 499–500

Kalter S, Metzger H, Todd W, et al: Excretion of urinary indoles in patients with recurrent dreams. Dis Nerv Syst 29:182–188, 1968

Kanzer M: An autobiographical legacy of Victor Tausk. Int J Psychoanal 52:423–430, 1971

Keiser S: Freud's concept of trauma and a specific ego function. J Am Psychoanal Assoc 15:789–794, 1967

Kellett WL: Wings as Eagles. Quanah, Tex, Nortex Press, 1976

Kirsch J: Affinities between Zen and analytical psychology. Psychologia 3:85–91, 1960

Kraft IA: Use of dreams in adolescent psychotherapy. Psychotherapy: Theory, Research and Practice 6:128–130, 1969

Langs RJ: Manifest dreams in adolescents: A controlled pilot study. J Nerv Ment Dis 145:43–52, 1967

Lowenstein RM: A post traumatic dream. Psychoanal Q 18:449–454, 1949

Mack JE: Nightmares, conflict, and ego development in childhood. Int J Psychoanal 46:403–428, 1965

Markowitz I, Bokert E, Sleser I, and Taylor G: A cybernetic model of dreaming: A basis for understanding the interpersonal context of children's dreams. Psychiat Q Suppl 41:57–68, 1967

Marshall JR: Treatment of night terrors associated with post-traumatic syndrome. Am J Psychiatry 132:293–295, 1975

Miller ML: Ego functioning in two types of dreams. Psychoanal Q 17:346–355, 1948

Nagara H (ed): Basic Psychoanalytic Concepts on the Theory of Dreams. New York, Basic Books, 1969

Neumann E: Art and the Creative Unconscious. Princeton, Princeton University Press, 1959

Ornitz EM, Ritvo ER, Walter RD: Dreaming sleep in autistic and schizophrenic children Am J Psychiat 122:419–424, 1965

Padgham CA: Colors experienced in dreams. Br J Psychol 66:25–28, 1975

Paulsen L: Dreams and fantasies of falling. J Anal Psychol 16:1–17, 1971

Pesikoff RB, Davis PC: Treatment of pavor nocturnus and somnambulism in children. Am J Psychiat 128:778–781, 1971

Piaget J: The affective unconscious and the cognitive unconscious. J Am Psychoanal Assoc 21:249–261, 1973

Podolsky S: Some problems related to children's sleep. Psychiat Quart Suppl 36:66–81, 1962

Rhine LE: Hidden Channels of the Mind. New York, William Sloan Associates, 1961

Root NN: Some remarks on anxiety: Dreams in latency and adolescence. J Am Psychoanal Assoc 10:303–322, 1962

Rossi EL: Self-reflection in dreams. Psychotherapy: Theory, Research and Practice 9:290–298, 1972

Sachs LJ: On crying, weeping and laughing as defences against sexual drives, with special consideration of adolescent giggling. Int J Psychoanal 54:477–484, 1973

Saul LJ: Embarrassment dreams of nakedness. Int J Psychoanal 47:552–558, 1966

Saul LJ, Curtis GC: Dream form and strength of impulse in dreams of falling and other dreams of descent. Int J Psychoanal 48:281–287, 1967

Sharp BB: Psychotherapy with adolescents. Pastoral Counselor 1:39–44, 1963

Sharpe EF: Dream Analysis. London, Hogarth, 1937

Shengold L: The metaphor of the mirror. J Am Psychoanal Assoc 22:97–115, 1974

Stewart WA: Comments on the manifest content of certain types of unusual dreams. Psychoanal Q 36:329–341, 1967

Steyn RW: Medical implications of polyglottism. Arch Gen Psychiatry 27:245–247, 1972

Suinn RM: Jungian personality typology and color dreaming. Psychiatr Q 40:659–666, 1966

Suinn RM: Anxiety and color dreaming. Mental Hygiene 51:27–29, 1967

Tauber ES, Green MR: Color in dreams. Am J Psychother 16:221–229, 1962

Tauber ES, Roffwarg HP, Herman J: The effects of longstanding perceptual alterations and the hallucinatory content of dreams. Psychophysiology 5:219, 1968

Ullman M, Krippner S, Vaughan A: Dream Telepathy. New York, Macmillan, 1973

von Franz ML: Interpretation of Fairy Tales. New York, Spring Publications, 1970

von Franz ML: Number and Time. (Trans: A Dykes) Evanston, Northwestern University Press, 1974

Walker W: The mediator. Unpublished diploma thesis, Inter-Regional Society of Jungian Analysts, 1975

Ward CH, Beck AT, Rascoe E: Typical dreams: Incidence among psychiatric patients. Arch Gen Psychiatry 5:116–125, 1961

Whitmont EC: The Symbolic Quest. New York, Putnam, 1969

Wilhelm R, Jung CG: The Secret of the Golden Flower. New York, Harcourt, Brace, 1962

Winget C, Kramer M, Whitman R: Dreams and demography. Can Psychiatr Assoc J 17:203–208, 1972

Wisdom JO: A hypothesis to explain trauma re-enactment dreams. Int. J Psychoanal 30:12–20, 1949

Woltmann AG:A contribution to the symbolic use of color in dreams. Psychoanal Rev 52:94–105, 1965

Yazmajian RV: Color in Dreams. Psychoanal Q 33: 176–193, 1964

Yazmajian RV: Dreams completely in color. J Am Psychoanal Assoc 16:32–47, 1968

PART I V

Enactments

For the good that I would I do not: but the evil which I would not, that I do.

Paul, *Romans* 8:19

16
Enactments

"Awareness of the projections and symbolic meanings involved enables us to *enact* rather than blindly *act out,*" according to Whitmont
(1969, p. 132). In Jung's use of the term *symbol,* the symbolic carrier is
not necessarily an idea or an image. It can have concrete form. After
his break with Freud, Jung spent time at Bollingen building model cities
with canals and streets on the lake shore. A child's game? A form to
add stable order to a mind that was alive with change? Later in life,
Jung became an accomplished carver of stone and a painter, always
giving some form to the images in his mind, giving them body.

If one "acts out," the unconscious complexes that are constellated possess the ego, leading to fascinations or repulsions toward
external persons or events. Although the person who is acting out may
feel he is breaking the bonds of restriction, he may simply be falling
unaware into the same complexes he seeks to escape. Enactment is
different. It is an "acting in," inward toward the symbolic, but an
inward meaning poured outward into the world, so that it is caught and
held in a symbolic form, as foamy seawater can be caught in a cup or a
strange fish can be drawn up from the depths and studied.

The ability to *enact* dream images rather than *act out* the complexes requires a sense of the symbolic attitude, an "as if" ability.
Fantasy is play, but it can also be harnessed to carry the contents of the
mind and allow them to develop symbolically, to seek their existence in
the outer world as symbols rather than as compulsions, neuroses,

fears, and fearful forms. If one already finds himself in such neurotic nets, the way out is the same: an experience of the symbolic nature of the situation, its meaning in the longer path of individuation. Much as the traumatic war dream begins to fade when finally it is entered by a symbolic element, the situations of life move through their impasses when the symbolic stance of enactment can be introduced.

Easy to say, hard to do. Yes. But to know the value of the symbolic mode is the essential beginning. Dreams repeatedly demonstrate such value. It is something that we have all experienced. It is therefore important to remember that dreams may be used not only for interpretation, they can form the basis for enactments.

PHYSICAL FORMS

Images from dreams can be put in physical forms. Like remembering a dream, such forms tend to lend stability to what otherwise may sink back into the unconscious with little impact on consciousness. The particular medium in which the symbol is embodied is not crucial. What does matter is that the dreamer put something of himself into the creation or selection of the form, just as Jung made model canals in the mud on the lake shore. The largest resistance that must be overcome is the fear of thinking oneself foolish or being seen as silly, a persona anxiety.

Paintings

Painting is a readily available way to enact a dream image in a physical form. It is important not to spend excessive time considering the artistic qualities of the work for that will constellate one's other critical standards from consciousness and will impede the flow of the unconscious imaginal process. The technique of painting imaginal pictures involves tapping that source of imaginal activity that we all experienced in childhood, when the picture came from inside, not from any learned ability to scrutinize and reporduce the external forms of the world.

One woman, in the course of a single night, painted three canvases, not from a desire to be artistic but to relieve an overwhelming sense of alienation. The first picture was red and fiery, with sexual symbols woven throughout, conveying the despair she felt of ever achieving a balance with the man she felt she loved. Once that sharp, harsh picture was in a permanent form, a cooler, more structured painting emerged on the second canvas. The third showed a calm, soft-eyed woman, painted in cool greens and blues, an image that was still not her waking ego but was the compensation to the angry pyrotechnic jaggedness of the initial painting of the night.

For paintings to come from the unconscious and adequately carry symbolic meaning, the center of consciousness during their production must lie somewhere closer to the unconscious than when painting is done according to conscious intention and standards. For example, symbolic painting that was once very helpful to me was done while I was in a state of real psychological need. Although I was painting a familiar object, I allowed my brush to act somewhat "of itself" as one would do with an object in active imagination. The result was that the object seemed to rotate in three different directions simultaneously, something that was physically impossible but could be represented in the plane of the painting. Further conviction that the painting came from the unconscious rather than as a conscious production was the uneasiness I felt after "finishing" it. Although it was late at night, I was unable to sleep. After several hours, I got up and looked at the painting. On impulse, I took out my pocket knife and made a small hole in the very center of the object. This was the "fourth"—the complement of the three rotations. It seemed that it could not be represented on the painting itself, but had to be a change in the ground of the representation, in the canvas. The tension was relieved at once, and I was able to sleep. This painting, done quickly, was of symbolic value for years, and its imagery continues to unfold.

Sandtray Projections

The sandtray in which pictures are constructed with small figures was developed by Lowenfeld (1964) in England and later adapted by Kalff (1971) of Zurich to Jungian principles of interpretation. It is a deceptively simple and effective way of projecting unconscious contents. The sand in the tray, which is $19.5 \times 28.5 \times 3$ inches, can be wet or dry. The child or adult who makes the picture is able to choose from a wide assortment of materials: small human figures of various sex, age, and dress; animals, tame and wild; vehicles; dwellings; trees; fences; fish and sea creatures; planes and ships; religious symbols; rocks; and ways of representing bodies of water—mirrors in the sand, actual water poured directly on the sand or placed in bowls, or strips of blue plastic that can be molded to indicate streams and rivers.

A large part of the effectiveness of sandtray projections derives from the fact that they almost completely circumvent any tendency to be artistic, avoiding excessive ego involvement. There is no recognized art form of placing toy figures in sand, so that the subject has no objective standard by which to judge his production. His contribution to the picture is merely one of selection and arrangement, as there are no criteria of artistic excellence, no brush technique, no skill in handling the medium. Furthermore, most children and adults have at some time in life enjoyed fantasy play in sand, often having built castles on the beach. There is therefore a precedent for imaginative, non-purposive activity with sand.

I have found sandtray pictures particularly useful in working with children and with some adults who do not easily give verbal material and dreams. The therapist limits himself to encouraging the patient, recording the order in which objects are chosen, and making notes about any story the patient is willing to tell about his construction. A Polaroid picture is made for the patient to keep, with a copy for the therapy records. In many cases little interpretation at all is used, as a series of pictures seems to hold unconscious images that are worked through in successive constructions. With adults, more interpretation may be done, particularly if the sandtray is used as a projective technique rather than a therapy device.

If a sandtray room is available, it offers a quick and efficient way to make rapid objectifications of unconscious imagery from dreams or to continue the action of a dream and develop it further. For persons who are inhibited in making symbolic forms in artistic materials, it avoids persona defenses.

Most sandtray projective pictures can be interpreted with the same principles that are used for dreams, with the precaution that they are more conscious in origin and do not as completely carry the imprimatur of origin in the central archetype process that produces dreams.

Poetry

Poetry carries such meaning that patients who write poetry often bring poems once they begin to feel safe in the analytic relationship. The imagery of poetry is more discursive than plastic forms, but it can embody more specific meaning. One person, for example, embodied a particularly important dream in this poem:

I am eye of no dimension:
Darkened room, illumined screen.
On screen a boy, one such as I
Observing river's steady sheen.

I am I (the screen no longer)
Watching river shimmering
Point to point of round horizon
Flowing river stately seen.

Ripples break the flowing waters
Clumps and masses roughening
Deeper, wider swells the river
Angry, heavy, moving thing.

(I engulfed by fear of drowning!)
(I a small and frightened thing!)

I am eye of no dimension:
Darkened room, illumined screen.
On screen a boy, one such as I,
Observing river's steady sheen.

Because poetry often carries such a sense of the person of the poet, it must be handled with care in psychotherapy, certainly more carefully than sandtray pictures and perhaps more carefully than paintings. If a patient is accustomed to writing poetry, it can often be suggested as a safe form of objectifying excessive unconscious contents that are pressing for release. Poems about dreams offer a rather structured way to allow the imagery to develop, and this technique of enactment may be preferable to less structured techniques such as active imagination in patients who lack effective ego strength. The container quality of the poetic form can easily be varied—from haiku, which requires compression and precision, to sonnets, which allow more expansive form but provide structure in syllable count, rhythm, and rhyme scheme. Free verse can be suggested if it is desired to loosen the patient's expression.

In a lighter vein, the following poem captured in an image the high hopes and actual awkwardness of a man attending his first Mensa meeting:

Adiadochokinetically,
The Mandarin frog
Jumps in the puddle
But bumps on a log.

Letters

Letters are an often overlooked device for objectifying dream images of real or subjective contents. Most people have never thought of the possibility of writing a letter to someone who is deceased, to an imaginary person, or to a figure from one of their own dreams. Such letters can be an extended and controlled form of imaginal work for persons who are too unstable to approach personified complexes directly with active imagination.

Letters to the dead are a particularly good device for resolving some fixations. It is not uncommon for neurotics to feel an unresolved sense of loss at the death of someone close to them, most often a parent to whom close feelings were not adequately expressed during life. One such case involved a young woman who for 5 years had been unable to put aside thoughts of her father's death. The night that he died, she had asked him by telephone to tell her mother that he, not the daughter, was responsible for the parents' financial difficulties. Although he worked the same night loading heavy equipment, she blamed the emotional impact of her telephone call for his death later that night of a heart attack. Her clinging to guilt about his death interfered with other relationships in her life and, in fantasy, gave her an elevated but negative role through her responsibility and guilt. In the second visit it was suggested that she write a letter to her dead father, just as if it would be mailed to him and he would read it. This she did, pouring out her guilt. It was then suggested, to her surprise, that she write the answering letter from her father to herself. By linking the image of her father with his own response to her, she was able to write a most realistic letter, very different from her more emotional fantasies. Her guilt quickly diminished, and she began to work on more immediate problems in her psychotherapy.

Letters can be written to dream figures, with answering letters from them, in the same fashion.

Jewelry and Personal items

The psychological meaning of jewelry is so ingrained in the culture that it is hardly apparent to us. Wedding and engagement rings are worn on the third finger of the left hand because the Romans believed that a channel ran directly from this finger to the heart, the seat of affections. Class rings are a reminder that one belongs to a certain group, and they can be a physical aid to the maintenance of a dominant ego identity based on that group identification, whether it is a high school class, a college class, or the classes of such professions as medicine and law. Honorary keys, such as Phi Beta Kappa keys, open nothing but symbolic doors, either in the mind of the holder of the key or in the image of himself reflected back from the eyes of others.

These same principles can be used in a more personal way. Symbolically meaningful items can carry complex meanings that arise in dream images. When such an item is carried sufficiently long in the everyday world, waking consciousness can be influenced through a series of minor enactments that may take place spontaneously.

One analysand had constructed for herself a mandalalike small pendant. Although the design itself had not come from a dream, its form carried for her imagery from actual dream material, slightly reworked by consciousness without driving off the meaning of the original images. Only after it was finished and she began to wear it did she note certain symbolic meanings that could be read into the design.

When symbolic meaning is embedded in items of jewelry, self-designed or chosen, problems may arise that are not present in such items when they are used in a nonsymbolic way. The use of the symbolic form, for example, must be a matter not of conscious choice (questions of style and adornment) but of a deeper choice about whether that symbol is appropriate for the conscious situation.

CARE AND NURTURING OF SYMBOLIC FORMS

Symbolic forms cannot be fabricated, they must appear. It is possible to put images in concrete form, as I have suggested, but it is not within the power of the ego to ensure that they retain their symbolic effect. The actual symbol (more precisely the "symbolic attitude toward an object") arises unconsciously through the transcendent function, producing in the symbol a unity of opposites that cannot be reconciled on rational conscious grounds. This should not be taken to mean that they cannot at any time be placed consciously together without conflict. A more conscious resolution may be possible at some future time. Until then the conflicting materials are carried by the symbol, whether it remains in imagery or is given an actual form, as in a painting. The production of a true symbol often means that the opposites it carries cannot otherwise be reconciled *at that time* and also *by the particular dominant ego image then in ascendancy.* The symbolic form is like a first rope secured across a gorge, a link to a new shore, tenuous, uncertain, capable of being broken. But if it endures, it focuses attention and energy so that eventually a permanent bridge may replace the rope, allowing easy and safe access between the two banks of the river. The rope is then no longer needed as a symbol, since the thing that it represented has been durably constructed. This movement from symbol to constructed psychic form is much of the process of Jungian analysis. It is reflected in the imagery of alchemy and, in a literary form, in Goethe's story of a bridge formed initially by a living snake, who is unable to accomplish the task except at noon, when (symbolically) consciousness is at its zenith (Metman, 1962). Later, the snake is transformed into a permanent bridge across the river.

During the time that a symbol or symbolic form must serve as a tenuous bridge between the current dominant ego image and the potential future ego states, the care of the symbol is particularly important. Since consciousness cannot by will invest any form with symbolic meaning, it is important not to depotentiate those symbols that have been spontaneously formed by the transcendent function. How are symbols nurtured? In much the same fashion as one would nurture a child or a small puppy or kitten—by giving them attention and not exposing them to tasks that are too great for their growing strength. Attention to a symbolic form is like food to an infant, conveying libido toward that part of the psyche that the symbol expresses. It is not necessary to devote great time to formal meditation on a symbol. If it is kept in the anteroom of consciousness and thought is allowed to fall on it spontaneously from time to time, the symbol is nourished.

The most frequent danger of depotentiating a living symbol is by using it excessively in consciousness, either as a defense against unwanted thoughts and affects or as coinage in interpersonal discussions. When used in such a defensive way, the symbol is asked to give the ego immediately those contents that it carries only symbolically. This is often an effort by the ego to avoid the painful tasks of actual growth and transformation, which involve images of the death/rebirth mythic cycle. This cycle is equally true when symmetrically reversed as the birth/redeath cycle—a form in which it is often experienced by the dominant ego image that must suffer deintegration to allow more comprehensive forms of itself to emerge.

The second danger to the symbol, excessive talking about the symbol, is a particular threat in people who are in psychoanalytic training. During my time of study at the Jung Institute in Zurich, the coffee conversations were often about dreams and symbolic material. More than once I experienced the loss of symbolic meaning that can occur from talking too much about a symbolic image rather than nourishing it in oneself. In most cases it was possible to revitalize the imagery, but the lesson was important. When one has a living symbol it is quite permissible to rely on the symbol tacitly, if not done defensively, and to talk to others from an ego image in which the symbol participates. It is dangerous to talk *of* the symbol to others, as it may then be mere persona coinage. The temenos of the psychoanalytic situation permits more talk of symbols than is safely possible in the everyday world.

ENACTMENT OF DREAMS

Enactments of dreams are possible in many forms: in hyp-notherapy, in active imagination or guided imagination, in dance, in dialogue with the analyst, in group therapy, in psychodrama, and (with more caution) in everyday situations and relationships. Since the dream is a symbolic statement, it may have wide relevance to life and may manifest further meanings in many situations if its imagery is kept accessible to consciousness. Obviously it is not desirable to spend all one's time in such symbolic activities; balance is required. Given balance, it is possible to do further work on dream images in the context of many life activities. However, the focus should always return to the ongoing series of dreams, since they give feedback in the form of further images. Return to the stream of dreaming prevents facile sub-stitution of a consciously known pattern for the subtle process of individuation—always a tempting substitution for the ego that would like to have things right now and right here, fixed and understood forever. True attention to the real here and now always reveals the presence of the individuation process that is shown so clearly in the images of dreams.

Imaginal Techniques

Techniques that rely heavily on the use of images can be called *imaginal techniques*. There are three principal forms and endless varia-tions. The three principal forms are hypnoanalysis, active imagination, and guided imagination. Imaginal techniques differ from rational problem-solving in permitting images to participate with some au-tonomy. They differ from ordinary imagination in their seriousness of purpose, in their service of individuation rather than escape, and in their putting some demand on the image to reveal itself in increasingly meaningful ways. Imaginal techniques constitute a halfway station be-tween our ordinary state of practical consciousness and the deep inner world of dreaming.

HYPNOANALYSIS

Hypnosis is a powerful tool for investigation of the mind (Crasil-neck and Hall, 1975). Hypnoanalysis is a specialized use of the hyp-notic interaction to probe the images of the analysand's mind. The ad-vantage of hypnotherapy (which involves two-person interaction) over solitary forms of self-hypnosis lies in the fact that hypnotherapy allows the analysand to identify more with the imaginal process in his own mind, since the therapist assumes the role of directing the imagery and attending to such practical matters as preventing interruptions. The therapist maintains the temenos or alchemical vas, the safe boundary, within which the patient can permit his mind to deintegrate through imaginal techniques.

Hypnotic age regression is an imaginal technique. When unverifiable memories are recovered, one does not know if they are actual memories or imaginal forms. Even with this uncertainty, they may aid the analysand in taking a different attitude toward the unalterable events of the past—their meaning but not their existence may change.

Dreams may be relived in the hypnotic state, with the therapist suggesting that the imaginal ego in the enactment of the dream perhaps take different attitudes than it did in the dream. Such changes in dreams must be used cautiously, however, or the process can become a mere exercise in the defense mechanism of *undoing*. Changes in the imagery are of little importance unless they significantly affect the tacit structure of the ego, as can occur in dreams. A safer procedure is to go through the entire dream in the hypnotic state and then *continue the dream* in the hypnotic state beyond the point of the dream's former termination.

The techniques of hypnosis are simple, but they are best learned under the guidance and supervision of a therapist skilled in hypnotic interventions in psychotherapy. The two major societies that represent responsible and ethical uses of hypnotherapy are the Society for Clinical and Experimental Hypnosis and the American Society of Clinical Hypnosis. Hypnosis by itself is not a form of professional practice like psychiatry or psychology, and many states have laws restricting its use to legally defined professions. A general rule to follow is that hypnosis should not be used by anyone who cannot take responsibility for any complications that may arise and who cannot treat the same problem by nonhypnotherapy techniques.

ACTIVE IMAGINATION

Jungian active imagination is not widely understood, although its principles are the basis for many techniques that are given other names. Jung early began to use active imagination in his own growth, and it is of great value in selected cases.

Active imagination is best described as a technique of using the imagination in a controlled way that (1) maintains maximum ego responsibility and (2) allows maximum freedom of the images to develop of themselves. We have all done active imagination as small children, but we usually have forgotten the experience. If one can remember, as a child, elaborating a fantasy to the point that it began to seem real, even to the point of becoming frightening, then one has had the childhood experience of treating fantasy as real, which is the basis of active imagination.

When I was a child, we had, just outside the door, a large sandbox, perhaps 8 feet square. I can remember as a small child playing in this sand with toy cars and trucks, losing myself in the play. However, a few years later, when I wished to reexperience that play, I was unable to contact that level of imagination again, even with the same toys and the same sand. It was not until adulthood and experience with active imagination that the imaginal dimension was again accessible at will. My childhood experiences in sand play seem to me the basis for what is used more intentionally as the sandtray projective technique described earlier.

Many writers, including Jungians, often lump together active imagination, the painting of imaginal pictures, and work with dance and the sandtray, as well as other imaginal techniques. However, I prefer to make distinctions among these techniques, since active imagination, in its pure state, allows the greatest amount of participation of the unconscious; any variant that introduces an enduring physical form, such as painting, restricts to some extent the freedom of the symbol in exchange for achieving a more permanent embodiment of the symbolic image.

Responsibility of the ego. In active imagination, the ego must treat the imaginal episode as if it were a real situation. Thus it is not permissible to say that it is "just imagination" and forego the moral choices that would have to be faced if the images were objects and persons in the everyday world. This rule is intended to entice the ego to participate in the imaginative situation in as complete a form as possible, not avoiding stresses between competing ego images by a mild dissociation under the permissive guise of it being "only imagination."

Respect for the object. In active imagination, the non-ego parts of the images are allowed to function with maximum autonomy. If one is being attacked by a dragon in active imagination, it is against the rules to say "only imagination" and turn the dragon into a poodle. Such transformations can be forced on the images, but not on the complexes that are personified in the images. To "know" that an imaginal dragon is "really" a helpful content of the mind is to relinquish the autonomy of the object, to abandon the imaginal ego, and to turn the whole process of active imagination into mere fantasy. If a dragon appears it must be faced in active imagination "as if" it is a real situation.

How can one know if active imagination is genuine and not fantasy or daydreaming? The most useful way to judge the authenticity of active imagination is that, like a dream, it will produce surprises. Fantasy is more controlled, being directed by the ego to its "as if" desires. Daydreaming is less directed, but it involves little ego responsibility. But active imagination, correctly done, goes beyond the sense of "I'm doing it" and shows that the imaginal objects and persons begin to act with surprising autonomy. For example, a woman's active imagination:

An unknown man [animus?] brought me out onto a small narrow stage. I was nude. I began to masturbate. He bent down and seemed to be "milking" my vulva. When he did this, a red flow (like menstrual blood) spewed out in two lines. I became repulsed and stopped the active imagination. But when I started the process again, the story exactly repeated itself [it seemed to have an autonomous form]. Again I stopped. When I started active imagination for the third time, it still repeated exactly as before, and I decided to let it run its course in spite of my dislike of the imagery. [She is able to interrupt active imagination, but if it is done with respect for the non-ego images, the autonomy and psychic reality of the other images are revealed in their repeating themselves three times in spite of the ego's dislike of the scene.]

The two red streams flowed away from the stage and then curved upward before touching the floor. As they arched upward they turned into shiny gold bands. [This suggests that the menstrual blood, one of the alchemical images of prima materia, is connected to the making of "gold," another image of the lapis or goal of alchemy.]

Off in the distance, in the direction the two bands were moving, there was some kind of structure that I at first had difficulty in seeing. It was itself very dark, and the area around it was black. But soon I saw that it was an intricately carved wooden shrine, such as that where an icon might be kept.

Moving from right to left of my visual space, the two arching gold bands moved straight toward the shrine's center, where they merged. The instant this happened, a bright white light emanated from the shrine's center. The white light was all that I could see.

This is an authentic experience of active imagination, the imagery of the shrine and the white light surprising the ego. Various uses of this experience were possible in her analysis: the need to reveal herself more openly (as nude on the stage), the acceptance of her sexuality (which had been largely in the persona), and the way in which despised and orphaned parts of herself (the "useless" menstrual blood) could give birth to an unexpected value (the gold) if she would permit the process to seek its natural goal. The white light, of course, is a frequent image of enlightenment in mystical literature.

GUIDED IMAGINATION

I have applied the term *guided imagination,* following Whitmont, to all those processes that partake of active imagination but involve some structure from outside, such as input from the therapist in hypnoanalysis. These can involve minimal influence on the imagery, in which case they are near to active imagination itself, or they can involve elaborate structures of imagery, as in some psychosynthesis exercises, autogenic training, or traditional Eastern sadhanas.

At a conference sponsored by the Sangreal Foundation I once had an opportunity to discuss with Lama Govinda, an authority on Buddhist philosophy (Govinda, 1969), the differences and similarities between Jungian psychoanalysis, a Western technique, and the traditional meditation practices of Buddhism, particularly in the Tibetan tradition. I felt that the most basic distinction was that Jungian active imagination begins with the personal images and gives them the right to express themselves, while in traditional Buddhist practice there are rigidly prescribed rules and forms, including the prescription of which images are to be the focus of meditation in a particular study. Govinda disagreed, however, and wisely commented that the traditional Buddhist images could only be approached in a individual way by each person, while if one pursued individual images deeply enough they inevitably touched the universal level that Jung referred to as the objective psyche.

Techniques of guided imagination have been developed for group use by Dr. Ruth T. Fry of the C. G. Jung Education Center, Houston, Texas. As used by her, they require careful attention to any disturbing reaction in a participant, which must then be dealt with individually if necessary. Images produced in this experience of guided imagination frequently make persons aware for the first time of the reality of the unconscious process.

Dance

Carolyn Grant Fay, M.A., also of the C. G. Jung Center, Houston, has for several years applied Jungian principles in dance therapy. In some persons, granting permission to use the body in movement, often with closed eyes, together with the affective stimulation of carefully selected music, permits imagery to come to consciousness in a safe and contained way. When done in a group setting, the dance time is followed by a discussion period in which images may be shared, although no one is pressured to reveal his imagery if it seems too personal—a respect for the "care and feeding of symbols."

Dialogue with the Analyst

One form of enactment of dream images that is often of value is to have analyst and patient carry on dialogue from the point of view of various characters in the dream. This permits the analysand to experience in an imaginal way some of the other possible dream ego identities that could have occurred in the dream itself. Since this takes place in the analytic container, it is possible to push insight further than is possible in some group therapy situations. This dialogue often helps the analysand understand, through observing the analyst's use of his own imaginal functions, the technique of active imagination.

Special Language

This use of dream images in analysis seems to occur almost without the intention of the analyst or the client. When a long series of dreams is analyzed, some dreams inevitably stand out as representative of recurring motifs in the analytic process. If a green snake has been a particularly meaningful image in the dream material of the patient, the analyst may find himself saying in reference to nondream material: "There's your green snake again!" Dream images become a shorthand for complicated groupings of insights and experiences, functioning somewhat as minor symbols for larger parts of the analytic enterprise. Such language is similar to references to meaningful past events that tend to occur in family discussions. A related use of such language is to identify confusing life situations by reference to the meaningful dream symbols.

Dreams in Group Psychotherapy

Jung himself was not enthusiastic about group psychotherapy, as is seen in his correspondence with Hans Illing (Adler and associates, 1953). Jung believed that group psychotherapy was not a substitute for individual psychoanalysis and that the danger of group therapy is in the patient getting stuck on the collective level. Jung acknowledged, however, that group therapy could be of value in the education of the social human being and that individual analysis ran a risk of neglecting social adaptation. Jung believed that individual psychoanalysis and group psychotherapy complement each other, which is consistent with my own experience.

Group therapy is a very useful container in which to explore some dream images through enactment techniques, although the limitation of time in group therapy prohibits attention to all dreams of each member. Selection is required. Many psychodrama techniques are of value in enactment of dreams in therapy groups, such as alter ego roles, stage direction from the therapist, and switching of roles. It is important to remember that the insights obtained in the use of dreams in group therapy may or may not coincide with an understanding of the dream itself. Since dream images are so rich in meaning, being based on personified psychological complexes, it is possible to derive meaningful insights that are of great value but that do not deplete the meanings of the dream itself. In addition to the enactment of dreams in group psychotherapy, the actual interpretative process may also be used in a group setting, with the additional material of cultural and personal amplifications from other members of the group

Frequently when dreams are enacted in group therapy, it is possible for the therapist or other members of the group to recognize that the aspects of the patient shown in his dream, often of a shadow nature, can also be seen in his habitual interaction within the group. The additional parallel to group behavior is a form of amplification of dream material that is unique to the group therapy setting. It often aids the patient in seeing the meaning of the dream in a nondefensive manner.

Dream Images in Everyday Life

Since dreams speak to the individuation process of the dreamer, which involves his actions in everyday life, images from dreams are of use in understanding and even initiating everyday activities, if the dreamer is intent on promoting the movement of his psyche through attention to symbols.

A young woman with many fears of a psychosomatic nature dreamed that a woman had only "two more Christmases" to live. She was afraid the dream was a portent of actual physical death, that her psychosomatic problems would lead to organic illness. In the dream she had looked shocked when she heard this pronouncement, and a man in the dream pointed toward a whole shelf of cookbooks and shook his head sadly, seeming to imply that the girl who was to die had never used any of the recipes available to her.

In addition to working on the dream symbolically, the dreamer in her waking life put forth great effort in cooking her meals. This was not a magical device, but simply a conscious enactment of a dream image in an attempt to stimulate that part of her personality that had resisted both the ordinary task of cooking for herself and the more crucial life task of putting into actual practice the "recipes" that she had acquired through reading and years of psychotherapy. Her cooking was an enactment of a dream image in everyday life. Her attitude to the dream was not unlike that of Socrates to his daimon—wondering whether actually to learn a new skill or take it symbolically, and giving at least some attention to the literal task.

Dream images can be used to help the dreamer identify the projected presence of complexes in everyday situations. If a dream image has shown in symbolic form the dream ego's fear of taking action, a conscious memory of the dream may serve as a cue for the waking ego in identifying the same attitude in itself in waking life. As in the dream, when the situation is recognized by the waking ego, there is the possibility of taking effective action that can lead to change. This is not simply a matter of choosing to act differently, since such change often comes against strong resistance. But as in the dreams, the ego's attitude toward a task often brings forth responses in the personality that are ordinarily not available to the ego.

Dreams in Close Relationships

There is an almost universal temptation to tell a friends or family members when one has dreamed of them. Often this is done lightly, as if the dream were a matter of no consequence. If one appreciates the meaningfulness of dreams, however, such communication must not be carried out without forethought. It is equivalent to offering to the other person a form of one's deeper consciousness, the dream, as a projective test. The friend may project into the dream complexes of his own and infer the dreamer's "real" attitude toward him that is not at all the dreamer's true feeling nor the meaning of the dream. The person to whom the dream is told almost never, unless he has been analyzed, thinks that his own image in the dream might be a subjective part of the dreamer's mind rather than the dreamer's secret attitude toward him or toward their relationship.

A woman dreamed the following:

> I was in a car with Bob and Charlie [men in her group psychotherapy]. The dream changed and I was in bed with my husband, who is also named Bob. He said that he was going to the kitchen for some wine and cheese, which I expected him to bring back to our bedroom. Then I realized that he was not coming back and was in the kitchen enjoying the wine and cheese by himself.

On awakening, she told her husband the dream, which (correctly) compensated her conscious feelings, showing that he was not sufficiently attentive to her needs. Instead of understanding the dream herself and relating to her husband differently, she expected him to understand the dream in the same way she did. Probably she hoped that he would take the dream as more "objective" and realize his error of ignoring her. Instead, the husband projected into her dream his own fears and insecurities. His reaction: "An automobile means intercourse; so you've wanted to be unfaithful to me with these men in your group!" A colossal argument followed. This is only one example of the difficulties that can arise from sharing dreams that have not been "digested" or sharing them with persons who are not attuned to understanding the subtle relationships between dream images and real persons.

Positive sharing of dreams with others requires that the relationship be strong enough to tolerate misunderstandings. The dream may, of course, be saying something negative about the relationship, perhaps something that the dreamer has not seen in his own dream. Unless the dreamer feels that the other person can be objective in examining himself and the relationship, it is best for the dreamer to accept his dream and then, on a different level, take responsibility for his part in the relationship of which the dream speaks. In those relationships where both persons understand the nature of dreams, and in which both are more committed to individuation than dependent on the relationship for support, the sharing of dreams can be a deep and moving experience. When such relationships are available, they carry much of what is achieved in psychoanalysis into the individuation process in the world. Ideally, marriage should allow for such psychological sharing, but openness should not be presumed simply because two people are married, although they may work toward achieving it.

REFERENCES

Adler G, Jaffé A, Hull RFC (eds): C. G. Jung Letters, Vol 2: 1951–1961. Princeton, Princeton University Press, 1953
Crasilneck HB, Hall JA: Clinical Hypnosis: Principles and Applications. New York, Grune & Stratton, 1975
Govinda A: The Psychological Attitude of Early Buddhist Philosopy. London, Rider, 1969
Jung CG: Memories, Dreams, and Reflections. New York, Vintage Books, 1965

Kalff DM: Sandplay: Mirror of a Child's Psyche. San Francisco, Browser Press, 1971
Lowenfeld M: The Non-Verbal Thinking of Children and Its Place in Psychology. London, Institute of Child Psychology, 1964
Metman E: The green snake and the fair lily (guild lecture no 41). London: Guild of Pastoral Psychology, 1962
Whitmont EC: The Symbolic Quest. New York, Putnam, 1969

Last Thoughts

The reader who has assimilated the material in this volume should have a clear vision of the outlines of Jungian dream interpretation and their relevance to both clinical and experimental work on dreaming. He should begin examining the dreams of his own clients in the light of Jungian principles, letting his own experience teach him still more.

I can but lament the necessity of leaving out much material. Each specimen dream stands for dozens more that could have been cited. Each dream discussed is taken from a series of dreams that might have been explored, revealing other facets of the individuation process of the dreamer.

I wish to make brief mention of two important areas that lie adjacent to questions of clinical use of dreams. Perhaps there are underground streams that connect these to clinical dream theory. The first is the problem of parapsychological research and the nature of dreaming. The second is the religious meaning of dreams, which is vital to a responsible depth psychology of religious counseling. Many writers have contributed to each of these questions, but space limitations have not permitted detailed reviews of their work nor extended examination of these problems.

Jung's theory is still little understood, and it is increasingly misunderstood. His conceptualization of the psychological complex, the archetype, and the compensatory function of the dream, and above all his symbolic grasp of the individuation process, outline a field of inquiry that has relevance for scientific study, for clinical applications in

349

psychotherapy, and for reopening of prematurely closed doors between the fields of science and religion. Jung appreciated more than any depth psychologist that man himself contains a religious dynamism that is no mere illusion of projected parental images. Neither science nor theology have opened these doors that Jung set ajar, although Dr. J. B. Rhine, the father of modern parapsychology, has spoken to this question as recently as April 1977 at a major theological seminary.

Perhaps I must reassure myself regarding the incompleteness of this volume with the thought that, like a dream, it shows what it shows, although it is part of a deeper process that surfaces elsewhere in other dreams, in other forms.

Index

Abenheimer, K.M., 117, 127
Abenson, M.H., 195
Achusimnutupalit, 270
Acting out, 331
Active imagination, 340–342
Actual dream, 261–271
    see also Dream(s)
    archetypal amplification of, 266–271
    exposition in, 264
    plot of, 264
    rational and irrational functions in
        relation to, 261
Adelson, J., 309
Adler, A., 45, 63–64, 67, 124, 138,
    305, 344
Adler, G., 29*n*
Adlerian theory, firstborns in, 222
Adolescent dreams, 306–307
Aeneid (Vergil), 5
Aeschylus, 4
Aesculapian sanctuaries, 4
Aesculapius, 4–5
Affect ego, 49
    see also Ego
Albertus Magnus, 13
Alchemical dreams, 319–321
Alcohol, as dream-depriving agent, 89
Alcoholic hallucinations, 94
Alcoholics, sex dreams of, 68

Alcoholism, REM or State 1 sleep in,
    210–211
Alert attentiveness, 78
Alexander, Franz, 32, 168*n*, 264
Alkindi, 7
Alliez, J., 302
Alpha activity, 79
Altman, L., 17
Altshuler, K.Z., 37, 87
Amann, A., 307
Amant, E., 306
Amenhotep IV, 35
American Society of Clinical Hypnosis,
    340
Amplification
    of actual dream, 265–271
    cultural, 266
    vs. free association, 29
    in Jungian theory, 129–131
    personal, 265
Analysand, eliciting dreams from,
    245–246
Analysis of Dreams, The (Boss), 56
Analyst
    dialog with, 344
    dreams of, 225–226
    psychological type of, 262
Analytical material, forgetting of,
    177–178